A Hundred Years Ago

Britain in the 1880s in Words and Photographs

by Colin Ford and Brian Harrison

Harvard University Press
Cambridge, Massachusetts
1983

Printed in Great Britain

Library of Congress Cataloging in Publication Data
Ford Colin, 1934–
  A Hundred Years Ago.

  Bibliography: p.
  Includes Index.
  1. Great Britain—Social life and customs—19th century.
I. Harrison, Brian Howard. II. Title.
DA560.F67 1983   941.081   82–15869
ISBN 0–674–42626–6

FRONTISPIECE *This photograph of Castle Garth,
Newcastle, won prizes in competitions in London,
Birmingham, Richmond and York. But how far do its
careful composition and elegant pictorial arrangement
invalidate its value as a historical document?* Lyddell
Sawyer, 1889 (Private Collection)

Contents

Sources of Photographs

Aberdeen Public Library 1.8, 5.11, 10.4; Barnardo Photo Library 2.8, 2.9, 2.12, 13.3; B.T. Batsford Ltd 1.22, 6.1, 10.7, 10.8; B.B.C. Hulton Picture Library 4.16; Beamish North of England Open Air Museum 6.12(c), 14.5; Bethnal Green Library 5.4; Birmingham Public Libraries, Local Studies Department 4.19, 5.9, 6.27, 7.5, 9.6, 12.6; Bodleian Library, Oxford 6.16; Bowes Museum, Barnard Castle 7.6; Boys' Brigade 2.13; Bradford Library Local Studies Department 8.15; British Rail (Eastern Region) 8.13; British Telecom 8.2–4; Bryant & May 9.2; Buckinghamshire County Record Office 9.4; Cadbury Brothers Ltd, Historical Records 4.6; Charterhouse School 3.8, 3.9; Chelmsford Public Library 9.5; Christ Church, Oxford 1.15; Christies, Manson & Woods Ltd 10.5; Colman and Rye Libraries of Local History, Norwich 4.20; Cricklade Museum 5.3; Croydon Public Library 4.8; Dublin Civic Museum (Old Dublin Society) 10.1; East Sussex County Library 6.18; Eastgate House Museum, Eastbourne 4.9; Edinburgh City Library 7.21; Eton College 14.4; Finlay & Co. Ltd 6.24; The Francis Frith Collection Ltd 1.11; Gernsheim Collection, University of Texas 8.14; Girton College, Cambridge 3.13; Greater London Record Office 13.6, 13.10; Greenwich Public Library 4.18, 5.10, 7.3, 7.4; Guildford Public Library 9.7; Gwynedd Archives Service 8.1; Hamilton Public Library 4.14; Hampshire County Museum Service 3.4, 5.6, 9.14; Harrogate Public Library 1.10; Home Office 11.1, 11.5, 11.6, 11.8; The Trustees, Ilfracombe Museum 7.29; International Museum of Photography, George Eastman House, New York 1.3; Isle of Wight County Record Office, Newport 1.24; John Lewis Partnership, Archives Department 4.15, 6.25; James Klugman Collection 9.1; Kodak Museum 1.5, 7.22; Lady Margaret Hall, Oxford 3.2; Leeds Public Library 4.12, 6.21; Lewes Historical Society 6.20; Lewisham Public Library 3.3; R.A. Lister & Co. 6.10; London Transport Executive 8.8, 8.11, 8.12; Mander and Mitchenson Theatre Collection 7.31, 7.33, 7.34; Mansell Collection 3.6, 10.9; Museum of London 1.25; National Army Museum 11.11, 11.12; National Library of Wales 6.14; National Monuments Record 4.13, 6.19, 6.26, 6.28, 7.32, 10.6; National Museum of Photography, Film and Television 1.2, 1.21 (a and b), 2.2, 2.5, 2.7, 3.5; National Portrait Gallery 1.6, 1.14, 1.16, 1.18, 1.19, 1.26, 2.6, 7.8, 7.35; National Railway Museum, York 10.11; Newcastle Public Library 5.8; Norfolk County Local Studies Library 9.9; John Oldfield Collection 11.9; Oxford City Library 1.9, 3.10, 5.2, 7.13, 8.9, 9.10; Pontefract Public Library 9.8; Private Collections *frontispiece*, 1.1, 1.2, 1.21 (a and b), 2.1, 2.3, 2.4, 3.12, 4.2, 4.3, 4.7, 5.5, 6.1, 6.3, 6.7, 6.12a, d, 6.17, 7.9, 7.14, 7.15, 7.17, 7.24, 7.26, 10.2, 10.3, 10.7, 10.8, 11.2, 11.3, 11.9, 11.10, 12.4, 13.1, 13.2, 13.5, 14.1, 14.2; Public Record Office 1.17, 1.23, 2.11, 3.1, 3.7, 4.5, 4.11, 5.1, 5.7, 5.12, 5.13, 6.4, 6.5, 6.11, 6.12(b), 7.10–12, 7.16, 7.18, 7.20, 7.25, 7.27, 7.30, 8.6, 8.16, 9.3, 9.11, 9.13, 10.10, 11.4, 11.7, 11.13, 11.14, 12.1–3, 13.4, 14.3; by gracious permission of Her Majesty the Queen 1.7, 4.4; Reading Museum of English Rural Life 6.2, 6.6, 6.8, 6.9; Roedean School 3.11; J. Sainsbury Ltd 6.22, 6.23; St Bartholomew's Hospital 1.20, 13.7, 13.8; Salvation Army 4.10, 5.14–16; Scarborough Public Library 7.28; Science Museum 6.3, 6.7, 6.12(a), 14.1; Shaftesbury Society 2.10; Strathclyde University 4.1, 6.15, 7.7; The Sutcliffe Gallery, Whitby, by agreement with Whitby Literary and Philosophical Society 1.1, 7.19, 8.10; Tower Hamlets Public Library 8.7; Tunbridge Wells Public Library 8.5; United Society for the Propagation of the Gospel 5.17, 5.18; Victoria and Albert Museum 3.15, 9.12; Walker Art Gallery, Liverpool 1.12, 1.13; Watney Mann Ltd 7.2; Weidenfeld & Nicolson 11.10, 13.2; Reece Winstone Collection 4.17

Acknowledgements

We gratefully acknowledge here the most generous help received from Dr I.S.L. Loudun of Wantage with the first part of Chapter 13; Dr Margaret Pelling of the Wellcome Unit for the History of Medicine at Oxford urged us to consult him, and we are most grateful to her for such good advice. Dr John Springhall, Dr Susan Budd and Dr Bill Lambert kindly allowed us to cite their Ph.D. theses at three points in the text, and Miss Mary Tabor of Stevenage gave permission to quote from the autobiographical recollections of her aunt, Mrs Rackham of Cambridge. Mrs Decima Curtis offered us the opportunity of reading the manuscript diaries of her great-aunt, Margaret 'Daisy' Norman, and kindly agreed to let us quote from them. Dr J.L. Lant of Cambridge, Mass., kindly sent us offprints of his articles on the ceremonial aspects of nineteenth-century monarchy, and in addition we have of course found his book, Insubstantial Pageant *(1979), most helpful. We would like too to thank the staff who work on the British Library's newspaper collection at Colindale, and those who service the typing rooms at the Bodleian Library, Oxford, and at the British Library in Bloomsbury. Brian Harrison's obligation to them extends well beyond this book and is steadily mounting; their always courteous and sometimes strenuous services lie behind every page which follows. The importance of having an experienced picture-researcher in compiling a book such as this cannot be over-emphasized. For the first three years of our work on* A Hundred Years Ago, *Philippa Lewis scoured the country and discovered many treasures we had never seen before. We owe her an immense debt of gratitude – and about half the pictures we reproduce. We are also deeply indebted to the owners of the photographs, who have often allowed us to use their unique originals. Although we have relied for the most part on publicly accessible collections, our range of illustrations would have been much impoverished without the generous cooperation of a number of private owners, among them Mr Bryan Brown, Mrs N. Buchanan, Mrs R. Clark, Lord Eliot, Mr D. Hebbert, Mrs H. Mildmay-White, Mr John Oldfield, Mr E.J. Sidery, Mrs M. Spark, Mr Roger Taylor, and the Verney family. Judy Nairn made very helpful stylistic suggestions, and we are grateful to Mr J.A. Kewell of Hove for his preliminary work on the index.*

Introduction: Photography

Chapter 1 # and Society

A hundred years ago, photography was no longer merely one of the nineteenth century's many new technological marvels. Since the discovery of the French daguerreotype (on metal) and the English calotype (on paper) had been announced in January 1839, it had changed in status from scientific wonder to lucrative profession and widely respected art-form. It had enjoyed huge commercial booms, notably the portraiture crazes of the 1850s and 1860s, and had seen the complete careers of some of its greatest artists. The partnership of D.O. Hill and Robert Adamson, for instance, who produced probably its first body of masterpieces, ended when the latter died tragically young in 1848; Julia Margaret Cameron, whose portraits were the most searchingly perceptive of the century, died in 1879. Yet in some respects photography had still not come of age. As one of its most skilled practitioners, 1.1 Frank Meadow Sutcliffe, pointed out, to succeed in it one needed to be an artist, chemist and mechanical engineer.[1] Thus, for its first half century, the new medium was barred to all but those able to invest heavily in time and money, namely comparatively well-off amateurs whose education and cultural awareness often led to high artistic goals, or professionals whose short cuts through the technical difficulties

1.1. Baiting lines at Runswick Bay, near Whitby, Yorkshire. A real fisher-girl in a real situation, but to nostalgic modern eyes the photograph looks as romantic as any Victorian painting, Frank Meadow Sutcliffe, c.1880

enabled them to produce portraits on what was virtually an assembly line.

During the 1880s, all this began to change as cameras improved in speed, mobility and convenience. Speed, brought by the invention of the dry plate, was perhaps the most important. The conventions of portraiture have always led sitters to adopt their most earnest expressions in the studio, and painters rarely show their subjects smiling. In the early days of photography, this was reinforced by the need for long exposures, for it was virtually impossible for subjects to look relaxed when forced to keep still for up to a minute at a time. The first daguerreotypes and calotypes had required exposure times of fifteen to twenty minutes, making portraits impractical, but in 1851 both processes began to be superseded by Frederick Scott Archer's wet collodion, using glass negatives and paper prints.

With very small glass plates, exposure times could be reduced to a matter of seconds and, as early as 1856, George Washington Wilson improved on this still further with his own accelerated 'developer'. Uncovering his camera's lens for only about one-tenth of a second, he took the first of what he called his 'quick exposure' pictures: clouds, moving water, ships at sea, 1.2 and a busy Princes Street, Edinburgh. In 1877, Eadweard Muybridge (an Englishman whose real name was Edward Muggeridge) used a battery of twelve cameras to prove that a galloping horse momentarily takes all four feet off the ground. 1.3

1.2. Two of the earliest 'instantaneous photographs'. Fishing boat at Yarmouth, Isle of Wight (LEFT); *Princes Street, Edinburgh* (RIGHT), *George Washington Wilson, c.1860*

The real breakthrough, though, came with the invention of the dry plate. Developed by various British experimenters throughout the 1870s, it was taken up by manufacturers towards the end of the decade. Sir Joseph Swan's company began selling them in 1877 and the famous 'Ilford' plate was introduced in 1879.

By the end of the decade it enjoyed the world's largest sale. Dry plates enabled Muybridge, at the University of Pennsylvania, to make many studies of movement, especially among human beings and animals. In France, Étienne Marey, inspired by meeting Muybridge in Paris, invented his *fusil photographique* ('photo-

1.4

1.3. Twelve photographs of 'Sallie Gardner', showing that a galloping horse lifts all four feet off the ground simultaneously, Eadweard Muybridge, 1878

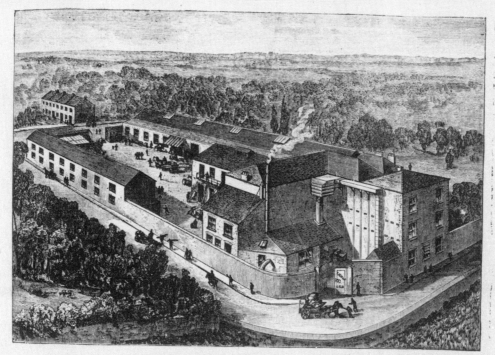

1.4. An advertisement for the best-selling dry plate in the world, made in Britain. 1888

graphic gun'), in which he mounted tiny glass plates in a disc to facilitate quick changing. When the American George Eastman introduced film, lighter and more flexible than glass, as a base for chemical emulsions, Marey was able to speed up still further and record the wing movements of birds in flight. His new apparatus, the Chronophotographe, was really the first moving picture camera; indeed, had he been a businessman or entertainer rather than a scientist, he might now be remembered as the inventor of the cinema. But that had to wait another ten years, and the true significance of photography in the 1880s was its growing ability to capture moments of unposed reality rather than actual movement.

1.5   Eastman's Kodak No. 1 camera, marketed in 1888 with the famous slogan 'You press the button, we do the rest,' used an exposure of only about one-twentieth of a second and was the first generally available hand

1.5. The first 'Kodak' camera, $3\frac{3}{4}''$ high × $3\frac{1}{4}''$ wide × $6\frac{1}{2}''$ long. Its shutter was set by pulling the string. 1888

camera. It was the beginning of a successful commercial campaign to make photography less exclusive, and the thousands of blurred photographs taken with it bear witness to the inexperience of most of those who bought it. Taken on a 100-exposure roll film, they have a characteristic circular shape, rather like F.C. Wratten's 7.22   pictures of the 1884 Boat Race. Another development of 1888 came with the first horse race in which a photo-finish occurred. Ernest Marks, of Plainfield, New Jersey, was able to hand the judges a negative within three minutes of the end of the race. It gradually became possible to capture fleeting facial expressions in a way which today, after years of candid photography, we take for granted. Queen Victoria, for instance, seems scarcely to have smiled in public after Prince

Albert's sudden death in 1861, but during the 1887 Golden Jubilee celebrations, a photographer caught her doing so.   1.6,7

The camera was becoming more flexible in other ways too: though photographs could not normally be taken after dark, electric light was just beginning to be used in some portrait studios in 1880, and the magnesium flash was developed during the decade, though its tendency to produce smoke was a drawback, only overcome by the addition of other chemicals in the mid 1890s. The camera was also better able to capture spontaneous movement now that it could be operated successfully when held in the hand. When the tripod was discarded for ordinary purposes, the camera became much more mobile, and photography far less expensive. In 1889, the *Photographic News* seemed to be looking back to a far-off dark age when it referred to the days when 'numerous loose parts to cameras were prevalent, and the different sections of the camera often needed so much fitting together and adjustment, that an amount of time which would now seem intolerable was lost over each picture.'[2]

As exposure times came down, and the cumbersome and restrictive tripod could be abandoned, the whole business of taking photographs became cleaner and more convenient. 'The last two or three years have witnessed a "great revival" in photography,' declared *The Cornhill Magazine* in May 1885. 'Modifications have been introduced which have rendered this truly fascinating art-science both cleaner, easier, and more certain, while they have further rendered possible the securing of effects previously undreamt of.' The main result was to 'render it possible for any person of ordinary intelligence and industry to produce good and even excellent pictures, with a less expenditure of time and labour than was formerly the case; and this without that soiling of the fingers, clothes and surroundings which had procured for photography the name of the "black art".' All this was due to the fact that 'During the last two years the manufacture of "dry plates" has   1.4 assumed colossal proportions, many thousands of dozens being turned out weekly during the summer months by each of the five or six large firms who have made their preparation a speciality. Almost every photographer, amateur or professional, purchases these wonderfully sensitive plates, and the exhibition of the so-called "instantaneous" picture secured by their means has almost ceased to excite our wonder.'[3]

These improvements produced an explosion in the number of photographs taken. In 1881 only 7,614 people were engaged in professional photography in England and Wales, but by 1891 their number had

HER MAJESTY THE QUEEN.
AN INSTANTANEOUS PHOTOGRAPH FROM LIFE.

HER MAJESTY'S GRACIOUS SMILE.

Charles Knight,
Court Photographer,   26, QUEEN'S ROAD,
                                   ALDERSHOT.

1,6,7. In most of her photographs, Queen Victoria, like the majority of her subjects, appears unsmiling. But, as one lady at court wrote: 'Those who never saw the Queen's smile can have little idea of the marvellous way in which it brightened and exhilarated the lines of the Queen's features in advancing years. It came very suddenly, in the form of a mild radiance over the whole face, a softening and raising of the lines of the lips, a flash of kindly light beaming from the eyes' (Lady Ponsonby). Victoria received a loyal address from the Mayor and Corporation of Newport, Isle of Wight, near her home at Osborne House, at the celebration of her Golden Jubilee

(BELOW). *A photographer was there to capture the royal smile. The detail from the photograph (LEFT) was issued in cabinet form, as an 'instantaneous Photograph from Life', six years later, Charles Knight, 1887*

risen to 12,397; in 1887, the *Photographic News* estimated that about 3,000 people in the United Kingdom (including Ireland) owned their own photographic businesses. More significant, at least for the status of the photograph as historical evidence, was the still faster rise in the number of amateurs; there were fourteen photographic clubs in 1880 but 256 in 1900. By 1890, 50,000 Kodak cameras had been sold and, by 1905, roughly one in ten of the population used a camera.[4] Even aristocratic ladies found it an acceptable substitute for the embroidery needle and the watercolour brush, and several of the pictures in this book were taken by them. A few women established portrait studios (Mrs E. Higgins, of Stamford, for instance) but their professional involvement was more often in the printing and developing rooms of what was becoming an industry.

Two Scottish companies typify the growth of the industry. In Dundee, James Valentine & Sons, who specialized in publishing views of Scotland, had forty employees producing some 3,000 prints a day. In Aberdeen, George Washington Wilson, described in the 1881 census as 'master photographer and town councillor', employed fifteen men, twenty-one women, two boys and two girls, and gave employment to 150 people

in the busy summer months.[5] By 1884, his premises spread over half an acre, and included elaborate processing equipment, changing and sensitizing rooms, glass-roofed toning and fixing rooms where printing frames were moved about on miniature tramways, and a portrait studio. On the ground floor of one building, women sorted the orders 'hourly arriving by post', and in another Wilson's daughter scanned the foreign journals, translating items which she thought might be of use to her father.[6]

New photographic periodicals and annuals were springing up to cater for this new interest. The oldest, called *The Journal of the Photographic Society of London* when it first appeared in March 1853, had in 1859 become, more simply, *The Photographic Journal*. Its publishers, the reputable Photographic Society of London, had also been founded in 1853 and boasted Queen Victoria and the Prince of Wales as patrons. Its chief interests were technical: apart from organizing an annual exhibition (which, in 1882, had 7,439 visitors), it had then, as now, little impact on the actual art of photography. By 1888, it had only 513 members, for many had left to form new clubs.[7] In London, for instance, the Camera Club (which also still exists today) was founded in 1885, and its premises included a

1.8. G.W. Wilson & Co.'s printing, enlarging and publishing works, St Swithin's, Aberdeen. Most of the employees seem to be women. c.1885

1.9,10. The Oxford headquarters of Taunt & Co., Photographers, from 1874 to 1895 (LEFT). Here and at their High Wycombe branch they advertised their services as 'Carvers and Gilders' and 'Picture Frame Makers', Henry Taunt, 1881. Yates's 'Tit Bits' Studio (ABOVE), an altogether more modest affair, also apparently supplemented its income with non-photographic business, Lonsdale Yates, c.1890

studio and enlarging room, a workshop and library, as well as dining and billiard rooms. Outside London, sixteen clubs were founded between 1880 and 1884, and a further eighty-eight between 1885 and 1889.[8] By the end of the decade, the *Photographic Journal*'s austerely technical reports of the Photographic Society meetings began to refer to embarrassing attempts by the more radical members to turn it away from technicalities and academic proprieties. Perhaps they were influenced by the example of the New English Art Club, which seceded from the Royal Academy of Fine Arts in 1886. They did not break through the Society's conservatism until the 1890s.[9]

Photographic retailing was also booming. Although the Yates family of Harrogate sold ice creams as well as taking photographs, Henry Taunt's Oxford shop was already a substantial affair in 1881. By the end of the decade, the Kodak camera was being advertised even in small non-specialist shops up and down the country. In a big city like Birmingham there were dozens of

1.11. Seaside scenes were always popular. Frith & Co.'s view of New Brighton sands, Cheshire, shows several beach photographers' booths

photographic retailers. As a recreation, photography was beginning to compete with the church and the pub. The manufacture of photographic equipment contributed to that boom in consumer goods which now modifies our traditional view of the period as one of economic depression. Parts of the countryside were in decline, unemployment was alarming, and the rate of economic growth was slowing down; but on the other hand opportunities for enjoyment were increasing – in holiday resorts and music halls, at the chain store and at home, on bicycles and in trains.

In the range and quality of its photographic evidence, then, the decade that began in the 1880s is the first in which Britain revealed itself to posterity with a visual completeness approaching the standard we now take for granted. And it is with the photograph as evidence that we are concerned in this book. Our discussion of the history of photography is intended only to help place the photographs in context and to try to illuminate their unique documentary value, to which historians have so far given surprisingly little attention. Partly, they have been properly cautious about *any* new forms of evidence. But there has also been a curious separation between the professional his-

torian, often displaying photographs on the page like postage stamps to decorate his prose or on a screen to spice his lecture, and the editor of photographic collections, whose commentary, largely antiquarian and nostalgic, merely provides captions for each picture. But the recovery of the past is difficult enough, without neglecting any major source of information. It is time that the photograph participated fully in that extraordinary expansion in the range of evidence available to historians which has been a remarkable feature of historical writing since the Second World War. If folksong, tape-recorded interviews, flags and banners, paintings, architecture, sculpture and ephemera of all sorts are now thought proper supplements to the historian's traditional written sources, so surely is the photograph.

Even where a photograph can tell us nothing new, it often lends impact to what we know already. It can alert the imagination of the historian, and make it easier for him to alert the imagination of his readers. It can sometimes produce a shock of recognition which prose cannot. In the 1880s, political orators, among others, were already becoming aware of this. When Henry Broadhurst, the trade union leader, was addressing the House of Commons on the need to en-franchise leaseholders, he distributed to fellow M.P.s photographs of the dilapidation of houses nearing the end of their lease. Gladstone, at a key moment in a speech on Home Rule delivered in Birmingham in November 1888, produced two photographs of Mitchelstown in the hope of discrediting official accounts of violent incidents there.[10]

Two aspects of photography will particularly interest the historian. One is the medium's technical evolution, commercial exploitation and stylistic development. As recently as 1955, the Gernsheims expressed surprise that the history of British photography had been 'so completely neglected'.[11] They had lighted upon an important aspect of modern British history which deserved setting in its contemporary context. This first aspect has already been briefly mentioned, and has also been widely discussed among the historians of photography. The second aspect is the impact of photography on society as a whole; it is difficult to assess, but it is at least as interesting, and has rather gone by default. Although by the 1880s the camera was making a major social impact, the words 'camera', 'photography' and 'film' rarely enter the indexes of historical textbooks concerned with the decade. At least four areas of major social influence for photography can be detected: those concerned with artistic activity, intellectual life, social class and politics. Each deserves a little consideration here.

As with so many technological revolutions – the internal combustion engine and the radio spring to mind – the camera's full social significance was not realized at the time. The artistic and scientific breakthrough which it represented was not recognized, nor was its full potential for capturing reality exploited. Most photographers did not at first feel able to stand on their own feet, and many yearned for the professional 1.12 and creative prestige of the artist. Peter Henry Emerson, for instance, was deeply influenced by the French painter of peasant scenes Jean François Millet, and 1.13 stayed on the houseboat of a painter friend, Thomas Goodall, when photographing on the Norfolk Broads. Frank Meadow Sutcliffe advised photographers, as late as 1916, to emulate painters. 'Unlike the art of painting,' he wrote, 'photography cannot look up to any old masters whose work the student may be sure is right. We photographers have no Rembrandts, no Franz Hals, no Constables, no Whistlers. So the student had better not look at photographs after all till his taste is perfectly broken in. It will be safer for him to look at pictures.'[12]

By so deferring to the values of the painter, the photographer at first seemed his ally rather than his rival. On portrait painting, in particular, his impact was at first beneficial. David Octavius Hill was one of many who used photographs as reference material, though nowadays it is his photographs we admire, not his paintings. Photographs soon entered into the painter's very process of composition, reducing the number of sittings for a portrait, enriching the raw material from which a painting could be worked up, and sometimes even being painted over. They also enabled painters and art-lovers to familiarize themselves with reproductions of paintings from many sources. In 1885, the German Braun Company was entrusted, to the displeasure of some British firms, with the task of photographing paintings in the National Gallery and, later, in Buckingham Palace. In 1894, when Gladstone proposed to confer baronetcies on G.F. Watts and Edward Burne-Jones, Queen Victoria gave her approval after 'having herself seen photographs of the latter's works wh[ich] show a g[rea]t power of composition and correct drawing, tho' his colouring, like Watts's, is not considered good.'[13]

Yet in the long run, the camera's impact on the painter who aimed at representation was disastrous. By 1859 the Royal Academy exhibition was completely lacking in miniatures, and by the 1880s this artform had almost disappeared. Some miniaturists, like Henry Collen, turned to photography instead. Eventually the camera's greater accuracy and versatility in portraying reality was to force artists away from representation altogether, but in the 1880s they were still fighting a losing battle to surpass its ability to render faithful impressions of reality.

Intellectual life also responded to the camera unobtrusively, and in many dimensions. In 1882 the *Photographic News*, discussing photography's contribution to science, described it as 'a maid-of-all-work, put upon on every occasion, to discharge all sorts of functions, whether menial or high-class.' It was employed at two levels: in the process of investigation, and in recording the results. As early as 1855 the Ordnance Survey had begun to experiment with photography in producing maps; it soon found that the camera made it possible simultaneously to increase accuracy while reducing staff. Muybridge and Marey made a considerable impact on British photographic periodicals during 1882 with their revelations about muscular action and motion in men and animals. And whereas at the beginning of the decade the *Photographic News* grumbled at the reluctance of doctors to use the camera in hospitals, by 1888 a contributor could say that it was being regularly employed to record symptoms, and that this was done far more accurately, and with far less

1.12,13. Victorian photographers and painters frequently collaborated. P.H. Emerson, Norfolk amateur photographer and polemicist, took his 'Setting the Bow Net' (ABOVE) while staying on the houseboat of a friend, the painter Thomas Goodall, 1885. Goodall's oil painting 'The Bow Net' (BELOW) may well be based on Emerson's photograph, but the viewpoint is slightly higher and the background softer and more romantic. 1886

1.14,15. 'All artists use photographs now', the Pre-Raphaelite painter Sir John Millais told Beatrix Potter (Journal, 9 February 1884). Later in the year she wrote: 'Papa has been photographing old Gladstone this morning at Mr. Millais'. The old person is evidently a great talker if once started ... They kept off politics of course, and talked about photography. Mr. Gladstone talked of it on a large scale, but not technically. What would it come to, how far would the art be carried, did Papa think people would ever be photographed in colours?' (Journal, 28 July 1884)

Millais often asked his friend Rupert Potter to take studies from his paintings (the famous 'Bubbles' among them) and declared that 'the professionals aren't fit to hold a candle to papa' (Beatrix Potter's Journal, 30 January 1884). Potter's photograph of W.E. Gladstone (LEFT) justifies such praise. It not only defines the powerful public figure, but suggests a vulnerability quite lacking in Millais' more bland and flattering portrait (BELOW). Seeing the painting at the Royal Academy, Disraeli said the missing characteristic was 'vindictiveness'! 1884

1.16. *The actor Henry Irving, aware how much photographs affected his public image, rigorously controlled their publication. This 'day dress' portrait is one that met with his approval, Alexander Bassano, 1887*

1.17. *The painter Andrew Gow, one of a published series of portraits of 'Royal Academicians in their Studios', Joseph P. Mayell, 1888*

discomfort to patients, than had ever been possible for the artist.[14]

As for the storing of evidence – archaeological, criminological, architectural, philanthropic – the camera was invaluable. As early as the 1850s, prison governors were keeping photographic records of prisoners, together with details of their criminal history, and by 1869 Dr Barnardo had begun using photographs of destitute children to advertise his cause. He sold these 'before and after' photographs in packets until 1877, when they were pronounced deceptive by arbitrators; thereafter, he employed them only for purposes of identification. By the 1860s Archibald MacLaren, pioneer in Britain of anthropometry and Prussian gymnastics, was using 'before and after' photographs of his military pupils. The Society for Photographing Relics of Old London, founded in 1875, had produced 120 carbon prints by 1886. In 1885 W. Jerome Harrison, a peripatetic science teacher, was urging Birmingham photographers to conduct local surveys; in 1892 he made a speech to the Photographic Society in London on the subject of a national record, and his paper delivered to the Chicago World's Congress of 1893 advocated an international survey. Several were begun in English counties, and in 1897 the National Photographic Record was established 'to obtain photographic records of all objects and scenes of interest in the British Isles, and to deposit them with explanatory notes, in the British Museum, where they may be safely stored, and be accessible to the public under proper regulations.'[15] Over 4,000 of these photographs, taken between 1897 and the Record's demise in 1910, are still in the museum.

On society as a whole the camera exerted an intangible but subtly pervasive influence by accentuating the pressures towards contemporaneity. Andrew Gow – painter of *The Last Days of Edward VI* (1880), *Cromwell at Dunbar* (1886) and *The Flight of James II after the Battle of the Boyne* (1888) – might still surround himself with historical bric-a-brac in his studio, but unbeknown to him, social change was gradually eroding the Victorians' profound consciousness of their own history. The camera was not solely responsible for this; intellectual specialization and the growth of academic professionalism among historians – symbolized by the founding of the *English Historical Review* in 1886 – were drawing history away from the general public. But it contributed to that speeding up of life which had begun with the industrial revolution and has continued ever since. It is one of the roots of our present-day preoccupation with the immediate and the here-and-now, with current affairs, 'instant history' and

perpetual innovation. In November 1884 the *Photographic News* was so impressed by the increased simplicity of the camera and its equipment that it envisaged the day when the two great barriers to the press reporter's use of the camera – its weight and the time taken to print the positive – would be removed; when that time came, the reporter would be able to dispense with the artist who was at present entrusted with providing illustrations. By August 1888 the paper had visions of the day when the stenographer and the journalistic photographer would hunt in couples, 'or, better still, every first-class reporter of the future will carry a camera as well as a note-book, and be, in fact, a photographic operator and a stenographer rolled into one!' Old hands were soon getting nostalgic for the days when cameras needed elaborate preparation before the photograph could be taken.[16]

The camera is associated with another deep-rooted modern tendency: that democratization of British society which has been one of its major themes for nearly two centuries. Queen Victoria had been well to the fore in developing a taste for photography in Britain. The foundation of George Wilson's success was his appointment in 1873 to 'the place and quality of photographer to Her Majesty in Scotland.' He was the seventh to earn the royal warrant, and there were to be forty more before the end of the reign.[17] While Prince Albert was still alive, the royal couple owned and used cameras, and a dark room was built for them at Windsor Castle under the supervision of Roger Fenton, a founder and first secretary of the Photographic Society. They visited its first exhibition in 1854, and agreed to become its patrons (though it did not become 'Royal' until 1893). The Queen avidly collected snapshots, and made up no less than forty-four albums of 'Portraits of Royal Children' between 1848 and the end of the century. Her rooms in the royal homes were stuffed with photographs, especially during widowhood, including many of the Prince Consort. She often gave portraits of herself as presents; to Lord Salisbury in 1886 when he handed over office to Gladstone; to the Duke of Edinburgh on his departure to command the Mediterranean Fleet 'the last new photograph of myself in a case'; and to the dying Emperor Frederick III of Germany, who kissed it 'but, a fit of coughing coming on, we left him.'[18] Cameras were favourite gifts to the Queen's relatives and children, many of whom took lessons at the London Stereoscopic School of Photography. Prince Alfred and the Princesses Helena and Beatrice were keen, the Prince of Wales rather less so. In 1885, however, the Princess of Wales, later Queen Alexandra, became the most enthusiastic royal

1.18 (ABOVE). *Queen Victoria's bedroom at Balmoral, with a photograph of the dead Prince Albert and a wreath, George Washington Wilson, c.1866*

1.19 (RIGHT). *Sir James Brooke, Victorian adventurer, painted in an eastern landscape by Sir Francis Grant, later President of the Royal Academy. 1847*

photographer and, with a Kodak hand camera presented by George Eastman, took many snapshots, some of which were included in public exhibitions in the 1890s and were published after the turn of the century.

The British governing élite had long enjoyed the double privilege of determining what records survived from their generation for posterity, and of employing artists who, often sycophantically, enhanced their beauty and social standing. In the early 1920s, just before his death, Willoughby de Broke drew a nostalgic but remarkable portrait of English provincial landed society as it had once been. He showed as little patience with the camera as with any other of the innovations which had occurred during his lifetime. For him, the snapshot had 'done more to impair the dignity of the English nation than any other recent invention.' Whereas even at its best a photograph could capture a sitter's appearance only at a particular moment, an

1.19 artist like Sir Francis Grant, the great painter of the

1.20. A nursing sister surrounded by prints, photographs and knick-knacks at St Bartholomew's Hospital, London. Undated, probably early 1890s

mid-Victorian English gentry, could employ his expertise as gentleman and foxhunter to bring out the mood and essence of his subject: 'He was of their class,' wrote de Broke; 'he knew how a well-bred man ought to sit on a well-bred horse, and he put him there, as few other artists ever could, plumb in the middle of the saddle.' Dismissing Queen Victoria's suspicion that photography would put an end to miniature portrait-painting, Alfred Chalon replied 'Ah, non Madame, photographie can't flattère'; he was wrong about miniatures but partially correct about photography, whose relative truthfulness made it easier for beautiful women in any social class to win a place in high society.[19] Photographs of such camera beauties as Mrs Cornwallis-West, Lillie Langtry and Mrs Luke Wheeler were widely disseminated.

The camera's democratizing impact was felt at more than one level: in addition to promoting a society where beauty could force its way through class bar-riers, it enabled the comparatively poor to own portraits, hitherto the preserve of the rich and leisured. As early as 1861 the *Photographic News* pointed out that photography had 'swept away many of the illiberal distinctions of rank and wealth' by enabling the poor man to possess as lifelike a portrait of his wife or child as any monarch. The anonymous hospital sister was as free as Queen Victoria to accumulate photographs among the knick-knacks on her mantelpiece. In 1887 the Princess of Wales visited the appallingly crippled 'Elephant Man' at the London Hospital and saw the collection of autographed portraits which gave him such pleasure; her signed photograph arrived from Marlborough House soon afterwards. 'Blessed be the inventor of photography!' wrote Thomas Carlyle's wife Jane in 1859: 'I set him above even the inventor of chloroform! It has given more positive pleasure to poor suffering humanity than anything that has "cast up" in my time or is like to. – this art by which even the "poor" can possess themselves of tolerable likenesses of their absent dear ones. . . . I have . . . photographs of old lovers! old friends, old servants, old dogs!' J.R. Green acknowledged the new situation in 1871: 'Any one who knows what the worth of family affection is among the lower classes, and who has seen the array of little portraits stuck over a labourer's fireplace . . . will perhaps feel with me that . . . the sixpenny photograph is doing more for the poor than all the philanthropists in the world.'[20]

Even the image of the past conveyed to posterity could be democratized now that so many people were involved in creating it. The 1880s were to see the end of the monopoly of the photographic expert, whether professional or amateur. The dry plate, the Kodak No. 1, and the new informality in photography made the propagandist for, and distinguished pioneer of, artistic photography P.H. Emerson abandon its practice, denying that it was an art form at all. Lewis Carroll gave up twenty-five years of highly skilled and intensive photography in 1880, and later dismissed all dry-plate photography as 'inferior, in artistic effect, to the now abandoned "wet plate".'[21] For a few years, at least, it seems that he was right. For more than a decade there were no great artist photographers, at least in Britain.

The camera was involved in the democratizing process in one further way: it rapidly became an adjunct to the politicians' publicity machine. At the general election of 1880 several candidates presented voters with their photographs when canvassing. 'This is decidedly a happy idea,' wrote the *Photographic News*, 'since the canvassers are able to bring, face to face with the candidate, all the electors, even those who are unwilling to go through the ordeal of a public meeting.' In London, magic lantern portraits of the local candidates were even projected onto a house with the aid of equipment in its front garden. At the general election of 1886, photographs of Gladstone were 'scattered broadcast throughout certain electoral districts,' and one candidate distributed a picture of a Tipperary mud cabin's interior in the hope of strengthening his appeal for justice to Ireland. Photographs could by then be readily bought in the shops; the camera had made Lord Randolph Churchill so generally recognizable that his European holiday in that year was by no means as private as he would have liked. All the paraphernalia of publicity accompanied Gladstone on his triumphal tour of the West Country in 1889, and when he was formally greeted by the local dignitaries at Romsey the *Daily News* correspondent noted that 'the inevitable photographer prepared his camera for a photograph of the scene.'[22]

We are by no means the first to recognize the historical importance of photographs, as the bibliography to this chapter testifies. Publishers in recent years have been only too eager to bring out collections of them. But many are antiquarian or topographical in purpose, whereas our theme is the history of the nation as a whole; we are concerned with local institutions and scenes only if they seem to illustrate some national development. Other photographic books are designed for connoisseurs, so that they can appreciate the value of surviving objects manufactured in the 1880s. Our aim is, by contrast, to recapture a past which has gone for ever – to use the photographs which will place the artefacts of the period in their contemporary setting.

There is a great deal to choose from. Contrary to the London Stereoscopic Company's optimistic quotation from the *Morning Post*, 'No one ever throws away a good Photograph,' many taken in the 1880s have in fact been lost, neglected or destroyed; others that we would find revealing could never be taken. Nonetheless, far more pictures survive than can possibly be reproduced in one volume. Going beyond already published photographs and those accessible in well-

1.21. The London Stereoscopic & Photographic Company's pocket calendar, with carbon print of a portrait of Mary Anderson, 1884. According to Beatrice Potter: 'Miss Mary Anderson charges the photographers £150 for every sitting she gives them' (Journal, 10 February 1884)

known national collections, we have found little-known material to illustrate neglected aspects of British society in institutions such as schools, companies, and religious organizations. We have also searched through many books of old photographs as well as consulting biographies and histories which include visual material. A particularly rich source has been the Public Record Office. As a result of the 1862 Fine Arts Copyright Act (25 & 26 Victoria, Cap. 68), photographers who wanted to establish copyright in their works lodged descriptions of them at Stationers' Hall and, in some cases, actual prints. Each of the thirty-nine illustrations in this book from the P.R.O. was originally such an attachment to a Memorandum for Registration under Copyright (Works of Art) Act, and many are published for the first time. Among the most striking finds from this source is J.A. Smythe's photograph of the cast of Gilbert and Sullivan's *The Mikado*, taken by electric light on stage at the Savoy Theatre in 1885, one of the first set of pictures ever made in such circumstances.

In selecting items for inclusion, we have aimed to reveal the full range of illumination which the camera can provide on the decade; where possible, we have therefore included material which simultaneously throws light on more than one aspect of British life.

Where both published and unpublished photographs exist to illustrate a point, we have chosen the unpublished. Wherever possible we have chosen pictures taken in the 1880s, though we cannot always be totally sure of the decade. Dating is a constant problem. Those who created or acquired photographs in the nineteenth and twentieth centuries often did not bother to caption them, assuming that all who saw them would recognize the subject, the occasion, and the place. Internal evidence, whether taken from objects shown (costume, architecture, vehicles, etc.) or from technical information (type of negative or print, speed of exposure) is often helpful, but needs to be supplemented by specialists in many different areas. Sometimes external evidence (where the photograph was located, documents found with it, and so on) can help. The least reliable clues – as with all forms of recent history – seem to be those supplied by human memory. Wherever we have been uncertain of the date of a photograph, we have referred to the problem in the caption. But we are only too aware that there will be errors.

We have also tried where possible to choose pictures whose human subjects are engaged in their daily business, and not staring fixedly into the camera. In a period where exposure times were still relatively long

7.30

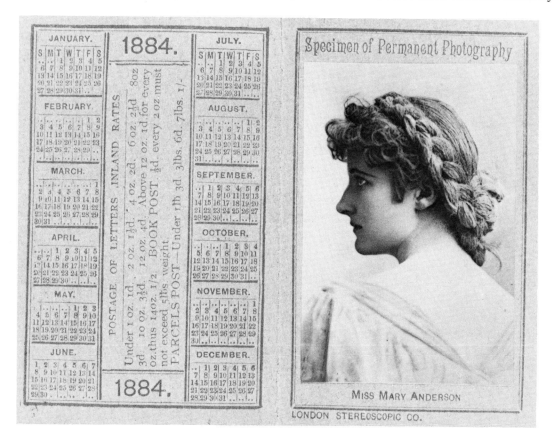

and equipment relatively cumbersome, this has not always been possible. There were also cultural inhibitions: 'Laundrymaids hanging out sheets, and carrying heavy baskets of clothes would make grand subjects,' Sutcliffe grumbled, 'if laundrymaids had not such objections to be photographed in anything but their Sunday garments.'[23] In some situations, though, formality is an asset – for instance, in studying ceremonial and public occasions, which were of major political and social importance in the 1880s. Their historical significance is often neglected because they seem so ephemeral, their effects so intangible.

Although we attach great importance to photographic evidence, we recognize that photographs alone cannot hope to illuminate all aspects of British society in the 1880s. For technical or cultural reasons, many aspects of behaviour elude the camera at any time. All societies discourage it in certain circumstances; few would be callous enough, for example, deliberately to photograph the precise moment of death, even when it occurs naturally – though pictures taken as mementos

14.2,3 after death were far more common in the 1880s than they are now. Nor was the camera as versatile as it is now; for example, it could not capture the colour and panoply so central to the political and social life of the day.

Furthermore photographers in the 1880s, like photographers in any generation, failed to bear the historian's requirements in mind. They pursued the dramatic, the unusual, the special, and (as far as they were technically able) the unexpected. By contrast, the events of greatest interest to the historian are often routine and continuous in nature, imperceptible in their processes of change and unexciting to the eye. The confidential and the unpredictable can rarely be photographed even today; then it was still more of a problem, given the slow speed of photographic materials and the relative privacy of government and of so many other aspects of British life. Perhaps the most significant political event of the decade was the assassination of Lord Frederick Cavendish in Phoenix Park in 1882, yet for several reasons no photograph could possibly have been taken; still less could the camera capture for posterity what is far more interesting to the historian – the way the political system reacted to that tragic moment in Anglo-Irish relations.

In the 1880s reticence was much more widespread than it is today: the pursuit of publicity seemed a radical cry, and rather vulgar. The ordinary citizen often felt a delicate sense of privacy and a pronounced distaste, unfamiliar to us, for notoriety. The distinguished photographer Frank Meadow Sutcliffe had been well

1.22. A picnic for the members of the Dundee East of Scotland Photographic Association in the Den of Airlie. 1882

1.23. At the mill, Goring, Berkshire. But the camera was becoming an acceptable substitute for the paintbrush, Henry Tripp, 1885

known in the Whitby area for over fifty years when he wrote of the local superstition that it was unlucky to be drawn or photographed: such reserve was particularly common, he said, 'among old people in outlying moor edge farms, and out of the way fishing villages'.[24] Despite politicians' increasing resort to the photograph, few even thought of this method of recording the inner processes of government, the mysteries of religious ceremonial or the intimacies of the home. Childbirth, whose agonies and dangers overshadowed so many women's lives, remained concealed from public view. As for politics, W.E. Gladstone – the decade's most prominent statesman and Liberal Prime Minister from 1880 to 1885 and again in 1886 – described his government of 1880 as 'a wild romance of politics, with a continual succession of hairbreadth escapes and strange accidents pressing upon one another.'[25] All too little of this can be captured in photographs, for privacy lies at the heart of the political process. Lord Salisbury,

Conservative leader and Prime Minister in 1885 and from 1886 to 1892, insisted that Cabinet proceedings should be confidential, and even forbade the taking of notes. Only in the late 1920s, with the invention of the 35mm camera, did press photographers like Dr Erich Salomon penetrate the inner councils of government, and then only for the brief moments when the political process itself was in temporary suspension.

When the Victorians allowed themselves to be photographed or painted, they adopted stiffly formal poses. With photographs, the reasons may have been partly technical, but it was also regarded as appropriate, especially at weddings, christenings, anniversaries, outings and funerals, for this has been described as 'an age which hardly knew how to question the psychic value of ceremony.' Yet however much people posed, froze or postured before the camera, it was still an instrument which 'observes, but does not select.'[26] We therefore concentrate in this

1.24,25. The slowness of the glass plates used for most 1880s negatives makes photographs taken in bad light, or when the subject was in movement, exceptional. (ABOVE) Newport, Isle of Wight, after an unusually heavy snowstorm. 1881. (RIGHT) Old houses, Aldgate. Published by the Society for Photographing Relics of Old London, 1883, Henry Dixon, possibly late 1870s

book on photographic rather than on other forms of visual evidence, such as drawing and painting. And, although buildings, furniture and other artefacts of the period have survived into our time, only contemporary photographs can give an idea of the way they were seen – and used – in the 1880s.

One further distortion would be encouraged by an analysis of the decade by means of photographs alone. Cameras needed plenty of light, and do not normally reveal a Britain which, particularly in winter, was smothered in snow, fog and rain. Henry Dixon, explaining in 1880 the slow progress being made by the Society for Photographing the Relics of Old London, pointed out that 'Each subject wants its special time of day, and special weather; so the work cannot be quickly done.' It is worth pointing out that a downward cycle in central England's January and July mean temperature had begun in the late 1860s, and persisted until the late 1880s, reaching a new peak in the early twentieth century. The mean temperature between 1881 and 1890, 47.9°F, was well below that for England and Wales between 1941 and 1970, 50°F. This is true for every month in the calendar.[27] Furthermore, in a relatively agricultural and outdoor society, bad weather damaged the economy, especially in Ireland, and by modern standards had an undue influence on the daily work of a great many people. Long after he had retired from the trade, George Howell, the prominent Labour leader of the 1880s, was sent into a depression by bad weather which would throw bricklayers out of work. So we must beware of a lingering regret for the long hot summers which shimmer in many Victorian photographs.

Nor should we pine for a lost world not yet overrun by cars and office blocks; horses, cobblestones and back alleys made towns at least as dangerous and dirty as

1.24

1.25

8.6

they are today, and probably more so. Photographs also encourage another form of nostalgia; they hide away the unrespectable elements in society, except where philanthropists or politicians have taken them up for their own specific purposes. Behind the lavishness of the fancy-dress ball and the elegance of aristocratic tailoring there were dreary and drudging aspects of life which were almost never photographed.

In the important areas which the camera did not penetrate, prose must take over. The photographs in this book are linked to a historical discussion which draws on evidence of many other types. We have no desire to launch a new school of 'visual history'. Such a term would be as misleading as 'oral history', for historical writing can no more be based primarily on photographs than on interviews. Other types of evidence will affect the historian's approach to visual material, and this in turn will lead him on to evidence of other types. Nonetheless from the outset the arrangement and even the content of the prose in this book have been moulded by the photographic evidence, which has played a far more central role in its development than that of mere stimulus or afterthought.

There are other difficulties, too. A decade is not in itself an obvious unit for historical analysis. The 1880s did not seem as distinctive at the time as they have come to feel in retrospect, and even this latter-day flavour is in many ways misleading. In most areas of life, tendencies from earlier decades persist, just as later conduct is anticipated. A decade is an arbitrarily abstracted segment of time, coarsely cutting through a continuous and complex series of events. Each area of national life has its own chronology, and by no means all saw significant changes during the 1880s – let alone changes which fell neatly between 1 January 1880 and 31 December 1889. We have therefore occasionally deliberately strayed outside our chosen period in search of photographs and other evidence where it can reasonably be taken to illustrate a situation which actually did prevail during the decade.

In writing about the 1880s, it would have been quite possible to adopt a chronological structure, as several excellent histories have done. But photographs focus on the individual and on his relationship to the environment; they impose a time-scale inevitably less integrated or precise than when institutions with their clear chronologies are the focus of attention. A chronological arrangement therefore seemed inappropriate, though we have tried to capture some of its merits by including a Chronology of Events (page 322). We were also unable to adopt the static 'social photograph' approach of T.H.S. Escott's valuable *England: Its People, Polity and Pursuits* (1885), which surveyed institutions and social groupings comprehensively but in no logical order. We lack the freedom of manoeuvre allowed by his six hundred pages of closely packed print and we are now perhaps in a better position to analyse long-term tendencies and change. Sixty years after Escott, Helen Lynd's penetrating *England in the Eighteen-Eighties* (1945) was preoccupied with social and economic change. So it dealt first with areas where change was occurring, and then with the social institutions which produced that change. But a rounded analysis of the decade must be equally concerned with tradition and stability. So, ultimately, it seemed best to follow the human life cycle from childhood to school and university, through marriage, church and chapel, work and leisure. After this follows a discussion of the social and political framework which shaped the individual's life in the 1880s; this section begins by outlining the fragmenting influences (mostly concerned with region and class), and moves on to the attitudes, institutions and personalities which brought stability and political cohesion. In conclusion, we deal with sickness, old age and death.

Throughout this volume, we have tried to combine two aims: to explore the opportunities offered to historians by evidence contained in photographs and to describe British society as it was in the 1880s. We have regarded the roles of historian and expert in photographs as equal, each being able to bring new knowledge to the other. Most of our illustrations have been chosen with these two aims in view, though some may have crept in simply because they were too good as photographs to leave out. Here, the economics of modern publishing are a problem. The number of illustrations, the available methods of reproduction, and sheer lack of space have sometimes inhibited us. But we still hope to give the reader a good idea of the quality of photographs of the period, and the types of photographs being taken: *cartes de visite*, formal records and family groups, 'art' photographs, action pictures, snapshots and so on. For the photographic evidence to be useful, the boundaries and conventions which constrained the photographer must be understood.

In an increasingly specialist world, one of history's major attractions is its continued pursuit of readability and breadth of scope. More and more, historians must collaborate with specialists in particular areas: psychology, economics, sociology, social anthropology, political science, literature, painting, photography. Our hope is that we will encourage people to look again at the many photographs and albums which still lie neglected in attics, cupboards, offices and libraries throughout the country. When this is done, a richer insight into the 1880s and other decades will be possible.

Our volume has one further objective: to stimulate interest in what Britain was like one hundred years ago. Its combination of prose and photographs should enable the reader to reach his own conclusions about the period and to be more independent of the authors' interests and outlook than is usually possible. Photographs can perhaps free the reader from subservience to the prose of any one historian; they can bring him closer to a valuable source of information about the period, and can allow him to monitor the writer's views by constant cross-reference to that source. We hope he will agree with some of our analyses, but we shall have failed in at least one of our objectives if he does not sometimes choose to disagree.

1.26. The front and back of a cabinet photograph of Queen Victoria presented to his customers by a Scarborough grocer, Bassano, 1887

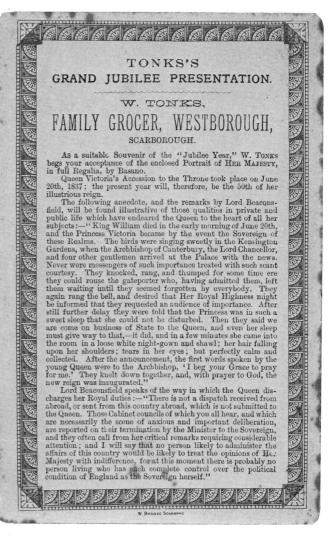

Chapter 2 *Childhood*

'The past is a foreign country: they do things differently there.'[1] This is particularly difficult to remember for so recent a period as the 1880s: language, conduct, environment and even some attitudes seem familiar. Yet in the area of childhood, the contrasts could hardly be greater. It was difficult in the 1880s even to get through the first year of life: in England and Wales between 1880 and 1889 an average of 142 infants under twelve months died annually per thousand live births, as compared with only 18 between 1965 and 1974. This was partly because the 2,646 midwives of England and Wales in 1881 (all female, and four-fifths over forty five) were not yet members of a profession with recognized standards. But the trend in infant mortality was improving, and figures were much worse in France, Germany, Italy, Austria and Russia.[2]

Although children often died after their first year, as Victorian novels frequently testify, there were by modern standards a great many young people in Britain; in 1881, 26 per cent of the population in England and Wales were under ten, 46 per cent under twenty (equivalent figures for 1975 were 15 per cent and 30 per cent).[3] This had immense implications for the whole experience of childhood; not only were there proportionately fewer adults in the world at large – there were also far more children within each family.

2.1. Village children from Holbeton, Devon, at school feast on Mothecombe Beach. Photographed by one of a growing number of aristocratic amateurs, Lady Georgiana Mildmay, c.1885

Family lessons, family games, family holidays, family newspapers, family functions of every kind made it unnecessary for the young child to venture very far outside the home for his major needs. The size of family has been falling almost continuously ever since. By 1900–9 women in England and Wales under forty five were bearing an average of 3.53 children, but only 1.98 by 1941. In 1911, 41 per cent of the households in England and Wales had five members or more, but only 16 per cent in 1966.[4]

The experience of childhood varied profoundly with class, region and gender. Middle-class parents were shielded from the less pleasant aspects of child-rearing and even from weaning by an army of nannies and nurses who often took great pride in their work. We know all too little about the history of child-rearing, but autobiographies so often record the child's deep affection for these women that it must frequently have been the middle-class parent, rather than the child, who suffered from emotional deprivation. Once weaned, the middle-class child required elaborate dressing (his clothes were hardly practical) and walking, at first in a perambulator. He had his equivalents of the top hat and tail or frock coat to mark him off from his contemporaries of a lower social grade, who ridiculed him when they got the chance: the children in Marchmont Street jeered at the brown stockings of the Pankhursts, then living in Russell Square, and when hats from Liberty's were acquired there were cries of 'What are your hats made of: hay, straw, cane of a chair?'

Recalling his upbringing as one of the nine children of a prosperous Jewish solicitor during the 1880s, Leonard Woolf decades later described how he was first attracted to books by the family nurse Vicary, who read aloud from the *Baptist Times* before a blazing fire in the nursery on the third floor in the family's Bloomsbury home. There were patriarchal Sunday lunches, annual expeditions in August to the country where a house was 'taken', and a stream of tutors – in drawing, elocution, German, piano-playing and other subjects – constantly arriving at the house. Yet Woolf's childhood was lived in the continuous knowledge that 'just beneath the surface of society lay a vast reservoir of uncivilised squalor and brutality.' On one occasion he was shocked to see the police dragging along a raving woman pursued by a mob: 'they were human beings, but they made me sick with terror and disgust in the pit of my small stomach.'[5]

Within the slums, sheer necessity forced many parents to look on their children as sources of cheap labour or income; for this and other reasons, in some parts of the country a man was reluctant to marry (much to the local clergyman's disgust) until his prospective wife was pregnant. The sheer size of the Victorian family readily converted it into a working unit, especially when agricultural and craft occupations provided the income. The major contribution made in the 1880s by James Murray's children in sorting the slips for the great *Oxford English Dictionary* – taking a run round the garden after each hour's work when engaged on a long stint – reminds us that middle-class children could also be enlisted by their parents. Furthermore the family firm was far more widespread, from the small shopkeeper upwards, and even where the head of the family worked outside the household, his connections and influence were often the route to employment for his children. Schooling became compulsory only in 1880 and the early statutory leaving age (not raised nationwide to fourteen till 1918) meant that only within the upper and middle classes was there the modern identification of childhood with recreation and education, and of adulthood with work. The concept of adolescence existed in the 1880s, but not the word 'teenager', let alone teenage culture. Largely for nutritional reasons, puberty arrived rather later in life, nor were there such powerful cultural pressures towards earlier intellectual maturity. Indeed, the word 'girl' seems to have been applied to unmarried women well past the age of childhood; the Girls' Friendly
2.4 Society was designed largely for young servants away from home, and its title at no stage seems to have embarrassed its young adult members. *Boy's Own Paper* saw itself as being read by young men up to the age of twenty four, and the major discrepancies between the classes in educational experience and age of entry into employment removed any sharp definition from the frontier between childhood and adulthood.

Even where working-class children were not employed in any formal sense, they were expected to carry out a great deal of tedious drudgery within the home; for if married women did not then go out to work, except in special areas like the Lancashire mill-town, their hands were full with a large family to bring up and difficult housekeeping tasks to complete. The suffragette Hannah Mitchell, born in 1871, recalled that her mother 'never seemed to realize how small and weak we were. She made us sweep and scrub, turn the heavy mangle on washing days and the still heavier churn on butter-making days.'[6] The home was not yet mechanized, so that the mother was often distracted by a host of domestic tasks; the elder children therefore often had to mind the younger – one reason for the high accident-rate. In England and Wales between 1881 and 1890, 821 boys and 552 girls out of every million aged between one and five died from falls, burns and scalds, drowning or vehicle accidents; boys were much more at risk in each of these categories. Drowning had already begun its dramatic decline, but not so falls, burns and scalds; vehicle accidents were to rise much higher between the wars.[7] These figures reflect a remoteness of parental control from younger children in day-to-day matters, but with older children it was different; they depended on parents and parental connections for getting employment, lacked the freedom of movement later brought by motor transport, and were unsupported by any distinctive youth-culture.

Nowhere does the camera fail the historian more seriously than in portraying childhood. Children were rarely as neat, innocent and tractable as those photographed in Bromley's 'Portrait and Equestrian 2.5 Studios' during 1887. Yet this was how late Victorian families liked to be remembered, idealized in dress, background, props and pose, and (as required by relatively long exposures) absolutely motionless. The less polished side of childhood in any class was photographed less frequently. Many families could not afford individual clothes for each member, and poverty as well as fashion dictated that skirts and pinafores should be worn by the young of both sexes. The ready-made clothing industry later dramatically reduced the housewife's sewing and mending tasks and made class contrasts less obvious both for adults and children.

In 1872 Disraeli pronounced England to be 'a domestic country. Here the home is revered and the hearth is sacred';[8] in the 1880s both political parties sought to gain the prestige involved in upholding family values, aided by a monarchy which had been setting an example to the nation since the 1840s. The Queen might dislike the politics of John Bright and Mr Gladstone, but she could share their unquestioning respect for domestic virtues. On the other hand, the prevalence of child cruelty and neglect made many humanitarians in the 1880s wonder whether the family should be so sacred as to escape all state supervision. Canon and Mrs Barnett, active in East End social work, sometimes virtually kidnapped the children they wished to rescue. The National Society for the Prevention of Cruelty to Children became a national organization in 1889; its 'Children's Charter' of that year made it easier for the courts to get evidence of cruelty within the family, and introduced new penalties for it, together with new restrictions on child labour. No doubt the austere and authoritarian Victorian paterfamilias existed in many middle-class families too, but Mrs Creighton reminds us that there were less formal patterns of child-rearing in the 1880s, when she recalls her husband as a Cambridge professor lying on the floor with several of his children on his back, rocking them violently up and down, and later (as Bishop of Peterborough) taking the whole family out for walks with him in the afternoons. James Murray played cat and mouse with his younger children in the 1880s, with a couple of them clinging to his coat-tails while he whirled them round.[9]

Parental authority was also being eroded by those who extended the regulation of children's working hours in factories, made primary education compulsory, and encouraged the growth of boarding schools. But there was resistance to the trend by those who believed that it mistakenly undermined family responsibility; Charlotte Mason's Parents' National Educational Union, founded in 1887, advocated education at home up to the age of eight, and she set up a training school for governesses at Ambleside in 1892. Mrs Sumner reinforced an Anglican conservatism by founding the Mothers' Union to uphold the traditional domestic social, religious and educational values. She emphasized the family role shared by women at all social levels, and complained in 1893 that 'there has been a tendency in all reformatory efforts to ignore the parents and the divine institution of home life'.[10]

The divergence between those who favoured and those who opposed interfering between parent and child should not be exaggerated. The N.S.P.C.C. disliked socialistic diagnoses of child cruelty at least as strongly as Mrs Sumner; Benjamin Waugh, the

Society's secretary, insisted that responsibility for children must lie squarely with the parents, and pointed out that there were plenty of good ones among the poor. Philanthropists believed so strongly in the Victorian family that when it broke down they organized substitutes (as in Dr Barnardo's 'village homes', where the children were trained to a trade): or they mobilized proxy parents like the Girls' Friendly Society's 'associates', who befriended young girls separated (usually by domestic service) from home. Legislation against child cruelty went through Parliament in 1889 as a non-party measure. Initiated by the Liberal M.P. A.J. Mundella, it was backed by the Conservative government, whose amendments aimed, significantly, at preserving (in Sir Richard Webster's words) 'the proper and legitimate control of the parent over the child'.[11]

Why this increased concern in the 1880s? Partly perhaps because the child, whose innocence had been exhilaratingly discovered by the romantics, had become (with Dickens) a vehicle for pathos and (with J.M. Barrie) an excuse for escaping from adulthood altogether. Twentieth-century Freudian psychology was to reverse this trend, but as long as the Victorian belief in 'original innocence' persisted, society's revulsion at the influence of the corrupting adult was accentuated. Reinforcing these general factors were specific structures growing out of the Anglo-American humanitarian movement, which had steadily been extending its range for over a century. The London society (founded in 1884) from which the N.S.P.C.C. emerged in 1889 was modelled on a Liverpool association itself inspired by American precedents. The N.S.P.C.C. received much encouragement and guidance from the Royal Society for the Prevention of Cruelty to Animals, founded sixty years earlier. The spread of birth control and the drop in the birth-rate may have reinforced this higher valuation of children. And in its pursuit of information which would, in Waugh's words, 'make the facts of child-life a science,' the N.S.P.C.C. was applying the lessons he had learned from T.H. Huxley on the London School Board, and was also displaying the British philanthropist's strongly empirical bias.

The 1880s were a decade of educational and philanthropic achievement, and photographs made their contribution. The Shaftesbury Society group was no doubt taken for propaganda purposes, but such a snapshot had value only in so far as it bore some relation to reality. Philanthropists valued the 'before and after' photograph, which reflected the prevailing belief that cleanliness was somehow related to godliness. Dr Barnardo pioneered it in 1870, and during the 1880s raised £67,694 a year, three times as much as in the

(marginal figure references) 2.8   2.4   2.10   2.9

1870s. Between 1886 and 1890 the Church of England Waifs and Strays Society (founded in 1881) nearly quadrupled the annual sums it had raised in its first five years.[12]

Nobody was more deeply involved in philanthropy than the seventh Earl of Shaftesbury, whose religion brought him friendships which cut across social class. He loved children, and the group photographed with him in 1883 almost evokes a smile from a face made severe by the betrayals he had experienced, the sights he had seen, and the austere beliefs he acted upon. The five boys had been tidied up, and were no doubt learning a trade which would immunize them against the moral defects which philanthropists thought were responsible for poverty. Emigration might carry them into a less crowded labour market; some of Shaftesbury's boys may well have been destined for Canada. But these Barnardo and Shaftesbury Society children were exceptional; most deprived children were cared for within the family network, very widely extended by modern standards, and orphans were often entrusted to a relative. In the 1880s, the extended family was a welfare system in itself.

The authorities were slow to appreciate the recreational needs of children beset by the cramped environment of town life; as late as 1911, 132 of the 605 children brought before Birmingham juvenile court for non-indictable offences were accused of playing football in the street. But the 1880s did see important pioneering developments in organizations for youth. Semi-military groups of boys flourished among Scots Presbyterians. The first Glasgow Company of the Boys' Brigade originated in October 1883 as an offshoot of the North Woodside Mission, and the movement rapidly caught on. By 1890 cleanliness, punctuality, discipline and good manners were being inculcated by 394 companies with 16,752 members, the great majority in Scotland; high spirits were being channelled into safe courses.[13] So successful an enterprise could hardly be left to the Nonconformists, and the Church of England responded in 1891 with the Church Lads' Brigade. These youth movements pioneered many features of the Boy Scouts (founded in 1907-8), whose creator Baden Powell originally wanted the two to amalgamate. Their recreational importance is obvious; they diffused more widely that tight organization of leisure time which had been drilling public school boys for a generation. Also obvious is their political importance, for they inculcated discipline, and their advent is an early sign that young people were emerging as a distinct social group – with their own needs, their own organizations, their own culture.

A decade which saw the publication of *Treasure Island* (1882), *King Solomon's Mines* (1885) and *Kidnapped* (1886) also did much for children's literature, but it was not until Kenneth Grahame's *The Golden Age* (1895) that children were approached through seeking to understand their imaginative life for its own sake instead of aiming to speed them on towards adulthood. Books for the young deserve discussion because they are read at a very impressionable age. There is no doubt some relation between imperialism and the excellent writing for boys to be found in Henty's *Union Jack* and the *Boy's Own Paper*. When Henty heard that British forces had been defeated at Majuba in 1881, he allegedly burst into tears, exclaiming that the disgrace could never be wiped out.

The *Boy's Own Paper*, founded in 1879 by the Religious Tract Society (together with the *Girl's Own Paper*, launched in the following year), proved so successful that it was soon able to subsidize the Society's mission work. Its three-columned, close-printed pages energetically promoted self-education, but varied the diet with plenty of adventure stories, coloured inserts, chess problems, poems, printed music, and engravings of gripping scenes. In 1881 the paper serialized Talbot Baines Reed's *The Fifth Form at St Dominic's*, which helped to transform the school story by omitting the moralism of *Tom Brown's Schooldays* while retaining its realism; it was published in book form in 1883. There were articles on British birds, 'Rugby Football, and How to Excel in It', and 'Goats and Goat-Keeping for Pleasure or Profit'. Readers' problems were vigorously tackled in a correspondence page – 'M' in the number for 10 June 1882, for instance, receiving the British Museum's pronouncement on the rubbings of medals he had enclosed with his inquiry, and 'Carion Crow' being rebuked for his mis-spelling and told that dormice could be purchased through the columns of *Exchange and Mart*.

The papers unquestioningly accept the customary separation of spheres between the sexes: whereas *Boy's Own Paper* feeds the boy with tales of fighting and adventure and discussion of scientific and technical subjects, *Girl's Own Paper* centres on the home, with articles on dress and domestic skills. Yet in other respects the papers closely resemble one another. They look alike in design, and both use historical and biographical articles to spur on their readers to emulate heroic figures; there were 4,956 entries weighing almost a ton when the *Girl's Own Paper* competition of 1884 asked for biographical notes on a hundred famous men.[14] Both papers were intensely patriotic, and encouraged the active, participating reader. The *Boy's Own Paper* target of £1,200 to buy two Boy's Own lifeboats was easily exceeded in 1882, and by July 1885 the paper had raised £149 towards the fund launched in April to commemorate General Gordon. Both papers encouraged hobbies of all kinds. By 1885 photography had become simple enough for a boy at Winston Churchill's Brighton prep school to be practising it: 'One of the boys has got a Camera,' Winston told his mother in a letter, 'and takes Photos very well, you must be taken when you come down.' By 1889 *Boy's Own Paper* felt able to organize a postal photographic competition; it received so many entries that the deadline was extended and the prize-money increased. The members of the Boy's Own Postal Photographic Club, organized in May 1890, inserted into its box, circulated monthly, not more than three prints for mutual criticism.[15]

No doubt these two children's publications catered primarily for the middle-class end of the market, though *Girl's Own Paper*'s circulation reached 250,000 soon after its launching. But the comic paper, originally designed for adults, was also making great strides. Ally Sloper, the first true British comic-strip hero, first appeared in 1867. The earliest comic directed at children, *Jack and Jill*, was launched in 1885; the first major one, Harmsworth's *Comic Cuts*, dates from 1890.

It is difficult to generalize about children's experience in the 1880s: they were deeply divided by social class and fragmented into relatively self-sufficient families. Their recollections were rarely written down and have aroused little interest among historians; nor had businessmen yet fully discovered their potential as independent consumers. They can perhaps most effectively be brought to life if three among them – Winston Churchill, Sylvia Pankhurst and J.H. Thomas – are taken for detailed discussion. These children are in no sense representative: indeed, it is precisely because they were unusual that we know so much about their early life. But their experience can perhaps usefully bring out some of the continuities and contrasts between the 1880s and today.

Winston Leonard Spencer-Churchill, born at Blenheim in 1874, the elder of two boys, enters the 1880s in the care of his beloved nanny Mrs Everest ('Woomany'). His parents show a continuous concern for his educational progress and improved conduct, and receive frequent and detailed reports on him from conscientious schoolmasters and tutors. But Lord and Lady Randolph Churchill are preoccupied with their social life: she is gay, young, and beautiful, and he is a rising politician consumed by an overriding ambition which he tries rather crudely to impart to his son in a series of exhortatory letters. Winston therefore admires them both only from afar; he follows his father's career closely in the newspapers, but neither parent responds when he repeatedly begs them to visit him at school, where he is boarded out from shortly before his eighth birthday. It is only from Woomany that he receives warm and motherly letters preoccupied with his health and happiness. By 1882 Lady Randolph is complaining that he has returned from school 'terribly slangy and loud'; her letters display a lively but distant amusement at her son's activities, and seldom respond to the abundance of affection which flows from him, though she occasionally mediates between him and his still more remote and sharply critical father. Winston endures his first prep school (at Ascot) for only two years; it is a place where those in disfavour attend the headmaster's study for weekly beatings which now seem repugnant in their brutality.[16] Winston departs in 1884, unhappy and ill, for a more humane boarding school in Brighton conveniently located near the family doctor Robson Roose, whose services prove invaluable when he sits up through the night during the crisis-point of Winston's pneumonia in 1886.

By this time, Winston has grown into an ebullient and active child – riding, building up his stamp collection, accumulating model soldiers eventually to the number of 1,500, and repeatedly begging his father for autographs which can be distributed to his friends. In 1887 he urges his mother to send him Rider Haggard's novels, and artlessly brings every weapon to bear ('I am nearly mad with suspense')[17] in his eagerness to attend the jubilee celebrations in London. He finds plenty to occupy him during the holidays – butterflies are a major interest by 1887 – and regards attempts at getting him to study during such periods as an intrusion. He is drilled in Greek and Euclid in the hope of getting to Winchester, but in 1888 Harrow is chosen as a second-best, and a regime of examinations descends. Throughout the decade he is constantly encouraged by parents and teachers to compare his own attainments with those of his contemporaries; there is continuous grading within school, together with traumatic external examinations which determine his long-term fate. The examination for entry to Harrow makes him sick afterwards, and his struggles to get into Sandhurst put severe strains on his relations with his parents.

By the end of the decade, Winston's schoolmasters and instructors are beginning to win the battle against his carelessness, unpunctuality and forgetfulness. His letters home, alternating between a rather stilted and orotund correctness – reflecting the struggle to appease his parents' distaste for his casual manner – and desperate, ill-written, breathless appeals (often surreptitiously sent to his mother), reinforced by shrill post-scripts, smart remarks, and the occasional rather untidy drawing, invariably seek replenishments for his exchequer. His mood swings, from an incurable optimism about the marks he is likely to get in forthcoming examinations and about the improvements which are always imminent in his conduct, to a profound gloom at his failure to please his parents. His interest in soldiering is consolidated by the manoeuvres of the Harrow Rifle Corps, and his enthusiasm for arranging his model soldiers in battle formation helps to convince Lord Randolph that Winston must go to Sandhurst. He joins the army class at Harrow and passes the preliminary examination for the R.M.C. in 1890, well imbued with the competitive spirit and launched on a career which will shortly become unusual in several respects.

Estelle Sylvia Pankhurst was born at 1 Drayton Terrace, Old Trafford, Manchester, in 1882, the second of the five children of the controversial radical lawyer Richard Marsden Pankhurst and his impulsive, vivacious, artistic and beautiful young wife Emmeline. Sylvia soon comes to see that her mother regards her as less attractive than her eldest sister Christabel, to whose prince she plays Cinderella at a memorable family pantomime during Christmas 1885. She follows Christabel about in admiring fascination, badly scorching an arm — one of three serious childhood injuries which left permanent effects — after falling in the fire when being chased round the big dining-table; the consolation a small black rabbit could offer proves short-lived, its early death 'making upon me an impression of awe and sorrow lasting through childhood.'[18] She is an artistic, imaginative, introspective, rather gloomy child with weak eyes, schooled early in life by upbringing and experience to bear pain without complaining. Her father in evening dress seems to her the perfection of manly beauty, as her mother puts in his diamond studs before some public function. But the children are fascinated also by his sincerity and zest for life; he interrupts his long extemporized story-tellings to the girls with statements about his ideals. 'Life is nothing without enthusiasms' is a saying of his which Sylvia will carry with her throughout a lifetime.

Emmeline Pankhurst is busy and distracted with other interests; she is ambitious, devoted to her husband, and short of money. She is often insensitive to Sylvia's needs and devolves much of her children's upbringing upon their Welsh nurse Susannah. The family moves to London in 1885 and Emmeline opens an artistic shop which fails to pay. Daily governesses are brought in. One of them reads Dickens aloud, and the murder of Nancy by Bill Sikes makes an indelible impression – 'for years I was haunted by visions of her beautiful face of agony and fear, confronting his brutal strength.' The death of Sylvia's four-year-old brother Frank in 1888 provides another reason for sadness; the doctors think it is croup, but the boy dies from diphtheria, and another vivid memory is implanted when Sylvia is taken to see his 'beautiful little white figure, with dark, still hair and long black lashes'.[19] By the end of the decade, Sylvia's mother is moving in progressive London circles and interesting herself in the feminist issue which will eventually make her name a household word. The children help out at the political meetings she organizes in the family's rented house in Russell Square, handing out leaflets and arranging the chairs. They are encouraged to give lectures to parents and relatives assembled; there are amateur dramatics and a family newspaper, *The Home News and Universal Mirror*; there are visits to the British Museum with Susannah, songs on Sunday with mother at the piano, and the beauty of the trees and lawns in the Square. But there is also plain food and compulsory porridge in the nursery; disputes inevitably result, together with the agony of displeasing her mother, whom Sylvia implores to 'help me to be good.' Half a century later, Sylvia will express her belief that 'children to-day are freer and franker than they were in our generation; they meet their elders on a more genial plane, and are the happier for it.'[20]

James Henry Thomas was born at 51 George Street, Newport, Monmouthshire in 1874, beside dockyard marshalling yards whose coal trucks could be heard shunting day and night. Brought up as the youngest of widow Ann Thomas's children, with three of the other six still living at home, he is disciplined by this determined, middle-aged woman, distinctly Tory in outlook, who struggles to keep herself and the children out of the workhouse. She provides for her family by taking in washing from the ships in dock, and obtains a mangle by hire-purchase, so that young Jim wakes up in the morning and falls asleep at night to the sound of its turning. When not at the mangle, she seems always to be busy at the ironing-board or bent over the wash-tub. A cocky and assertive child, the eight-year-old Jim is taken aback when excluded from St Paul's Church School's treat of the year, the Whitsun outing, on the ground that his best clothes are not good enough to keep up the school's reputation.

Determined to help out at home, at the age of nine he takes a part-time job (35 hours a week) with Phillips the chemist – running errands, keeping the shop clean and taking a pride in his polishing of the firm's brass name-plate; he also somehow finds the time on Tuesday evenings for the church Bible class. At the age of twelve he becomes a full-time employee at the chemist's, but soon leaves to take a series of jobs before beginning at fifteen as an engine cleaner in the Great Western Railway's shop on the Alexandria Docks. His earliest duty is to run through the dark streets and alleys in the early mornings, waking up the drivers and firemen, but he graduates to engine-cleaning after a year, and takes great pride in his work. At eighteen he passes his fireman's exams, and goes for a short time in his new role to Barnstaple, returning to Newport within the year.

Even as an engine driver Jim Thomas shows that he can stand up to the employers, successfully insisting that the cleaners cannot do their job adequately if their tallow ration is reduced from three ounces to two. He now begins a strenuous course of miscellaneous reading and follows his driver into the trade union movement. His sense of social grievance is reinforced by a more personal resentment shortly before his twenty-first birthday, when he is astonished to find that he is not Ann Thomas's son at all, but her grandson, and that his mother lives in Newport but will not acknowledge him because she now has a husband and family. Somehow he discovers her address and stands in front of the house, gazing at it, but venturing no further. This shock does nothing to remove that sense of personal insecurity which will pursue him through life – at first making, and then breaking, his political future. But Jim has already met his future wife Agnes Hill, one year older than himself, at St Paul's Church School. At seventeen she had lost her father in an explosion aboard ship. Her calm and quiet manner gives him the companionship he needs: as he recalled at the end of his career, 'from first to last she has believed in me.' He soon finds that he can put over his views effectively at meetings, and 'Young Thomas' is launched on his rise to fame.[21]

The description of these three very different youthful experiences has unconsciously moved us forward from childhood into education, which now deserves more extended discussion: for the 1880s saw the climax of a great crusade to get the children into school.

2.2. Countless middle- and upper-class boys were photographed in idealized sailors' dress in front of this painted background, Elliott & Fry, undated

2.3 (RIGHT). 'Baby Eliot' and nurse. Mrs Mitchell, at Port Eliot, Cornwall. The photographer was an aristocratic lady amateur, Carolyn Rhadigund Eliot, 1886

2.4 (BELOW). A meeting of the Wembland Girls' Friendly Society. These young domestic servants were photographed by Lady Georgiana Mildmay, c.1885

2.5 (LEFT). *In their Sunday best dresses, two children pose in front of the painted backcloth of the 'Portrait and Equestrian Studios', Bromley, Kent, E. Davey Lavender, 1887*

2.6 (BELOW). *'Safr-Kali, one of the Prince of Wales's Indian Elephants (female)'. From the first issue of* The Graphic *to be illustrated with half-tone photographs, 5 September 1885*

2.7 (ABOVE). *Spick and span, and in the care of a benevolent philanthropist: Lady Breadalbane's Waifs, 1884*

2.8 (BELOW). *Learning a trade to combat poverty and moral defects. Boy cobblers at Dr Barnardo's, Roderick Johnstone(?), c.1890*

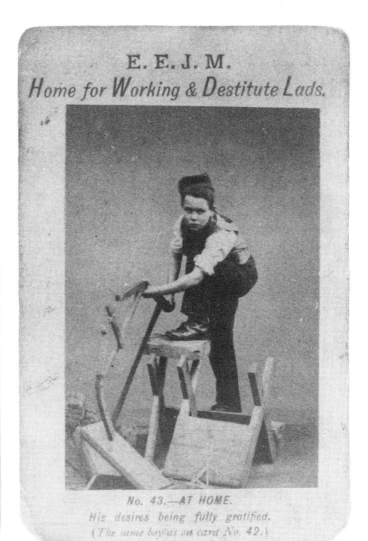

No. 42.—FROM LAMBETH.
Craving for Admission and Employment.
(*The same boy as on card No. 43.*)

No. 43.—AT HOME.
His desires being fully gratified.
(*The same boy as on card No. 42.*)

2.9 (ABOVE). *A Lambeth boy at the East End Juvenile Mission. These 'before and after' cards were later discredited and Dr Barnardo abandoned them, Thomas Barnes(?), 1870*

2.10 (LEFT). *Four boys from a Shaftesbury Home in East London, perhaps photographed for propaganda purposes, J. Bender, date unknown but probably 1880s*

2.11 Lord Shaftesbury himself. The great philanthropist with five of his 'Shaftesbury Lads', William Broughton, 1883

2.12 (ABOVE). *The first fifty Barnardo's boys to be sent to Canada by Dr Barnardo, not an agency, Thomas Barnes(?), 1882*

2.13 (BELOW). *The original Boys' Brigade, founded in North Woodside, Scotland, in 1883. The earliest surviving photograph, 1885*

Education
and Newspapers
Chapter 3

Education does not happen only in school; it is breathed in from the environment. In the 1880s the proportion of country to town children was continuously falling – and urbanization itself has profound educational consequences. A country child almost instinctively understands nature, animals, crops and the weather; the town child is compensated with a diversity of experience which makes him quick-thinking and literate. Victorian Britain witnessed a town-based thirst for literacy which can now be seen only in less developed countries. Educational opportunity had to be grasped whenever it presented itself, and elementary-school pupils were often by modern standards quite old. Education also happens within the family, especially in a society where work (in craft or agriculture) can be done in or near the home by children or apprentices taken into the household. But factory employment and compulsory schooling eroded the family's educational role; between 1871 and 1891 children between ten and fifteen contributed a diminishing proportion of the workforce in almost every industry.[1]

The Education Act of 1870 aimed at universal elementary education. The schooling of any one child in the 1880s, however, depended heavily on its religious denomination, sex and social class. Religion was involved because religious organizations before

1870 had built up an impressive array of voluntary schools. Sex was relevant because sex-based contrasts in curriculum were even more prominent in the 1880s than they are now. As for social class, working-class parents before 1870 had relied on the 'dame school' or (in slum areas) the 'ragged school', and many of these survived into the 1880s. They were austere: walls are bare, desks battered, facilities minimal. Often run for profit and free from state inspection, dame schools provided none of the health and welfare facilities which modern schoolchildren enjoy. Sunday schools had also been central to the voluntary system. Run by an army of unsung heroes and heroines in their spare time, they rescued many working people from illiteracy and helped place religion at the centre of Victorian social life. Far more people were influenced by them than attended at any one time. In 1887 2,222,000 children went to Anglican Sunday schools in England and Wales, and 3,006,000 attended Sunday schools of other denominations. These are high figures for a population aged five to fourteen of only 6,619,000 in 1891. Nonetheless the 1880s saw the Sunday schools entering on their long decline; for a few more decades their membership continued to grow faster than church membership, but state-provided elementary education could now offer formidable competition.[2]

Until 1870 – largely because the Victorians feared a Frenchified and centralized regimentation and uniformity – the state did not feel obliged to create a national framework of primary education. But when schooling

3.1. 'The Dame's School' – re-touched photograph, prettified scene, and a dying form of education. From 'Pictures from Life in Field and Fen', P.H. Emerson, 1885

3.1

3.3
3.4

3.5

was improving so fast among Britain's commercial rivals (most notably in Germany and the United States), voluntary provision seemed insufficient. The 1870 Act left denominational schools untouched where they met the local need adequately: elsewhere, locally-elected 3.6 school boards were empowered to build 'board' schools from the rates and provide a non-denominational education for the children not being educated elsewhere. This yoking together of voluntary and state educational systems nourished many late Victorian disputes. Nonconformists feared the Anglican voluntary schools, whose resources were so much larger. Their distrust of the predominantly Anglican state which had persecuted their ancestors did not prevent them from championing the board schools, which seemed likely to gain the upper hand so long as the Anglican schools could be deprived of public subsidies.

The 1870 Education Act launched a crusade for education into the remotest areas – into the sparsely 3.7 populated St Kilda, for example, where only a state-sponsored system could have coped. The task was immense, if only because there were so many children. Between 1870 and 1888 the number on the registers of inspected elementary schools in England and Wales rose from 1,152,000 to 4,688,000, and elementary education was made compulsory in 1880. By 1882 the inspected schools accounted for at least 63 per cent of children between five and thirteen.[3] In 1888, 86 per cent of those in the inspected schools were aged between five and thirteen, but as many as 10 per cent were under five. The inspected schools were small – averaging at 200 in 1872, 244 in 1888 – which was expensive, but made discipline easier.[4] The financial structure required an annual inspection of every child, but with such large numbers it sometimes became so crude as virtually to insult the teachers. Unimaginative direction from central government ensured that teachers, school boards and politicians were the main sources of improvement in the system.

To staff this educational revolution an army of teachers had to be recruited; the increase was formidable, both by European standards and in absolute terms (37,714 in the inspected schools of England and Wales in 1872 and 100,401 in 1888); no such increase in pupils and teachers was occurring at this time in France, Belgium, Austria, Italy or the Netherlands.[5] The major growth-period occurred in the 1870s, when the number of teachers in inspected schools in England and Wales more than doubled, but their ranks continued to swell between 1880 and 1888 (by 33 per cent). This increase is reflected in the rising proportion of teachers to the population of England and Wales

aged between three and twenty: one for 68 in 1871, one for 56 in 1891. The proportion of certificated teachers remained roughly constant between 1880 and 1888 at nearly half the total teaching staff.[6]

These new posts offered many opportunities for social ascent. Self-educated working men had long been able to climb socially through shopkeeping, temperance lecturing and preaching; now they could become pupil-teachers, and from there they could aspire to the salary for certificated principal and assistant teachers of £119 (for men) and £72 (for women), as averaged in 1883. The number of pupil-teachers doubled in the 1870s and stabilized in the 1880s at about 29,000 in England and Wales.[7] In this incidental way, some of the best brains were creamed off from the working class. There were opportunities too for women, who filled two-thirds of the teaching posts in 1888. Public education also enabled them to obtain experience in community life; female householders had gained the vote in municipal elections in 1869 and in school board elections a year later. Women could be voted on to the boards: it was an election of 1870 which brought together the founders of that important middle-class secondary school venture, the Girls' Public Day School Trust, and in 1887 there were at least ninety-eight women on school boards in England and Wales. Women were enabled to vote in county council elections in 1888, but few came forward for local posts: the first woman poor law guardian was not elected till 1875, though in 1889 two women were elected to the first London County Council and at least seventy-six were operating as poor law guardians in England, Wales and Scotland.[8]

School attendance levels improved greatly, with London setting the pace. Teachers were keen to assist, if only because attendance had a bearing on salaries. In the inspected elementary schools of England and Wales, the level rose slowly from 68 per cent in 1872 to 77 per cent in 1888; by the Edwardian period it was as high as in the 1950s – that is, between 85 and 90 per cent.[9] Many gaunt, hunger-pinched parents were prosecuted for not sending their children to school; they had to be persuaded that education was more important than customary family duties. Toughness was required from school attendance officers, and many had served in the army or police. Some parents saw the curriculum as excessively academic, and felt insulted by the teachers' efforts at improving their children's hygiene and manners. But such efforts were less an imposing of middle-class standards on working people than a building upon traditions of respectability within the working class. Charles Booth, the late Victorian social investigator, praised the new board schools for civilizing both parents and children. 'Habits of cleanliness and of order have been formed; a higher standard of dress and of decency have [*sic*] been attained, and this reacts upon the homes; and when children who have themselves been to school become parents, they accept and are ready to uphold the system, and support the authority of the teachers.' He saw the new London board schools, with their distinctive Queen Anne architecture, as standing up in slum areas like sentinels, 'keeping watch and ward over the interests of the generation that is to replace our own.'[10] The teacher was beginning to replace the clergyman as the local cultural leader, and in a community with relatively few public buildings and recreations, schools were used for more than purely educational purposes.

This educational revolution was expensive; it demanded an increasing share of a gross national product much smaller than our own, created by adults who constituted a much smaller proportion of the population. During the 1870s expenditure on the inspected elementary schools in England and Wales had nearly tripled, and by 1880 rates and taxes were contributing over half the cost.[11] The average rate raised for elementary education rose markedly during the decade, and the Department of Education's expenditure rose by 45 per cent. Free schooling crept in, so to speak, by the back door. The 'school pence' (28 per cent of the inspected elementary schools' total income in 1882) were hard to collect, if only because it was difficult to single out the parents who could afford to pay;[12] besides, the system might hurt the sensitive child or discourage attendance by those who most needed schooling. Abolition of the parental contribution after 1891 therefore arrived more because of administrative necessity than from enthusiasm for its principle.

Discipline was rigorous by modern standards, but it needs to be judged in the context of poorer resources, higher pupil–teacher ratios, the scale of the educational problem being tackled, and the severer parental control which then prevailed in all social classes. The pupil–teacher ratio varied markedly between schools but was as high as 55 per teacher in 1882, falling to 47 by 1888.[13] Illiteracy had been almost conquered by the 1880s. At the 1885 general election only 4 per cent of the United Kingdom electors were illiterate; half were Irish, but even in Ireland the improvement during the 1880s was dramatic. The decline continued – to 2.7 per cent in 1886 and 0.6 per cent in 1906. The percentage of prisoners in the local gaols of England and Wales who could neither read nor write also fell – from 35 in 1868/9 to 25 in 1887/8.[14]

Socialists might condemn the social system of the 1880s, but it had at least presented them with a potential readership. Furthermore, schools enabled the state to approach children for other purposes: in the 1880s it became clear that the poorest could not be educated without welfare measures. Schoolteachers were often made into socialists by the sheer recognition that starving pupils could not study effectively. Free meals had been integral to Barnardo's educational programme for his free ragged schools in the 1870s; a free meal for all children was part of the Fabian Society's platform from 1884, and in 1889 charities were already providing them to half the 43,888 children at London elementary schools who went habitually in want of food.[15] It was also increasingly recognized that problems of school attendance were often problems of poverty; the attendance officer became an expert on slum conditions and was much consulted by Charles Booth when preparing his famous survey of the London poor.

Still, the private sector in elementary education remained attractive to the wealthier parent. There is a modern ring about Joseph Edmondson's remarks to the Sheffield Liberal H.J. Wilson in 1877: after praising the new board schools and expressing the hope that children from all social classes would one day be educated together, he went on to urge Wilson to 'look a little at the sanitary part of the question. There is a want of cleanliness among many of the children attending Board schools that would make me hesitate . . . There is something in the dialect that might be acquired by association with working class children. It might require great watchfulness at home to counterbalance this danger.' He did not mention the fleas and other insects which alarmed the well-to-do parent. The young Pankhursts, when living in Russell Square, were kept well away from the local board school; the family servant said that the pupils would be 'rough', and that the girls would get things in their hair if they were sent there. For Mrs Pankhurst they were 'too highly strung' to be taught with a class of others, and would 'lose all originality'.[16]

No wonder so many middle- and upper-class children were educated at home; in 1868 about a tenth of Oxford and Cambridge entrants had been tutored privately, and about the same proportion thirty years later.[17] Life in an aristocratic family was an education in itself, and political aspirations or intellectual interests were often encouraged early. Disraeli was frequently impressed in old age by the intelligence of the Cecil children at Hatfield: 'five boys,' he told Lady Bradford in 1879, 'the youngest quite an urchin, hardly breeched but giving his opinion on public affairs like his brothers. The *Standard* is his favourite paper, but he did not approve of its leading article on Russia of that day, "the tone too sarcastic!!!".' Lord Salisbury trained his children at home in precise speech with his familiar question 'Would you mind defining?',[18] and at many aristocratic dining-tables the intellectual pace was formidable. As for middle-class family life, Charlotte Yonge's novels contain long passages of highly academic drawing-room gossip. The governess or private tutor reinforced the family's educational resources, especially for girls. But by the 1880s the reformed public school system had made considerable headway, and even girls were being despatched to female versions of Arnold's Rugby.

The independent schools fostered individual ambition and mutual cooperation through team games, increasingly at the expense of intellectual distinction. This was partly because such qualities suited the military needs of a growing empire: public schools contributed 33 per cent of Woolwich's entrants in 1883, 79 per cent in 1896–1900: Sandhurst's percentage rose from 12 to 55 in the same period. The armed services claimed a fifth of the 206 boys who entered Rugby and Harrow in 1880 and whose later occupations are known, and careers overseas claimed another tenth. Games kept the boys occupied without resorting to the traditional rural sports involving cruelty to animals; they also probably explain the late Victorian decline in the traditional riot between public school and town boys. At Charterhouse games and photography reinforced one another as recreations: it was one of several public schools with photographic clubs by 1886, and several shots of its sporting activities survive.[19] Athletic qualifications became increasingly important in a schoolmaster, and sport helped the public school to perpetuate the rural ideals associated with the concept of the English gentleman.

3.8,9

The suffering caused by bullying and sport to a boy who was not good at games can well be imagined. Neville Chamberlain, who entered Rugby in April 1882 as 'a slender dark-haired boy, rather pale, quiet and shy', hated school for the rest of his life, and never saw Rugby again except when changing trains.[20] The whole subject was ventilated in *The Times* after a letter from 'Etoniensis' in 1889 had complained that older boys at Eton bullied younger ones into sporting activity. Two things are surprising about this controversy: that *The Times* assigned so much space to it at all; and that, although attacks were launched against many aspects of a letter from 'A Well-Known Old Harrovian', nobody contested the impertinent question 'Why is it that the French young man is such a weakling in

everything manly when compared with the English? Because he loathes games.' Lord Robert Cecil and others denied that games-playing promotes morality: in his day 'the reputed wickedness in the high places of athleticism' had done 'more harm than anything else.'[21]

Nonetheless this was a period of great national pride in the public schools. Their headmasters were an elite in themselves: the Butler, Vaughan, Temple and Gilkes families intermarried and became an important subsection of Victorian Britain's powerful intellectual aristocracy. Public school histories were written, school songs and poetry compiled in abundance. In the 1880s nostalgia rather than resentment was their old boys' most publicized mood.

The fact that Neville Chamberlain, son of a Birmingham Unitarian screw-manufacturer, should attend Rugby at all is significant. Today public schools are often seen as socially divisive, but in the 1880s they helped to dissolve the barrier between aristocracy and commercial elite – though this often involved encouraging the sons of businessmen away from commerce and into the professions. Likewise the sons of prosperous dissenters were tempted by public schools into an Anglican world which would give them the classical education they needed for entering the ancient universities, from which dissenters had largely been excluded by religious tests till 1871. From there, nonconformists could at last penetrate the highest levels of politics and government. Another young Unitarian, Frederick Lawrence, later the Labour peer Lord Pethick-Lawrence, who entered Eton in 1885, later recalled that, despite several years of unhappiness, 'from the standpoint of worldly promotion my Eton schooldays have been of incalculable benefit to me in after life. Old Etonians have stood by me on many occasions, and have often extended their friendship to me even when I was vigorously attacking their privileges.' Fifty of the 206 Rugby and Harrow entrants in 1880 embarked, as he did, on careers in law, administration and politics, and forty-seven went into business.[22]

The classics, which still provided the backbone of the public school curriculum, were taught by nearly two-thirds of Eton's masters in 1884, leaving the remaining third for the whole of mathematics, science and modern languages;[23] they prepared the ground for law, politics, scholarship and the Church, and linked school and university through a private language used only within the elite. Only when the Labour M.P. Will Crooks requested translation of the Latin tag 'in pari materia' in the House of Commons did they lose their prominence in parliamentary oratory. But they were unimaginatively taught, with excessive stress on syntax and grammar; 'even the literal meaning of the sentences generally escaped me,' Fred Lawrence recalled, 'and of the tremendous human issues of the drama I never had the foggiest notion.' Many public schoolboys in the 1880s would have shared George Orwell's doubts 'whether classical education ever has been or can be successfully carried on without corporal punishment.'[24] Yet sometimes the system fostered a broad culture and a lifelong affection for the classics which enriched both imperialist attitudes on the right and libertarian attitudes on the left. Gladstone throughout his life turned to them whenever political business was not too pressing: it was one of the significant differences between him and that up-and-coming radical leader of the early 1880s, Joseph Chamberlain (Neville's father), whose education had been severely practical.

Provincial dissenters like John Bright and scientists like T. H. Huxley frontally attacked this classical bias. Charles Darwin, grand old man of English science till he died in 1882, nursed a lifelong grievance against his Shrewsbury headmaster Dr Butler, who had rebuked him as a schoolboy for wasting time on chemistry; when asked by Galton in 1873 whether his public school education had any peculiar merits, he replied 'none whatever,' and described its chief omissions as 'no mathematics or modern languages, nor any habits of observation or reasoning.'[25] Businessmen were perturbed at British inferiority in modern languages and in technical and commercial subjects; as the Royal Commission on the Depression in Trade and Industry pointed out in 1886, 'in the matter of education we seem to be particularly deficient as compared with some of our foreign competitors.' It is hardly surprising that only eighteen of Rugby and Harrow's 206 entrants in 1880 went into science and medicine.[26] Yet the public school system still had life in it. At Uppingham, Thring was free to pursue his solitary course till he died in 1887; convinced that 'every boy can do something well,' he hated education to be dominated by examinations and introduced several new subjects into the curriculum.[27]

3.8

The most striking innovations in secondary education occurred in girls' schools. The boarding school was emancipating in so far as it removed the girl from the narrowing influence of her family circle and rescued the woman from the trade of governess, embarrassingly located as it was midway between master and servant. In the 1880s the Girls' Public Day School Trust, founded in 1872, established fifteen new schools for the

middle classes, bringing its total in 1890 to thirty-four (catering for 6,540 girls, mostly in respectable London suburbs and smaller non-industrial provincial towns). Frances Buss at North London Collegiate School and Dorothea Beale at Cheltenham Ladies' College were steadily raising funds and overcoming the disbelief in women's higher education.

Menstruation among women, like masturbation among men, was regarded as physically debilitating. But whereas masturbation was held to be avoidable, menstruation clearly was not; this was made into an excuse for encouraging women into invalidism and discouraging them from sustained intellectual activity, for which allegedly nature had not intended them. Similar ideas governed what was called the 'physical force argument' against woman suffrage – the idea that effective government requires an electorate which represents the preponderance of physical force in the community. The suffragist Joseph Cowen rightly countered it in 1884 by arguing that woman is weaker than man largely because 'the enervating habits we have imposed on her have impaired her physical powers, and then we cite to her detriment the weakness which our customs have created.'[28] In this situation, sport at girls' boarding schools did not spring merely from attempts to imitate boys' public schools: it was integral to women's educational emancipation.

3.11.12

Educated girls were hardly likely to content themselves with a narrowly domestic existence. 'It is usual for the whole family to congregate in one room,' wrote Emily Davies, pioneer of women's education at Cambridge, discussing women's family life in 1878, 'every one carrying on her individual occupation in suspense, so to speak, liable at any moment to be called off from it for something else, trifling or important, as the case may be. Naturally enough, these half-occupied people prey upon each other.'[29] Here at the highest social level was that same dissipation of intellect which affected the working woman who had sole responsibility for rearing her hordes of young children, or the (probably female) telephonist distracted by a succession of incoming calls. The upper-class girl even lacked the freedom of movement of her working-class counterpart: the chaperon survived long after evangelicals, humanitarians, and the gas-light had dispelled coarseness from most respectable urban streets and from the social functions which had given her birth. And the teashops, restaurants and women's clubs which later extended women's freedom did not yet exist. Many years later, Beatrice Webb recalled the 'pleasurable but somewhat feverish anticipation of endless distraction' in the 1870s at the beginning of a London season whose main purpose was to marry off daughters to suitable husbands.[30] Only through rejection of this world could Beatrice's major intellectual and political achievements become possible.

A fortunate few did escape. Improvements in girls' secondary education naturally built up pressure for their higher education; much was done for them through the University Extension movement. Women were first admitted into London University in the 1870s and the Royal Holloway College was founded for them in 1883 by Thomas Holloway, patent medicine manufacturer and philanthropist. At Oxford and Cambridge, the new women's colleges were not yet fully incorporated into the university; in 1882 they housed under 200 undergraduates. But each of these gained opportunities for physical exercise together with all the liberation involved in having a room of one's own, and therefore a potential for intellectual achievement. The strength of character women undergraduates then required sometimes made it difficult for the early colleges to maintain discipline. Nonetheless, in 1887 Agneta Ramsay was placed above the Senior Classic at Cambridge, and three years later Philippa Fawcett was placed above the Senior Wrangler.

3.2,13

The fashion designer did not yet hold sway in the 1880s, and women's clothes were more varied. But dress reform was an important aspect of emancipation, though less influential among feminists in Britain than in Europe or America. The Rational Dress Society, founded in 1881, favoured garments with legs, arguing that 'clothing should follow and Drapery not contradict, the natural lines of the body.' The pursuit of simplicity by William Morris and his disciples, and the growth of tennis and cycling, worked in the same direction. Health was becoming more important. In 1884 the International Health Exhibition held in London included a section on hygienic dress; on the opening day Edwin Chadwick, the great sanitary reformer of the 1840s, utilitarian and progressive to the last, wore 'a suit of sanitary woollen clothing as devised by Dr Jaeger', who was promoting natural dyes and the wearing of 'natural' (i.e. woollen) clothing next the skin.[31]

9.12

3.14

3.2

The group at Lady Margaret Hall in 1888 includes the anti-suffragist Gertrude Bell, the future traveller and expert on the Middle East; her career shows that higher education did not necessarily encourage feminist views. Influential women had no need of the vote; Octavia Hill, best-known of the housing reformers, strongly opposed woman suffrage, and so many men and women shared her view that no formal anti-

suffragist organization was required until 1908. Signatories to the appeal against its introduction published in *The Nineteenth Century* in 1889 included the wives of many distinguished men in church and state, who claimed that 'the emancipating process has now reached the limits fixed by the physical constitution of women.'[32] The decade actually saw a major feminist reverse when William Woodall failed to get a clause on their behalf incorporated into the Bill enfranchising agricultural labourers in 1884; suffragists were so demoralized and divided that their movement did not revive until the Edwardian period. It was one of the tragedies of the decade that Lydia Becker – who for twenty years had lacerated anti-suffrage arguments in her *Women's Suffrage Journal* and addressed with her unwearied courage an endless sequence of public meetings – should have died in 1890 with her reform still well below the political horizon.

Most suffragists were still campaigning only to remove disqualification from the existing franchise; on this basis, only woman householders would get the vote – that is, propertied spinsters, widows (and, opponents argued, prostitutes), but not wives. The vote was eventually to be won only on the more democratic platform of adult suffrage. R.B. Haldane summed up the situation only too clearly in 1890: M.P.s disliked the existing woman suffrage Bills, and the feminist movement was ill-organized, insufficiently economic in its concerns, and predominantly middle-class.[33]

Women's commonest jobs in the 1880s (apart from housekeeping and child-rearing) were humble: the three largest were domestic service (45 per cent of the female workforce in Great Britain in 1881), textiles (19 per cent) and clothing (17 per cent). In England and Wales in 1881 they outnumbered men in several occupations outside the factory: domestic service, teaching, laundering and boardinghouse-keeping, for example, as well as the factory-based boxmaking and textile manufacture.[34] Women's trade unionism, which had led a struggling and precarious existence since 1874, gained a major asset in 1886 when Lady Dilke took over the leadership and gradually eroded the more sectarian of its feminist attitudes. But in that year an analysis of 600,000 wage-earners showed an average weekly rate almost exactly half that of the men; rough estimates counted only 36,900 unionized women workers, almost all in the textile trades. A woman T.U.C. delegate who expressed concern in 1883 at the lack of female employment was told amid laughter that the remedy was to 'get married'; in all social classes, this remained the expected vocation. Between 1896 and 1900 women still accounted for only 8 per cent of the

9.2

total trade union membership (compare 26 per cent in 1970–74), and the great days for growth were postponed to the Edwardian period.[35]

As for middle-class careers, substantial progress was made only in schoolteaching, though women doctors were gaining ground; of the 87 women entitled to register as medical practitioners in the United Kingdom in December 1889, only 14 had qualified before 1880. But their impact in Britain was diluted by their geographical spread; of the 70 qualified by February 1889 whose locations are known, 16 had gone to India (9 as medical missionaries) and 16 more were also overseas. Those who settled in Britain made for the big towns, with 3 in Edinburgh and 23 in London; this left only 12 for the rest of the United Kingdom. In 1895 Alice Gordon analysed the careers of the 1,486 graduates of Girton and Newnham Colleges (Cambridge), Somerville (Oxford), and Alexandra College (Dublin) on whom details were available: 680 were teaching and 208 had married; of the rest, only 11 were in medicine, 8–9 in government employment and one in law. The entirely male procession leaving Balliol College hall shows how small was the outward impact made on the university by the women's colleges, most of which were located well away from the city centre. The university still dominated Oxford, and was the major local source of employment until the growth of motor manufacturing in the 1920s. The procession, instinct with the dignity of the university, passes through the quadrangle where on summer evenings the 'ruddy light of the windows, and . . . broken notes of music and laughter' inspired Arnold Toynbee in 1875 to see Oxford as a place where, 'after all, one's ideal of happy life is nearer being realized than anywhere else . . . the ideal of gentle, equable, intellectual intercourse.'[36]

Yet it was because Toynbee's energies were not totally absorbed by 'gentle, equable, intellectual intercourse' that he became a national figure who inspired important work in the university settlements. Toynbee Hall, founded by Canon Barnett in 1884, was quickly followed by Oxford House (1884), Caius (1887), St Hilda's (1889) and Mansfield House (1890). Barnett aimed to transplant Oxford college club-life directly into the slums, with the ultimate objective of creating a university of East London which could weld together the social classes and bring culture to the poor. The ideal was not fully realized, but at least a nucleus of educated men was introduced into the area; Toynbee Hall was the base for many a middle-class radical foray into local institutions and sponsored several social investigations. Charles Booth once told a Toynbee Hall

audience that these had inspired his own major breakthrough in social survey technique.

But Toynbee's influence was wider even than this. His conduct and ideas, together with those of his colleague T.H. Green, helped to broaden out Liberal theory beyond a mere negative opposition to the state. The privileged male exclusiveness which linked Oxford so firmly to the London clubs and elite professions did not deter Green from helping women's higher education locally. He was also among the earliest to withdraw from college bachelor life into one of the large late Victorian North Oxford suburban houses which were being built for those dons who were now free to marry. For despite the university's unchanging appearance, major reforms had occurred there and in Cambridge, giving the university a clearer footing vis-à-vis its constituent colleges, and freeing endowments for wider purposes.

The Liberals were by no means in complete control at Oxford and Cambridge in the 1880s: the Canning Club was one of the Oxford debating societies whose vigour anticipated the Conservative revival in the nation at large. Founded in 1860, it declined until Curzon revived it as secretary in 1880. The Oxford Conservatives organized themselves into a new club, the Strafford, which secured the election of four of the six Union presidents between Michaelmas 1888 and Trinity 1890. 'The youth of England is on our side,' claimed the young Tory Democrat Randolph Churchill; his morale was much boosted in 1884 by an undergraduate deputation from the Cambridge University Carlton, which shared his desire to democratize the party's structure.[37] Prominence in these clubs was less important to a political career than success in the Oxford and Cambridge Unions. Curzon became president of the Oxford Union in 1880, and it was difficult to find good Liberal speakers. The pre-eminent figure at the Cambridge Union in the eighties was J.K. Stephen, president in 1881, who spoke only on the Conservative side; in 1884 socialism was rejected by 399 votes to 58. At a time when the political parties drew their new blood from the two ancient universities, Liberals had reason for concern.

Oxford and Cambridge were influencing a wider world in other ways. Since the 1850s they had been extending their sway over middle-class education through their local examinations. In 1878 the two universities together examined 8,765 candidates; by 1898 the figure had risen to 25,077. The University Extension movement was growing apace; in Michaelmas term 1880, the Cambridge Local Lectures Syndicate operated from thirteen centres attended by

2,510 students; ten years later, these figures had risen to fifty and 6,398, respectively.[38] The movement also helped to promote new provincial English universities: the first, the Victoria University, was founded in 1884 to integrate the colleges separately developed at Manchester, Liverpool, and Leeds.

The provincial universities owed much to civic, national and denominational pride, but much also to distaste for the classical and clerical bias of Oxford and Cambridge. When the young Lord Ernle criticized T.H. Huxley for bitterness in controversy, Huxley replied in a 'mood of half-comic, half-serious ferocity' that Ernle was 'not old enough to remember when men like Lyell and Murchison were not considered fit to lick the dust off the boots of a curate. I should like to get my heel into their mouths and scr-r-unch it round.'[39] Huxley championed the new university at Birmingham, which followed German and American models and gave science unusual prominence. Students at these centres of learning, whose numbers were rising fast in the late 1880s, differed from Oxford and Cambridge undergraduates: they were a mixture of young ladies in pursuit of culture, trainee teachers, foremen and technicians taking night classes, with a hard core of dedicated candidates for the London external degree.

The government, through its grants to the Royal Society, directly supported scientific research, and in the 1870s the number of applicants more than doubled, to 231; in the 1880s it again rose sharply, to 325.[40] But the close intermeshing of government and universities is mainly a twentieth-century story. Karl Marx argued that modern industry 'makes science a productive force distinct from labour and presses it into the service of capital,'[41] but in Britain the pressure did not come from commerce, where science was very much a practical, rule-of-thumb affair. Nowhere was the gulf between industry and the universities wider than in Wales, where the colleges set up in the 1880s owed little in finance or location to the major sources of Welsh wealth. Schoolmasters were the prime products of the decidedly non-industrial colleges at Aberystwyth (45 per cent) and Bangor (59 per cent) in their first twenty-five and twenty years, respectively; they were closely followed by ministers of religion (25 per cent at Aberystwyth, 16 per cent at Bangor). National and cultural factors were the overriding influences here. In Scotland, too, the relationship between industry and the universities was less fruitful than might have been expected, partly because the universities had been established well before the industrial revolution; but they were outstanding for their breadth of recruitment, with one university per million inhabitants in the 1880s as compared with only one per six million in England.[42]

From elementary school to university, the prestige of the written examination in the 1880s was immense. This was because the ancient universities, where it had originated, also enjoyed great prestige, and because the examination promised emancipation – to women from their long intellectual subordination, to the hardworking and the talented from aristocratic privilege and corruption, to professional men from low standards and indiscriminate recruitment. Memory-testing, the routinizing and standardizing of teaching, the cramping of originality in teacher and pupil – these were the legitimate objections raised by Auberon Herbert's 'Protest' against examinations published in *The Nineteenth Century* for 1888. But what should replace them? This was the familiar problem encountered by the fifteen members of the House of Lords and the ninety-six M.P.s who signed the Protest, together with many other famous names. Their own alternatives were feeble, and some of their respondents, including Joseph Chamberlain, preferred examinations, with all their evils, to privilege and patronage. Furthermore Herbert's protest was linked to the view that women's physique could not possibly tolerate the strain of men's examinations. But the campaign against 'over-pressure' in education during the 1880s was not entirely without fruit; the crudest form of mass-testing took place in the elementary schools through the system of 'payment by results', but it steadily lost intellectual respectability during the decade. Important statistical research was also conducted in 1888–90 by the Oxford mathematician F.Y. Edgeworth on the limits within which examination results might be expected to vary, but his work was not followed up for decades. Neither of these developments resulted in the abandonment of examinations as such; on the contrary, they merely assisted in their further refinement.

Adult education was not confined to universities or even to university extension classes. Much of what now happens in polytechnics, secondary schools and universities then happened in the workshop, the church, the public library, the mechanics' institute, the political meeting, the debating society, and above all through the newspaper and periodical. Much of the scholarship nowadays buried in academic journals was then published in the great weekly, monthly and quarterly reviews such as *The Spectator*, *The Nineteenth Century* and *The Fortnightly Review*, which also serialized many of the great Victorian novels.

From the 1850s, improvements in newspaper technology and the removal of 'taxes on knowledge' produced a massive growth in the readership of daily and evening newspapers. This ended the supremacy of *The Times* in circulation and boosted the number of United Kingdom daily papers from 14 in 1846 to 158 in 1880 and 180 in 1890; it also launched the *Daily Telegraph* and *Standard* on their great careers as mass-circulation dailies. By about 1888 the *Telegraph* had reached 300,000, and the *Standard* 255,000 by 1889. These figures were far higher than anything seen before, whereas *The Times* declined from 60,000 in 1879 to 40,000 in 1890. Evening papers were also booming, and sales of the Sundays, led by *Lloyd's Weekly News* with 900,000 in 1890, were impressive. The number of newsagents in England and Wales almost doubled during the 1880s: this flood of newsprint is only one aspect of a dramatic growth in the amount of paper flowing through society as a whole.[43]

The consequence of all this for the economy was considerable: in one week of 1886, 49 per cent of *The Times*, 51 per cent of the *Standard* and 61 per cent of the *Daily Telegraph* consisted of advertisements. Of the non-advertising space, 17 per cent in *The Times* and the *Standard* and 15 per cent in the *Telegraph* went on commercial and shipping news. Even this was not sufficient: the number of trade journals rose from one (*The Pawnbrokers' Gazette*) in 1851 to 119 in 1880. The 54 specialist weeklies of 1851 grew to 794 in 1880,[44] and the photographic press can perhaps be taken to illustrate the continued growth of specialism during the decade. The *Photographic News*, founded in 1858 as the first of the photographic periodicals, was quickly followed in 1860 by the *British Journal of Photography*. Their mood in the 1880s is one of self-confidence, tinged with mild sarcasm at the backward-looking institutions and individuals who fail to see the potential of this new technology. Thrustingly enthusiastic, they

1.4   bulge with advertisements for the newest equipment; confident in their editorials that it will improve still further, they predict several technical innovations well before they actually appear. It was a situation which inevitably encouraged the emergence of several more photographic papers during the decade.

The reasons for this impressive expansion in press sales are complex: the spread of literacy is both cause and consequence of the newspaper boom, but improved technology – leading to reductions in price and quicker reporting – is also relevant at many levels, especially with the provincial press. From the mid-Victorian period, the telegraph was tautening the lines of communication throughout Europe. Public interest in foreign affairs was greatly stimulated by the increased speed of reporting; foreign news absorbed 8 per

cent of the *Daily Telegraph*'s non-advertisement space in April 1886, 9 per cent of *The Times*'s and 12 per cent of the *Standard*'s.[45] The major London newspapers and press agencies had special wires to European capitals, and from the 1860s the major provincial papers had theirs to London. Through London offices and London correspondents, supplemented by the Press Association (founded in 1868), the provincial papers set the pace in the mid-Victorian pressure for publicity in government. This speeding-up in news-gathering ensured that the two provincial dailies of 1846 had by 1880 become 88, with 52 evening papers. They gave more news for a penny than their London equivalents because they supplemented foreign and London news with local. Likewise the London suburban papers grew from one in 1846 to 104 in 1880. Simultaneously London publications were invading the provinces, owing to improvements in delivery methods; in 1876 W.H. Smith organized 'newspaper trains' to leave the termini at 5.15 or 5.30 every morning, and procured adjustments in the time of going to press. Given that the newspapers were folded and sorted *en route*, these changes ensured that London dailies could reach Birmingham by 7.30, Bristol just after 9, York by 10, and Liverpool soon after 11.[46]

Photography accentuated the impression of immediacy which the press was increasingly able to convey. Illustrations, according to one observer in 1890, were becoming 'more a matter of course in magazines and newspapers'.[47] These were not actual photographs. Although the principle of half-tone reproduction had been known as early as 1852, photographs still had to be converted into woodcuts, or the cheaper zincotypes, before being printed. Woodburytypes (convincing reproductions made on a printing press) and carbon prints had been available from 1864; but as neither could be printed directly on to the page, they were not suitable for mass publications. The first newspaper half-tone appeared in New York in March 1880, in London not until 1885. It was an isolated example: the   2.6 first illustrated daily (the *Daily Graphic*) was not launched till 1890, and the first paper illustrated only with photographs (the *Daily Mirror*) not till 1904.

All this energy and enterprise was accompanied by political influence, and although in 1884 Gladstone's private secretary opposed ennobling journalists, they were rapidly rising in status. Frederick Greenwood claimed in 1890 that the political influence of the press must decline with the increased complexity of government and the rising number of newspapers,[48] but no such trend was yet apparent. The actions of every government were restrained by the knowledge that

Labouchere's *Truth* lurked in the shadows to pounce on political scandals and financial swindles. The articles of W.T. Stead in his influential penny London paper the *Pall Mall Gazette* on the state of British defences and on 'The Truth about the Navy' helped push up late Victorian expenditure on armaments: his attack on Sir Charles Dilke after he had been cited as co-respondent in a divorce case in 1886 prevented any recovery in the career of this major radical politician: and his campaign against Lord Clanricarde's ruthless evictions in 1886 helped to shift even Conservative opinion against irresponsible Irish landlordism.

8.16

An ambitious politician like Lord Randolph Churchill was almost obsessed with the press. In 1883, before delivering his three much-publicized Edinburgh speeches, he sent the text to *The Times* and was then tortured by the fear that the speeches would be printed in the wrong order: it was an experiment he decided never to repeat, but he continued to cultivate his newspaper links as energetically as ever. Early in the morning after Churchill's dramatic resignation as Chancellor of the Exchequer in December 1886, Lord Salisbury, the Prime Minister, told his wife 'if I know my man, it will be in *The Times* this morning.' It was. Churchill's career was wrecked, and as the Queen heard of his resignation only from the newspapers, recovery was unlikely.[49] Churchill was quite correct, though, to perceive the need for the Conservative Party to project itself more effectively now that the electorate had been enlarged.

Newspaper growth also owed much to another innovation. Investigative journalism took a big leap forward in the 1880s. Repudiating the old anonymity, W.T. Stead thought the reporter should 'be universally accessible' and 'know everyone and . . . hear everything'. In 1885 he launched a sensational investigation into London's underworld, 'carried out on the sound journalistic principle of the universal interview.'[50] It was neither the first nor the last newspaper social survey of the 1880s: a census of religion was promoted in the provincial press in 1881, and another (of London) launched the *British Weekly* in 1886. But Stead's was the first inquiry to make a sensation. Behind his innovations lay a passionately held political philosophy. He was heir to the optimistic mid-Victorian Liberal vision of the journalist as crusader for the open society: as the expert in analysing public opinion: and therefore as the indispensable aid to politicians in a democratizing political system.

A rather breathless enthusiasm for universal interrogation informs his well-known article of 1886 on the profession. Instead of the close world of confidential conversations between politicians and trusted journal-

ists – epitomized by Delane's supremacy in the mid-Victorian *Times* – Stead envisages a much more open relationship. He regards politicians as amateurs in assessing public opinion, and envisages a nationwide network of between 600 and 1,000 informants who could be instantly consulted by editors about local attitudes on any issue. The newspaper editor, 'filled with his central fire, saturated with his ideas,' would then co-ordinate the results and enjoy all the prestige of being 'the latest to interrogate the democracy.' Parliament would be kept continuously responsive to public opinion between elections, and the newspaper 'would . . . be a great secular or civic church and democratic university . . . the very soul of our national unity.'[51]

By the 1880s politicians were already feeling the need to protect themselves against this journalistic onslaught. Though they talked in public more frequently, this does not mean that they talked more freely; indeed, Dilke thought that Gladstone's relatively uninhibited conversation on diplomatic matters was a sign that he came from an earlier generation whose political elite had less to fear from press intrusion. Parnell was particularly good at submerging himself below the journalist's horizon, though even he was inconvenienced by enterprising reporters prowling about South London. In January 1884 John Bright could hardly contain his impatience with the new publicity after spending three hours in sitting for Mr Blake Wirgman so that his portrait could be used for the *Graphic*: 'I wish I had finished with photographers, artists, sculptors and interviewers and newspaper people,' he grumbled in his diary: 'they have given me not a little trouble – and will not leave me "obscure".' In July 1886 the press, gaining entrance by way of the garden, surprised the Conservative statesman W.H. Smith at the home of Lord Salisbury, who was in the midst of cabinet making; 'it is really quite intolerable,' he told his wife; 'these vermin are omnipresent and it is hopeless to attempt to escape observation.' Gladstone felt a certain exhilaration in publicity, but even he was complaining to Hartington by December 1885 (in the midst of the Home Rule crisis) that 'the whole stream of public excitement is now turned upon me, and I am pestered with incessant telegrams which there is no defence against, but either suicide or Parnell's method of self-concealment'; he felt 'so battered with telegrams that I hardly know whether I stand on my head or my heels.'[52]

Still, it did at first seem that Liberal ideals were, broadly speaking, being realized by these developments. By modern standards, newspapers in the 1880s provided readers with abundant information about Parliament:

such reports occupied 23 per cent of *The Times*'s non-advertising space from 5 to 10 April 1886, 18 per cent of the *Daily Telegraph*'s and the *Standard*'s.[53] Extra-parliamentary speeches were long, reflective and often printed in full. All this greatly broadened out the area of 'informed opinion' in Britain. The daily press in the 1880s was dominated by penny papers such as the Conservative *Daily Telegraph* and the Liberal *Daily News*. These, like the threepenny *Times*, which in prestige surpassed them all, were by modern standards short on headlines and long on exhaustive parliamentary reports. Joseph Arch, the agricultural labourers' trade union leader, formed his opinions from newspaper reports of Gladstone's and Bright's speeches – though he added a comment which usefully sets a limit to press influence: 'It was a case of like to like; I got what I wanted in the speeches, they gave me reasons for feeling and thinking in the way I already did.' The young Lloyd George walked fourteen miles to Portmadoc and back to get a London paper with a full report of a Gladstone Midlothian speech at the 1880 general election, and later heard it read aloud to an audience by his Uncle Richard.[54]

Radicals had long seen publicity and open government as aids to political progress. An impressive sequence of nationwide pressure groups from the anti-slavery movement onwards had flooded the country with propaganda and helped to convert general elections from contests about personalities and local interest-groups into debates on national values and policy. The Liberal agitation against Disraeli's foreign policy between 1876 and 1880 began in the provincial press and threatened the governing elite with the intrusion of public opinion into the formulation of foreign policy. The extent of the intrusion was unprecedented – hence the Queen's almost hysterical disgust, which increased her existing prejudice against the Liberal leader Mr Gladstone. The press seemed to be turning the whole nation into a schoolroom – even on matters hitherto confidential – just as radicals had long desired. Far more information on politics was being made available. In 1880 the Liberal journalist T.W. Reid claimed that 'today the visitor to the [parliamentary] lobby will find it overrun with the representatives of newspapers great and small.' The London correspondents included more than one M.P. among their number. Reid welcomed these developments because 'we have to educate our masters in something more than the three R's.'[55]

After 1880 there seemed to be penetration even into the very heart of government: Gladstone's Cabinet of 1880–85 was decidedly leaky, and the Queen repeatedly protested against Chamberlain's use of the press to outwit his Whig opponents there. In May 1880 his fellow-radical Sir Charles Dilke used his influence with the *Daily News* to head off a proposed initiative on Irish coercion by his colleague W.E. Forster. Defending himself in February 1885 against Gladstone's rebuke, Chamberlain claimed that 'popular government is inconsistent with the reticence which official etiquette formerly imposed on speakers . . . Now the platform has become one of the most powerful and indispensable instruments of Government.'[56] Gladstone was not above manipulating the press himself, as indicated by his private contacts with John Morley, editor of the *Pall Mall Gazette* from 1880 to 1883. Ironically Gladstone's son Herbert later in 1885 employed similar means to outmanoeuvre Chamberlain by informing T.W. Reid of his father's radical ideas on Irish government.

So energetic and self-confident a press had some hope of promoting that clash of argument, that 'education by collision', which Liberals favoured. So dominant were Liberal ideas in the mid-Victorian period that even the Conservatives were influenced by them. J.S. Mill thought political institutions should be judged by 'the degree in which they promote the general mental advancement of the community, including under that phrase advancement in intellect, in virtue, and in practical activity and efficiency.'[57] In 1867 the Liberal journalist Walter Bagehot condemned Louis Napoleon's autocratic regime in France because it 'is not a *teaching* government':[58] its intentions might be benevolent, but it did not train the citizen in political thinking or develop his sense of public responsibility. Similar motives lay behind the Liberal enthusiasm for local self-government: the community might lose thereby in efficiency, but it would gain through the spread of administrative experience. Mill, the radical philosopher whose *Representative Government* (1861) is the classic formulation of these ideas, even proposed introducing an examination as a preliminary qualifying test for voters.

It is hardly surprising that of the United Kingdom's 1,376 daily and weekly papers in 1880, as many as 482 avowed themselves Liberal; 564 claimed to be neutral or independent, and only 330 Conservative.[59] By 1880 Liberals dominated the London press agencies, together with the London and provincial newspapers. Yet in many respects the 1880s saw ominous developments for those who believed in the Liberal vision of the press. It was not simply that the Conservatives were beginning to mobilize – though Disraeli's encouragement of the *National Review*, founded in 1881 as a rival to the predominantly Liberal monthlies, was a foretaste of that; it was more that there was what Gladstone in 1885 described as a 'prevailing disposition to make a luxury of panics.'[60] These were forced on the reader with the aid of the multiple headline which Stead introduced in his *Pall Mall Gazette* in 1881 and employed to break up the long blocks of prose which had hitherto been customary.

Stead's political preoccupations made him in some ways traditional as a journalist. It was George Newnes (founder of *Tit-Bits*) who pioneered the entertainment of the semi-literate reader; Alfred Harmsworth was much influenced by him when launching his first paper, the weekly *Answers to Correspondents*, in 1888. His energy and ambition, coupled with his brother Harold's financial sense, brought fame to a newspaper proprietor who, according to an informed biographer, 'knew no Latin or Greek . . . had very hazy notions of history . . . was well acquainted with no modern languages.'[61] This commercialization of the press increased its preoccupation with the habits of the rich, and with crimes, disasters and death; from now on, the

commuters and clerks hurrying past in the street were to be titillated rather than instructed. The press had begun to cater for the needs of the commuter – for the quick and entertaining reading required by the District Railway's passengers as they moved from Parsons Green to the City and back; on entering the station, they were greeted by advertisements for the *Standard* and the *Illustrated Church Times*. Readers were also wooed by the prize competitions introduced by Newnes in 1880 and by Stead in 1886. 3.15 8.11

These developments should not be viewed too sourly, for the new papers were merely providing entertainment which had earlier been obtained by other means; they were tempting into buying and reading newspapers people who had never thought of doing so before. Still, the tendency was a far cry from the calm deliberation on national policy, the cultivation of the reason through the informed study of the facts, which had been the ideal of the mid-Victorian Liberal. It was a tendency which would be carried much further in later decades.

3.2. A group of women undergraduates at Lady Margaret Hall, Oxford. Gertrude Bell is in profile in the centre row, third from the right. 1888

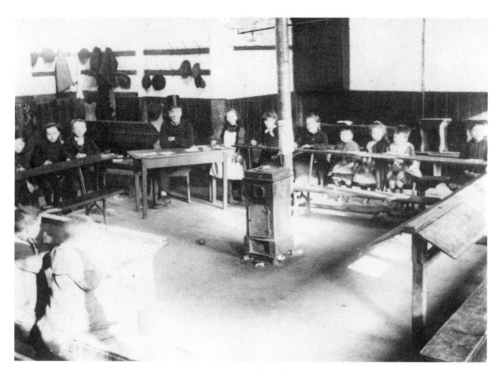

3.3.4. *City and country schools in the 1880s. In a private school in Deptford, London (LEFT), a few smartly dressed children sit round a stove with their top-hatted teacher. At the British System Public School, Sarum Hill, Hampshire (BELOW), crowds of boys gather round the 'Giant Stride' in the playground, while the girls look out of the school windows. Dates unknown*

3.5 (RIGHT). *A Methodist Sunday School class, Forest Side, Nottingham, Richardson(?), 1880*

3.6 (BELOW). *A Board School. The blackboard preaches: 'It is only by labour that thought can be made healthy, and only by thought that labour can be made happy' (Ruskin). Date unknown*

3.7. Schooling on the remote Scottish island of St Kilda, where the educational system arrived in 1884, Norman McLeod (published by G.W. Wilson & Co.), 1886

3.8 (ABOVE LEFT). *The chemistry laboratory at Charterhouse School, with the chemistry master, the Rev. S.D. Titmus, 1888/9*

3.9 (BELOW LEFT). *Charterhouse moved from London to its new Surrey home, designed by P.C. Hardwick, in 1872. An Old Carthusians' football match. 1884*

3.10 (ABOVE). *An Oxford University degree procession leaving Balliol College hall to proceed to the Sheldonian Theatre, Henry Taunt, undated*

3.11 (BELOW). *Members of Roedean School Archery Club with one of the school's founders, Millicent Lawrence. 1890*

3.12 (LEFT). *The 'Warriors' at Halliwick School for Girls. 1890*

3.13 (BELOW). *The Fire Brigade, Girton College, Cambridge University, founded in 1869 (Newnham College was founded in 1871). 1887*

3.14 (LEFT). *Dr Gustav Jaeger, promoter of natural dyes and textiles, in his 'suit of sanitary woollen clothing',*
H. Brandseph, undated

3.15 (ABOVE). *The magazine vendor, Ludgate Circus, London:*
'Tit-Bits was her greatest sale' said the photographer, Paul
Martin. 1893

Chapter 4 *Home and Family*

4.3 The wedding of Ernest Fletcher and Annie Wright at Clay Cross in 1884 was an Anglican ceremony, as were 707 out of every 1000 marriages in England and Wales that year: 43 were Roman Catholic and 119 of other denominations.[1] Registry office ceremonies (131) were comparatively rare, for weddings were then – even more than now – occasions for formal dress, family celebration, bouquets and somewhat embarrassed joviality amidst conspicuous expenditure. The camera probably helped to consolidate home life and middle-class values by viewing major domestic events through the professional photographer's middle-class eye.

Personal attraction between bride and bridegroom was a less important factor in the 1880s than it would be now. Marriages, at least in the landowning classes, were often 'arranged' so that fortunes could be built up and estates consolidated; through the wedding ceremony, relationships were reaffirmed between landlord, tenants and neighbours, manufacturer and employees. Likewise, royal weddings cemented ties within the nation and between nations. Monarchy and aristocracy in the 1880s assuaged some of the thirst for glamour which was later transferred to the film star; but apart from the military uniforms, the wedding group of Prin-

4.4 cess Beatrice and Prince Henry of Battenberg resembles its middle-class counterparts. Queen Victoria, who

4.1. A crofter and his family at Whiting Bay, Scotland, Matthew Morrison, 1888

rejected aristocratic extravagance for middle-class morality, no doubt approved. She knew how to stabilize monarchy by emphasizing family values. Until 1887 even the innocent party in divorce was excluded from the Court, a policy which stemmed more from concern for the monarchy than from any puritanism on the Queen's part. She disliked dynastic marriages unaccompanied by affection. The sufferings of her eldest daughter, briefly Empress of Germany, illustrated the personal difficulties likely to result in an age of mounting nationalism from intermarriage between royal families which even in Britain still wielded considerable political power.

If only for technical reasons, the camera in the 1880s was unlikely to penetrate very far indoors, let alone into rooms where the Victorians undressed – though already by 1889 four men were appearing in a Manchester court for sending obscene photographs through the post. Photographs now available can tell us nothing of the fears, agonies and dangers of childbirth which threatened the lives of so many late Victorian women. Openness about sexual matters is a recent development; Lady Pethick-Lawrence was not alone among those who had been young in the 1880s and who later deplored 'the tangle of emotion which I and many others of my generation have had with much difficulty to unwind.' Sylvia Pankhurst explains how even her mother, progressive as she was in the 1880s, failed at this hurdle: when her daughter Adela had been asked some strange questions by boys in

Russell Square, Mrs Pankhurst tried to sort out the matter: ' "Father says I ought to talk to you," she began; but she did not get very much further, and never again reverted to the subject, leaving us as free from knowledge as before.' Bertrand Russell, born in 1872, learned what he could about sex from friends of his own age and from a page boy 'rather more knowing than we were'. Miss Loane, the East End nurse, found respectable Edwardian working-class mothers ready to boast that 'I've brought up my children that innocent they don't know *nothing.*' The mothers were probably ill-informed, but their children almost certainly knew less than they do now. Sex was no doubt freely discussed in the male atmosphere of music-hall, London club and country pub – but in public, reticence was the rule. When Lord Randolph Churchill in Parliament in March 1890 described the Pigott forgeries, which *The Times* had published as incriminating Parnell in Irish violence, as produced by 'a thing, a reptile, a monster. Pigott … a ghastly, bloody, rotten, foetus – Pigott! Pigott! Pigott!!!', there was an audible gasp of horror.[2]

'To seek out the most vital facts of life is still in England a perilous task,' wrote Havelock Ellis, the pioneer of systematic sex research in Britain. But reticence by no means indicates abstinence. The physique of the Victorians was not so very different from our own; the contrast is more a matter of appearance and situations. If we look at three areas of sexual activity outside marriage – masturbation, homosexuality and prostitution – we find unfamiliar public attitudes, but no evidence of diminished incidence; indeed, prostitution seems to have been more widespread.

We know almost nothing about the incidence of, or attitudes to, masturbation among women in any class or among either sex in the working class. We can only speculate that working-class conduct was modified by lack of privacy, by exclusion from semi-monastic boarding schools and above all by a shorter interval between puberty and marriage. Whereas improved diet caused a long-term lowering of the age of puberty for all classes, the fall was less pronounced within the working class, who were also less likely – for social reasons – to postpone marriage. In 1881 two upper-class areas of London, St George's, Hanover Square, and Kensington, show a higher percentage unmarried within each age-group between fifteen and thirty-five, than in the poorer areas of Whitechapel and St Giles. As for male aristocrats, their mean age at marriage in 1875–99 was as high as thirty.[3]

Rather more can be said about the middle class, because masturbation was much discussed (usually

under the euphemism 'immorality') among public-school masters. E.B. Pusey, the Oxford High Church clergyman, claimed in 1877 that only about 10 per cent abstained before coming to confession, and that 24 per cent practised alone, 66 per cent with others; his figures accord quite well with Kinsey's for a later generation. Pusey's estimate was accepted by Edward Lyttelton, headmaster of Eton, who took the matter very seriously; but he shared the general tendency of commentators at the time to pronounce, as Havelock Ellis complained, 'in a dogmatic and off-hand manner which is far from scientific.'[4] A.S. Dyer, author of *Plain Words to Young Men upon an Avoided Subject*, predicted disease, moral decay, unfitness for marriage and divine retribution as deserved punishments, but the more horrific medical arguments against masturbation were being heard less frequently. The association with insanity was contested, though as late as 1912 Freud did not rule out masturbation as a possible cause of severe mental illness. In the 1870s Sir James Paget, the Queen's surgeon, thought it no more harmful than sexual intercourse, Lyttelton took a middle and somewhat unworldly position, claiming that it weakened morality and intellect, yet should be more freely discussed between boys and adults.[5]

The Rev. J.M. Wilson, headmaster of Clifton College, in his controversial presidential address to the Education Society in 1881 advocated filling the schoolboy's time with sporting and other activities, together with closer relationships between masters and boys. In the subsequent discussion, some correspondents took up the orthodox position on masturbation, but the editors of the Society's *Journal* wondered whether an emphasis on athletics might not worsen the problem, which should be tackled through parental warning and co-education in day-schools. Even more daringly, 'Olim Etonensis' accused schoolmasters of ignorance on the whole topic and doubted whether masturbation was really so harmful; he recalled that at Eton it had been current among boys who were now 'Cabinet Ministers, statesmen, officers, clergymen, country gentlemen, &c'. He thought it best to keep the boys occupied, arrange school buildings sensibly and let well alone. Nor did he share the assumptions made by the advocates of sex education that the habit was caused by ignorance, and was something to worry about. Here he was at one with Havelock Ellis, whose *Auto-Erotism* (1899) recognized the prevalence of masturbation but denied that it 'can produce any evil results beyond slight functional disturbances'. Ellis felt that expressions of horror merely buried the facts more deeply and thereby worsened the problem.[6]

With homosexuality too there is progress towards empirically-based understanding in the 1880s, but no evidence of reduced incidence. Havelock Ellis later alleged that sexual inversion (which he carefully distinguished from occasional homosexual activity) affected 5 per cent of middle-class men and was often associated with artistic and acting ability. There were about a hundred committals annually in England and Wales for sodomy, bestiality and attempts to commit 'unnatural misdemeanours' in the 1880s, but homosexuality was far more widespread than these figures suggest: in the London parks, guardsmen and others pursued a vigorous trade in male prostitution, while the Cleveland Street scandal shows that post office boys were involved in homosexual brothels with a decidedly aristocratic clientèle. Urban life made it easier for homosexuals to meet one another, but they were driven further underground in 1885 when the legislation against sodomy (whether with male or female), a felony punishable by up to ten years' penal servitude, was supplemented by making intercourse between males, even in private, punishable by up to two years' hard labour. The law had nothing to say on lesbian relationships, about which even less was known, though Havelock Ellis in 1897 ventured the figure of 10 per cent for its incidence among the educated middle class.[7]

The great strides in research on the subject during the 1880s were being made in Germany, Austria and France, but Englishmen were beginning to write intelligently about it – most notably the socialist Edward Carpenter, to whom it had come as a revelation in the 1880s that many men had the same leanings as himself, and J.A. Symonds, the well-known and homosexual historian of the Renaissance, whose chapter on Greek Love in his *Studies of the Greek Poets* lost him the Oxford Chair of poetry in 1877. He had already written a study of homosexuality in classical times but dared not publish it till 1883, and then only for private circulation. His *A Problem in Modern Ethics* (1891) provides an entirely factual and scholarly analysis. Using the Austrian psychologist Krafft-Ebing's term 'urning' where we would say 'homosexual', he points out that 'the line of division between the sexes, even in adult life, is a subtle one,' and stresses the illogicality and harmfulness of British legislation on the subject; an over-populated society, he claims, can hardly be injured by a small number of homosexual men. Like Havelock Ellis, whose *Sexual Inversion* (1897) he helped to compile, Symonds thought that incidence might be diminished if co-education replaced the semi-monastic public school. Here is one root of the twentieth cen-

tury's partial disenchantment with the public schools, then in their heyday: one source of that individualism in personal conduct which has accompanied the twentieth-century growth of collectivism in public affairs.

Prostitution, at least as prevalent in the 1880s as now, was at last being discussed more publicly. Since 1869, Josephine Butler had been attacking the state-regulated traffic which existed in some seaports and garrison towns, and shocked her contemporaries by discussing the most unladylike topics in public. Her villains were not the humble servicemen who used the prostitute, but the authorities who assumed that sin was inevitable and that women must gratify male desires. Press censorship did not prevent her from getting the system suspended in 1883 and abolished in 1886. By then, W.T. Stead had fully publicized London prostitution and the trade in young girls with his *Pall Mall Gazette* articles of 1885; Mrs Butler saw these as 'the grand unveiling of hell'. The wealthy London 'Minotaur', who boasted of seducing 2,000 virgins, was sensationally described. Karl Marx saw prostitution as the inevitable consequence of capitalist exploitation: for him, bourgeois marriage was 'in reality a system of wives in common'. When provincial employers and employees mobilized themselves against such evils, Marx's daughter Eleanor doubted whether much impact would be made on one class 'literally in a position to buy ... the *bodies* of the other'. By contrast, Stead and Mrs Butler adopted a moralistic and anti-aristocratic standpoint, blaming the London clubs where the anonymous author of the erotic autobiography *My Secret Life* spent so much of his time. 'Money will open every female's legs,' he wrote.[8]

Parliament raised the age of consent for young girls from thirteen to sixteen, and the National Vigilance Association was formed to outlaw indecent literature and the seduction of children; it successfully campaigned in the late 1880s against the sale of Zola's novels in Britain. Courageous and high-minded people like Mrs Butler or Mr Gladstone (who, in fulfilment of a vow taken as a young man, alarmed his secretaries in the 1880s by walking the West End streets trying to reclaim prostitutes) probably made little impact, because their diagnosis was so superficial. Major social changes were needed to discourage the trade on what might be described as the 'supply' side. In the absence of adequate pay, welfare schemes, or male protection, women were periodically thrown into a poverty from which only prostitution seemed able to rescue them. Official standards of sexual conduct ensured that, once a woman had broken the code, she was 'ruined' and therefore had little to lose by offending further. The illegitimacy figures show that fornication was common enough, and, where marriage did not result, prostitution might well be the mother's only resort. In several rural counties – Shropshire, Cumberland, Westmorland, Hereford and Norfolk – the illegitimacy rate in the ten-year period between 1878 and 1887 was markedly above the national average. Between 1881 and 1885 there were 48 illegitimate births per 1,000 live births in England and Wales; this is comparable with twentieth-century figures until the 1960s, when the rate began to rise fast. The unmarried woman was ridiculed if she did not combine pre-marital abstinence with the acquisition of a husband. As the music-hall song put it: 'I never say "nay" – yet he gallops away, and I must wait for another year.'[9]

As for the 'demand' side, prostitution flourished on the declining, but still close, relationship between property and marriage; at the higher social levels, the arranged marriage was common. Landownership, the key to social prestige, was concentrated within families through the primogeniture system. In this situation, the couple could not hold property jointly; the wife's father therefore provided her with a substantial sum on marriage, in return for which the husband made a 'settlement' upon her which allowed limited financial independence. To the extent that this system freed the wife from complete dependence on the husband, it increased the daughter's dependence on her father. In 1882 the married woman gained a full right to the ownership of her own property. The husband's greater wealth ensured that he became the child's natural guardian, though legislation in 1886 recognized the mother as natural guardian of the child on the father's death. Reform in the law of guardianship moved during the nineteenth century towards recognizing the claims of the wife, and during the twentieth century towards protecting the interests of the child.

This interaction between property and marriage helps to explain why a separation of spheres was so widespread among the upper classes: friction between a couple who had married for reasons other than affection could be minimized by assigning them distinct roles and by winking at unobtrusive adultery on both sides. As Beatrice Webb recalled, 'a duchess, especially if she came from a princely family, might exchange her insignificant duke for a powerful marquis as a habitual companion without causing the slightest dent in her social acceptability' whereas 'Mrs Smith' could not. The Countess of Warwick described 'the kind of freemasonry of conduct' which prevailed in her circle. 'We could be and do as we liked according to the code.

The unforgivable sin was to give away any member of our group. That was class loyalty ...'[10]

Prostitution also stemmed from the virtual impossibility of divorce. Where landed estates were indivisible, marriage must be indissoluble. Involvement in divorce cases was a serious enough matter to wreck the careers of two prominent politicians – Dilke and Parnell – in the 1880s. Divorces per 10,000 of the married population in England and Wales were rising slowly but steadily, from 2.02 in 1861 to 5.01 in 1901; but the figures for the 1880s were lower than in the nine other European countries (and the U.S.A.) for which statistics are available. Figures as low as this cannot indicate the number of broken marriages, and are compatible with a higher, rather than a lower, level of 'permissiveness' than our own. When the marriage failed, its façade could be preserved with the aid of the mistress or prostitute: or (as with many working people) cohabitation with a new partner could result. Only a sixth of the divorces in England and Wales in 1871 occurred within the working class, mostly among skilled operatives.[11] Divorce has become more common in the twentieth century partly because others have gained access to legal facilities that had once been confined to the rich.

Prostitution also flourished on the prevalence of the single state. Nowadays, as in the medieval period, matrimony is entered into early and is almost universal. Even the Victorians assumed that every woman would marry, and marry happily, otherwise she would be a failure. Yet in 1881 there were 316,100 more women than men in England and Wales between the ages of 15 and 39, a disproportion which actually increased during the decade; the scarcity of husbands was increased by widespread bachelorhood, which at that time carried no stigma. Postponement of marriage was becoming more common even among younger people of both sexes. In the 1880s many occupations were or had recently been incompatible with matrimony – those of soldiers, sailors and dons at Oxford or Cambridge, for example. In 1881 41 per cent of the men in England and Wales between 20 and 45 were single, 9 per cent of those over 45. The proportions of each sex unmarried within each age-group in 1881 are higher than those for 1971 in every category except women over 65. In the age-groups between 20 and 45, the contrast is very marked; whereas in 1881 78 per cent of the men and 67 per cent of the women between 20 and 25 were unmarried, in 1971 these figures fall to 63 per cent and 40 per cent, respectively. One similarity between the two years persists, though; in the younger age-groups, a higher percentage of women were married than men – a contrast partly explained by the male tendency to marry women younger than themselves.[12]

Bachelorhood by no means entailed sexual inexperience. Prostitution, a major problem in seaports and in university and garrison towns, was encouraged by the fact that the imbalance between the sexes was much greater in some areas than aggregate national figures would suggest. In 1881 there were 108.3 women for 100 men in the towns of England and Wales, but only 99.8 in rural areas, largely because country girls went to the towns for their domestic service; this contrast, very marked in the age-group between 10 and 20, diminished between 20 and 25 because young men were by then moving into the towns in search of work. Between the ages of 25 and 45 the sex-balance was restored, but the disparity reappears in later life, perhaps because towns offered more employment for older women. This patchy geographical imbalance appears strongly in the distribution of women voters on borough electoral rolls of 1885: only the woman householder – that is, the unmarried or widowed woman – could qualify, and the percentage within the municipal electorate ranges all the way from Swansea, with 4.5, to Great Torrington, with 28.8. It was, in general, in the spas, seaside resorts and country towns that women were strongest in the municipal electorate, and in the industrial towns and seaports that they were weakest.[13]

Even to the happily married man in the 1880s, prostitutes were tempting, given his wife's repeated pregnancies; but this cause of prostitution was already in decline. By the 1890s many of the modern methods of contraception were available, and the large family was ceasing to be an index of wealth. The number of births per thousand women between the ages of 15 and 44 in England and Wales shows a clear decline only from the 1880s. These overall figures mask major class-contrasts: educated people had smaller families than the workers as a whole, and skilled and textile operatives had smaller families than miners, agricultural labourers and unskilled workers. Such differentials had major consequences for social mobility, and therefore for politics in the coming generation. But to judge from advertisements in the general area of sex, the chief preoccupation was not with birth control but with restoring lost sexual vigour; high fertility in the 1880s, like the modern balance of payments, was an indicator of national and individual virility. Fighting strength in warfare was a major consideration, an attitude so deeply entrenched that most British feminists dared not repudiate motherhood as woman's predes-

tined role, and opposed that reduction in the birth rate which has subsequently achieved so much for women's emancipation. Late Victorian doctors enlarged upon the terrible diseases resulting from artificial contraception. It was widely thought that only the immoral would use such devices until the Bradlaugh–Besant trial of 1877 advertised Knowlton's birth-control manual, *The Fruits of Philosophy*; its annual sales jumped from 1,000 before the trial to 185,000 in the three years after it.[14]

The publicizing of contraceptive techniques perhaps enabled some parents to give effect to a long-felt desire for fewer children, but this cannot be the whole explanation for the declining birth rate because alternative methods had long been known: coitus interruptus, prolonged weaning and abortion. The incidence of abortion is unknown, but it was certainly far greater than committals for attempting to procure miscarriage (a mere 15 in 1883, 17 in 1888 in England and Wales).[15] It was a topic much discussed among the groups of women whose mutual help complemented the male society of club and pub. More important than technique was probably the curbing of family size encouraged by compulsory education (which made children less lucrative), and by improvements in child care and nutrition, rising real living standards, and the spread of respectable styles of life. Philosophies of birth control had long attracted self-educated skilled working men eager to shape their own destiny. It was a form of thrift or temperance which would ensure that expenditure did not outrun income. 'It still remains unrecognised', wrote J.S. Mill, the agnostic and radical spokesman, in his *Liberty* (1859), 'that to bring a child into existence without a fair prospect of being able, not only to provide food for its body, but instruction and training for its mind, is a moral crime, both against the unfortunate offspring and against society.'[16]

The camera reveals more about the external appearance of domestic day-to-day life than about its inner reality. The *Tit-Bits* villa epitomizes lower-middle-class 4.5 suburbia in the 1880s. Its plate-glass windows, Venetian blinds, pot-plants, decorative ironwork and polychromatic brick show technical innovation strengthening the association between art, ornamentation and social aspiration. From the 1870s onwards, the Artisans', Labourers' and General Dwellings Company collected together people on the margin between middle and working class into London suburbs like Shaftesbury Park (Wandsworth), Noel Park (Hornsey), and Queen's Park (Kilburn), where respectability was upheld through excluding pubs and pawnshops and letting out small, well-maintained, sanitary houses.

4.6 Cadbury's Bournville, launched in 1879, was merely the latest of the benevolent employers' industrial villages. They showed a proper respect for factory hierarchies. Bournville epitomizes the prevailing ideal of countrified townscape which was springing up in so many suburbs of the 1880s: in the middle-class estates of north Oxford, for example, or in Bedford Park, London, with its rather larger houses and gardens. Smaller middle-class families meant smaller houses, and at the same time the Queen Anne style was eroding pretentiousness. Building societies from the 1850s onwards diffused the idea of house purchase more widely, and the 1880s saw one of their three boom periods; total assets in Great Britain rose from £54,300,000 to £69,900,000 between 1880 and 1889, and the number of societies from 1,853 in 1880 to 4,472 in 1890. The movement now had nearly 650,000 members, but a property-owning democracy had not yet been created, and progress was not to be so rapid again till the 1920s.[17]

Prestige projects like Kensington's Imperial Institute and Manchester's Town Hall – not to mention the heavy bankers' buildings customary for commercial firms – gave plenty of scope for the grandiose, but it was small-scale suburban housing which offered the most interesting architectural developments of the 1880s. Norman Shaw's Dutch gables and vernacular brickwork were eminently suited to the cottage estates modelled on Bedford Park. From his office came many of the architects who developed the new, less pretentious, domestic styles so well suited to the expanding hordes of city clerks and civil servants. The Queen Anne style reappears in the houses built for Alfred Marshall and T.H. Green, breaking up the rigidities of Victorian Gothic and itself dissolving in the 1890s into further suburban novelties. These styles were founded on close observation of older English architectural practice, and aimed at harmonizing building materials with the surrounding landscape.

The fixed and identifiable home was the mark of only the respectable working class. In 1881 the census enumerators found 10,924 vagrants (4,309 of them women) in England and Wales; a quarter were in barns 4.7-9 and sheds and the rest in caravans, tents and the open air. Many were 'tramping' in search of work and using the trade unions' nationwide network of pub staging-posts on recognized routes, but some were true vagrants, for whom shelters could hardly be said even to 4.10 provide a proper bed. Housing density varied markedly from town to town, but the overall figure in 1881 was 5.38 human occupants per inhabited home in England and Wales, for 1891 5.32 – as compared with 2.74 for

Great Britain in 1975. The poorest working people lived in grim slums and tenements; heroic struggles 4.11,12 were often made to keep up appearances and preserve decency, but privacy was almost completely lacking. Even when staying with respectable working-class relatives in Bacup in the 1880s, Beatrice Webb found it impossible to keep up her diary because 'these folk live all day in "coompany"', and were constantly in and out of each other's houses.[18] The practice of 'flitting' to avoid paying the rent was common; cramped conditions fomented family disputes and a burning desire for more space. The street inevitably became an extension of homes which were too small to accommodate so many children, so much washing, so many animals. Many slum families had but recently arrived from the countryside, and realized only slowly that animals could no longer be kept in or near the home.

The family and the neighbourhood helped to mitigate some of the uncertainties of slum existence. Most working people suffered poverty at three stages in the life-cycle: in childhood, in early parenthood, and in old age. Assistance is now provided by the state at each of these points whereas in the 1880s it came primarily from the extended family, a very flexible instrument. Old people helped young parents with child-minding and even accommodation, and housed older children as lodgers during a crisis; young people gave a hand to the old when necessary; wives and children worked to maintain unemployed husbands and parents. When families were large and when distant relatives kept in touch, this almost tribal system could often prevent the burden on any one individual from becoming intolerable. It was a declining birth rate as well as socialism which created the welfare state.

Where the family failed, neighbours might step in. In 1886 Beatrice Webb commented sourly on the East End's 'low level of monotonous yet excited life; the regular recurrence to street sensations, quarrels and fights; the greedy street-bargaining, and the petty theft and gambling'.[19] But violence and vendettas were the obverse of the tight personal relationships that developed in such communities – part of the entertainment occurring at one's very door while sitting with pipe or drink as the womenfolk gossiped and the children swarmed on the pavement. The poor helped one another in ways which were less advertised but often more timely and better directed than the charity of the rich. Through gossip, women could often get local news essential to the family's welfare. Many facilities now enjoyed individually were then available only communally: the street was a playground for the children and a place for hanging out washing, lavatories were shared, pubs provided comforts absent from the individual home. The slum was rarely photographed because respectable people kept away, and the occupants could not begin to photograph themselves. These areas threatened public health as well as public order, and were coloured black on Charles Booth's map of London housing densities.

Many working people lived in rented accommodation; receipts from land and buildings accounted for 14 per cent of United Kingdom national income in the 1880s, compared with only 5 per cent in the 1950s. The state had not begun closely regulating rents, and in the 1880s Octavia Hill fought to keep it out of housing by encouraging respectability in the tenant and professionalism in the rent-collector. When the poorest class enters a house, said a Clerkenwell medical officer in 1883, 'the locks and handles of doors become toys for the children, and are soon demolished. The drain taps are sold at the bone and bottle shops, those left are never kept on; the closets are stopped up and the pans are broken.'[20] The problem was partly educational and still affects populations unaccustomed to fixed accommodation. It could not be tackled by landlords in pursuit of profit, by philanthropic housing schemes, or even by enlightened employers like Lord Leverhulme, who launched his factory estate at Port Sunlight in 1888, or the Cadburys who pushed Bournville further forward in the 1890s.

The 800,000 houses built by private enterprise in Great Britain between 1880 and 1889 in no way equalled the totals of the 1870s or 1890s and were quite insufficient.[21] When the newly formed London County Council moved towards the solution ultimately adopted – the provision of subsidized housing by the local authority – distinguished architects began at last to concern themselves with working-class housing needs instead of catering primarily for the aristocratic, bourgeois and religious whim. Young socialistic disciples of Philip Webb joined the L.C.C. architect's department after its foundation in 1888 to devise pioneer re-housing schemes in Boundary Street, Bethnal Green, Millbank and elsewhere. Living in 'flats', which had already attracted middle-class tenants at Kensington and Victoria by the 1880s, and had long been common among working people in Scotland, now became equally so among English working people, though technical factors fortunately made it difficult as yet to build very high. The Housing Act of 1890 was a major codifying and consolidating measure which looked to the state and the municipality for improvement, rather than to self-help. This pragmatic advance into socialism was limited in scope: it by no means

involved the way of life envisaged by Annie Besant in *Fabian Essays*, whereby servants would be employed and meals would be eaten in common; the new public housing merely accommodated private family units side-by-side.

In the 1880s family life was usually photographed only out of doors. We know that most cooking was done on a kitchen range – or at the baker's for special meals – because gas was only just coming into use for this purpose, and the slot meter was not invented till the end of the decade. The range was laboriously cleaned with black lead; lighting in all but the wealthiest homes was by oil lamps; food often went bad; illness was recurrent; children crowded round, demanding attention; furniture was riddled with nooks and crannies collecting dust and surfaces needing polish; dirt, insects and dust were everywhere, there were no detergents, and water often had to be specially heated and carried about. Housekeeping was, in other words, monotonous, complex and backbreaking, and middle-class observers flitting in and out of working-class homes often misunderstood the problems and skills of the housewife in such an environment. Much was said about the need for better knowledge of domestic economy, and the London School Board made some attempt to teach it, but little practical guidance was given. The good housewife needed to know where food could be obtained for nothing – off hedgerows and in the fields – and which herbs and spices could liven up a monotonous diet. She was constantly balancing conflicting priorities in time and resources, 'making do' with inadequate funds and clothing which could not be replaced. She could hardly take on a job as well; to some extent the home was her empire, and the men were often encouraged to spend their leisure time elsewhere. Sex-segregation in leisure complemented sex-segregation in work. The late Victorian music-hall might rhapsodize about courtship but it had few illusions about marriage.

The real test of the working-class housewife's expertise lay in the purchase of food and clothes. She had to be alert, because poverty forced her towards secondhand or cheap goods. It was also essential to 'be known' to local shopkeepers who could provide credit during a strike, illness or unemployment. The 7,681 male and 1,278 female pawnbrokers of England and Wales in 1881 gave the poor man's budget a necessary flexibility, and acted as intermediaries between the declining and the rising members of society.[22] This was a world where very little was thrown away, and where clothes and furniture were handed down from generation to generation, from family to family, or sold in the

4.1

4.14

4.13, 15

4.17

numerous secondhand shops. The continued vitality of small-scale trading blurred any clear distinction between 'middle' and 'working' class. Shopping was in some ways more sociable and entertaining than it is now. Zest for a bargain was by no means confined to the stock exchange, and the commercial patter of the market place even led to more than one career on the socialist platform.

4.18   In the 1880s the seller was still at least as mobile as the purchaser. Hawkers and tradesmen called at the home, often with distinctive uniform, equipment and cry, and stores were prepared to deliver. Street traders were fighting a tough battle with shopkeepers whose fixed location increased their overheads, and with municipal authorities eager for hygiene. Wakes and fairs were being superseded by shops, but something was lost in the process: here, as elsewhere, work and recreation were drawing apart. From the 1840s, the larger retailers favoured legislation concerning hours of work to restrict competition from their smaller rivals. In 1885 the recently-formed Shop Hours Labour League found that whereas the fashionable London shops closed relatively early, those in the London suburbs and provincial towns opened for between thirteen and fifteen hours on weekdays and between fourteen and seventeen on Saturdays. The Shop Hours Regulation Act (1886) limited the working day of young shop assistants, but was ineffective until inspection provisions were introduced in 1892.

4.19,20   Housekeeping was getting easier because packaged foods and cleaning materials were becoming readily available and were widely advertised. Mazawattee packet tea, for example, was first put on a mass-production basis in 1884; by the end of the century packet tea dominated the retailing trade. The industrial revolution had begun the process of diversifying diet which was still going strong in the 1880s. Mobility of the population, improved retailing, better real wages, increased liquidity of resources and international trading all extended access to new foods, and average annual imports of sugar, grain, meat, butter and cheese all rose fast. Production for a mass market required standardization even of non-branded foods; for example, by the 1880s many of the old local varieties of cheese were being reclassified by the dairy schools and sold after a much shorter maturing period. Legislation to curb

adulteration became effective only after 1874, and initially affected but a few items. As for middle-class housekeeping, an army of drudges emancipated their betters from much of the hard and routine work, but 4.2 put in its place all the personal and financial worries involved in administering a staff of servants, all the consequent loss of privacy, and (for the richer and unmarried woman) all the tedium of life without a role. There must have been many trapped, intelligent women in the 1880s who could have written, as did the future suffragette Lady Constance Lytton to her eldest sister in 1899, that life 'seems like *waiting*, not like actually *living*.'[23]

But there was a brighter side: plenty of opportunities for fun cropped up when families were large, relatives abundant, and recreation was taken largely at home or in the street. Family newspapers were common, and the eleven children of James Murray the lexicographer even managed to support a home amateur debating society, with its own minute-books, for two years in the 1880s.[24] Many recreations took place, strange as this 5.4-6 may now seem, in a religious context – at seasonal festivals, church outings and family celebrations. And here we return to our starting-point: the Protestant faith was rooted in the family. There were family prayers, family Bibles, family services; religion and marriage were so integrally bound up that divorce law was very much a matter for the Church.

Although in most parts of the country a certain discredit still attached to civil marriage, it was becoming more common. It was already prevalent in 'frontier' areas, or for local or denominational reasons – especially in the northern border counties, Wales and southwest England; in London and the south-east on the other hand (where it is now most widespread) it was relatively unusual. Mixed marriages were rare; even in political matters the wife was expected to adopt her husband's views, and woman suffrage was opposed on the ground that it would open up disputes within the family. The plot of Mrs Humphry Ward's influential novel *Robert Elsmere* (1888) could even centre on the disruption of a marriage by religious disagreement: Catherine, told by her husband Robert that he had lost his faith, 'grew paler and paler' and almost immediately he 'felt through every fibre the coldness, the irresponsiveness of those fingers lying in his.'[25]

4.2. These two maids, 'Dixon' and 'Sayer', were only part of the full staff complement in a middle-class Kent household, William Boyer, probably before 1880

4.3.4. *A wedding was as much an occasion for stuffed shirts and stiff poses in the 1880s as now. Ernest Fletcher, master builder, and Annie Wright, owner of a milliner's and draper's shop (RIGHT), were married at Clay Cross, Derbyshire, Seaman & Sons, 1884. Princess Beatrice, Queen Victoria's youngest daughter, married Prince Henry of Battenberg at Osborne House, Isle of Wight (BELOW), G. Mullins, 1885*

4,5,6. *Solid housing for the lower middle class. Private Mellish* (LEFT) *won his Dulwich home in a competition organized by Tit-Bits magazine, 1884. Almost as lucky were the occupiers of one of the first 143 Cadbury's houses built at Bournville* (BELOW). *Each had a garden three times the area of the house and was sold to a Cadbury's employee on a 999 years' lease. 1879*

4.7,8. *Flimsy roofs for vagrants and tramps (of whom 10,924 were recorded in England and Wales in 1881). 'Brusher' Mills (RIGHT), a New Forest snake-catcher, was photographed outside his cone-shaped hut of tree branches and turf by S. Harvey some time in the 1880s. The gipsies (BELOW) were photographed with their insubstantial tent on Mitcham Common by F.C.L. Wratten, 1881*

4.9. Watts' Poor Travellers' Charity, Eastbourne, gave 'lodging, entertainment and four pence each' to six travellers a day. 1881

4.10. The Salvation Army's shelter in Burns Street, Liverpool. Undated, possibly later than the 1880s

4.11,12. *Grim slums and tenements in Leeds. The workman's backyard at 17 Otley Road (*LEFT*) has a dog kennel and outside lavatory. 1887. The children of such a poor workman might well have nowhere better to play than Pounders Court (*BELOW*). Undated*

4.13,14. *Two domestic interiors. The Chubbs' richly furnished drawing room at 14 Woburn Square, London* (LEFT) *called for much dusting and polishing.* 1890. *The Scottish kitchen* (BELOW) *was plainer, but its cooking range meant a lot of work.* 1880

4.15 (LEFT). *The warehouse of Heelas, Sons & Co., Reading, 287 feet long and stuffed to the rafters with furniture, Sydney & Ernest Whyte, 1887*

4.16 (BELOW LEFT). *Covent Garden market, women shelling walnuts. 1890*

4.17 (BELOW). *Jessel's, St Augustine's Parade, Bristol. One of the thousands of pawnbrokers who helped the poor to stretch their meagre budgets. Undated*

4.18 (ABOVE). *Delivering milk, Greenwich. From a series of lantern slides used by the Baptist preacher and lecturer C.H. Spurgeon, George R. Sims(?), 1884*

4.19 (ABOVE RIGHT). *Posters at Soho Hill, Birmingham. Alongside advertisements for Blackpool, Kennedy the Mesmerist, and Bovril is one for portrait photographers Powls & May: 'Cartes de Visite from 4/6 per dozen, Cabinets 7/6', J. Benjamin Stone, 1889*

4.20 (BELOW RIGHT). *Die-stamping penny mustard tins on belt-driven presses in J.J. Colman's Norwich works, A.E. Coe, undated*

Chapter 5 *Church and Chapel*

Public worship 'not only meets the spiritual needs of our nature, but has become a deep-seated habit of society,' said the *Nonconformist and Independent* in 1882, commenting on a press census on the subject. It is not necessary to hold that it is in 'our nature' to feel 'spiritual needs' in order to comprehend the attractions of religion in the 1880s. It flourished on sentiment and tradition, on recollections of much-loved parents and teachers in childhood; 'the secret of our emotions never lies in the bare object,' wrote George Eliot, 'but in its subtle relations to our own past.'[1] Many areas were still traditionalist and deferential in outlook, and the Church of England met their needs. It gave hope to people suffering from shocking deprivation, offered social discipline to a violent and only precariously ordered society, prepared the mind for the sudden and unexpected death which was then so common, and provided explanation for what must often have seemed an unjust and disorganized world.

Yet it was the strength of religion in Britain that, unusually in Europe, it could also attract the radical, discontented, thrusting type of personality. Nonconformist chapels resounded with the challenge which Liberalism, industry and the towns had thrown down to the complacent, deferential Anglican and aristocrat-

5.1. Roman Catholic pilgrims and racks of crutches left by healed cripples outside the chapel at Knock, southern Ireland, Millard Robinson, 1880

ic world of the countryside. And through the Catholic, Presbyterian and Methodist churches, religion could also mobilize the resentments and loyalties of subordinate social groups. Although atheism was much discussed in the 1880s because of Bradlaugh's attempts to get into Parliament, it was in fact rare. At its peak in 1880, the National Secular Society, the major atheist organization, had an affiliated membership of only 6,000; during the eighties it had between fifty and a hundred branches. Yet in 1891 there were 24,232 Anglican clergymen in England and Wales, 2,511 Roman Catholic priests, and 10,057 other Christian ministers, reinforced by 9,313 home missionaries, 4,678 nuns, and 7,851 church and chapel officials, not to mention the lay followers.[2]

Religious organizations then sponsored many activities which would now be seen as purely secular in nature. Churches and chapels had already lost their record-keeping, fact-collecting, archival role, but they were still able to tempt large congregations for patriotic, recreational or family reasons, as well as lend dignity to major moments in the life of nation, community and individual. The 1881 newspaper survey investigated seventy eight towns and districts (total population 3,629,200) and estimated that 30 per cent of those enumerated attended services at some time on Sunday. The *British Weekly*'s census of London's religious observance, which ignored missions and understated Roman Catholic attendance, found a quarter of the population at worship on 24 October 1886.

These are high figures when one allows for illness, old age and other detaining factors; in compiling his 1851 religious census, Mann claimed that 70 per cent would be the maximum possible attendance on a Sunday.[3]

Particularly exhilarating for Christians was what the *Nonconformist and Independent* called 'the marvellous growth of the Free Churches since the beginning of the present century'. By comparison with 1851, Anglican attendances in 1881 were up by 40 per cent, other religious groupings by 48 per cent; Anglican sittings were up 38 per cent, the others up by 86 per cent. Methodists and Nonconformists were almost keeping up with the increase in population. Anglican confirmations rose by 50 per cent between 1872 and 1881, and by 21 per cent between 1881 and 1891. In the provinces of Canterbury and York, an annual average of 296 males and 437 females per thousand living aged fifteen were confirmed in the years 1880–89; equivalent figures for 1950–59 were only 238 and 350, respectively.[4]

Religion profoundly influenced the politics of the 1880s. Ritualism, religious education, burial rites, disestablishment were major questions; and even secular issues like imperial expansion, home rule for Ireland, or the conduct of foreign policy, readily acquired religious overtones. Both the Prime Ministers of the decade were devout men. Mrs Gladstone took a delight in hearing the psalms of thanksgiving which issued from her husband at the news of his electoral triumph in 1880; on meeting Parliament in that year he felt 'that the Almighty has employed me for His purposes in a manner larger or more special than before.' When Mrs Humphry Ward met him to discuss her novel *Robert Elsmere*, which assumed that a civilized society could survive without Christian dogma, she found him charming, but 'at times he looked stern and angry and white to a degree, so that I wondered sometimes how I had the courage to go on – the drawn brows were so formidable.'[5]

Lord Salisbury was more reticent about his faith, but to the end of his life he read as much theology as history and science. Even a young ambitious politician like Lord Randolph Churchill, speaking in May 1880, thought that he and his party had something to gain by an advocacy which involved hurling the atheist Bradlaugh's *Impeachment of the House of Brunswick* on to the floor of the House of Commons and trampling on it. There were probably about fifty atheist M.P.s, including Joseph Chamberlain, during the decade, but only Bradlaugh dared admit such a conviction publicly. While church and state by the 1880s were less intimately linked than in Gladstone's young days, and

the House of Commons was no longer overtly Anglican, the bishops were still closely integrated with the ruling elite (though new recruits came increasingly from the sons of clergymen and professional people). Church patronage was still one of the Prime Minister's most time-consuming responsibilities; 'a vacant See is a great excitement to Mr G[ladstone],' wrote Hamilton, his private secretary, in 1884; 'indeed I believe it excites him far more than a political crisis.'[6]

Religion dominated education and communication. In the absence of radio and television, ideas were moulded by the lecture, the book and the periodical – all profoundly influenced by the pulpit. Religious leaders were trained orators in an age which admired public speaking, and were often the most articulate and cultivated men in their communities. Church and chapel were in themselves a huge 'open university' whose courses were accessible to all in an age when few had the time or resources to pursue a formal education beyond thirteen. The young Hannah Mitchell in her late Victorian Derbyshire village took pains to improve her vocabulary by listening attentively to the clergyman's addresses, and many whose weekdays were intellectually starved broadened themselves out on Sunday by moving on from sermon to sermon. 'To my father, who started to preach at the age of fifteen as a "local preacher",' wrote Ellen Wilkinson, 'chapel meant everything. There he was taught to read, was lent books. It was his only contact with education, its pulpit his only means of self-expression.'[7]

Religion also dominated the voluntary schools, which in 1880 were teaching 72 per cent of the children in average attendance at inspected elementary schools in England and Wales. Between 1880 and 1889 attendance at the board schools, which filled the gaps left by the voluntary system, continued its rapid climb (by 85 per cent); it also rose (by 14 per cent) at the voluntary schools, though much more slowly than in the 1870s. Expenditure per child in average attendance was much higher throughout the decade at the board schools, which were larger (averaging at 302 pupils in 1888, as compared with the voluntary schools' 152). But the voluntary schools could draw on a large fund of dedication and unpaid effort.[8] As for religion in the nineteenth-century public schools, no less than four of their headmasters became Archbishops of Canterbury, and in 1884 a third of Eton's schoolmasters were in orders, though a dwindling proportion of public schoolboys was entering the Church (nine of the 206 Rugby and Harrow boys arriving in 1880).[9] Both the major universities were closely tied to the established church, and the intellectual reviews abounded in theological discussion. At least a quarter of the magazines published in the United Kingdom in 1881 were religious in purpose. Nor is there any evidence of absolute decline, or much evidence of relative decline, in the proportion (15 per cent) of books published during the 1880s in the category which *The Publisher's Circular* labelled 'theology, sermons, Biblical'.[10]

Aldous Huxley once claimed that all religions provide the same essential benefits to their supporters: 'good luck and protection against the powers of evil; and ... an excuse for a bit of fun in company.' Even purely religious occasions – a baptism in the Thames or a children's special service at Llandudno, for example – were full of interest for a society relatively starved of recreation. They attracted a large attendance; before Mrs Freeth, the last Baptist convert to be baptized in the Thames, entered the water in September 1890, there were hymns and an impressive sermon from Mr Piggott of Swindon. She and another convert were 'gently submerged backwards' and then carried off 'in a covered conveyance, and driven to a house in the town, where they received attention.'[11] The recreational aspects of late Victorian religion flourished on an increasing belief in the humanity of Christ which earlier generations would have considered heretical; and on a growth in ceremonial which would earlier have been branded as Papist. In these circumstances the church could begin to compete with the pub in its colour, music and culture. Canon Barnett in the East End relied on pictures and lectures to collect the large, culture-starved congregations which his sermons could never win. Religion was protected from its rivals by sabbatarian regulation and moral censorship of theatre, music-hall and public house. Choirs and musical instruments could often be heard only at church and chapel, and impresarios toured Lancashire Nonconformist chapels searching for talent; the famous music-hall performer Marie Lloyd made her debut in the 1880s with a temperance song at a London mission meeting. All this activity helped produce an outburst of church-hall building in the 1880s, when half of those in existence today were built; by 1890, no well-run country parish could do without one.[12]

For many people, religion in the 1880s was simply good fun, not just for its own sake but because it offered young people week-night entertainment such as Bands of Hope, Girls' Friendly Societies and Boys' Brigades, as well as regular outings and festivals. The Barnetts experimented with such functions among the roughest of East End populations. When trying to curb one street entertainment which had got out of hand, they found

themselves pelted with missiles. Urged by her husband to walk slowly away from the scene, in the hope that the aim would be poor, Mrs Barnett recalled her assailants' final insult: 'and it's us as pays you' – ignorant, she comments, 'of the financial basis of the Established Church'. The civilizing mission which the Methodists had embarked upon in the mining districts so many years before was still being carried on by churches of all denominations, often through their schools and mission stations. The Mothers' Union, founded by Mrs Sumner in 1885, had 157,668 members and associates by July 1889, and the Nonconformists developed their own equivalents.[13] Evangelists, temperance lecturers and missionaries held lantern-slide meetings, and C.H. Spurgeon the Baptist leader commissioned a series of photographs of South London in 1884, some of which are used in this book. Churches and chapels combined business with pleasure by offering friendships, customers, partners in marriage or business. Their often gloomy present-day aspect gives no hint of their important social role a hundred years ago.

Religion and commerce reinforced one another. Commerce (it was thought) civilized, humanized and pacified people and called out those qualities of integrity, industry and thrift which Christians admired. By joining a congregation one opted for the right company, adopted the correct patterns of expenditure and built up creditworthiness. This was a society which greatly valued 'character' – a word which was even used to describe the employer's written reference. Without a 'character', without 'being known' in the district, life was insecure indeed. In a society without a welfare state, the religious community was a welfare state in miniature. Members were encouraged in self-help and mutual aid – not least in resisting the formidable temptation offered by strong, cheap alcoholic drinks in pubs ablaze with entertainment. Preachers dramatized the clear choice between alternative ways of life, pub and chapel; it required courage, self-control and independence to seek a middle way. Hence the prominence of teetotalism; the Church of England Temperance Society was booming in the 1880s, and many chapels encouraged local temperance societies and Bands of Hope. Teetotalism both encouraged and was encouraged by the rising consumption of tea (from 1.54 pounds per head per year in the 1840s to 4.86 pounds per head in the 1880s). Coffee consumption somewhat declined over the same period, but sugar bounded ahead from an average of 19.45 pounds per head in the 1840s to 68.09 pounds in the 1880s.[14] With its music, processions, outings and lectures, the temperance movement mobilized the respectable, increased the incentives to sobriety and lent colour to drab lives.

Puritan attitudes deeply permeated working-class life. For Beatrice Webb in 1884, the dissenting faith of the East Lancashire millhands 'seemed to absorb the entire nature, to claim as its own all the energy unused in the actual struggle for existence.' She felt as though she were 'living through a page of puritan history; felt that I saw the actual thing, human beings governed by one idea; devotion to Christ, with no struggle or thought about the world.'[15] The miner or fisherman likely to die at any moment: the countryman constantly reminded in his daily work of the Bible stories: the craftsman struggling to maintain his respectability – situations like these lent religion its genuinely popular following.

The late Victorian moralistic diagnosis of poverty involved the churches at more than one level in social questions which would now be seen as entirely secular in nature. Thrift, the protection against poverty, was promoted by friendly societies, which began as informal groups of people attached to pubs or (from the 1830s) temperance organizations. Character was investigated before admission was granted, and the rule-books enshrined the values of respectability. By the 1880s friendly societies were shedding their rituals and growing into huge national financial organizations; in 1887 they had 3,600,000 members and funds of £20,000,000. In devising any social welfare scheme, reformers had to reckon with the distaste felt by respectable working men for indiscriminate hand-outs to the thriftless and shiftless. Friendly societies were well rooted in their communities through the annual branch festival of 'club day'. Seebohm Rowntree in the late 1890s found villages near York where 'in some of the Foresters' Societies, officers dress in the full costume of Robin Hood and his men, each carrying his bow and arrow.' Eager for working-class recruits in the 1880s, the Conservative Party reproduced many of the friendly society's major features in its popular organization, the Primrose League, founded in 1883. Even the trade unions, whose membership in the 1880s was far smaller than the friendly societies', were permeated by the ideas of thrift and self-help. The total annual expenditure of the 234 unions supplying information in 1889 was £706,233, of which three-fifths went on unemployment, sick, accident, funeral and superannuation benefit, and only a tenth on dispute benefit.[16]

Behind these and other institutions of the 1880s lies a mood of scarcity, an intense awareness of the niggardliness of nature which led the economist W.S.

Jevons (like Archbishop Benson) to store bits of string in his desk drawers and stuff wrapping paper behind his bookcases, and the philosopher John Stuart Mill to urge the repayment of the national debt before British fuel supplies ran out. The related idea that time is precious caused Darwin to live in horror of his notes being destroyed by fire or his manuscripts being lost. Resources were scarce, dangers were lurking, life was short. The phrase 'work while it is day, for the night cometh', with all its resonances, echoed through society and was acted upon even by those who had shed the Christian faith. As Chancellor of the Exchequer, Gladstone carried these attitudes into his management of the national economy; 'treasury control', with its insistence on scrimping and saving, assumed an analogy between the budgets of individual and nation. The Post Office Savings Banks, which owed so much to Gladstone, doubled their deposits within each of the century's last three decades and in 1885–9 for the first time overtook those of the Trustee Savings Banks. Henry Fawcett as Postmaster General between 1880 and 1884 was keen to encourage thrift, and introduced several devices to promote it, including savings stamps in 1880. Post Office Savings Bank branches increased from 6,233 in 1880 to 9,353 in 1889, whereas Trustee Savings Bank branches fell from 442 to 346, though their total assets continued to grow slowly. Other banks were opening up new branches, and insurance company assets went up by 31 per cent between 1880 and 1889.[17]

A great incentive to thrift was the spectre of the workhouse; local authorities in England and Wales spent an average of £6,700,000 annually on poor relief between 1884 and 1890 (15 per cent of their total budget). For many it seemed the ultimate degradation to enter that institution and receive a pauper's burial. Mrs Barnett recalled how the chairman of the East End poor law guardians often snapped out 'the house' before an applicant for outdoor relief had even finished stating his case. 'The House, is it?' said one applicant: 'I'll give yer the House,' and whipped out a bottle to strike the chairman.[18] Yet so harsh a system could have survived only if others besides those in authority believed that the individual was responsible for his own poverty; as soon as that belief withered, the whole system collapsed.

Charity was the other face of the moralistic interpretation of poverty: the idea that the rich would exercise a stewardship for their wealth, and would discriminate, when voluntarily parting with it, between the 'deserving' and the 'undeserving'. This was the mood of the Charity Organisation Society (C.O.S.),

5.12

founded to systematize charity in 1869. Its ideas were sharpened during the 1880s by the Social Darwinist concern to avoid perpetuating weaker strains in the population. Herbert Spencer in his influential *Man Versus the State* (1884) claimed that indiscriminate relief would discourage self-help, and claimed that 'protection of the vicious poor involves aggression on the virtuous poor.'[19] The C.O.S. ideal was one of friendship between giver and receiver; the detailed social casework which resulted tempted many conscientious people into grappling personally with the problem of poverty, so the C.O.S. is important in the history of social work as a profession. The courage and self-sacrifice required from its adherents can now be only imagined. It was not simply the fleas and vermin they picked up on their visits to the poor: they also had to steel themselves to face the unpopularity involved in refusing help to people obviously in need. Canon Barnett repudiated the indiscriminate charity of his predecessor, so his East End vicarage was sometimes besieged by mobs throwing missiles; eventually he had a door cut from his house to the church, so that he could slip out when necessary to fetch the police. 'I don't 'old with such close ways in people as pretend to be yer friends,' grumbled one of his parishioners.[20] Similarly, Octavia Hill's attempt to solve the housing problem through fostering respectability often meant braving intense unpopularity, for example in the Deptford Buildings whose inhabitants' strong sense of privacy caused her such trouble in the 1880s.

This short-term parsimony seemed necessary if poverty was to be eliminated in the long run through the spread of the respectable ideal. But the Barnetts illustrate how supporters of the C.O.S. often moved beyond it. By 1888 Barnett had become impatient with the Society's negative outlook, which was neither winning round public opinion nor organizing charity effectively; he therefore gradually withdrew. The C.O.S. shared the modern belief that poverty can be eliminated, but its remedy seemed too slow-moving, and its practical, empirical mood blinded it to the long-term and structural causes of poverty. It seemed actually to be inflaming class relations; by 1890 Cardinal Manning, drawing upon a rich vein of Roman Catholic social thought, welcomed indiscriminate charity as 'the lightening [*sic*] conductor which saves us. And as to the waste and wisdom [of donations] I am content that many unworthy should share rather than one worthy case be without help.'[21]

More congenial to us today is the sense of personal responsibility for improving social conditions common to many philanthropists, whether supporters of the C.O.S. or not. They did not shield themselves from the realities of poverty behind an army of social workers, nor was their redistribution of wealth required by law. Throughout his life Gladstone voluntarily devoted a tenth of his income to charity, and had little patience with those who made donations only on their deathbeds. Philanthropy was inspired by a genuine desire to relieve suffering, combined with an assuaging of personal guilt – whether about loss of faith, privileged class position or some personal failing. If the churches opposed a socialistic compulsory redistribution of wealth, they also tried to inculcate in the rich the idea that wealth is a trust. Charity was a source of power in a society which took a pride in its voluntary action and participatory political system, and leading philanthropists like the Baroness Burdett-Coutts were well-known public figures. Voluntarism even inspired important social investigation, now so often the responsibility of government; Charles Booth's ambitious survey of London life and labour was financed entirely from private resources.

The C.O.S. was radical for its day in rejecting the traditionalist, largely self-regarding, sentimental and often patronizing practice of indiscriminate charity which palliated suffering without offering a cure. The ideal of the open-handed gentleman – generous and hospitable, willingly assuming the financial responsibilities of his station – was nonetheless backward-looking in assuming that the poor will be always with us. Here was the antithesis of thrift: a generosity which asked no questions, responded instinctively and spontaneously, and surrounded itself with a penumbra of begging letters, importunate relatives and hangers-on seeking tips and legacies. When in 1886 Churchill referred in a speech to Rosebery's 'enormous and unlimited wealth', Rosebery rebuked him with the complaint that thousands of mendicant pens would now be sharpened. Parliamentary candidates were usually expected to give generously to local good causes and even to individual electors. L.R. Phelps, an Oxford don active in local poor law relief, described in 1905 how 'every October sees two distinct streams flow into Oxford. One follows the lines of railway, floods the station, flows over into cabs, and loses itself in the various colleges: the other comes rippling along the high roads, runs silently down into the lower parts of the town, and forms a dark, stagnant pool in the common lodging-houses ... probably few undergraduates have any idea how eagerly their return to Oxford is awaited by a perfect army of beggars and tramps.'[22] In a society whose contrasts in wealth were impressive, the poor clustered round the rich, eager with expectation. Phelps's remedy was to ensure efficient and systematic local relief through the poor law system and to issue C.O.S. warnings against indiscriminate giving.

Philanthropists intensely disliked the new socialism of the 1880s; Dr Barnardo's fund-raising appeals spoke of Russian nihilism and German socialism as 'the forces of the enemy' and pointed out that 'every boy rescued from the gutter is one dangerous man the less.' The dislike was mutual; the pioneer socialists of the 1880s challenged charitable activity all along the line, and debated publicly with philanthropists on several noisy occasions. When the future Lord Swaythling told the future Labour leader George Lansbury in 1889 that he gave away a tenth of his income to the poor, Lansbury replied: 'We Socialists want to prevent you getting the nine-tenths.'[23] Whereas the philanthropists often saw the nation as a mere collection of individuals, or at best of family groups, socialists likened the nation as a whole to a family. Socialists also resented the intrusiveness of reformers like Octavia Hill who thought they could distinguish between 'deserving' and 'undeserving'; so crude a polarity ignored the complexity of human circumstances, they thought, together with the structural factors now responsible for poverty. Marshall's use of the term 'unemployment' in 1888 brought it into currency among economists.

Socialists also questioned the ideal of thrift, which for them merely required working people to relieve the rich of their social duties. They dwelt upon the narrowness of the frugal mind, and wondered whether spending, rather than saving, might not be the best way out of a depression; of all wastes, the greatest was surely the waste of labour involved in mass unemployment. This did not prevent individual socialists from practising thrift personally on an impressive scale. As a young Scotsman seeking his fortune in London after 1885 later recalled, 'I used to buy myself whatever food I wanted around the slums of King's Cross, but I used to receive my staple food, oatmeal, sent to me from home, and I always paid for it. Of course, I could not afford tea or coffee, but I found hot water quite as good as tea from the point of view of food, and that it tastes as well when once you have grown used to it'; the Scotsman's name was Ramsay MacDonald.[24]

One religious movement of the 1880s did seem to unite charity to a perception of the real needs of the poor: the Salvation Army, which sought the earthly as well as the celestial millennium and seemed to promise a really vigorous attack on social problems. Its provision of food, work and shelter was supplemented by the attempt to rouse the conscience of society as a whole; it devised quite ambitious schemes for labour colonies to cure unemployment. It was by no means the only Victorian institution to place improving mottoes on its walls, but with phrases as direct as 'there's no friend like Jesus,' 'practical religion' had arrived with a vengeance. Its unorthodox methods – involving a national network of disciplined cadres speaking directly to the poor – must at first have seemed highly subversive. It is hardly surprising that when a hostile 'Skeleton Army' emerged from pubs and slums, it sometimes received discreet encouragement from the authorities. The Army faced over sixty riots between 1878 and 1891, especially in the smaller towns of the South of England. The lawsuit *Beatty v. Gillbanks* (1882) decided that when disturbances of this kind occurred, the Army could not fairly be accused of encouraging tumultuous assembly – a major landmark in safeguarding the right of public meeting. The authorities in such places then fell back on by-laws and administrative methods to achieve the same result.[25]

Still, the Army slowly gained widespread acceptance. The *Nonconformist and Independent* census of 1881 showed that in the seventy-eight enumerated areas the Army had already won six per cent of total religious attendance, and by 1886 it was organizing impressive outdoor processions for its international congress. Its officers and employees increased from 363 in 1880 to 3,135 in 1893, and its centres of work quadrupled between 1881 and 1891.[26] Its military paraphernalia and extreme (some said vulgar) evangelicalism were not the Army's only eccentricities: in 1875 it gave women an equal place with men among its officers. Part of its attraction was the way in which it combined recreation with uplift. The young men who joined its first brass band must have relished the uniforms, the colour and the chance to play an instrument in public. It is perhaps not entirely incongruous that the Marylebone corps in 1888 should include the future circus impresario Bertram Mills.

Regional contrasts are as important in religion as in other areas in the 1880s. In most parts of the English countryside the Church of England was supreme. The rural rectory nestled up to the great house, reflecting the alliance between parson and local landlord; 'the unity between Church and State', wrote T.H.S. Escott, 'is typified in the administration of an English village at every turn.' The clergyman brought university culture into the remotest parts of England. Country vicars often carried out duties far broader in scope than the purely parochial: the historical profession in the 1880s owed an immense amount to the scholarly activities of two country clergymen, William Stubbs and Mandell Creighton. While Stubbs was revolutionizing the study

5.14–16

5.13

5.16

of medieval charters, Creighton at Embleton vicarage was steadily compiling his multi-volumed *History of the Papacy* in between parishioners' interruptions. And of the 174 contributors to the *Oxford English Dictionary* between 1858 and 1884, at least twenty two were clergymen. Sometimes the country priest even assumed the roles of doctor and lawyer, and was entrusted with safeguarding the savings of his parishioners.[27]

In the towns, especially in the provincial industrial towns, Anglicanism was less strong. The established church in the 1880s was threatened simultaneously by agricultural depression and by political dissenters thirsting for disestablishment, yet it proved surprisingly resilient. With bishops and archbishops as energetic as Benson, as scholarly as Lightfoot, and as politically astute as Tait, and with a political champion as unobtrusively resolute as Gladstone, it could outmanoeuvre its enemies. As with its ally the Conservative Party, its resistance to Liberal assault gained much from the growing estrangement between middle and working class; and like the House of Lords and the public schools, it was helping to knit together the aristocracy and the bourgeoisie.

When allied with nationalism in the 1880s, religion established really popular roots. In Ireland, Scotland and Wales Anglicanism was weak. Catholicism was the Irish national faith, though in Ulster the Apprentice Boys could display their popular Protestantism with a parade of cultural symbols. Taunting the Catholics was quite widespread also in areas of Irish immigration like South Lancashire and London, especially on Guy Fawkes' Day. The furious riots of 1869 between Lancashire Catholics and Protestants were but a recent memory. Presbyterianism was the Scottish national and established religion – so that disestablishment there was an entirely domestic affair. In Wales, Anglicanism was the established church; national sentiment therefore centred on the dissenting chapel, which *The Treasury* described in 1881 as 'the social centre around which its adherents gather ... school, lyceum, club, church, all in one ...' In Wales, unlike Ireland and Scotland, religious dissent and nationalist feeling were consolidated by a distinctive and popular language. These strands came together in the Welsh Sunday Closing Act of 1881, Parliament's first important acknowledgement that Wales might need separate legislation. 'Where there is a distinctly formed Welsh opinion upon a given subject which affects Wales alone,' said Gladstone, '... I know of no reason why a respectful regard should not be paid to that opinion.' Gladstone was well aware that 'the back-bone of the Liberal party lies in the Nonconformists of England and Wales, and the Presbyterians of Scotland.'[28] His major objective after 1886, which he came nearer to achieving in Wales than in Scotland, was to create a sense of Celtic solidarity behind a Home Rule measure which would conciliate the Catholics in Ireland.

In the 1880s Christianity seemed to be spreading abroad as well as at home; through their missionaries, the churches attracted to themselves all the glamour of empire. Missionary news seemed exciting to British Christians who never left their home town, and fundraising was an important church and chapel activity. In 1885 there were fifty eight British national missions with a total annual income of £1,316,798; the smallest sects saw missionary work as proof of their vitality. In 1886 missionary staff included 3,000 ordained Europeans, and 815 other European male and 2,430 female workers, together with 2,370 ordained natives and 26,800 other natives.[29] Civilizing and humanitarian motives were much more powerful driving forces than the idea that the heathen must be saved from damnation; indeed, the theological and liturgical disputes among Christians at home often seemed irrelevant when set beside the immediate and huge problems faced in the mission field.

So unaware of religious decline were Christians in the 1880s that many still felt free to quarrel among themselves; political dissenters fought the established church, and the saintly Bishop King of Lincoln was tried in 1889 for ritualistic practices. Even the vitality of the atheists testifies to the strength of religion, for they shared the Christian's intense interest in the subject; both were on the same side when confronted by indifference. Secularists are quite often recruited from those who are disillusioned with the most vigorous religious groupings of the day: from the nonconformists in the nineteenth century and from the Catholics in the twentieth. Victorian secularism did no more than carry to an extreme the freethinking involved in nonconformity; in the Liberal politics of Northampton, for instance, in the 1880s, secularists and nonconformists worked together. Bradlaugh shared the earnestness and high moral aspirations of Christian leaders and carried out many of their pastoral functions for his followers. Lord Randolph Churchill libelled the atheists in 1883 when he described them as 'for the most part ... the residuum, the rabble and the scum of the population ... persons to whom all restraint – religious, moral, or legal – is odious and intolerable';[30] in reality, atheism, particularly in the London area, attracted just the sort of respectable and educated working man who elsewhere lent nonconformity its popular base.

Bradlaugh took a pride in the freethinker's superior morality; this was prudent, for, as Renan said, 'a man should never take two liberties with popular prejudices at the same time.' But the secularist also believed that his morality originated in motives higher than the Christian's; it certainly sprang more exclusively from the puritan strains within the working class. Posterity, rather than God, was his final court of appeal, and this produced a high-mindedness which a small minority even of secularists found intolerable: G.W. Foote's weekly *Freethinker* printed cartoons ridiculing the Bible story and articles with titles like 'On the Advantages of Going to Hell'. But this was not the mood of secularism as a whole. There was never much danger in the 1880s of Cardinal Manning's great fear being realized – of the British Left taking a continental and vigorously anti-clerical direction: Anglican methods of self-defence were too shrewd, and nonconformist Liberals too influential, for that to happen.

So Escott could point out that 'the spirit of organisation is visible within the pale of every creed. On all sides there is hurrying to and fro, much parade of the machinery of faith, much insistence upon its routine business and its spectacular effects.' Charles Gore's influential collection of essays by high churchmen, *Lux Mundi* (1889), was optimistic. It recognized that the Church must make terms with prevailing modes of thought, and had no difficulty in admitting that 'evolution is in the air . . . the category of the age' or in accepting the Higher Criticism.[31] Far from conflicting with theology, science seemed to be operating on a different plane; through revealing the regularities of the universe, it was enhancing the glory of God, just as the need for Biblical interpretation was extending the functions of the Church. Furthermore industrial conflict made the Church seem even more central as an arbiter, a reconciler, and an inspiration to higher motives.

Lux Mundi could also have pointed out that education did not seem to be extending a secular rationality at the pace anticipated by early Victorian Liberals: indeed, intellectual specialization was forcing even educated people, including scientists, to take more and more on trust, and to defer to the expert. Positivism, like other attempts to secure morality and social discipline without the aid of religious belief, had made little progress. At Cambridge the philosopher Henry Sidgwick and the psychologist James Ward were worrying about how morality could be securely founded without divine prescription; indeed, Sidgwick went through a mental crisis on the issue in 1887–8. The new secular religions from which mid-Victorian progressives had anticipated so much seemed to lack the necessary sanctions for morality.

But *Lux Mundi*'s optimistic view of Christianity's situation was not universally accepted; it shocked conservative churchmen like Liddon and Pusey, and reinforced their pessimism. Gladstone saw unbelief as a threat to Christianity more serious than any disputes between Christians. Social and moral reformers began to urge them to unite behind their causes, and T.H. Green even urged that a lost faith was best recovered by acting as though it had never departed. Yet a reunion of Christians which empties their belief of theological content actually accelerates decline; by 1902 William James claimed that 'today, rightly or wrongly, helpfulness in general human affairs is . . . deemed an essential element of worth in character; and to be of some public or private use is also reckoned as a species of divine service.'[32] There was little now to distinguish the Christian from the humanitarian agnostic. Reunion among Methodists, the most dynamic breeding ground of early Victorian religious growth, did not prevent their proportion of the total population from stagnating in the 1880s and then moving towards its dramatic twentieth-century downturn. By 1890 the voluntary schools' proportion of total elementary-school attendance in England and Wales had fallen to 61 per cent; it was to fall much farther in coming decades.[33]

Religious energies were taking secular directions. The political prophets – Carlyle, Ruskin, J.A. Froude – who made such an impact on earlier generations of Victorians were transitional figures who created excitement because they carried the fervour of religion into the secular sphere. But by the 1880s they were going out of fashion except within the labour movement, and even there they were increasingly required to grapple with economic science and legislative detail. Beatrice Webb says that in the mid nineteenth century 'the impulse of self-subordinating service was transferred, consciously and overtly, from God to man.' What she calls 'a new consciousness of sin among men of intellect and men of property' encouraged them towards political and reforming activity. In Chamberlain's Birmingham, for example, she found plenty of earnestness in 1884, but political conviction had supplanted religious faith.[34] It was a transition which she personally had made, together with two men she greatly admired, Charles Booth and Joseph Chamberlain. The 'political conversion' channelled energies hitherto religious into imperialism, art, woman suffrage, social reform or socialism without any conscious repudiation of religion, because all these movements were at first seen as in their various ways promoting Christ's Kingdom. Political parties, increasingly programmatic in nature, could gain renewed impetus from catering for these causes.

A mass entertainment industry was also emerging; instead of reinforcing religious observance, recreation increasingly moved into competition with it. Light-weight stories, illustrations and advertisements began ousting the theological content from late Victorian Methodist periodicals. The attractions of the pub, already seen as a threat to religion, were reinforced by music-halls, sporting facilities, excursions, holiday resorts, and many other claims on spare time. The survey of religious attendance at Bristol in 1881 found that whereas 40.6 per cent of the population attended divine worship on Sundays, 50.6 per cent entered drinking places on a Saturday night. Christians were in a dilemma: either they appropriated these entertainments and in effect secularized their chapels and churches: or they repudiated the new leisure, and lost their congregations. If one surveys later developments from their own point of view, the Dean and Chapter of Worcester were perhaps not so very foolish when they excluded the Three Choirs Festival's orchestra and soloists from their cathedral in 1875. A foretaste of the future was provided in October 1890 by Christ Church, New Street, Birmingham, which wired up its pulpit to the telephone exchange and relayed the service (including appeals in aid of the choir and organ fund) to London and elsewhere. *The Baptist* raised the practical objection that worshippers by telephone could easily evade the collection, and there was something more than mere obscurantism in those members of the congregation who saw the innovation as 'an encouragement to idleness and ... a desecration.'[35]

A further threat to religious observance, growing at least since the industrial revolution, was the hurrying life of great cities; they sheltered their inhabitants from natural hazards, slackened the ties of community, and encouraged that relativist and materialist outlook which kills religious commitment. Town dwellers were unlikely to appreciate the essentially rural background of the New Testament message, and the population shifts encouraged by industrialization – first from south to north, then (from the late nineteenth century) from north to south – severed the religious connections which stemmed from local residence; these were not always resumed on arrival at the new abode, partly because church and chapel building could not keep pace with population movements. The *British Weekly* in 1886 estimated that in London alone about a million people never attended religious services. Willoughby de Broke noted in the 1920s how easy it then was for a bishop to inspect the whole of his diocese; but the railways and roads which made this possible had simultaneously rendered such inspection necessary because they had disrupted those local power-structures where the rector's authority had once been unchallenged.[36]

These long-term secularizing developments were at first masked by the fact that industrialization threw up a new entrepreneurial class which found nonconformity ideally suited to its needs. But by the 1880s the fires were burning out, and some nonconformists were even gravitating towards Conservatism and the established church. Religion received no substantial new source of recruits. For many late Victorians the loss of faith was gradual and painless, hardly even perceived. But to many of the more thoughtful and conscientious minds of the day it was an agonizing process – so central had religion been to their upbringing, social life and moral values. Mr Grey (*alias* T.H. Green) in Mrs Humphry Ward's *Robert Elsmere* was a man who never advertised his feelings, yet he declares 'with a wonderful manly tenderness' that 'to him who has once been a Christian of the old sort, the parting with the Christian mythology is the rending asunder of bones and marrow. It means parting with half the confidence, half the joy, of life!'[37]

5.2. A Bible stall finds its home among the amusements and sideshows of St Giles' Fair, Oxford, Henry Taunt, undated

5.3. Mrs Freeth receiving the last Baptist baptism in the River Thames, at Hatchetts, near Cricklade, Wiltshire, Henry Taunt, 1890

Baptising at Cricklade.

5.4.5. *A hundred years ago, religion had an important social role. A horse-drawn outing prepares to leave Bethnal Green Christian Community Memorial Hall and Free Library* (RIGHT). *The Children's Special Service Mission gathers round the word 'Love', spelled out on the beach at Llandudno* (BELOW). *Both photographs, undated, may actually have been taken in the 1890s*

5.6.7. *Religious activities provided recreation for all. Children are especially prominent among the crowds at the temperance rally, Basingstoke, Hampshire (ABOVE), as is the banner of the Primitive Methodist Band of Hope. Undated. Heavy rain fails to stop the raising of the maypole at the May Festival (LEFT), Temple Sowerby, Westmorland, Abel Macdonald, 1884*

5.8–10. The virtues of teetotalism were urged on all. Many travellers patronized temperance refreshment rooms (ABOVE LEFT) and hotels such as Corbett's in Birmingham (BELOW LEFT). The Church of England Temperance Society's tea stall (BELOW) is set up outside St Alphege's Church, Greenwich, to catch August Bank Holiday trippers. Photographs by Wetherall, undated; J. Benjamin Stone, 1887; G.R. Sims(?), 1884

5.11,12. *The Lord High Commissioner's procession to the Free Church of Scotland General Assembly, Princes Street, Edinburgh* (ABOVE). *G.W. Wilson & Co., 1883. Meeting of the High Court of the Ancient Order of Foresters, Leicester* (RIGHT), *convened by W.G. Seville. 1886*

5.13 (OPPOSITE). *An impressive procession leaving the Salvation Army's International Congress, Congress Hall, Clapton, John Madison, 1886*

5.14–16. *By the end of the 1880s, the energetic Salvation Army
had gained widespread success and acceptance. Its headquarters in
Bethnal Green Road, East London (ABOVE), c.1890, a prison gate
home (ABOVE RIGHT), undated and probably later still, and one of the
Salvation Army's earliest brass bands (BELOW RIGHT)*

5.17,18. Christianity was spread abroad through the activities of missionaries in many lands. C.R. Tyrwhitt (LEFT), with four African boys in Zanzibar. Mr Viner and Mr Travers (ABOVE), members of the Universities Mission to Central Africa, in the Mission's London Office. Both photographs c.1890

Chapter 6 # *Work*

In her old age Teresa Billington-Greig recalled her childhood in the 1880s at Blackburn, the great weaving centre, where the knocker-up began the day by hitting the window with the bundle of umbrella-wires on his long pole. 'Then the march of the clogs would begin and resound in all the industrial parts of the town – a great army in the grey morning or the half dark of the winter evening ... figures marked by the same grey sameness: shawls sheltering the women, caps and scarves the men, – of all ages from 11 years – and all smelling of the dusty, oily smell of the cotton mills.'[1]

We know more about the history of trade unions and labour organizations than about what happened as a matter of routine inside the factory and workshop, let alone in open-air occupations. For many in the 1880s the days were filled with the backbreaking, grinding labour traditionally involved in getting food from soil and sea. Equipment was primitive, so work was dirty, dreary, dull, repetitive and exposed to the elements. In 1881 fishing, agriculture, horticulture and forestry in Great Britain still absorbed 18 per cent of the occupied male and three per cent of the occupied female workforce.[2] But census figures are crude indicators; they ignore part-time, seasonal or spare-time employment, particularly of women, who often worked side by side with men. Their labour would now seem unacceptably heavy; to that extent, at least, we have moved away since the 1880s from equality between the sexes. Part-time craft and other labour by women had long ensured – in town and country – that the family was not completely at the mercy of conditions in any one trade. Children getting in the harvest (which was one of the reasons for longer school holidays in the summer) worsened the rural teacher's attendance problem. The family had its own internal counter-cyclical safeguards against poverty and unemployment, however inadequate, long before such things were dreamt of as a matter of national policy.

Work might be hard but it could also be companionable and a source of pride: in the 1880s the artisan was often photographed holding the tools which were integral to his personality. It was assumed that a skill once acquired would be a source of livelihood for a lifetime. Although Henry Broadhurst gave up being a stonemason in favour of political and trade union activity in 1872, he tells us thirty years later that he still kept his tools by him in case they might be needed, and often dreamed that he was using them.[3] The dreariness of work was also often relieved by a competitive element; teams of drinking and teetotal mowers competed, neighbouring communities matched their skills, and there was the age-old excitement involved in pitting oneself against nature. Success brought respect for one's skill and celebration within the community; work and leisure were not clearly distinct.

6.2

6.1. Women hauliers working at the pithead, Abergorky Colliery, South Wales. 1880

Country life should not be romanticized, least of all in the 1880s during the agricultural depression. Wheat acreage in Great Britain declined by 21 per cent between 1876/80 and 1886/90 and did not recover till the Second World War. In Ireland the fall was even more dramatic: 42 per cent. Barley acreage also decreased markedly. Immense suffering followed from switching out of cereal farming; Denmark chose the alternative of increasing competitiveness through improved processing and marketing arrangements.[4] Given the continuing strength of the landed interest in politics and the class system, the political parties inevitably felt the need to offer remedies. Though tempted by protectionism, Conservatives in the 1880s never succumbed; they did, however, set up a Board of Agriculture to specialize in rural problems. Liberals attacked rural ignorance, servility and traditionalism, and recommended smallholdings, local self-government and disestablishment. More important as remedies were the spontaneous commercial developments. The gross output of poultry, oats, potatoes, fruit and vegetables either declined more slowly or actually rose during the period. Between 1877 and 1887 there was a dramatic increase in market garden and orchard acreage in Great Britain; protected from overseas competition by their transport advantages, the growers of fruit and vegetables supplied town dwellers who enjoyed a rising real income. Apart from the specialized fruit-growing areas in the west of England, the counties with the highest proportion of market garden acreage in Great Britain in 1882 were all near conurbations. As for orchards, Hereford, Devon, Somerset, Kent, Worcester and Gloucester contributed a far higher proportion of Great Britain's total acreage than any other county.[5]

There was no serious decline in the output of livestock. The falling price of cereals cheapened cattle feed, and agriculture in the north and west of England suffered much less than in the south and east. Throughout the 1880s cattle-breeding continued to provide an excuse for major semi-recreational occasions; booths were set up, special drink licences issued, and streets transformed from thoroughfares into places for gossip and entertainment. Cattle judging at auctions was highly professional, and observed by shrewd audiences. Darwin's *Origin of Species* in 1859 had been able to draw on a wealth of rural expertise: 'breeders habitually speak of an animal's organisation', he wrote, 'as something quite plastic, which they can model almost as they please.' By 1881 an army of people were caring for animals in England and Wales – 7,511 vets and farriers, 2,233 horse proprietors,

6.4, 5

breeders and dealers, and 40,863 grooms, horse-keepers and horse-breakers.[6] In agriculture, as elsewhere, an occupational loyalty joined employer to employee, and created pressure groups such as the protectionist Fair Trade Movement, which cut across class allegiances; rural tenants and labourers had long been sceptical of the urban do-gooding radicals who claimed to be their champions.

Many town dwellers had only recently shed their country connections, and there was much recreational and even occupational interchange between town and country. Rural labour often entered industry during a boom and withdrew during harvest time. The local economies of the Welsh hill country, the Scottish highlands and western Ireland rested on a seasonal harvesting migration into the lowlands and England. After 1860, armies of townsfolk gathered the fruit and hop harvests in Kent, Sussex, Herefordshire and Worcestershire. Hop-picking gave a regular holiday to London working people; the acreage assigned to hops averaged at 66,000 in Great Britain for the 1880s, and in 1890 (by which time it had begun to fall) 40–50,000 'strangers' from the London slums came to pick hops in a good season. They lived in 'hopper houses' of brick and tile, or brick and corrugated iron, with cooking houses;[7] here was yet another bond between the brewers and working people, another obstacle for the temperance movement to overcome.

6.3

Looking back over the decade, John Wrightson claimed in 1890 that 'never has there been a period of greater activity of thought, of proposed alterations, of attention to agricultural matters, than we have witnessed during the last ten years.' Traditional skills were gradually being superseded by machinery, and town and country were being drawn together by the need to service the new equipment. Urban fashions spread quickly into the countryside, and distinctively rural dress was in decline; Escott noticed that it was 'seldom seen now' among children.[8]

6.7–9

Nowhere were improvements more adventurous than in the milk trade. The size of the English national dairy herd was growing, and there was a rising average net yield per cow and heifer in milk and in calf. Per capita daily consumption of milk was low – only about a fifth of a pint in London in 1886.[9] But from the 1860s Lawrence's cooler made it easier to transport milk for long distances; by the 1870s the Londoner was supplied from the country rather than from town-fed cows, and at about the same time condensed milk came on to the market. So a declining proportion of the milk produced entered the cheese and butter trades, and these too were being transformed. 'It is scarcely too

4.18

much to say that modern dairying arose during the "Eighties",' said Wrightson.[10] Partly because of Danish competition, butter manufacturing and packing processes improved and the centrifugal cream separator (invented in 1877) made slow advances, though not till 1913 did the Royal Show see its first trial of milking machinery. Science was beginning to make a major impact on agriculture; the first specialized dairy school in Britain was founded at Worleston, Cheshire, in 1886, and by 1888 certificates were being awarded by the British Dairy Institute; during the 1890s there was considerable progress in cheese-making as a result of Dr F. Lloyd's researches.

Catching and valuing fish – an important industry in Scotland and the West of England – was a skilful business. Seafaring was integral to the national traditions, and in 1880 the United Kingdom had 19,938 registered sailing and 5,247 steam merchant ships. Profits rose in the fishing industry with the spread of the fleeting system, whereby fishing fleets remained at sea for long periods and were serviced by carrier vessels; but working conditions worsened to such an extent that half Grimsby's apprentice lads in 1885–90 had to be recruited from public institutions. The whole system could be enforced in the 1880s only through imprisoning deserters, and shocked Joseph Chamberlain when he observed it from the Board of Trade.[11] Towards the end of the 1880s, new steam trawlers set out from ports like Fleetwood and Aberdeen to the rich waters of the north-west Atlantic, and this entailed longer and longer voyages. On the other hand, preparing and marketing the fish was one of the trades open to women.

Britain's massive industrial supremacy during the 1880s rested on a great deal of backbreaking work. Far from dispensing with manual and craft labour, industrialization in many areas actually extended it, while exposing it continuously to the threat of mechanization and consequent redundancy; railway building, for instance, still required an army of labourers. The scale of the British industrial achievement needs emphasis. In 1880 the United Kingdom produced twice as much crude steel as Germany, and more than three times as much as France: operated seven times as many cotton spindles as Germany in 1890, seven times as many as Russia and nine times as many as France: produced more pig iron in 1880 than twelve European countries combined, including Germany, Russia, Belgium and France: and achieved an annual average coal output in the 1880s more than twice that of Germany and eight times as large as France.[12] Coal was the major source of energy, one of the many loads which had to be humped around. Rup-

tures were widespread in the 1880s, and advertisements for different makes of truss were common. The camera can shed little light on the miner's trade, whose geography and peculiar dangers isolated its members into distinct, tightly-knit communities. Women had been excluded from the coal face since 1842, but they could still work amidst the dust and dirt of the pithead.

Factory occupations accounted for only one-sixth of London's adult labour force up to the 1890s.[13] The political and cultural influence of the craftsman was even greater than his numbers; life in the workshop was often compatible with self-education, and the craftsman was relatively well-organized in trade unions, which shared many of the employer's attitudes. Compilers of the census often found it difficult to distinguish between employer and employee, and in many trades the craftsman did his own retailing. In a small firm, employer and employee often had more in common with one another than did the skilled and unskilled labourer. Far from ousting people at sixty-five, these crafts treasured the expertise of the old, who often gained more in experience than they lost in agility. Owning their own equipment and trained in a long apprenticeship, such craftsmen helped to colour working-class politics with the individualism and enthusiasm for hard work and enterprise which lay at the root of popular Liberalism; this was the essence of politics in a city of small workshops like Birmingham, and these were the men who flocked to hear Mr Gladstone. Occupational pride is reflected in Birmingham's welcome to the Queen on her visit of 1887; she described its two ceremonial arches in her journal as 'very remarkable'.[14] Craftsman and labourer diverged markedly in the level and regularity of their wages. Even when employed in a factory, a male boot and shoemaker in 1886 could expect an average wage of 24s. 3d. for a full week's work, a brassfounder 29s. 7d., and a coach and carriage builder 26s. 6d. – as compared with only 13s. 4d. for an agricultural labourer.[15]

Marx predicted that mechanization would gradually render intelligence and skill redundant except in the employer, but his forecast was only partially borne out. New products were being manufactured on a mass scale, and packaging was monotonous, labour-intensive and often done by women. On the other hand new skilled trades – clerks, engineers, foremen, technicians of all kinds – simultaneously appeared, and the alleged 'great depression' saw considerable industrial growth and innovation. There were problems, of course: protective tariff barriers were erected by Germany in 1879, Russia in 1881–2, France and Austria–Hungary in 1882, Italy in 1888. The proportion of British exports by value sent to the protected countries fell from 53 per cent in 1870 to 46 per cent in 1890. Businessmen like S. Cunliffe Lister the Bradford silk manufacturer launched a movement for 'fair trade', or tariff reform, and rural protectionism (never completely killed off by the repeal of the Corn Laws in 1846) revived and made progress within the Conservative Party. For a time the movement tempted even so ambitious and rising a politician as Lord Randolph Churchill, and the minority report of the Royal Commission on the Depression of Trade and Industry in 1886 recommended a 10–15 per cent tariff on all manufactured goods from overseas, together with colonial preference. At the 1887 colonial conference Hofmeyr, the Afrikaans delegate, suggested a 2 per cent duty on foreign goods to help finance the navy.

When trade revived in the late 1880s, the protectionist movement went into decline and did not revive till 1903. This was partly because so many country people could still remember the Hungry Forties before free trade was introduced; a working man confronted Walter Long at the 1885 general election and told him that as a boy he'd had only two barley bannocks to eat throughout the day. Hence the popularity of Gladstone, Bright and the Liberal Party's free trade platform. Free trade also had the advantage of providing cheap food and raw materials for an urban population. It encouraged a general expansion in international markets, which benefited a nation whose wealth was increasingly drawn from the 'invisible exports' of shipping, insurance and financial services. It was in the City that the great nineteenth-century fortunes were made; of the nation's millionaires who died in 1880–99, 39.0 per cent were from the commercial sector, and 41.8 per cent of the half-millionaires; manufacturing contributed only 37.3 per cent and 38.0 per cent, respectively. The tonnage of shipping built and registered in the United Kingdom rose fast in the mid-Victorian period, together with net shipping earnings from the rest of the world; the figures levelled out in the 1880s, but did not collapse, and the rise was maintained in the index for United Kingdom exports and re-exports. The gross merchant tonnage built in the United Kingdom rose in the 1880s by 32 per cent, as fast as in the 1870s, and the percentage built for foreigners also rose – from 11.2 per cent in the 1870s to 15.2 per cent in the 1880s. Furthermore this prosperity accompanied the great transition from sail to steam; of the gross merchant tonnage built in the United Kingdom, sailing ships contributed 32 per cent

in the 1870s, 24 per cent in the 1880s, and 16 per cent in the 1890s.[16] There was immense investment in dockyards, services and transport. London's extensive mid-Victorian dock-building continued; the Albert Dock opened in 1880 and Tilbury Docks in 1886.

Interest rates and equity prices may have fallen in the 1880s, unemployment may have risen, and the increase in industrial production may have slackened – but it was inevitable that newly-industrializing countries like Germany and the United States should show higher growth rates, if only because new industries, with their rapid expansion, profoundly affect aggregate growth rates. Besides, a nation's economic history needs to be seen in absolute as well as relative terms, and industrial production continued to rise impressively throughout the 1880s. Figures for the rate of growth in national income and real income per head, as well as for exports and output per man-hour, compare well with those for any decade between 1860 and 1960. Expansion occurred even in one of the most depressed sectors of the economy, agriculture; and in so far as the agricultural depression moved labour from country to town, it promoted a move from low- to high-productivity sectors. The gross national income of Great Britain rose by 23 per cent between 1881 and 1891, largely due to increased revenue from mining, manufactures, building, transport and rents; average annual taxable income continued to rise in each quinquennium – by 4 per cent in 1880–84, 5 per cent in 1885–89. And what sometimes looks like lack of enterprise was often simply behaviour reflecting Britain's easy access to cheap fuel, cheap labour and capital equipment whose age made it cheap to operate because free from heavy depreciation charges. In the 1880s British mines were booming, there was a rise of 50 per cent in the quantity of gas sold to consumers in Great Britain, and petroleum imports (overwhelmingly for home consumption) increased threefold. There was, in other words, a curious disjunction in the 1880s between what people said and what was actually happening. The idea that there was a depression owed much to the fact that profits were now being distributed more widely; although fewer fortunes over £2,000 a year were being created, for many sections of the population the 'great depression' did not exist.[17]

Most British manufacturing firms in the 1880s were family businesses, but there was a growing number of private companies with a limited number of shareholders which made no appeal for public subscription; and there was a major broadening out in facilities for raising capital. In the limited liability companies launched from the 1850s, share denominations had originally been high, and only in the 1880s did it become normal for companies to issue £1 shares, fully paid-up. The number of limited liability company registrations rose fast – from 6,111 in 1866–74 to 9,551 in 1875–83. Between April 1884 and April 1890 the number of joint stock companies carrying on business rose by 53 per cent and the amount of their paid-up capital by 63 per cent.[18] This steadily increased the numbers directly interested in commercial and industrial profits. Indeed, the Royal Commission wondered whether the Limited Liability Acts were encouraging excessive speculation, and whether this explained the outstripping of demand by supply. Limited liability assisted another major change: the increase in size of firm. Though the number of Lancashire cotton-spinning firms rose only from 639 to 657 between 1884 and 1914, the number of their spindles nearly doubled. Mergers were particularly common in the food and drink trades in the 1880s; their incidence rose markedly with the trade cycle towards the end of the decade.[19]

6.16,18 Technical feats now became possible which increased national pride and the pride of the new skilled worker in his job; photographs inevitably resulted. 'Above all things, it is the era of material triumphs,' wrote Escott proudly: 'the miraculous feats of our engineers, the immense development of machinery, the mastery which on every hand man seems to be acquiring over nature, have brought with them to Englishmen a sense of boundless power.' On the day the Prince 6.17 of Wales opened the Forth Bridge, a *Times* leader described it as 'the greatest feat of engineering that the world has ever seen' and compared it favourably with the Eiffel Tower. Even more impressive in some ways was the Manchester Ship Canal, conceived in 1882, begun in 1887. Commenting on the first eighteen months' work, W.M. Acworth felt it 'probably safe to say that, never since the world began, has so much been done in so short a time to change the face of Nature over five-and-thirty miles of country.' This was also the decade which saw the completion of the Severn and Mersey Tunnels. Invention and technical achievement were boosted by the Patent Act (1883) which increased the number of United Kingdom patent applications from a total of 28,190 (68 per cent granted) in 1878–82 to 91,439 (51 per cent granted) in 1885–9.[20] Escott saw the profession of civil engineer as 'one which appeals with peculiar force to the imagination and ambition of the youth of the day' and which 'gratifies that adventurous instinct which is the heritage of the English race.' It is hardly surprising that, despite mechanization and the rising size of firms,

employees so often shared their employers' political outlook, even in the large factories of the Lancashire cotton district.[21]

Urbanization and mechanization may have been dissolving the old occupational, regional, religious and status divisions within the working class, but fresh divisions were replacing them. The managers, clerks and new types of technician required by larger and more complex firms often worked in small groups and enjoyed close contact with their employers, whose life- 6.19 style and politics they readily imitated. Late Victorian merchant banks were almost entirely concerned with financing foreign and government loans, but both in London and in the manufacturing districts, adventurous entrepreneurship needed the backing of extensive professional services. Their history has yet to be adequately recorded, but the early socialists were well aware of them; the Socialist League's manifesto of 1885 denounced the wastefulness of an economic system which employed 'whole armies of clerks, travellers, shopmen, advertisers, and what not, merely for the sake of shifting money from one person's pocket to another's.'[22]

Doctors were the first to uphold their professional standards through a self-regulating corporation which attracted customers only by the quality of its services; solicitors, architects, accountants and others followed suit. Through pursuing professional status, wider and wider social groups aimed at rising in society; the process still continues. In the 1880s charters were granted to the Institute of Chartered Accountants (1880), the surveyors (1881) and the Institute of Chemistry (1884). The growth of limited liability and government regulation entailed the growth of accountancy, and several professional bodies emerged after 1853. The English ones merged into the Institute in 1880, but its supremacy did not last for long; a splinter group broke off to become the Society of Incorporated Accountants and Auditors (founded in 1885) and thereby forced the Institute to listen to their views. It was a pattern which often recurred in the history of the professions: dissidents with a genuine grievance were usually re-absorbed into a broadened and invigorated parent organization. Splits also resulted from specialization; whereas the property and finance of an early-nineteenth-century firm could be handled by a single attorney, by the 1880s both a chartered surveyor and a chartered accountant might be needed. Even without the teachers, numbers employed in the professions rose by 103 per cent between 1841 and 1881, whereas in the same period the population of England and Wales rose by only 63 per cent.[23]

6.19   Behind all this paperwork lay a boom in commercial clerks, whose numbers in England and Wales nearly tripled between 1841 and 1881; in addition there were the office clerk, the typewriter (patented in the United States in 1867), the filing system, and shorthand. Commercial manufacture of the typewriter began in 1873, and the Board of Inland Revenue introduced it into the civil service during the 1880s. Isaac Pitman's lifelong campaign for spelling reform failed, but the 1880s saw the climax of the contest between his own and other shorthand systems. Business firms knew that time was money; as many new books (forty-nine) on shorthand were published in the 1880s as in the 1830s, and more than in any other decade between 1800 and 1949. The first international congress was held in London in 1887 and shorthand's possibilities for women were recognized. By 1896 Lecky could report that 'the new and growing industry of typewriting, for which their flexible fingers are peculiarly adapted, is chiefly in their hands.'[24]

The service sector was expanding fast in the 1880s, the first decade to show signs of a mass market for consumer goods. Shops were increasingly mediating between producer and consumer. Markets and travelling salesmen were dwindling, big retail combines increasing. The Co-operative Retail Society was created by working people and, with 547,000 members, achieved sales of over £15 million in 1881; ten years later, both figures had doubled. Lock-up shops were increasing faster than the population, and in 1891 in England and Wales there were more shopkeepers in every category (except 'general shopkeeper') than in 1881; some of these increases were substantial –

6.20, 22–4   stationers up by 43 per cent, grocers 40 per cent, greengrocers/fruiterers 38 per cent, poulterers/fishmongers 38 per cent, ironmongers 33 per cent and so on. New types of shop were also appearing: for example, by 1881 there were probably about 3,000 photographers in the United Kingdom owning their own businesses, with about 5,000 employees, mostly women.[25]

Photographs demonstrate the considerable pride that was taken in the display of goods. A panoply of
6.20   carcases adorned the butchers' shops; health considerations did not yet segregate them off from the street, and the distinction between street-stall and shop was
1.25   not yet complete. Imports of Australian and American tinned meat increased fast in the 1870s, but were pushed out in the 1880s by imports of chilled meat from the U.S.A. and frozen meat from South America, Australia and New Zealand. In February 1880 the S.S. *Strathleven* arrived in London from Sydney and Mel-

bourne with forty tons of beef and mutton, and in 1882 the S.S. *Dunedin* carried the first import of frozen New Zealand meat. The first successful dockside refrigerated store, set up in 1882 in London, was followed the next year by the first provincial store (in Liverpool). In each decade from the 1860s to the 1890s, the annual import of meat rose impressively, by 190 per cent in the 1870s, 62 per cent in the 1880s and 84 per cent in the 1890s. Per capita consumption of all meat rose steadily during the same period, as did the proportion contributed by imported meat.[26] Traditional butchers refused to distribute the imported goods, so multiple butchering firms grew up and combined importing   6.21 with retailing; based at first mainly on London, the Midlands and the Liverpool area, these firms – Eastmans, Nelson's River Plate Meat Company, and others – began by carrying on a somewhat inferior trade.

There were also major changes in the retailing of other foods. Around 1880 America began exporting tinned vegetables (mainly tomatoes) to England, and by the 1890s improved canning and drying methods had made California and New York State fruits cheap and plentiful, though bananas and citrus fruit were still in the luxury category. More fruit was also being grown at home, much of it consumed by working people in the less nutritious form of jam. The frying machine, invented apparently by the engineer John Rouse of Oldham in 1880, created the fish and chip trade, illustrating how technical factors often influenced food retailing.[27] In 1869, science actually produced a new food, margarine, and its consumption as a cheap form of butter rose fast.

Personal service on a scale which is now unfamiliar was the objective even of multiple retailing firms; it lay at the basis of the largest occupation for women, domestic service, but the same ideal motivated the shop assistant, who by modern standards knew a great deal about his wares. Customers received personal attention, and goods were delivered by a fleet of vans. The number of retail firms with ten or more branches increased in the 1880s faster than at any time between 1876 and 1920. In 1880 there were only 1,564 multiple stores: by 1900 there were 11,645. Lipton opened his first shop in Glasgow in 1876, and food multiples like Sainsbury's moved forward fast during the 1880s.[28] Their hallmarks – plate-glass windows and frequently repeated brand names, gilt sign-   6.22, 23 boards and hanging lamps – were also seen on the street-corner public houses of the day. The retailer's   7.2 genteel reticence was being abandoned for the pursuit of cash payment and a mass market. Shopkeepers began living away from their premises and gave more

4.19
6.22
6.24

attention to advertisement, packaged goods, cheapness and convenience, less to the old retailing skills. Next door to Sainsbury's is Marks and Spencer's 'Original Half Penny Bazaar', but variety chain stores grew rapidly only in the Edwardian period. Clothing and footwear shops and newsagents/stationers (many on railway stations) were multiples already established in 1880, and new arrivals during the decade were chemists, and tobacconists like Finlays of Newcastle and Salmon and Gluckstein of London. All this entailed, in retailing as in manufacturing, splitting off the manager's function from the owner's, the decline of the family firm, and a division of labour which required more routine paperwork and fewer of the traditional skills from the employee.

6.25

Also new were the large department stores, which catered for a widely scattered but well-to-do clientèle rather than for the masses. Usually beginning as drapers, haberdashers or silk merchants, they evolved through the amalgamation of separate shops; the uniform façade usually appeared only after a fire or major reconstruction. The great city stores were often built up on the basis of a fiercely individualist puritanism which involved long working hours and careful accounting, both very necessary in the 1880s when the annual average of bankruptcies in England and Wales – stable in the 1870s – began rising rapidly; three times as many people were declared insolvent in the second half of the decade as in the first. After chapel one Sunday in 1890, the rising young politician David Lloyd George caught a glimpse of the money to be made from such enterprises by visiting 'a young Welshman who keeps a drapery establishment in Oxford St[reet]' who at the age of thirty-three lived in Regent's Park with a snobbish wife, liveried butler and paintings which Lloyd George valued at £10,000: his name was D.H. Evans.[29] Plate-glass windows in West End streets presented a constantly changing exhibition of goods which could be surveyed at leisure from carriage or pavement. The shopper's energies could be recouped at one of the A.B.C. teashops, launched in 1880, where a

woman could for the first time eat unaccompanied in public, or at one of the restaurants in the new department stores. J. Lyons began his career with a stall at the Newcastle Jubilee exhibition in 1887, and between 1881 and 1891 the number of coffee- and eating-house keepers rose from 8,173 to 11,535 in England and Wales.[30] The licensing laws were encouraging a separation between eating and drinking, and the old inns and hostelries were gradually abandoning meals to the new hotels and restaurants.

6.26, 28

This was a decade of vigorous advertising. Looking back over his life in 1911, the positivist Frederic Harrison complained that life had 'become a vast, incessant, ubiquitous biograph, whirling round ever before our eyes in order to puff somebody's wares.' In 1885 trumpets heralded the opening of Lewis's Birmingham store, which concentrated on low-price goods and transported its customers to upper floors by a hydraulic lift 'in the shape of an ornamental cage, richly upholstered'.[31] And in the following year the chairman of Pears Soap, T.J. Barratt, annexed to advertising the prestige of art by purchasing Millais's *Bubbles*. Supplementing the hoarding was the sandwichman, living testimony to the abundance of cheap labour in the 1880s. Advertisements enlivened the culture of the streets and conveyed information on new products. Venos Soap, Epps's Cocoa, Bird's Custard Powder, Autumn Grain Cake Flour and Libby's Compressed Beef were diversifying diet and easing the housewife's task at the same time as Lewis's boots, trousers and hats made respectability more accessible to the masses. Advertisers also encouraged materialism, commercialism and even (in the absence of adequate regulation) deception. But behind this advertising boom lay the major fact that, if more slowly than in earlier decades, prosperity was still growing. More important, falling prices and improved marketing and importing ensured that wealth was distributed more widely. So in the 1880s work may often have been hard and hours may still have been long, but for many it had begun to bring a better return.

6.27

4.19

6.2–4. *Agricultural life. A woman worker in the turnip fields, Herefordshire* (ABOVE LEFT)*, Sir George Clausen, undated. 'Bin men' at Long's Farm in the Kent hopfields* (ABOVE RIGHT)*, William Boyer, c.1888. Mr Walbank and his two prize oxen, Berwick-upon-Tweed, Northumberland* (BELOW)*, G. & I. Hall, 1882*

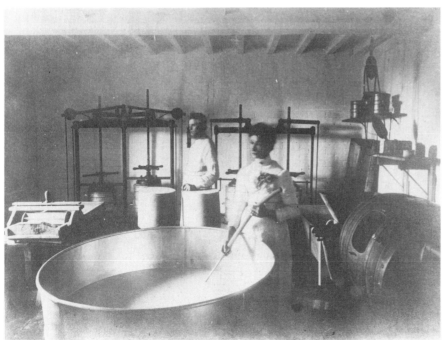

6.5,6. *Dairy farming in Wiltshire. The auction
ring at Stocktonbury during Lord Wilton's sale of
his prize calf 'Lord Wilton'* (ABOVE), *Edward J.
Evans, 1884. Manual labour, with some
mechanical aids, in the cheese-making room,
Windmill Farm, Blunsden, Wilts* (LEFT). *Undated*

6.7,8. *Traditional agricultural skills were gradually being superseded by the arrival of machinery on the farms. Horse-drawn plough and team of three ploughmen at Brazier's Farm, Sandwich, Kent (ABOVE), William Boyer, c.1888. Darby's 'Pedestrian Broadside Digger' (BELOW), introduced in 1879, also apparently needed three workmen. Undated*

6.9,10. *Agricultural machinery.
Demonstrating the use of the 'patent Sheep
Shearing Machine' made by E.J. Reeves &
Son* (LEFT). *Undated. Manufacturing farm
machinery in the machine shop of R.A. Lister
& Co.* (BELOW). 1888/9

6.11. *Conditions worsened in the fishing industry as the fleets stayed longer at sea. Aboard a whaler, Walter Livingstone, 1889*

6.12. *Proud of the tools of their trade. Mr Moat, basket-maker* (ABOVE LEFT), *William Boyer, undated. Pit-brow woman, Wigan* (ABOVE RIGHT), *Herbert Wragg, 1886. Robert Ferguson, cobbler* (BELOW LEFT), *Rev. James Pattison, undated. Mr Williams, carpenter* (BELOW RIGHT), *William Boyer, undated*

6.13,14. Labour was cheap and plentiful, indoors and out. A wheelwright's shop and yard, Elmstead Market, Essex (ABOVE). Undated. A spinning mill at Llanidloes, Montgomeryshire, Wales (BELOW). Undated

6.15,16. *Victorian technology induced a special pride in the labourers who produced its results. Metal workers at a brass foundry and copper smiths, Dyers Wynd, Paisley, Scotland* (LEFT), *Matthew Morrison, c.1890. Labourers erecting a new gasholder, St Ebbe's Oxford* (BELOW). *1880s*

6.17,18. *Railways continued to expand throughout the decade.
The partially completed Forth Bridge* (LEFT), *designed by John
Fowler and Benjamin Baker, built between 1882 and 1889,
Thomas Annan, 1888. Locomotive built at the Brighton works
of the London, Brighton & South Coast Railway* (BELOW
LEFT). *Undated*

6.19. *Expanding industry demanded an army of managers and
clerks. The head office of Pears Ltd, New Oxford Street, London*
(BELOW). *1888*

6.20,21. *The consumption of meat rose steadily throughout the 1880s. Butchers arranged their stock proudly* (RIGHT) *as at Lewes, Sussex, Edward Reeves, undated. But these displays gave no hint of the far from hygienic conditions in slaughterhouses such as one in Leeds* (BELOW), *Waring Ltd, undated*

6.22,23. 'High class provisions'.
Sainsburys, founded in 1869, opened the
first of many modern suburban branches
in 1882 at High Street, Croydon (LEFT),
c.1892. Its new interior design, using
mosaics and marble, was unchanged when
the Guildford branch (BELOW) opened.
1906

6.24. One of Salmon & Gluckstein's lavish shopfronts, typical of the 1880s, when the firm was founded. 1898

6.25. George Pratt's early department store in Streatham, which he took over in 1868/9, Thomson, c.1880

6.26,28. *Hotels and restaurants were springing up
everywhere. Two 1880s dining rooms in the Strand, London.
Queen Victoria Vegetarian Restaurant* (ABOVE LEFT), *Bedford
Lemere, c.1886. Savoy Hotel, restaurant interior designed by
Collinson & Lock* (ABOVE), *Bedford Lemere, 1889*

6.27. (BELOW LEFT). *Some thirty sandwichmen about to
parade the streets of Birmingham advertising Clarke's 'Thunder
Clouds' tobacco, J. Benjamin Stone, undated*

Chapter 7 **Recreation**

Work and leisure are not clearly distinct in any society, and this was particularly true in the Britain of the 1880s, when the employer's direct influence extended well beyond the factory gates. The factory itself could readily be turned into a recreation centre in communities short of large meeting-places, and in the mill towns of late Victorian Lancashire it was often the departure point for works outings and excursions. Mrs Billington-Greig recalled how even the community's timekeeping was governed by factory hooters in Blackburn: 'at the opening and closing of the working day the horns or buzzers sounded through the town, and again at the dinner hour. Housewives checked their clocks and timed their cooking by the horns and knew one of them from the other – Coddingtons, or Henlys or Yates.'[1] Employers wanted sober, honest, punctual and loyal employees, and often sponsored clubs to encourage the new athletic sports and team games at the expense of the less healthy or more time-wasting traditional recreations.

Photography was involved with recreation at two levels. Because the camera was initially seen as a plaything, it was often used to record leisure occasions; leisure abounds in those 'special' events which seem worth perpetuating, whereas the routines of work were less frequently inspiring. But photography was also

becoming a recreation in its own right. So numerous did the amateurs become in the 1880s that for some   1.22 professionals they constituted a threat, though others argued that they provided a recruiting-ground for ideas and personnel. A good-humoured rivalry between amateurs and professionals runs continuously through the specialist periodicals of the 1880s, a decade in which some felt that the art had become sufficiently respectable and technically accomplished to justify the creation of a national photographic portrait gallery.

Traditional recreations often involved small groups – family, relatives, street and neighbourhood; they required no elaborate apparatus and attracted few spectators. Conversation in the 1880s was still a major pastime at all social levels. At the country-house party and in the middle-class drawing room it was often elegant and erudite: riddles, epigrams and repartee were stored away in commonplace books and diaries for further use and enjoyment. As for working people, 'they had hundreds of proverbs and sayings,' says Flora Thompson of the Lark Rise cottagers, 'and their talk was stiff with simile.' Nothing in the street life and gossip circles of the slum was more savoured than the timely retort or the vivid account of an accident or a death. But the educated onlooker often noticed only the gambling, drinking and fighting: 'This morning I walked along Billingsgate to the London Docks,' wrote Beatrice Webb in May 1887. 'Crowded with loungers smoking villainous tobacco; coarse talk with the clash of the halfpenny on the pavement every now and

7.1. Robert Cripps and trophies, all won riding 'Humber' machines. But, said The Times *in 1882, 'the young fellow of nerve' preferred bicycles to tricycles, A.F. Cox, 1885*

again. Bestial content or hopeless discontent on their faces.' Leonard Woolf told his readers in 1960 that 'those who have never seen the inhabitants of a nineteenth-century London slum can have no idea of the state to which dirt, drink, and economics can reduce human beings.'[2]

It was not only drink that drew customers to the corner pub, but good talk, combined with smoking and observing street life. In some areas the pub was a place only for men, and for disreputable sports or brothels which the camera could not record. Instead,

7.2 photographers captured its grandiose exterior, the splendour of the brewers' drays and the tempting displays of barrels and bottles. Interiors were sometimes palatial, with frosted glass and baroque pilasters, or stuffed with objects of interest to a specialist clientèle. Nineteenth-century publicans pioneered many new recreations, but by the 1880s the temperance movement had established the freedom not to drink, and had set up alternative entertainments. It harassed the drink trade through licensing restrictions, though figures for consumption of alcohol per head did not decline appreciably until the twentieth century. Some social reformers favoured a less direct attack; in alliance with Emma Cons, the aged philanthropist Samuel Morley discovered in the Old Vic an enemy to the pub far more powerful than the temperance meetings he had sponsored as a young man. Pub life merged with street life. Photographers cap-

7.3–5 tured the many kerbside entertainments of the day: barrel organs, the sellers of ginger cakes and ice-cream, the acrobats and musicians – trades which required little more than enterprise, a voice and a small stock of

7.6 tools. Travelling musicians still visited the countryside too; so greatly had travel improved, said Escott, that 'the new ditties which the pantomimes popularize in the capital are dispersed throughout the provinces by itinerant organ-grinders before many months or weeks are over.'[3]

Clubs were central to recreation at all social levels. By their very nature they are exclusive, private, and akin to the home, and their interiors can rarely be photographed without intrusion. At the summit were the great institutions in Pall Mall and St James's Street – symbols of the London-based establishment, targets for radical criticism, dominating the intellectual and political world. At the Reform, the Carlton, the Athenaeum, White's and Crockford's, a privileged few informally took decisions which profoundly affected the British people as a whole. The elite was small: in 1898 the Athenaeum had only 1,200 members, the Reform 1,400, the Carlton 1,800, Brooks's 600 and

White's 750, and some of these memberships overlapped.[4] In addition, a rich complex of dining clubs, discussion groups and societies in London, Oxford and Cambridge groomed rising young politicians such as George Nathaniel Curzon. The House of Commons was itself a sort of club, a meeting place and social centre for the elite of the land. Hence the disgust aroused by the obstructive tactics of Irish M.P.s in the early 1880s; it seemed a breach of decorum. Hence also the half-hostile, half-admiring response evoked in newcomers to the parliamentary class during the 1880s – nonconformists, radical manufacturers and working men.

By the 1880s the London clubs were beginning to abandon their coordinating role to the rapidly-growing party machines. But at the constituency level, clubs were becoming if anything more important to the political parties, as a way of consolidating their supporters from the expanded electorate, and as a source of volunteers and canvassers; seventeen of Rochdale's twenty-nine clubs in 1885 were political.[5] Since the 1860s the Conservatives in the constituencies had been founding clubs whose representatives met annually in a conference which is the ancestor of the modern Conservative Party conference. More skilful than the Liberals in harnessing recreation to politics, less inhibited by any temperance connection, the Conservatives were able to consolidate a working-class following, as demonstrated by their urban successes at the 1885 general election. In a more home-centred and richly entertained twentieth-century Britain, the constituency clubs eventually faded away into mere party branches. The middle-class officials who ran Joseph Chamberlain's Liberal clubs in Birmingham, organized on a national scale from 1877 by the National Liberal Federation, were devotees of a radical philosophy which saw no clash of interest between urban employer and employee. But Liberals had less need of clubs than the Conservatives because the chapel or the reforming movement's local branch were usually quite sufficient to meet their needs.

For the middle and working classes, there were specialist organizations, such as the debating societies which reared statesmen as distinguished as Bonar Law and Joseph Chamberlain himself. Even photography provided an excuse for forming clubs. The first had been founded in 1852, and the Photographic Society of Great Britain followed in 1853; by the 1880s it had become somewhat unadventurous – holding periodic meetings where rather heavily technical papers were discussed, and organizing an annual exhibition for amateurs and professionals. In 1885 the Camera Club, which combined 'the ordinary advantages of a club with the appliances and conveniences of a photographic and scientific society', was launched in London. The Photographic Convention of the United Kingdom, founded in 1886, held an annual gathering in a different town each year. The number of local camera clubs grew fast from the mid 1880s: whereas there were only about twenty in the United Kingdom in 1880, by the end of 1890 there were at least 176.[6] Freemasonry too prospered in the decade; far from being anti-clerical (as on the continent), it was patronized by the most ardent of Anglicans – for example by the Conservative politician Sir Edward Clarke, who formed a lodge (named after himself) for the members of his old school, the City of London College. Collectively the freemasons could put on an impressive display, and even royalty donned their elaborate uniform.

In the London of the 1880s a hive of working men's clubs combined recreation with serious political discussion in a male aura of tobacco smoke, gas jets and beer. On special occasions they could stage spectacular parades in the London streets with their colourful banners; like the temperance and friendly societies, they enabled politicians to make contact with working people and mobilize them for political purposes. By 1898 about one man in thirteen aged twenty and over belonged to one of the 3,990 associations affiliated to the Working Men's Club and Institute Union (a rise from 2,160 in 1887). The London radical clubs helped to push Liberals leftwards in the 1880s by uniting them with radicals and socialists, and mixing them with anarchists, secularists, republicans, and continental refugees of every type. By comparison with the Athenaeum's eight guineas in 1898 and Brooks's eleven guineas, nearly three quarters of the 3,990 working men's associations in 1898 charged less than a pound for a subscription. Emphasizing the status of its members, the Working Men's Club and Institute Union pointed out that in 1895 1,936 members in 307 of its clubs were town or county councillors or held some other public position.[7]

Working men's clubs flourished most in the towns: in 1889 only 4 per cent were in Ireland, 4 per cent in Scotland and 2 per cent in Wales, whereas 23 per cent were in Lancashire, 17 per cent in Yorkshire and 15 per cent in the London and City police districts.[8] Pub, club and street life were more closely linked with the countryside at a time when towns were smaller and people had often only recently arrived in them, and road traffic was horse-drawn; the brewer provided regular country holidays and operated at the centre of the agricultural interest. Animals were important in

the many rural and even urban sports which persisted into the 1880s. In Canon Barnett's time, for instance, Whitechapel boys were still getting their fun by goading the beasts *en route* for the slaughterhouse, which Barnett tried to get re-sited. All classes were attracted as spectators and participants to the 'sporting life' which linked aristocracy and people, and the Prince of Wales gazes complacently out of many sporting photographs in late Victorian albums.

The camera can as yet capture none of the excitement involved in such sports, but it can shed light on the male empire which opened out from the dining room in the nineteenth-century country house, where the gun-room played so central a role. Between 1867 and 1900 the second Marquess of Ripon killed no less than 370,728 head of game; feats like this were commemorated by the trophies which clustered round the walls above the billiard table and the easy chairs. An army of licensed gamekeepers (an annual average of nearly 6,000 in England and Scotland in 1881–5) serviced these activities. Between 1881 and 1885 an annual average of 47,146 permits to kill game was issued in England, half as many again as in 1856–60; in Scotland, the increase was still greater.[9] Inspired by a heady mixture of humanitarianism, puritanism and concern for the farmer whose crops the game was plundering, radicals seized their opportunity to attack the aristocracy by opposing the game laws. John Bright, the grand old man at the head of the Liberal Party's radical section in the 1880s, had made a major speech on the subject as long ago as 1845. The Ground Game Act (1880) helped to remedy the tenant farmers' grievances by giving them an equal right with their landlords to kill and take ground game; but poaching, whose absence from the photographs should not lead us to ignore its major role in rural and class relations, remained an offence, and poaching in gangs by night was still a felony. In November 1888, for example, forty poachers were surprised by gamekeepers one night on the Duke of Portland's estate at Welbeck, and eleven were arrested.

'The turf and the operations essential or subsidiary to it possess more of a universal power in society ... than anything else,' wrote Escott in 1885. 'It is the ruling passion.' The Prince of Wales seldom missed an important race-meeting; here the aristocracy presided over a gathering of all classes. Newmarket, spoken of in English racing circles as 'head-quarters', was 'the capital of turfdom' in 1880: with its thirty-one courses on the heath, it ran 236 races in 1879, and was the nominal seat of the Jockey Club. The aristocratic stewards to whom the Club delegated its despotic powers, including the authority to disqualify trainers, jockeys or horses from recognized grounds, had complete control over a sport which the railways were making increasingly popular. At Ascot and Goodwood, fashionable people displayed their finery towards the end of the London season. Derby Day, the most popular race-meeting, was observed as a holiday in London; the House of Commons continued to adjourn for it until 1892. From the 1870s enclosed racecourses were introduced with an entrance fee, and sporting papers gained a wide circulation. *Bell's Life* had been launched in 1820, *The Field* in 1852 and *Sporting Life* in 1859; by 1881, *Sporting Life* had a circulation of 100,000. In 1904 a Lancashire observer noticed 'the extraordinarily intimate knowledge which the men of these parts possess of the pedigrees, the achievements, and the capacities of some hundreds of horses.'[10]

For many country people in the 1880s foxhunting was a passion. Even in the early 1920s Willoughby de Broke could still describe the Master of Fox Hounds as 'a considerable public figure' in rural areas, better known than the lord lieutenant, the bishop and the chairman of the county council. That mouthpiece of agricultural Toryism in the 1880s, Henry Chaplin, was noted for drawing horses on the order paper during a parliamentary committee. After a late-night sitting of the House of Commons, he would engage a special train to carry him from King's Cross to a remote spot in the Burton country. 'From the train would then emerge a young gentleman in red coat and leathers,' writes his biographer: 'up the bank he clambered, where his hack and groom were waiting for him on the top: and away he galloped to the meet of his hounds.' Rich and poor could share in the enjoyments of the hunt, to which Lord Randolph Churchill, defeated in his political ambitions, retreated in his last years. Something akin to a father–son relationship could build up between the young aristocrat and the countryman who taught him how to hunt, shoot and fish. Willoughby de Broke was 'initiated ... into the whole art of venery ... with a keen sense of tradition' by Jesse Eales, the head gamekeeper at Compton Verney; with him he had killed his first pheasant, duck, partridge, hare, rabbit, rook and fish – 'there never existed a finer pedagogue.'[11]

The other blood sports suffered from the sustained humanitarian attack on cruelty to animals which had begun with assaults on cockfighting and bull-baiting earlier in the century. By the 1880s the Royal Society for the Prevention of Cruelty to Animals had broadened out (under its skilful and energetic secretary John Colam) from a London-based association into a nation-wide pressure group. It developed the educational and propagandist aspects of its work at the expense of the purely repressive; in 1886 it had eighty inspectors, and in that year helped get the courts to impose 5,648 fines for offences against the Animal Cruelty Acts, under which there were 46,430 prosecutions during the ten years between 1880 and 1889. The nature of the problem was changing; by the 1870s humanitarians were moving on from attacking a medieval rural brutality towards rooting out modern urban threats to animals in mine and laboratory. The R.S.P.C.A. also had to concern itself with protecting rural species threatened by the urban tourist and sportsman, and would soon be preoccupied with the two major twentieth-century threats to British animals – vivisection and the mass production of animals for food. Although an average of thirty-one people in England and Wales died annually from rabies between 1880 and 1889, animals were ceasing to threaten man's safety and livelihood, and were becoming mere pets or exhibits, objects of curiosity and exploitation.[12]

Urban recreations involving animals had to become more formal and confined, with more emphasis on observation than participation. Circus men in their memoirs dwelt on the hazards and hardships involved in conveying animals round the inadequate road-system, but improved transport made it easier to take the audience to the animals, rather than the other way round. By the 1880s three large and five or six smaller menageries were still travelling about by road, but some circus men were creating fixed establishments. Here the animals were prized primarily for their quaintness, but in London's Zoo science supplemented mere curiosity, though natural surroundings were not yet provided. A new Lion House was built in 1876 and a Reptile House in 1883, and 188 new species and subspecies of bird were accommodated between 1881 and 1890. The arrival in 1876 of the animals collected in India by the Prince of Wales sent attendance shooting up to over 900,000, a total not exceeded till 1912, despite the acquisition of the first gorilla in 1887. The Zoo had become a living encyclopedia which illustrated Darwin's evolutionary theory, as well as a place of mass entertainment.

Industrialization weakened the fairground's commercial but boosted its recreational role. Trading increasingly took place in lock-up shops and auction-rooms, but the fairground's exhibitions of 'wonders of the world' were becoming more exotic. Scientific marvels and strange phenomena from distant parts began to appear; an imitation South African savage periodically startled bystanders at Oxford's St Giles' Fair in

1878 'by rushing forth and brandishing what the proprietor informed his hearers was the leg of his sister.' Technology was applied after the 1860s, notably by Frederick Savage of King's Lynn, who invented and manufactured fairground machinery as well as agricultural equipment. The steam-powered roundabout first appeared at St Giles' Fair in the 1860s; in 1882 it was being rivalled by a sea-on-land roundabout and in 1889 by a 'trapeze railway' or 'aerial flight'.[13]

Recreation flourished on a vital and active community life. By our standards, towns were smaller, transport was more difficult or costly, entertainments were less varied and more communal. Loyalties and traditions were more frequently reinforced through religious ceremonial and through formal political and municipal functions. The Lord Mayor's Show (attacked in 1887 by the radical trade unionist John Burns for advertising the charity of the rich in an unjust social system), the raising of the maypole and the May Day procession and festival integrated the community. They gave all age-groups an excuse for dressing up, enabled local dignitaries to emphasize their status, and allowed religious institutions to capitalize upon festivals which had once been pagan in nature. On these occasions the vicar's unmarried daughters, key figures in rural social work at this time, went into action and mobilized people of goodwill through organizations like the Mothers' Union and Girls' Friendly Society, the earliest formal organizations for women and young people.

Inventions are as central to recreational as to industrial history. New sports arise because of their inherent attractions, but also because commercially promoted, and because they meet a new social need. In 1891 Sidney Low pointed out that with urbanization 'the athlete waxes as the sportsman wanes.'[14] The whole urban population did not of course become athletes, but many were happy to watch the athletic feats of others. Towns were by now collecting together large groups of people and fixing their working hours while separating them from open space; for this situation, mass spectator sport was almost ideally designed. The Victorians were more effective in redistributing leisure time than wealth between the social classes. The Factory Act of 1867 gave women a compulsory half-holiday on Saturdays, and union pressure helped to spread the 54-hour working week during the 1870s. During the 1880s, trade depression and unemployment slowed down this trend, though several firms introduced paid annual holidays. But the important step had by then been taken: the standardization of the Saturday afternoon as leisure period at precisely the

time when improved transport made it easy to collect Britain's increasingly urban population in one place for recreation, and when sophisticated postal and telegraph services made it possible to organize a national network of competitions.

The late Victorian consolidation of the 'week-end' through the spread of the Saturday half-holiday was the obverse of the attack on 'Saint Monday' – that is, on unpredictable absenteeism at the start of the week. Likewise the textile districts' 'wakes week' aimed at making the factory's annual timetable more predictable. Week-end leisure time was safeguarded from another direction through the sabbatarian movement, which by the 1880s had eliminated many recreational rivals to church and chapel but had also firmly attacked week-end labour. Sabbatarians had 2,083 people in the United Kingdom fined for offences against the Lord's Day Observance Act in 1886, and influenced at least the outward aspects of upper-class conduct. But they were never strong enough to root out Sunday newspapers (very influential with working people) or the East End's Petticoat Lane market, or to ensure local churchgoing. Winnington-Ingram once described the Sunday of the typical East End working man: it began with late rising, followed by a visit to the pub for a drink. Then there was a big lunch, rest, and tea, followed by a walk to see relatives or friends, then early to bed, so as to make up for a late Saturday night. 'Let us face facts then,' he said, 'it is that Sunday you have got to turn into a day of spiritual rest and worship.'[15]

In 1886 the Lord's Day Observance Society complained that 'in high places, and in circles which are designated "society", it has grown into a common thing that some famous singer or thaumaturgist or musician should be invited to amuse the guests, or that some popular personage should be made the lion of the evening.' Escott found Sunday dinner parties 'universal' by 1885; here, as with the growth of the week-end, the Prince of Wales set the trend. 'Dined at Marlborough House,' wrote Gladstone in May 1885 of a visit to the Prince. 'They were most kind and pleasant. But it is so unsundaylike and unrestful.'[16] From the 1850s the anti-sabbatarian National Sunday League campaigned for the Sunday opening of art galleries and museums, and attracted support from intellectuals, artists and progressive Christians. Canon Barnett failed completely in his attack on Sunday markets in Petticoat Lane, and by the 1880s was trying the alternative tactic of holding Sunday art exhibitions in the belief that artistic refinement would foster religion. Yet the Victorian Sunday survived the 1880s, partly because of the trade unions' purely secular defence of it, partly because the National Sunday League aroused suspicion by its secularist connections, partly because of society's sheer inertia when it comes to major changes in its leisure habits.

In 1881 and 1891 the census reveals increasing numbers of employees, mostly male, servicing the new leisure. Rules had to be enforced, equipment and sporting grounds maintained. Football is perhaps the most striking example of growth. After the rules had been formulated in the 1840s, they were diffused throughout the country by public schoolboys returning home from boarding school; the first eleven finals of the Football Association (founded in 1863) were all won by public school amateurs. The Football Association had 10 affiliated clubs in 1867, 50 by 1871, 1,000 by 1888 and 10,000 by 1905. From 1871 all competitors for the F.A. Cup had to play within nationally-supervised rules, and in 1882 laws were agreed on for the whole of the United Kingdom. The competitive principle, increasingly criticized in the worlds of industry and education, triumphed completely in the world of sport. An equation between physical exertion and moral development was readily made; a quarter of the football clubs in the 1870s and 1880s originated with religious organizations, and most of the earliest professional players came from the skilled rather than from the unskilled workers – clerks, railwaymen and especially railway clerks being prominent in promoting the early clubs.[17]

Whereas in the 1870s it was southern England which produced the strongest football teams, during the 1880s the northern and midland urban sides, financed by gate-money collected from mass working-class audiences, began to mobilize themselves, most notably Blackburn Rovers and Preston North End. It remained relatively easy for the amateur to get into English football teams right up to 1900, but already by the end of the 1870s transfers of players were occurring (by the 1890s transfer fees were common), and with the growth of professionalism the referee needed to be given new powers. The supremacy of the middle-class amateur was first threatened by the working men of Darwen and Nottingham Forest in 1879; it was terminated by Blackburn Olympic in 1883. Between then and 1915, northern clubs won the F.A. Cup on twenty-one occasions and midland clubs on eleven. In 1885, after some resistance, the F.A. recognized professionalism in football. The wearing of colours and suitably inscribed cards had become common by the mid 1880s, and Saturday evening football special editions were spreading in the north. A provincial newspaper such as the *Preston Herald* could assign a complete

seven-column page to pre-match coverage in 1888 when the local team was playing in the Cup Final. Huge football crowds began to gather; from the 1870s, the Final brought swarms of visitors to London from the north for the first time since the Great Exhibition of 1851, and by 1880 it was attracting a gate of 6,000. Football specials on the railways had become a regular feature by the early 1880s, and 17,000 attended the match between West Bromwich Albion and Preston North End at the Oval in 1888; later on, the numbers went much higher, and, as the crowds got larger, the proportion of women and middle-class spectators diminished.[18]

By 1870 all but five English counties had formed   7.16
cricket clubs, often with help from the local nobility. M.C.C. membership rose threefold between 1870 and 1890, the year when its new pavilion was built; all ten presidents between 1880 and 1889 were either aristocrats or titled. The well-known politician Sir Henry James regularly collected the old boys of Cheltenham College into an eleven to play the school, and country house parties were then large enough for two   10.3
teams to be made up from the guests. But in cricket, as elsewhere, there was a strong drive towards professionalism; between 1885 and 1900 the Gentlemen lost all but four of the annual Gentlemen versus Players matches at Lord's and all but five of the twenty-three played elsewhere.

This was one of many late Victorian opportunities for the aristocracy to mix more widely within the community. Perhaps because it required no elaborate equipment and could therefore attract all classes, cricket became immensely popular. W.G. Grace's rep-   7.17
utation had already been made by 1880; with his black beard, big red face and great bulk, he became a national figure. The first Anglo-Australian test match   7.16
occurred in 1884, and publicity was descending with a vengeance. On 12 July 1889 the *Photographic News* complained of the delays at lunchtime when pictures of the teams were taken, and suggested that each club should employ its own photographer, equip him well, and encourage him to take shots of the game as it was actually being played, because 'excepting the pictures of the University boating crews, no photographs are so uninteresting as those of cricketing teams.'

More obviously suited to the country house was croquet, which attracted women and older people; but   13.1
lawn tennis, invented in 1874 and equally adapted for   7.15
both sexes, made great strides during the 1880s. Like cycling, it promoted greater freedom in women's dress. Wimbledon, which had begun as a croquet club, annexed lawn tennis in 1877 and launched its famous

annual championship meetings, but the camera could not yet capture the faster play. Golf, always a democratic game in Scotland, became rather exclusive when imported to England in the late nineteenth century. Balfour was a prominent player in the 1880s, and politicians began to forgather at Mitcham and other South London greens; but the real explosion of golf in Britain did not take place until the 1890s.

The new urban recreation involved more than merely watching others exerting themselves. The internal combustion engine had not yet divorced movement from exercise, and there were plenty of water sports. Captain Matthew Webb, the first to swim the Channel in 1875, had no successor till 1911, but his achievement helped to popularize swimming, which was organized competitively from 1886 through the Amateur Swimming Association; its rules were copied throughout the world. Nude bathing was so common among Whitby boys at the time that it does not seem to have startled bystanders in Frank Sutcliffe's famous 'Water Rats' of 1886; here the camera was itself making history as well as merely recording it. The boys had escaped from George Bonwick, attendance officer of the Whitby School Board, and knew that he would not plunge in after them; the Prince of Wales saw the photograph exhibited in London and had an enlargement hung in Marlborough House. Local authority expenditure on public baths, which made all-the-year-round swimming easier, rose threefold between 1884 and 1900.[19]

Rowing, long popular in the leading schools and universities, attracted Sir Charles Dilke throughout his life, and from about 1882 caused him to abandon any week-ending away from the Thames. Much popular recreation at this time consisted simply in the poor and not-so-poor watching the rich enjoy themselves. This is not surprising because by comparison the rich young man was expertly instructed, and (if only for nutritional reasons) better built. Around the year 1880, public school boys aged eleven were on average about five inches taller than children of the same age in industrial schools. Lord Brabazon in 1886 said that the person of average height who walked through the slum districts of South and East London 'will find himself a head taller than those around him; he will see on all sides pale faces, stunted figures, debilitated forms, narrow chests.' The L.C.C.'s medical officer in 1904 noted a significant correlation between the height and fitness of poor children at the ages of ten or eleven, and the state of the trade-cycle at the time of their birth.[20] The upper-class male was therefore as likely to excel the lower orders in sport as his sister (free from teenage drudgery and early

marriage, and as well fed as her brother) excelled them in beauty.

Technology and commercial enterprise collaborated in the 1880s to extend the range of late Victorian recreation as well as its quality, as the history of cycling illustrates. The number of makers and dealers in bicycles and tricycles in England and Wales rose tenfold between 1881 and 1891. The tricycle was at first the favourite, if only because it was in some ways more compatible with sedateness and security; Viscount Bury claimed in 1885 that it had 'established itself as a necessary of daily life ... Wherever there are active lads and healthy young ladies there are sure to be tricycles.' But *The Times* pointed out in 1882 that of the two, 'bicycling will always have the greater charm for the young fellow of nerve.'[21] It took some time before the bicycle assumed its modern shape, and (given the prevailing fashions) earlier versions could be mounted by women only at serious moral and physical risk. But it eventually triumphed and in the longer term (like the teashop) helped to extend freedom of movement for women.

In 1885 Viscount Bury estimated the number of regular cyclists at between 300,000 and 400,000. Two national organizations – the Cyclists' Touring Club and the National Cyclists' Union – catered for them, as well as several specialist newspapers, and almost every town and large village had its own club. This particular recreation (unlike some of its successors) seems to have begun higher up in society and quickly percolated down. 'It is now by no means uncommon', wrote Viscount Bury, 'to see, in the neighbourhood of towns, mechanics making their way home from their work on the bicycle.' Photographic periodicals of the 1880s frequently recommend their readers to combine the two new recreations. The tricycle and bicycle were not only pleasurable in themselves: they could enable the photographer to be more frequently in the right place at the right moment.[22] It was a golden age, for county councils were assuming responsibility for maintaining roads that had not yet been polluted by the dust and fumes of the first motor cars; indeed, cycling, together with excursions by rail and steamer, was one of the roots of the late Victorian and Edwardian rediscovery of rural England.

Leisure was now sufficiently important to justify, not merely specialized buildings, but recreational towns and even cities, for the seaside resort had now arrived in earnest. Nowhere was the architects' new Queen Anne style more appropriate. Brighton was busily transforming itself from fishing port to seaside resort and acquiring its paraphernalia of modest guest houses

and grandiose hotels. 'English watering-places', wrote
Escott, 'are the most determinedly go-ahead places on
the face of the earth. No sort of improvement is
introduced in architecture or drainage which is not
immediately taken up.' These developments owe something to the new-found safety of British coasts from
overseas attack, much to improved transport, most of
all to the working man's rising real income and the
extension of paid holidays. Margaret Lonsdale found
Margate's autumn crowds in the early 1880s composed of 'mainly ... the lower class of London trades-
people,' and noted that 'never a word of pure Queen's
English meets our ears.' In earlier generations, remarkably few Englishmen ever saw the sea; but during the
mid-Victorian period the promenade, the guest house

7.25,28,29
7.23,25
and the seaside hotel evolved to cater for the new influx, together with Punch and Judy shows, bathing
machines and fairground entertainments. Bournemouth grew even faster than Brighton, doubling its size
in each of the decades between 1861 and 1891. Still
more impressive must have been the rise in the number
of visitors; Blackpool in 1871 had just over 6,000 inhabitants, but it was welcoming 600,000 holiday-
makers during the season. Here as elsewhere, tourists
were bridging the gulf between town and country. In
1907 Edmund Gosse recalled the Devon rock pools he
had seen filled with natural life in his childhood: 'these
rock-basins', he wrote, '... exist no longer, they are all
profaned, and emptied, and vulgarized. An army of
"collectors" has passed over them, and ravaged every
corner of them.'[23] To the jaundiced eye, cheap railway
excursions, steamer trips and bicycles made the
countryside more accessible but in the long term less
worth visiting.

The explosion of leisure in the 1880s had important
though intangible political consequences. There were
no English equivalents of Michael Cusack's patriotic
revival of old native Irish games like hurling and Gaelic
football through the Gaelic Athletic Association, founded in 1884; but conservatism must have gained by the
rule-making, self-discipline and aristocratic leadership
and patronage associated with so many of these sports.
By the 1880s there were signs of that modern situation
whereby competitiveness is more vigorous and more
acceptable in leisure than in work, and whereby effort
at work is largely motivated by the desire to enrich
leisure. Attention was receding from politics and religion, which had themselves long been major sources
of recreation. During one week in April 1886, analysis
showed that five newspapers gave much more of their
non-advertising space to parliamentary reports than to
sport, but two of them gave more coverage to sport

than to foreign news. The political pottery and brass-
ware which decorated so many Victorian mantel-
shelves was making way for the sporting trophy. The
old Chartist Thomas Cooper deplored the fact that sport
should so preoccupy the working man from whose
enfranchisement radicals had expected so much. Obsessed with greyhound-racing, pigeon-fancying and
horse-racing, 'working men had ceased to think,' he
wrote, 'and wanted to hear no thoughtful talk ... To
one who has striven hard, the greater part of his life, to
instruct and elevate them, and who has suffered and
borne imprisonment for them, all this was more painful
than I care to tell.'[24]

7.1

7.12

It may not be coincidental that at the same time as
mass spectator sport was advancing into recreation,
violence was retreating from politics. The Ballot Act of
1872, the assault on electoral corruption by legislation
in 1883, and the transcending of local political vendettas by national party programmes were partly responsible. But perhaps the football stadium deserves some of
the credit, for it was channelling the early Victorian
hustings and mob violence into less damaging rivalries.
The rival Catholic-immigrant and Protestant-native
football teams – Glasgow's Celtic and Rangers and
Edinburgh's Hibernians and Heart of Midlothian – may
have prevented as much violence as they promoted. It
might even be argued that political maturity could
arrive only when the parties attracted loyalties less
tribal in nature.

It is a sign of recreation's vitality in the 1880s that
the more literary and artistic types of enjoyment
flourished too. *The Times* in 1882 noted the great increase in every type of out-of-season diversion in London, and the consequent incursion of foreigners: 'for
every art gallery the metropolis once had between May
and August, it now has four or five ... New theatres rise
on every side.' Professionalization made rapid progress
in all the arts. Architects were turning for representation to the Royal Institute of British Architects, then
transforming itself from a London society into a national body, and examining more candidates. By 1880
membership had risen to 719 (about 11 per cent of the
profession); in 1900 it was 1,633 (about 15 per cent),
and the proportion rose fast thereafter. Professionalism
stemmed partly from the increased complexity of artistic and intellectual work. Architects now had to work
closely with members of other new professions such as
engineers and quantity surveyors, and to give more
attention to interior planning, less to the façade. There
were new types of specialist structure: the board school,
the free library, the public baths, each with its own
requirements. Buildings had become more complex by

7.31,32

the 1870s, with lifts, fireproofing, sanitary facilities, heating and ventilation. Later came electric lighting, with which Lord Salisbury was already experimenting at Hatfield in the early 1880s. 'When the lights collapsed,' his daughter recalled, 'his voice could be heard through the darkness amidst the general outcry of laughter and dismay, commenting meditatively upon the answer thus supplied to some as yet undetermined problem of current and resistance.'[25]

As for the painters, Whistler in his battle with Ruskin over *Nocturnes* in 1877 gave himself credit for professional status without spelling out the nature of the technical skills involved; it could not therefore be judged whether they were equivalent to those which made professionalism acceptable elsewhere. His gospel of 'art for art's sake', put forward in his Prince's Hall lecture of 1885, staked out a remarkably arrogant claim for the artist's autonomy from his society. But most British painters had not yet distanced themselves from the lay public by abandoning the pursuit of representation; more or less surreptitiously, they made use of photographs in the course of their work, as did William Powell Frith. Sir John Millais (one of whose portraits of Gladstone strongly resembles Rupert Potter's photograph of 1884) freely admitted his debt to the camera, which also contributed to the perspective of Corot, Degas, Manet and Delacroix among many others.

Annual attendance at the Royal Academy's summer exhibition averaged at 355,000 between 1879 and 1899, and the 1880s saw a striking rise in the number of works submitted. Its president Frederick Leighton received a baronetcy in 1886 and ten years later was the first British artist to be raised to the peerage. Gladstone offered baronetcies in 1885 to Watts (who declined) and Millais (who accepted). In 1887 the President of the Royal Institute of Painters in Watercolours, Sir James Linton, wanted an order of 'the rose' created to honour those in arts and letters, but there were political and other difficulties; Jowett's rather similar scheme of 1887 for honouring men of literature and science also came to nothing, and the Order of Merit was not established till 1902. The number of painters, sculptors and engravers seems to have been rising during the decade, largely because of increased recruitment from women; some at least of the 7,962 painters and 832 sculptors in England and Wales in 1881 could afford large studios filled with expensive furnishings.[26]

Escott found London artists less bohemian than the French, but he mentioned the prevailing 'vague and unreasoning prejudice' against a 'certain aroma of social and moral laxity'.[27] Artists may also have become suspect through socialistic connections; the influence of the art critic John Ruskin on the rising labour movement was immense, and the revolutionary left owed much to William Morris. Not until 1886 did the English impressionists influenced by the French confront the Academy by organizing themselves into the New English Art Club. But once art was safely old, it lost its subversive quality, and an international art market was emerging whose clients were proliferating faster than the objects they pursued. During the 1880s Parliament spent £6,500,000 on national galleries and museums in Dublin, Edinburgh and London; between 1870 and 1890, public and private benefactions enabled the National Gallery to increase its holdings by 50 per cent. Not to be outdone, the great provincial city councils subsidized similar institutions from the rates; the Birmingham Museum and Art Gallery, for instance, opened in 1885, and by 1889 was attracting almost a million visitors a year.[28]

Music too was booming; the number of musicians in England and Wales increased between 1881 and 1891 by 51 per cent; women musicians increased still faster, by 68 per cent. Audiences for orchestral and chamber music came largely from the well-to-do; private recitals were still common in upper-class social life, and concert orchestras flourished at respectable resorts like Southport and Buxton. Foreigners were prominent; of the 25,546 musicians and music teachers listed in the 1881 census of England and Wales, 1,240 came from Italy and 880 from the German Empire,[29] and English performers often assumed foreign pseudonyms; but dependence on Germans and Italians was beginning to wane. From the 1870s the Three Choirs Festival broadened its repertoire to include British composers, and in 1880 Parry's *Prometheus* was performed at Gloucester. Edward Elgar joined the first violins at the 1881 festival and heard Dvořák conduct his *Stabat Mater* and D Major Symphony at Worcester in 1884. He was much impressed, and was greatly influenced by the festival's oratorios. Father Knight gave him Newman's *Dream of Gerontius* as a wedding present in 1889, and transcribed into it the markings General Gordon had made on his copy.

The revival of English music has been dated from the founding of the Guildhall School (1880) and the Royal College (1883), but it rested securely on the rediscovery of folk music by a generation of perceptive country vicars. In 1889 the Rev. S. Baring-Gould published a collection of songs and tunes obtained from Devon singers; the Church of England's system of benefices still made it possible to appoint cultivated and intelligent men to areas which would otherwise have been cut off from academic study. The folk-music and folklore movements gained a considerable impetus from Baring-Gould and from the Rev. C.L. Marson, who brought Cecil Sharp down from London in 1903 to record folk songs in his parish of Hambridge in Somerset.

The revival also owed a great deal to the remarkable expansion in popular music-making. Britain was then by far the largest importer of pianos, and in addition in 1890 more than thirty native firms were making at least 50,000 a year. Annual production tripled between 1870 and 1900, and Britain led the world until Germany overtook her in 1890; the U.S.A. overtook both in the early twentieth century. The piano was an important status symbol, by no means confined to middle-class parlours.[30]

Violin playing and choral singing were also increasing. Two energetic, gifted mid-Victorian teachers, J.P. Hullah and John Curwen, diffused both enthusiasm and skill in choral music. Curwen's 'tonic sol-fa' system, propagated by *The Tonic Sol-Fa Reporter* and (from 1879) by the Tonic Sol-Fa College, made it much easier to teach sight reading. Groups of singers burgeoned at nonconformist chapels and schools throughout the country, but especially in Wales, with the great competitions at the national Eisteddfod. Welsh choirs sang Welsh songs to the Queen in Sir Theodore Martin's garden at Llangollen in 1889: 'it is wonderful how well these choirs sing,' she wrote, ' being composed merely of shopkeepers and flannel weavers.'[31] In England and Scotland, too, chapels began to allow Sunday afternoon religious and even secular music; their choirs progressed, as their experience and numbers grew, from part-songs to cantatas to oratorios. The great oratorios provided performers with all the exhilaration involved in a combined musical and religious experience, for many were then believers. Technique was refined with the aid of competitions. Mary Wakefield's music festivals at Kendal were widely imitated in the north of England after 1885, and chapels competed in their musical productions as vigorously as in doctrine and liturgy.

Nonconformist chapels, factories and temperance societies used the brass band for marshalling recruits into the ranks of the respectable. Feelings often ran high at the annual contests at Belle Vue, Manchester, and competition was so great that two graded sections had to be formed after 1886. The *Brass Band News* (launched in 1881) reported on at least two hundred competitions a year, and one firm of music publishers in 1887 had over 5,000 brass bands on its books.[32]

5.6,16

Bands were most common in the north of England, but towards the end of the decade the Salvation Army helped to broaden out their regional appeal. Although in technical opportunity late Victorian music was by our standards impoverished, it was in some ways more central to daily life – whether religious, military or domestic.

As the son of a bandmaster at the Royal Military College, trained at the Chapel Royal, and gaining some of his earliest experience in the small choral societies which met in private houses, Arthur Sullivan emerged from a threefold world of popular musical opportunity. The 1880s firmly established his peculiar brand of light opera in Britain, and the prosperity of the late Victorian theatre was boosted by his greatest successes – *Patience* (1881), *The Mikado* (1884) and *The Gondoliers* (1889). The attraction of the Savoy Operas lay in their tuneful music, Gilbert's witty librettos and the combination of escapism (through settings in distant lands or faraway historical epochs) and up-to-the-minute, not-too-subversive digs at contemporary British institutions, interlarded with a strong sense of the ridiculous. Sullivan, knighted in 1883, was generously patronized by the Prince of Wales; his forty-first birthday celebrations in the same year anticipated the contribution soon to be made by electronics to musical appreciation when a performance of *Iolanthe* at the Savoy Theatre was relayed to his dinner party (which the Prince attended) by electrophone.

7.30

By 1892 there were 200 English theatres, 950 concert-halls, galleries, public halls and gardens and 160 music-halls in an industry with 350,000 employees. London was completely dominant; almost a third of all the actors in England and Wales worked there. Music-halls catered for recreation-starved urban audiences, and in the 1880s entered on their greatest period; in 1892 the thirty-five largest of those in London catered for a nightly audience of 45,000.[33] The most famous performers – Dan Leno, Marie Lloyd, Little Tich, and others – leapt into fame from obscure London backgrounds. Indulgent towards the rich, they recorded the lucky windfall or surprise inheritance more readily than the daily routine of work. But their fatalistic songs also retailed the sufferings of the East End poor to West End audiences consisting of university students, white collar workers, clerks, guards officers, sporting aristocrats, and even the Prince of Wales himself; the music-hall season reached its peak on boat-race night. Escott thought London society 'stage-struck' by a form of entertainment which operated on the frontier that separated 'conventional respectability from downright dissoluteness'.[34] The

7.31,32

7.33-5

music-hall originated as a recreation for the working class and a sprinkling of bohemians, but as the halls grew larger the interaction between audience and performer diminished and the chairman, who had linked the two, disappeared. By the end of the century, production was being undertaken by professionals who made huge profits.

Meanwhile actors were segregating themselves from popular recreation and becoming respectable, so that the Home Secretary W.V. Harcourt felt it necessary in 1884 to defend itinerant shows against attempts to suppress them: 'the "patter" of the showman', he said, 'is one of the most interesting and delightful specimens of indigenous wit and vernacular eloquence which remains to us.'[35] More and more players were housed in permanent theatres, and their profession recruited more and more women: by 1891 there were 3,625 male and 3,696 female actors in England and Wales. Pin-up photographs advertised the leading woman performers, though as the *Photographic News* pointed out in 1885 the camera could hardly do full justice to Mrs Langtry, for example, because 'powerless where fascination of manner and charms of conversation are concerned.'[36] W.S. Gilbert was particularly careful to preserve the proprieties at the Savoy Theatre. 'Society' actresses like Mrs Langtry (debut 1881) and Mrs Patrick Campbell (debut 1888) brought glamour to the stage, and the marriage of Earl Bruce and Dolly Tester in 1884 was the first of many between aristocrats and actresses. Undergraduate interest is reflected in the launching of Oxford University Dramatic Society in 1885. Actors were beginning to emerge from their professional clubs and pubs, and to move out from the areas of London where they had long segregated themselves. Standards of dramatic criticism, hitherto very poor in Britain, began to improve towards the end of the decade, and Ibsen made a major impact. Irving was offered a knighthood by Gladstone in 1883, but the supremacy of the actor-manager was being challenged, and virtuoso solo performances were going out of fashion.

One drawback of respectability was the theatre's increasing exclusiveness, especially in the West End, where evening dress was becoming fashionable. The Bancrofts, who retired with a fortune in 1885, had banished the pit from their rebuilt Haymarket, and with it the cheap seats for poorer customers. Here, as in painting, the people and the arts were drawing apart. Literature was in a similar case: although the long-standing dominance of classical culture at the highest social levels was breaking down in the 1880s, the spread of literacy was accompanied by new efforts to segregate the cultivated from the masses. For centuries the Bible, *Pilgrim's Progress*, Shakespeare and Milton had influenced outlook and language regardless of class, and even Dickens and Thackeray had been enjoyed at all social levels. But the followings of Swinburne, Arnold, Pater, Wilde and the Pre-Raphaelites were self-consciously limited; they may have revived British literary criticism with an infusion of European influences – from Germany, France, Russia and even Scandinavia – but they contributed towards a fragmentation of culture which was 'horizontal', or class-determined. The 'social novel', which revived in the 1880s, in some ways bridged the class divide; for example Walter Besant's *All Sorts and Conditions of Men* (1882) powerfully influenced charitable and literary circles and set the tone for popular slum novels. On the other hand the realism of Zola, whose *Nana* had been published in translation by Vizetelly in 1885, and of other social novelists advertised the lack of cultivation prevailing in what later social novelists were to describe as the 'ghetto' or 'abyss'.

The 1880s saw a great expansion in the choice and availability of reading matter. The 1881 census lists 2,982 male and 452 female authors, editors and journalists – figures which by 1891 had shot up to 5,111 and 660, respectively. The production of books (including new editions) rose steadily from an annual average of 4,929 in 1870–74 to 5,839 in 1885–9.[37] There was between 1881 and 1891 an impressive increase too (37 per cent) in the number of booksellers in England and Wales, and prominent authors such as Thomas Hardy, Walter Besant and Rider Haggard serialized their work in the press through new fiction syndication agencies like Tillotson's of Bolton. Poetry had given way to the novel as vehicle of the deepest feeling, and fiction accounted for 10 per cent of titles published in 1880–84, 18 per cent in 1885–9.

There was a rapidly growing market for low-priced and ephemeral novels to cater for tastes in the romantic and sensational which in earlier generations had been satisfied by other routes; by 1890 there was already much interchange between the cheap presses of Britain and America. Books had once been scarce and highly prized commodities, read relatively frequently by relatively few, and handed down from one generation to another through inheritance and through the once ubiquitous second-hand bookshop. But during the 1880s the modern cheap collections and reprints began appearing: John Morley edited two important series, *English Men of Letters* and *Twelve English Statesmen*, and J.M. Dent was moving towards creating Everyman's Library.

1.16

The middle classes had for some time been supporting subscription libraries like Mudie's, but in the 1880s local authorities made increasing use of their power to finance free libraries from the rates: 48 were started in the 1870s, 65 in the 1880s, 153 in the 1890s. Nearly half had less than 10,000 books each; only Leeds, Manchester, Birmingham and Liverpool had more than 100,000. Municipal expenditure on public libraries and museums trebled between the mid 1880s and the early 1900s; outside the industrial north the expansion was aided by philanthropists, notably the American steel millionaire Andrew Carnegie. Between 1875/7 and 1884/5 the percentage of the British population with access to municipal libraries rose from 16 to 23, and the number of volumes per head of the population served rose from 0.04 to 0.07.[38] The Library Association was founded in 1877, and from the late 1880s librarians – like other middle-class groups, becoming more professional – began entrenching themselves behind its local branches. A succession of periodicals catered for them during the decade, and from 1885 professional examinations were held. 'The modern library is the resort of the learner, not of the learned,' commented *The Times* on the twelfth annual meeting of the Library Association: 'hence a totally new conception has arisen of the librarian's functions.'[39]

The decade saw at least two major developments in the compilation of reference books. The publisher George Smith launched *The Dictionary of National Biography* in 1882, and the sixty-three volumes in its first series appeared at quarterly intervals between 1885 and 1900. They contained 29,104 memoirs – a major achievement owing much to Leslie Stephen, who edited the first twenty-one volumes single-handed. The immense *Oxford English Dictionary* also profited greatly from the remarkable energy and determination of one man; James Murray did not originate the project, but once the Oxford University Press had engaged him as editor in 1879 it began making substantial progress. A sequence of almost heartbreaking disputes in the 1880s failed to break Murray's insistence on maintaining the highest academic standards. Driven on by his religious convictions and borne up by the support of his family, he orchestrated from the abundant pigeonholes of the corrugated iron 'scriptorium' in his garden the 510 readers who were active in researching for the *Dictionary* by 1881. He did the preliminary groundwork so well that when a four-volume supplement was planned in the 1970s, no major change in format was required. This was, in a sense, a great middle-class enterprise: Murray himself

retained his Congregationalist and radical political convictions to the end, and the 174 volunteer contributors between 1858 and 1884 included such prominent middle-class figures as Leslie Stephen, Charlotte Yonge and Mrs T.H. Green. It was also a major Anglo-American undertaking, for 13 of the 174 were drawn from the United States. The first instalment (A–AUG) appeared in January 1884, and by November 1889 the *Dictionary* had got as far as CAST–CLIVY; its future was made secure only in the 1890s, however, and it was not completed till 1928, thirteen years after Murray's death.[40]

Despite these major collaborative and integrating enterprises, the 1880s saw an increasing 'vertical' fragmentation between subjects of study. Learned journals – vehicles of academic professionalism – threatened the more widely circulated quarterly, monthly, fortnightly and weekly reviews. Between 1880 and 1889, 6,624 new books and editions appeared in the category 'educational, classical, philological' (11 per cent of the total); scientific and technical works accounted for a further 6 per cent, 'political and social economy' for 3 per cent, medicine and surgery for 3 per cent, law for 2 per cent. The decade did not see any lasting change in the proportion of books published in particular subject areas, though there were considerable fluctuations within it.

The impressive growth in all academic studies can be illustrated through briefly discussing three of them: geography, history and economics. Of the total publications of the decade, about 5 per cent were assigned by *The Publisher's Circular* to voyages, travels and geographical research and 8 per cent to 'history, biography &c'.[41] Geography was studied with growing professionalism, and gained much from the increased interest in empire. J.S. Keltie's report of 1885 on geography teaching overseas was the turning-point in improving the situation in British schools, and in universities the dynamic influence was Halford Mackinder, co-founder of the Geographical Association in 1893.

Academic professionalism entailed segregation from the lay public. 'Though I cared in the highest degree for the approbation of such men as Lyell and Hooker, who were my friends,' wrote Darwin in his autobiography, 'I did not care much about the general public.' Even one of the decade's most readable historians, J.R. Seeley, intensely disliked the literary approach, and in the hands of William Stubbs and Mandell Creighton the profession grew still more austere. With his *Select Charters* (1870), Stubbs helped to build the close study of constitutional documents into Oxford's new History

School; the book went through three new editions during the 1880s, and there were also new editions of his three-volume *Constitutional History of England*. His work was aimed very much at fellow professionals, as was the *History of the Papacy* of Mandell Creighton, who in 1882 pronounced history 'a branch of science, not of novel writing'. As a tactful Dixie Professor of History at Cambridge, he was able to introduce something of Oxford's documentary approach in the syllabus reforms of 1885; and as first editor of the *English Historical Review* he believed (as he told Gladstone in 1887) that 'the combination of readableness and research is so difficult as to be almost impossible.'[42]

The career of the Cambridge economist Alfred Marshall again illustrates the tendency during the decade towards vertical fragmentation between subjects. One day in winter 1881–2 he descended from the roof of their small Palermo hotel and told his wife he had just discovered the notion of 'elasticity of demand'. His election to the chair of political economy at Cambridge in 1884, together with his inaugural lecture of 1885, marked a point of divergence between economics and history. Marshall espoused 'scientific' economics, as opposed to J.S. Mill's 'literary' variant, and was repaid for this and for his promotion by a running fire of criticism from William Cunningham, his more historically-minded rival for the chair. Marshall took great pains

with his students, valuing the mathematicians among them more than all his other pupils put together; he selected the leaders of the new professional economics with great care, and helped to finance an economics library from his own pocket. Steering his subject away from history, he established its academic existence in its own right. His writings, unlike Mill's, were designed primarily for academics; unlike his predecessor Henry Fawcett, he exerted considerable direct influence over the work of his colleagues.[43]

Yet all this achievement entailed a certain diminishment – an intellectual fragmentation and a loss of contact with the intelligent layman. The cultivated 'man of letters', with leisure and a private income but no university post, was doomed to fade out of scholarly life. Nor was there now much room for the amateur. In biology, the advent of a Germanic professionalism in the 1870s created periodicals like the *Journal of Physiology* (1878) and *Annals of Botany* (1887), and drove a wedge between the researchers who worked under university professors and the amateur naturalists and collectors who had earlier contributed so much to their subject. In this situation, the leading practitioners in different areas of knowledge found it increasingly difficult to communicate with one another and with the general public, and literary culture was doomed to lose its central position in public affairs.

7.2. A newly redecorated 'gin palace'. The White Horse, Edmonton, Middlesex. 1880s

7.3,4. *South London street life in two of the lantern slides commissioned by Baptist preacher C.H. Spurgeon. The ginger cake seller* (RIGHT) *and the 'hokey pokey' (ice cream) stall* (BELOW) *at Greenwich on August Bank Holiday, George R. Sims(?), 1884*

7.5,6. *Street entertainers were plentiful and popular. An escapologist* (LEFT) *performs on a patch of waste ground in the centre of Birmingham, c.1890. As so often in public places, the audience is exclusively male. Itinerant Italian musicians* (BELOW) *serenade two children and a servant at Seaton Carew, County Durham, Rev. James Pattison, 1890 or a little later*

7.7,8. Thousands of licensed gamekeepers helped to satisfy the upper classes' passion for shooting. At The Forge, Paisley (ABOVE), Matthew Morrison, undated. The Prince of Wales seems to have shot on virtually every estate in the land. At Mount Edgcumbe, Cornwall (RIGHT), Frederick Argall, 1887

7.9. *Hunting trophies decorated the male-dominated parts of the country house. The billiards room Port Eliot, Cornwall* (BELOW), *Carolyn Rhadigund Eliot, undated*

7.10,11. *Freemasonry appealed to the middle and upper*
classes: Procession of the Grand Provincial Lodge,
Caernarvon Castle, Wales (ABOVE), *Thomas Mills,*
1888. The Prince of Wales (RIGHT; CENTRE), *with his*
brother Arthur, Duke of Connaught (LEFT), *and his*
eldest son, Prince Albert Victor (RIGHT), *J.L. Russell,*
1885

7.12,13. *Entertainment for the working classes. A crowd of men and boys waiting for the result of the Derby outside the Fleet Street office of the* Sporting Life *newspaper* (ABOVE), *W.J. Belton, 1880. Sideshows, including marionettes and performing dogs and monkeys, at St Giles' Fair, Oxford* (BELOW), *Henry Taunt, 1885*

7.14,15. *Country house sporting activities. The hunt* (ABOVE) *with a crowd of riders, dogs and followers at Glynde House, Sussex.*
1881. *Lawn tennis* (BELOW), *invented in 1874, promoted freedom in women's dress. 1882*

7.16. International cricket:
Surrey County Cricket Club
v. the Australians at the
Oval, M.C. Rimmer, 1888

7.17. Village cricket: Mr A.
Harcourt M.P. with the
Nuneham Courtenay Cricket
Club XI, Henry Taunt, 1888

7.18. Exclusive golf: Arthur
Balfour (CENTRE), with Lord
Elcho (LEFT) and Mr F.G.
Faithfull, Charles Emery,
1888

7.19 (ABOVE LEFT). 'Water Rats',
*Whitby Harbour, Yorkshire. One of the
best-known photographs of the 1880s,
Frank Meadow Sutcliffe, 1886*

7.20 (BELOW LEFT). *'Water Rats' in the
River Medway, Maidstone, Kent. Taken
three years earlier than Sutcliffe's famous
photograph, John Clarke, 1883*

7.21 (ABOVE). *More and more local
authorities were building public baths for
year-round swimming. Warrender
swimming pool, Edinburgh. 1888*

7.22 (RIGHT). *The Oxford and Cambridge
Boat Race: (a) Clearing the course, (b) The
race, (c) Steamers following, (d) After the
race, Frederick Wratten, 1884*

7.23 (ABOVE LEFT). *Punch and Judy show on the lower
esplanade, west of the West Pier, Brighton, Sussex. 1884*

7.24 (BELOW LEFT). *The tricycle, safe and secure for 'active
lads and healthy young ladies'. Undated*

7.25 (ABOVE). *Modest guest houses, bathing machines and
beach entertainers at Sandown, Isle of Wight, F. Nutt, 1887*

7.26. In transition from fishing port to seaside resort. The beach at Brighton, Sussex. Prior to 1886

7.27.   Well-dressed paddlers, with buckets, spades, toy yacht and shrimping net, Robert Slingsby, 1885

7.28 (ABOVE LEFT). *The East Yorkshire seaside resort of Scarborough, with its particularly Grand Hotel, completed in 1887, J. Valentine, undated*

7.29 (BELOW LEFT). *Lewis's Dining Rooms, Ilfracombe, Devon, probably with Mrs Anne Lewis, the owner from 1885 to 1890, and her father. Undated*

7.30 (BELOW). *Gilbert and Sullivan's 'The Mikado', first performed at the Savoy Theatre in March 1885. Rupert D'Oyly Carte's theatre, designed by C.J. Phipps, opened in 1881 and was the first to be lit by electricity. This is one of the earliest stage photographs taken by electric light, J.A. Smythe, 1885*

7.31. The early music halls were merely rooms added to taverns. Deacon's Music Hall, near Sadler's Wells, was demolished in 1891

7.32. Throughout the decade, purpose-built music halls became more ambitious. The Tivoli in the Strand, designed by Walter Emden, was opened in 1890

7.33–5. *Three of the new stars of the 1880s music hall:* (TOP LEFT) *Vesta Tilley, before she adopted the full costume of a male impersonator, Symonds & Co., late 1880s;* (ABOVE RIGHT) *'Little Tich' in Budapest, J. Steiner, undated;* (BELOW) *Marie Lloyd on her first visit to New York, Schloss & Co., 1890*

Chapter 8 *Regional Loyalties*

When we move on from the individual to his political environment, we enter an exclusive world which the camera could seldom penetrate; but this remoteness did not prevent the politician from profoundly influencing the daily life of the ordinary citizen. To realize this, one need only recall the international conflicts which did not occur (between Russia and Britain in 1885, for instance), the civil wars which did not happen (Anglo-Irish confrontation), and the disputes which did not prove irreconcilable (between Anglican and Nonconformist, labour and capital). After conflicts have been resolved, it is easy to forget how serious they seemed at the time; yet in the 1880s, as now, there was much in contemporary society to alarm the timid and even the not-so-timid. The politician's reconciling and integrating role needs to be seen in the context of the decade's tendencies towards vertical fragmentation (of region and nationality) and, less serious, towards horizontal fragmentation (of class); these two tendencies will be analysed in this chapter and the next.

8.14   When Mr Gladstone looked out of his railway carriage window in Lancashire in 1885, the society he surveyed was being transformed in almost every way. Massive improvements in transport were in some respects uniting the nation and drawing it closer to other nations. The Atlantic cable had been completed in

8.1. W.E. Gladstone addresses a political meeting on the slopes of Mount Snowdon. Lloyd George and Tom Ellis are also on the platform. 1892

1866, the Suez Canal in 1869, the cable to India in 1870, to Australia via Singapore in 1871. Messages no longer had to be transmitted through face-to-face contact, and within the United Kingdom the 1880s saw an increase of 138 per cent in the number of telegrams despatched. At the beginning of the decade, the telephone was a mere novelty, first taken up by the rich. Visitors to Hatfield House saw their host, Lord Salisbury, testing his equipment by reciting 'hey diddle diddle, the cat and the fiddle; the cow jumped over the moon' from strategic parts of the house. As late as 1886 Birmingham telephone exchange had only 312 subscribers. Yet by 1882 Viscount Bury could note that an instrument regarded five years earlier as a scientific toy now ensured that 'every great office in London, and in a hundred cities besides, is in telephonic communication with its correspondents'.[1] Regularity, punctuality and regimentation were required from the operator, and this pointed to women; in the longer 8.2 term, the telephone encouraged the same qualities in society as a whole.

The Post Office was keen on innovation and dressed 8.3, 4 its employees in uniforms like the police and the army. Henry Fawcett's blindness did not prevent him, as Postmaster General between 1880 and 1884, from displaying considerable imagination and administrative flair. His many reforms include extending to the whole country a system of good conduct stripes; they were worth a shilling a week, and up to three could be earned. Postmen enjoyed all the prestige flowing from a secure post, and high standards of discipline and punctuality were insisted upon. They were carrying more and more mail: 55 per cent more letters and 100 per cent more newspaper packets in the United Kingdom than in the 1870s. Postal orders were introduced in 1880 and the parcel post in 1883. Postcard deliveries were also buoyant, especially in economical Scotland. To every person in England and Wales, Post Office deliveries rose from 53.6 items in 1881 to 77.1 in 1891; from 42.0 to 57.9 in Scotland, and from 23.0 to 32.9 in Ireland. Like free trade itself, such developments seemed to promise a world of continuous improvement, prosperity and peace: increased communication must bring increased understanding. 'Think what a softening of domestic exile,' Gladstone exclaimed in 1891 of the reformed postal system, 'what an aid in keeping warm the feel of family affection, in mitigating the rude breach in the circle of the hearth.'[2]

The Post Office thrived on improved travel by sea and land. The 1870s saw a massive conversion of ships to steam and of railways to steel. Capital expenditure on transport in that decade absorbed 4 per cent of Britain's national income, the highest of the century, and in 1882 steamers first overtook sailing-ships in tonnage.[3] Safety at sea was improving. Samuel Plimsoll's flamboyant attempts in the 1870s to prevent commercial craft from being overloaded were followed up by Joseph Chamberlain as President of the Board of Trade from 1880. The number of floating lights and lighthouses on the United Kingdom coastline increased by 14 per cent between 1861 and 1879, and there were dramatic improvements in lighting technology. The Royal National Lifeboat Institution, growing fast under its able secretary Charles Dibdin, raised more than £44,000 a year in the 1880s; in 1880–89 it managed 266 lifeboat stations, more than at any other time in its history. Despite all these efforts, in the United Kingdom in the twelve years between 1875 and 1886, on an annual average 727 ships (607 of them sailing ships) were totally lost at sea, and 1,958 people perished in total and partial wrecks.[4]

9.11

This was the great age of the railway; in the United Kingdom an average of 225 miles of new lines were opened in each year of the decade, though the figure was falling and the emphasis was on branch and link lines rather than on creating new trunk routes. Punctuality and standardization – Greenwich Mean Time and the standard gauge – were steadily spreading, and a network of rail links was gradually taming the English countryside and penetrating it with urban values. Railways could still attract well-to-do passengers, but the range of their clientèle was broadening. In Great

8.10–13

8.5

Britain in 1870–79 they carried an annual average of 462,000,000 passengers (excluding season-ticket holders), but 676,000,000 in 1880–89; the annual average of passenger and goods mileage also rose, but rather less quickly. These increases owed something to political pressures: the railway companies were unpopular, and were forced into improving their passenger service instead of loading their trains to capacity. More money was needed for equipment, and – because coal and labour (two of the major costs) fell more slowly than the general average of prices – the overall profit-margins contracted.[5]

The new methods of transport should not be unduly emphasized, if only because the old remained so popular. Long-distance walking remained common even in large cities because commuters could often afford nothing else, and because business firms could not dispense with their messengers until the advent of the telephone; only in the twentieth century did it become relatively unusual to walk to school, to work or to play. Again, rural transport still depended heavily on animals; railways actually increased the number of short-distance road journeys – hence the number of horse-drawn vehicles. An extensive network of country carriers linked the villages to the railheads and market towns, transporting both goods and passengers with the aid of a horse which had to be well cared for, a dog which needed to be ferocious in defence of the baggage, and a system of inns conveniently located near the market place.[6] Among the rich, carriage ownership grew from four to fourteen per thousand in the population between 1840 and 1870 (compare a car ownership in Great Britain of 252 per thousand in 1975), partly because of eagerness to attain 'carriage folk' status. Thereafter the figures went into decline; the rising cost of horsefeed in a crowded island, the shortage of carriage space in crowded cities, and the sheer congestion on the London streets were among the factors responsible. Noise, smell and danger are not peculiar to modern roads; horses are difficult to control in traffic, and with horse-drawn vehicles the proportion of useful space is relatively small. Anyone tempted to cross the road at Oxford Circus in 1888 would need to keep his wits about him. Lord Salisbury prided himself on being able to get from Downing Street to King's Cross in seventeen minutes, but his daughter explains that 'the daily challenge to London traffic was his outlet for the sporting instinct.'[7]

8.6

Any removal of barriers to the free movement of traffic aroused enthusiasm in the 1880s. Rural footpaths were vigorously defended against landowners' encroachment, and Londoners were exasperated by the fact that as late as 1879 there were at least 150 gates barring entry to exclusive residential areas. The collection of the last tolls at Putney Bridge in 1888 and at East Ferry Road, Millwall, in 1889 was seen as an occasion sufficiently important to justify a photograph, and the opening at Woolwich in 1889 of the metropolitan area's first free ferry was the excuse for what *The Times* called 'a grand gala day', with a procession half a mile long, bands, banners and a banquet for 200.[8]

8.7, 8

More people were travelling. In more traditional societies, work is close to the home and life is usually lived near the place where one is born. But by the 1880s inner-city overcrowding and improved suburban transport services encouraged two forms of commuter conveyance: the tram and the workmen's train. Britain made little original contribution at this time, but quite rapidly applied innovations developed in the United States and Germany. Between 1878 and 1886 tramway mileage in Great Britain rose from 237 to 779.[9] Oxford had successfully excluded the main-line railway earlier in the century, yet by the 1880s the horse-drawn tram had penetrated its very heart. In this city the redistribution of urban population from centre to periphery had not gone very far, but it was common enough elsewhere. Germany's electric tram was first installed at Portrush in 1883, and in the following year the American cable haulage system for trams was adopted in Birmingham, Edinburgh and elsewhere. Railway companies opened stations in isolated suburban locations; a cluster of houses usually followed, occupied by people like those who attended the Baptist chapel of the Rev. H. Oakley, at Upper Tooting. He told Charles Booth that 'they go into their work wearing a tophat and frock coat between 8 and 10 in the morning and get back about 7 in the evening.'[10] The Metropolitan Railway reached Chesham in 1889, and the South London tube between the City and Stockwell opened in 1890.

8.9

8.11

8.12

The number of third-class passengers was rising rapidly, and other companies had to follow the Midland Railway after it provided third-class accommodation on all its trains in 1872, abolished the second class in 1874, and upholstered all third-class carriages from 1875. By 1882, 85 per cent of United Kingdom passengers, exclusive of season-ticket holders, were travelling third class. The cheap morning fare rescued the working man who could afford neither to live in the centre nor to travel to the periphery. In 1882, 25,671 daily return workmen's tickets were issued per day in London, and in the following year the Cheap Trains Act extended this suburban migration by compelling rail-

8.13

way companies to introduce workmen's fares as and when the Board of Trade required.[11]

Urban commuting, gas lighting and longer office hours helped to alter mealtimes. The day had once been divided by two major meals, breakfast and dinner, but during the nineteenth century the timing of breakfast gradually became earlier, whereas dinner was gradually postponed. This left a widening gap in the middle of the day for two new meals, lunch and tea. Breakfast could then become lighter and less social – at least in middle- and upper-class families; Lord Houghton in the 1880s was one of the last to hold the sort of breakfast-party which began at ten and filled half the morning. Lunch was becoming a relatively unsocial, business-like occasion by comparison with tea, whereas it was at evening dinner that most entertaining now took place. But there were of course regional and class variations, and in the north of England 'high tea' remained the main meal of the day, with perhaps a snack for 'supper' shortly before going to bed.[12]

In addition to these changes in the arrangement of the day, there were changes in its pace: the telegraph – with all its implications for rapid press-reporting – together with faster railway travel, telephones, and improved postal services all combined to speed up the tempo of life, and to increase the pressures for standardizing practice. Railway timetables had for some time been inculcating punctuality more widely in society, and the process was now carried to its logical conclusion when politicians acted upon a suggestion made in a letter to *The Times* on 14 May 1880. 'Clerk to Justices' claimed that during the recent general election, polling had occurred at slightly different times in different places, whereas Greenwich time was now kept almost throughout England. Greenwich time, he said, should be made legal time. Within a month, the Statutes (Definition of Time) Bill had been introduced into Parliament, and rapidly went through all its stages without debate. Four years later, in Washington, delegates from twenty-five countries at the International Meridian Conference adopted Greenwich as the initial meridian for longitude.

Behind the improvements in transport lay a greatly improved knowledge of the United Kingdom's geography. The Ordnance Survey attracted little attention at the time, nor has it interested historians since, though T.P. White in 1886 pronounced it 'the most perfect and elaborate map-making machinery in the world'. Work began on the famous one-inch survey in 1791; and the final sheet of the one-inch map of England and Wales was published in 1870. By the 1880s, photographic processes were intimately involved in the whole business of producing maps. By 1885, with a headquarters at Southampton and field commands scattered throughout the country, the survey had 3,240 military and civil employees and cost £180,000 a year to run. It also carried out specific tasks for government such as the United Kingdom cadastral survey, launched in 1880 with a large addition to its staff. The geological survey too was making rapid progress after its reorganization under Andrew Ramsay in the 1870s; its maps were at that time the best in the world. By 1881 only small areas remained to be covered by the six-inch survey – in East Anglia, Lincolnshire, and the fell country of Yorkshire, Northumberland and Cumberland. Its staff, which in 1882 numbered only fifty-seven, completed the one-inch survey of the solid geology of England and Wales in 1883.[13]

Voluntary action supplemented the state in scientific and social investigations. It was during the 1880s, for instance, that major surveys of bird migration got under way. Questionnaires sent to 126 lighthouses and lightships in 1886 achieved a 60 per cent response, and through mobilizing the many amateurs scattered throughout the country in large federations like the Union Jack Field Club, maps invaluable to the ornithologist could be prepared; this did something to bridge the gap which had opened up in the 1870s between the universities and the spare-time naturalist. As for marine biology, smaller establishments attached to the universities of Liverpool and St Andrews preceded the foundation of the state-aided Plymouth marine laboratory in 1888.[14]

Faster travel did not win universal acclaim; Cobbett had grumbled at it in the 1820s, and in the 1830s the railway had many enemies. 'We do not ride on the railroad,' wrote the American rationalist H.D. Thoreau in 1854: 'it rides upon us.' Accidents were another problem, especially for women, because their emancipation caused them to travel more widely. Whereas in the 1870s women accounted for only 15 per cent of those killed on the roads and 7 per cent of those killed on the railways, by 1916 these figures had risen to 22 per cent and 10 per cent respectively; by 1967 women were contributing 30 per cent of all road accidents. But the objection to faster travel usually centred on the values associated with it. Scepticism about modern progress was natural to an educated class profoundly influenced by evangelical views. In 1861 Matthew Arnold feared the triviality threatening contemporaries who 'see all sights from pole to pole, and glance, and nod, and bustle by, and never once possess our soul before we die.' Escott in 1885 condemned the British aristocrats who 'pass their existence in a per-

petual round of visits,' 'flit from mansion to mansion during the country-house season' and 'know no peace during the London season.' Many socialists in the 1880s wanted more simplicity and shared Thoreau's distaste for the haste of modern life, his scepticism about its preoccupation with news and communication. 'Give me back the days when Emerson, Thoreau and Whitman were our high priests,' exclaimed Ramsay MacDonald many years later, when Labour Prime Minister, to an aged H.S. Salt (Thoreau's biographer): 'a new ideal of life was about: a simplicity in outward things, and a fineness in the texture of inward thoughts.'[15]

Yet to the millions who used them, the new facilities must have seemed a blessing, at least in the short term. They assisted the large-scale migrations which economic growth was encouraging, especially from country to town and increasingly from north to south. The industrial revolution created several boom areas (mostly in the north) which sucked in a relatively young and male population seeking its fortune; by the 1880s the last of these booms – the further expansion of the South Wales coalfields, and the iron and steel industry's shift to Cleveland and the north-east and north-west coasts – were well under way. Civilizing these 'frontier' districts was a major task; the threat to decency there seemed so great, the structures of authority so fragile, that rigid and narrow attitudes (elsewhere gradually being shed) built up to reinforce what was called the 'nonconformist conscience'.

Suburban settlements on the fringe of industrial and commercial centres were beginning to rival the boom areas in expansion. The six counties with the highest population growth in 1881–91 were Middlesex (51 per cent), Essex (38 per cent), Glamorgan (34 per cent), Surrey (24 per cent), Monmouthshire (17 per cent) and Durham (17 per cent). A similar mixture appears in the list of the fastest-growing towns: Leyton (133 per cent) comes first, then Willesden (122 per cent), Tottenham (95 per cent), Ystradyfodwg (Rhondda) (59 per cent), West Ham (59 per cent) and Cardiff (56 per cent). One in nine inhabitants of England and Wales lived in London in 1801, one in seven in 1881; but London's expansion occurred entirely on the periphery, and the central areas were actually falling in population. The decennial rate of growth in the English centres of early industrialism – Lancashire and the West Riding of Yorkshire – was already declining. Manchester was expanding less rapidly than the London area, and even Birmingham was slowing down.[16]

Improved communication in the 1880s encouraged moves towards imperial unity, just as faster transport at home created nationwide organizations and social movements, and smoothed out regional contrasts in Britain itself. 'The circumstances which surround different classes and individuals, and shape their characters,' said J.S. Mill in 1859, 'are daily becoming more assimilated.'[17] But easier contact does not necessarily improve relations; by throwing disparate cultures together, it may actually worsen them. Whereas imperial federation was seen as a preliminary to unification, federalism within the United Kingdom was viewed as a preservative against disintegration.

Regional contrasts were still very marked. Dialect poets were in their heyday between the 1860s and the 1890s, and even the political elite was not yet sufficiently integrated to speak with the same accent. Mrs Humphry Ward in the 1890s found Lord Derby 'a typical North-countryman', well able to tell a story in dialect: Henry Fawcett's biographer doubted whether he ever saw the difference between 'February' and Wiltshire's 'Febuwerry': and Gladstone's strong Lancashire accent did not go unnoticed when he visited Oxford in 1890. When the radical M.P. Joseph Cowen arrived at Westminster from Newcastle in 1874, his speeches simply were not understood. Boys sent as farm servants to the north of England from late Victorian Lark Rise were glad to return at the end of the year from what seemed to them a foreign country, whose speech they could scarcely comprehend. Mandell Creighton even noticed, as a Northumberland vicar in the 1870s, that each local occupation had its own patois, the fisherfolk, for instance, using a vocabulary very different from that of the hinds. He was very conscious of Northumberland's distinctiveness, even in patterns of landownership, and in 1884 envisaged working on a history of the Border Country before it was too late; 'under the influence of modern institutions,' he wrote, 'of the railway and the school inspector, the old provincial character of England was doomed to destruction.'[18] Schoolmasters everywhere were inculcating 'correct' speech – so that dialect writers like Edwin Waugh, Ben Brierley and John Hartley were popular as quaint entertainers rather than as promoting vital provincial speech-forms.

Wages varied markedly. In 1886, whereas a carpenter in the south-west earned 4s. 1d. for a nine-hour day, in London and the Home Counties he would earn 6s. 2d.: and whereas Nottinghamshire and Derby coal hewers earned 5s. 4d. a day in 1888, Somerset hewers earned only 3s. 3d. Nor were these contrasts offset by regional variations in living costs or family earnings. Good standards of productivity in the high-wage industrial areas concentrated investment there, so that

wage differentials would have become even wider but for extensive labour migration. Trade unions were not in a position to erode these differentials because they were strongest in the industrial areas, as becomes clear when membership is expressed as a percentage of local population: Northumberland comes first with 11 per cent, then Durham (11 per cent), Lancashire (9 per cent), East Riding (7 per cent), Leicestershire (7 per cent), Derbyshire (7 per cent), South Wales and Monmouth (7 per cent).[19] Only towards the end of the decade were powerful unions formed among the low paid.

Community ties were strong. Each village and county had its special character and distrusted its neighbours. Walter Long felt a loyalty to the Wiltshire electors which is perhaps now less familiar; in 1889 he told them that his family had represented them in Parliament for 500 years and that defeat would 'be a bitter blow to me . . . I regard myself as inseparably connected with my native county.' The national political parties trod gingerly when trying to organize supporters at the local level. The choice of rural M.P.s was often 'arranged' by the local hierarchy to ensure a harmonious compromise, and until 1880 more than a quarter of the parliamentary seats in Britain remained uncontested. Even the choice of a bishop needed to take account of the diocese's precise religious flavour; the local low church elements were offended, for instance, when the moderately high churchman MacLagan was made Archbishop of York in 1891. Bishop Walsham How, struggling to raise funds for his cathedral at Wakefield, found that local Anglican loyalties were channelled entirely into the smaller-scale religious needs of individual Yorkshire towns.[20]

The jealousy between pairs of Victorian provincial cities – Liverpool and Manchester, Bradford and Leeds, Edinburgh and Glasgow – is proverbial. Small northern townships laboured to build a town hall which would put their neighbour's in the shade. The positive aspect of these rivalries can be seen in the remarkable career of Joseph Chamberlain, Mayor of Birmingham from 1873 to 1876. Local municipalization and slum clearance owed much to his civic pride, to his vision of his city as metropolis of the Midlands. 'There is one eternal refrain in a Chamberlain-Kenrick household,' wrote Beatrice Webb in 1884: 'Birmingham society is superior in earnestness, sincerity and natural intelligence, to any society in the United Kingdom!'[21]

These small-scale local rivalries were transcended by four long-standing and overriding polarities in Britain during the 1880s: the gulfs between town and country, London and the provincial cities, Britons and

8.15

immigrants, and Englishmen and the other native races. The first – the continuing schism between town and country – Marx saw as 'the greatest division of material and mental labour': a division which had profoundly affected earlier polarities between Anglican and Nonconformist, Whig and Tory. In European countries with a town-based aristocracy, it was the countryside which gave birth to Liberalism; but in Britain the aristocracy was rooted in the countryside, and it was from the towns that Liberal movements for emancipation were launched. The repeal of the Corn Laws in 1846 saw rural protectionists succumb before Richard Cobden's free traders, who alleged a coincidence of interest between the manufacturers and the nation as a whole. In 1881 Joseph Cowen could still describe the towns as 'the backbone of the nation', just as Cobden would have done: 'they give it strength[,] cohesion, vitality. Scattered populations are usually ignorant, and oppression is always most easily established over them.'[22] Some towns were still struggling against local aristocratic control – Whitehaven against the Lowthers, for example, or Mansfield against the Dukes of Portland. There were even signs of a protectionist revival in the 1880s, though John Bright, once a leading Anti-Corn Law Leaguer, was still politically active.

Nonetheless the old dichotomy between town and country was waning; most major British cities had long since shaken off aristocratic control. The country house had once been a rural retreat from the life of public duty, but in 1885 Escott noticed that it was becoming 'but a London house, with a change of natural environment and pursuits': frequent visits were made to the capital by the owners, frequent visits from it by their guests.[23] This stemmed partly from easier transport, partly from the Victorian marriage between land and commerce. Rural Conservatives were gaining urban recruits and urban Liberals were expanding their rural frontiers by championing freedom of speech, employment, and belief in opposition to the tyranny of squire and parson. Liberalism flourished in the 'open' villages (most of them outside south-eastern England), where no landlord was paramount, where a more independent and often nonconformist spirit could prosper, where craft trades flourished or pastoral farming ensured a scattered pattern of residence. It championed the liberties of dissent, the attack on superstition and deference, the wider distribution of land, the defence of footpaths, and the promotion of education, temperance and progress. For long after the 1880s Liberals remained the major source of progressive ideas in the countryside.

But no political party in the 1880s could afford to base itself exclusively on a rural platform. The thirteen counties whose population declined between 1881 and 1891 (eight of them Welsh) were predominantly rural. Agriculture's share in the income of the United Kingdom fell faster in the 1880s than in any previous decade – from 11.9 per cent in 1875/84 to 8.7 per cent in 1885/94.[24] During the 1880s the Conservative Party negotiated a marriage between commercial and landed groupings which encouraged the growth of a mass urban party machine. When the agricultural labourers were enfranchised in 1884, a redistribution of seats greatly strengthened the political influence of the towns. A few predominantly rural movements – the Mothers' Union, for example, or the Girls' Friendly Society – launched surprisingly successful counter-attacks in defence of their values, but the future lay with the expanding suburbs.

2.4

Townsmen were soon in a position to move from strident urban self-defence to benevolent and even patronizing rural conservation. In 1887 the prominent Liberal politician James Bryce got Parliament to prevent a railway being built from Ambleside to Keswick. Octavia Hill's promotion of urban parks developed an interest which naturally moved forward to the formation in 1895 of the National Trust. Conservation also extended to folk-dancing, folk-music, wild flowers and wild animals. The first British nature reserve was created in 1888 when the Breydon Society bought one of the best of the Norfolk broads to safeguard its birds, and in the following year some Croydon women founded the organization which later gave rise to the Royal Society for the Protection of Birds. Observing birds instead of shooting them became a respectable masculine activity, championed by Charles Dixon's influential *Rural Bird Life* (1880). The countryside had been tamed.

Town and country ceased to conflict partly because they were merging in the suburb; here, up to a point, was realized William Morris's aim (echoing Marx) for 'the town to be impregnated with the beauty of the country, and the country with the intelligence and vivid life of the town.'[25] When the central areas decanted themselves into the suburbs, something was done towards tackling those twin nightmares of the late Victorian politician: urban over-population and rural depopulation. The Hampsteads and the Wimbledons penetrated the countryside with urban values and enabled wealthier businessmen to acquire the rural accoutrements of gentility. Suburban railways followed them and consolidated the territory gained; and in the twentieth century, radio, television and the

8.11

motor car completely overlaid the old dichotomy between town and country.

But a second polarity – that between London and the provincial cities – persisted longer. The triumph of the towns in the nineteenth century enabled them to enjoy the luxury of mutual rivalry. After the industrial revolution, town versus country could no longer simply be equated with London versus the kingdom. Manchester's power was reflected in the repeal of the Corn Laws, just as Birmingham's greatness was advertised by the career of Joseph Chamberlain. Although Chamberlain operated from Westminster after 1876, he never forsook his Birmingham base, and it was many years before he lost his suspicion of metropolitan and aristocratic ways. Britain's historic contrast between south-east and north-west was increasingly reflected in the conflict between the two major political parties. The Liberals' election victory of 1880 was seen by many as a triumph for the provinces over metropolitan clubs and journalists. The Liberal Party relied more and more on Wales, Scotland, Ireland and the industrial north of England; in this, as in so much else, it was largely followed by the Labour Party, which always owed more to the radical and largely nonconformist idealism of the provinces than to the rationalistic and secularist mood of London's socialism.

Provincial jealousy was nourished by London's conspicuous expenditure. This was where the great fortunes were made; twenty-one of the fifty-four millionaires who died between 1880 and 1899 came from the area, and that was only the tip of the capital's iceberg of wealth. Schedule D tax assessments for the ten London boroughs totalled £88 million (£26 per head); next on the list were Liverpool, with only £11 million (£20 per head), and Manchester with £10 million (£25 per head).

London's relative opulence can be illustrated from the history of photography. In 1891 there were sixty-three specialist shops selling photographic goods in the United Kingdom; thirty-six were in the London postal districts, and the large towns accounted for the rest. It was natural for the towns to cater earliest for new specialist requirements, and for the largest town to cater best of all. A similar pattern can be detected in the distribution of non-specialist shops selling photographic goods in the same year. The list is incomplete, but of 176 shops listed in the United Kingdom, thirty were in the London postal districts, and no other town scored more than Birmingham's six; county and industrial towns, seaports and seaside resorts account for the rest. Except in the resort towns, provincial photographers also (often undeservedly) lost customers to the larger towns and to London, so that they frequently found it necessary to establish a London studio in self-defence. 'There are hundreds of the public who never think of being photographed elsewhere than at the largest town in their neighbourhood,' wrote C.B. Barnes in 1888: 'if within twenty miles of the metropolis, they usually have their photographs taken there.'[26]

The provinces also had moralistic reasons for disliking London. It was sited within a predominantly Conservative region, and (as the centre of government) was the place where compromises were inevitably arranged. Such conduct of affairs was uncongenial to the idealist bred in dynamic and industrial cities. The provincial man's anti-aristocratic, self-helping and often dissenting and puritan outlook generated a single-minded resistance to the state, together with a pursuit of all-or-nothing policies, which provoked exciting splits in numerous social movements. Indignant provincials in the 1880s fuelled the feminist demand for disaffiliation from the Liberal Party, the anti-vivisectionist crusade, the attack on London brothels by W.T. Stead in 1885, and the assault on London clubland which lay behind Josephine Butler's campaign against state-regulated prostitution. Stead aimed to generate in London that community sense of moral responsibility to which provincial radicalism owed so much. 'I am a north countryman,' he told his supporters in August 1885, ' – and north countrymen, as a rule, do not think much of Londoners.'[27]

The gulf between London and the provinces within a reforming movement could be bridged only by very skilful leadership. Like Richard Cobden's attack on the Corn Laws in the 1840s, James Stansfeld's campaign against state-regulated prostitution in the 1880s ably channelled provincial idealism and moral indignation behind arguments and methods which would impress the metropolitan political elite; he got the Contagious Diseases Acts suspended in 1883 and abolished in 1886. Likewise William Tebb managed to unite provincials and Londoners in his successful London Society for the Abolition of Compulsory Vaccination, founded in 1880. Yet Manchester no longer thinks today what the world thinks tomorrow; provincial prosperity and self-confidence have declined, and the Labour Party's crusade for social justice and working-class dignity has pushed regional jealousies into second place.

There has been no such decline in the third polarity of the 1880s – between the immigrant and the host nation. Britain then had a reputation for welcoming immigrants. The number of inhabitants born in England and Wales per foreign-born inhabitant (149 in

1881) had fallen at every census since 1841. Resident immigrants in 1881 were almost all in towns, 51 per cent of them in London, 39 per cent in the forty-six great provincial towns, especially in seaports like Liverpool, Hull and Cardiff, but also in Manchester and Birmingham. It was rare at this time to see a coloured person; of the 117,999 immigrants who were foreign by nationality (68 per cent of the total in England and Wales), 84 per cent came from Europe and 16 per cent from the United States.[28]

Many of the Europeans were Jews fleeing from persecution; they huddled together in limited areas of London's East End, where two-thirds disembarked in the 1880s.[29] The view of them as allies of exploitative financial institutions explains the consistent strain of anti-semitism running through British radicalism from Cobbett onwards. The identification of many Jews both with early socialism and with the sweating of labour in the East End clothing trade provided further excuses for prejudice, but some opposition to immigration on the left stemmed then (as now) simply from desire to gain control over the economy. Though we may now reject the phrasing of Graham Wallas's plea in *Fabian Essays* for 'a law of aliens' to exclude 'the human rubbish which the military empires of the continent are so ready to shoot upon any open space,'[30] we less readily reject his associated belief that the attack on poverty requires some control over the size of the labour force. But racial prejudice was never officially espoused by the political parties, largely because the pattern of immigration was so regionalized, and because Jewish immigrants had wealthy allies in political and banking circles who relieved their poverty in an impressive and systematic way.

The Jews' ready identification with urban and industrial life helped to integrate them into British society, though at the price of weakening their distinctive culture and religious observance. Conversely, the anti-capitalists among them gained acceptance through their major contribution to the British labour movement. Entrepreneurial Jews aimed at a respectable and inconspicuous affluence, moving westwards across London to prosperous villas in St John's Wood, Hammersmith and Hampstead. They also moved into manufacturing communities like Manchester and Birmingham and into seaside resorts like Bournemouth and Blackpool. They branched out into the professions and even, with the Prince of Wales's encouragement, into high society.

Welsh and Scots immigrants into England were also successfully integrated. This was partly because no significant clash of cultures was involved, partly because

numbers were so small. Between 1881 and 1891 only 4.8 per cent of London's immigrants came from Scotland, compared with 11.9 per cent from abroad. The 253,528 Scots-born residents in England and Wales in 1881 were widely scattered: 243 out of every 1,000 were in the London area, 220 in Lancashire, 97 in Durham, 92 in Northumberland, 76 in Yorkshire and 48 in Cumberland. Four of the ten Prime Ministers between 1852 and 1908 were Scottish: Aberdeen, Gladstone, Rosebery and Campbell-Bannerman. Four of the late Victorian and Edwardian archbishops also came from Scotland: Tait, Davidson, MacLagan and Lang. Carlyle, James Mill, Ruskin and Macaulay were among the many Scotsmen who made their literary reputations in England. Scots and Welsh immigrants congregated in their many Presbyterian and Calvinistic Methodist chapels in English cities. Scotland's population rose by 150 per cent between 1801 and 1891, yet when expressed as a percentage of the population of England and Wales, it fell from 18.1 per cent to 13.9 per cent between 1801 and 1891, partly because (for Scotsmen) England's streets were paved with gold.[31]

Irish immigrants posed more serious problems because they were more numerous, rural, Catholic, and often migrant – *en route* for the United States or aiming to return home. As part of the group which Marx saw as 'the light infantry of capital, thrown by it, according to its needs, now to this point, now to that,' their nomad labour was used on construction sites, docks, railway building and agriculture. The 1881 census shows them clustering in the high-wage northern manufacturing and mining areas, in London and in the Scottish lowlands. Their arrival exempted industrialists from the need to pay wages high enough to tempt English workers into such areas. Irish drinking bouts and fights offended their Protestant neighbours, and helped to generate the strong British anti-Irish and Unionist vote which counterbalanced the Irish settlers' nationalist and Liberal loyalties. 'I believe the anti-Irish feeling is very strong with our best friends – the respectable artisans and non-Conformists,' Chamberlain told his fellow-radical Labouchere in January 1886.[32] This belief no doubt influenced his crucially important decision later in the year to oppose Gladstone's first Home Rule Bill.

The last of the four polarities of the 1880s lay in the friction between Englishmen and the other inhabitants of the British Isles. Then, as now, politicians laboured to hold the entire population together in a unified nation-state which would promote their joint economic prosperity without infringing their regional and cultural identity. The continuing importance of these relationships was at first masked in the twentieth century by the success of the Labour Party, two devastating world wars, preoccupation with the problems of empire, and independence for Eire in 1922.

The Liberal Party was traditionally enthusiastic for popular participation in government, instinctively wary of excessive concentrations of power, and sympathetic to overseas nationalist movements. Party inclinations therefore tempted Gladstone to encourage Welsh, Scottish and Irish aspirations, quite apart from his personal commitment to national self-determination. But the individualist, thrifty, and in some ways simple-minded peasant distaste for central government was relatively strong in such areas; these semi-nationalist movements, particularly in Ireland, threatened to out-flank Gladstone's party and encourage separation. Gladstone's crusade for Irish Home Rule after 1886 was unifying in a fourfold sense: it aimed at welding together the Union and re-creating the Liberal-Irish political alliance, but it also brought together the fragmenting elements of an attenuated political party through an exhilarating crusade, and unified the United Kingdom through making general elections moments for debate on national policy rather than on local personalities and issues.

But could enough non-Irish voters be won for Home Rule? Could they ultimately be convinced that only through concession to Irish demands would the Union be preserved? Would this not stimulate similar agitations in Wales and Scotland? A Scottish Home Rule Association was, after all, launched in 1886. Gladstone's was a dangerous course, but his assets were formidable: single-minded mastery of legislative detail, skill at detecting shifts in public opinion and at turning them to his purpose, brilliance at putting over a case in and out of Parliament, redoubtable determination, courage and energy.

In the late 1870s, agricultural depression and the importing of American grain inflamed the political temperature among the small-scale peasant farmers of Wales, the Scottish highlands and Ireland. Long-standing resentments against aristocratic landlordism were stirred up. But in Wales the problem was less serious for British governments than in Ireland because Welsh lines of communication led directly into England instead of forming a closed system, and because industrialization had divided the country into two halves. The south shared all England's urban and industrial problems, and its rapidly-expanding mining areas could easily absorb surplus population from the distressed agricultural north, whereas distressed Irish peasants had no such alternative. Furthermore, English squires were less alien in Wales than in Ireland: they more frequently resided on their estates, and were better integrated through their Protestantism and through patronizing such cultural functions as the Eisteddfod, which was conducted in English.

Welsh national self-awareness was growing, but could be fully satisfied in several ways without separation, especially through educational reform. In 1880 the Aberdare Committee asserted that 'Wales has a distinct nationality of its own,' and recommended a separate university system. The colleges founded at Aberystwyth in 1872, at Cardiff in 1883, and at Bangor in 1884 were united by royal charter in 1893 into the University of Wales, by which time the Welsh Intermediate Education Act (1889) had authorized the establishment of secondary schools.[33]

The union with England would have threatened the distinctive cultural traditions of Wales only if their appeal had been either narrower or wider. The Welsh language was not common to all Welshmen, nor was it diminishing in appeal to the point where intellectuals feared its extinction. Those who spoke it (Welsh only, 30.4 per cent of those aged two and over; bilingual, 24.1 per cent in 1891)[34] were largely concentrated outside the mining areas which were gaining so many English-speaking immigrants at this time. Furthermore, the population of the more rural and Welsh-speaking counties was either declining or increasing only slowly. The vernacular had not been integral to the national cultural revival in the mid-Victorian period, when dialects and minority languages were less highly prized than they are now, and there was no sense of persecution; during the 1880s Welsh even began spreading among the educated, and the first university chair of Celtic (at Oxford) was established in 1877. The Society for the Utilisation of the Welsh Language in Education was founded in 1885, and the ban on using it in school was lifted in 1888. Much cultural activity took place in nonconformist chapels; these the Liberals took care to cultivate through promising temperance and burial reform, and even disestablishment of the Anglican Church in Wales.

Gladstone was remarkably successful in attracting loyalty in the principality without doing much of substance to earn it. He unobtrusively resisted disestablishment and did little for temperance, that other favourite national cause, apart from supporting the Welsh Sunday Closing Bill of 1881. But he did live in Wales, and in a speech at Swansea in 1887 pronounced it a nation; in 1892 he was even prepared to climb a thousand feet up a hillside in Snowdonia to address a meeting of hymn-singing miners. For these small services, the 8.1

Welsh at the 1885 general election were prepared to sweep the Conservatives out of all but four of the thirty-four national seats, and after 1886 to give Gladstone much more generous backing for Irish Home Rule than the Scots. The explanation is partly to be found in the fact that he paid Welshmen the same compliment that he paid to working men: he took them into his political confidence, took the trouble to address them. Leading British statesmen like Lord Randolph Churchill and Lord Salisbury therefore had to follow; even the Queen visited the country in 1889 and regretted the neglect felt by 'this naturally *sensitive* and warm hearted people' at the Prince of Wales's failure to make the five-hour journey there from London.[35] So much of the politics of the 1880s is concerned with status, so little (by modern standards) with material welfare.

Gladstone also acted on his belief in equality of treatment; he supported educational reforms and appointed Welshmen to Anglican sees in the principality. No doubt also the magic of his oratory, which had never quite lost its youthful evangelical tone, bewitched those nonconformist chapelgoers who relished a high-toned dramatic sense in their public speakers. The Welsh were ideally suited by a Liberal Party which championed the rights of small nationalities, catered for dissent, and allowed small sub-groupings in its midst to campaign for particular interests. From 1886 the Liberal M.P. T.E. Ellis was able to build up a semi-independent grouping within the Liberal Party which promoted national causes and voted occasionally with the Conservatives. So the young semi-nationalist dissenters like David Lloyd George who got themselves returned for many Welsh seats after 1886 had little to complain of, and in the 1880s no serious attempt was made to secure independence.

The harsh environment and tough living conditions of the Scottish highlands might well have nourished a nationalist movement. Indeed, after 1882 there was a revolt there which superficially resembled events in Ireland. The Highland Land League was formed by crofters complaining of high rents, insecure tenure and frequent eviction, and four Crofter candidates were returned at the 1885 general election. Their independence of the Liberal Party and their popular basis in some ways anticipate the Labour Party. Emigration caused a net loss to Scotland's population of 218,000 between 1881 and 1891,[36] yet the Crofters' Act of 1886, which gave security of tenure and fair rents, brought the movement to an end, and in 1892 the Crofters merged into the Liberal Party. Nor was it ever a nationalist movement, for Scotland, like Wales, was politically and economically divided between north

and south; the industrialized south had more in common with England than with the highlands. Since the thirteenth century, long before the Union, the primacy had gone to the English-speaking lowlands. Scotland's distinctive language (Gaelic) was, again as in Wales, largely confined to the rural north; but in contrast, it was spoken by a mere 6 per cent in 1891. It was not persecuted; the Gaelic Society of Inverness was founded in 1871, and in 1878 the Scottish Code allowed the teaching of Gaelic. Scotland again resembled Wales in being overwhelmingly Protestant, but the established church there was the Presbyterian Church of the Scottish people. Disestablishment movements, unlike the Welsh, did not therefore take on an anti-English flavour, and militarism found an outlet in collaborating with the English in running the Empire overseas; 8.1 per cent of the N.C.O.s and other ranks in the British army in the 1880s were Scotsmen.[37]

Industrialization extended Scotland's ties with England; as in Wales, it occurred in the Anglicized areas (the lowlands), and in 1881, 92,000 of the country's inhabitants (2.5 per cent) had been born in England and Wales.[38] The Queen herself was among the immigrants, at least for much of the year. She established her home at Balmoral in 1855, and spent a total of seven years in Scotland. In 1866 she created her second son Duke of Edinburgh, the first royal dukedom to bear a Scottish title, and in 1881 her fourth son (one of whose christian names was Duncan, as 'a compliment to dear Scotland')[39] Duke of Albany. Franchise reform in 1832 firmly established the Liberal Party in the country, and thereafter at only one general election (1900) before 1914 did the Conservative Party win a majority of Scottish seats.

Here, as in Wales, the Liberal Party – with its dissenting connections and sympathy with rural radicalism – satisfied local needs. Again as in Wales, symbolic actions by Gladstone (his Midlothian campaigns in 1879–80, for example) seem to have been far more important in consolidating Liberal support than any measures of substance; Gladstone in his 1880 government was not at all responsive to Lord Rosebery's pressures for Scottish causes, though Liberals created the Scottish Office in 1885 and gave Cabinet status to the Secretary for Scotland in 1892. The Conservatives extended the role of the Scottish Office in 1887, and the volume of correspondence received there trebled between 1885 and 1890. Although nationalist feeling was strong enough by 1889 to remove the phrase 'North Britain' from Campbell-Bannerman's letter-heading, it no more threatened the union with England than did Welsh nationalism.

Gladstone found it more difficult in Scotland than in Wales to unite Liberals behind Irish Home Rule. 5.9 per cent of Scotland's population in 1881 was Irish-born; Scottish Protestantism was therefore all the more militant, and when Ulster Protestants organized themselves into the Ulster Loyalist Anti-Repeal Union in January 1886, they immediately made contact with anti-Catholic Protestants in Britain. James Henderson, one of the Ulster Protestant leaders, told a Newry meeting in February of his belief that 'if we can stir up the religious feeling in Scotland we have won the battle ... Scotland ... is the stronghold of Mr Gladstone.' At the 1886 general election, when Home Rule first became a major issue in Scotland, the percentage there voting Conservative or Liberal Unionist shot up from 33.9 to 44.8; twenty-eight Unionists therefore accompanied the thirty-nine Liberal M.P.s to Westminster.[40] The Conservative Party was thereby re-established north of the border, and although Edwardian Liberals recovered their former supremacy in seats, they could not do the same in votes. After 1886, then, Scottish politics were dominated by two English-based parties; to that extent the decade saw the Anglo-Scottish union consolidated rather than fragmented.

8.16 Very different was the situation in Ireland, where the English connection was symbolized for many by brutal evictions and gross inequalities in wealth. The Irish proportion of the United Kingdom's inhabitants declined from 32.6 per cent in 1821 to only 12.5 per cent in 1891. During the 1880s the population fell faster than at any time in the century apart from the period of the Great Famine, yet that of the United Kingdom as a whole was still growing fast.[41] When Sir Charles Dilke walked with Lord Spencer, the Viceroy, to the Strawberry Gardens on a Sunday in May 1885, he was struck with the hostile mood of passers-by. 'Who killed Myles Joyce?' they cried, referring to a young man hanged in 1882 for (subsequently disputed) participation in the Maamstrasna murders of that year. For Joseph Chamberlain in 1885, Irish government was 'founded on the bayonets of 30,000 soldiers encamped permanently as in a hostile country' – a bureaucratized, centralized, undemocratic regime akin to the Russian and Austrian empires.[42] Although 18.3 per cent of the N.C.O.s and other ranks in the British army whose origins were reported in the 1880s were Irish, British governments did not allow Irishmen to join British civilians in the volunteer movement, and Irish M.P.s more than once drew attention to the contrast.[43]

To British statesmen, Ireland seemed an alien and exasperating country which defeated their good inten-

tions; as the Queen told Earl Cowper in 1880, 'the more one does for the Irish the more unruly and ungrateful they seem to be.'[44] In the franchise reform debates in 1884, the prominent Conservative W.H. Smith even made the Irishman's mud-cabin an objection to granting him the vote, and in 1886 the Conservative leader Lord Salisbury was indiscreet enough to liken the situations of Irishmen and Hottentots. Prime Ministers rarely visited Ireland; neither Disraeli nor Lord Salisbury ever went there, and Queen Victoria, who spent only five weeks in the country, peppered her journal with grumbles about disloyalty. No statesman (except perhaps Lord Randolph Churchill) grappled as energetically as Gladstone with the Irish problem, and even he was curiously reluctant to take the country's M.P.s into his confidence when framing legislation.

Anglo-Irish relations were inflamed in the early 1880s by nationalist conduct. Particularly offensive was the assault by the nationalist M.P.s on the House of Commons. Even Englishmen as radical as Chamberlain or Bright had directed their reforming campaigns towards Parliament and had used constitutional weapons; radicals were therefore as shocked as their fellow politicians by obstructionism, and still more by the extremist violence in Ireland itself. The Irish M.P.s, with their interminable speeches in the early hours of the morning, were breaking the rules of a great debating club which was widely respected within British society. After Gladstone announced on 31 January 1881 that the government intended to carry its Coercion Bill at that sitting whatever the resistance, the Irish responded with forty-one hours of filibustering and exhausted the patience of many observers inside and outside Parliament. On 2 February, the Speaker, acting against all precedent, closed the debate. 'Never was there such a state of things,' wrote the Queen; she thought that nationalist insolence in saying that the Prime Minister was not to be heard 'passes belief', and went on to tell Gladstone how anxious she was about it all, and how eagerly she was following events. In August she told Gladstone that House of Commons proceedings were 'of a most disgraceful character', though nothing better could be expected 'from so many members of such low and revolutionary kinds who are now in the House of Commons.'[45] When the closure was introduced in 1882 the government's control over parliamentary time greatly increased, to be supplemented in 1887 by the guillotine.

The Queen in her indignation, as so often during her reign, spoke for a very wide section of British public opinion – so much so that one of Home Rule's attractions after 1886, even for some Liberals, was that it would expel from Westminster the Irish M.P.s who were, in Granville's phrase of 1885, 'introducing the dry rot into our institutions.' In reviewing the obstruction of the 1880s at the end of his life, the Liberal statesman James Bryce recorded that for him it 'marked the end of an epoch, the end of the old, dignified, constitutionally regular, and gentlemanly House of Commons, in which everyone was on his good behaviour and felt the force of great traditions.'[46]

Ever responsive to public opinion, the radical leader Joseph Chamberlain felt the need by 1881 to complain publicly of Irish nationalist methods. 'If this agitation had followed English precedent,' he argued at Liverpool in October, 'if its leaders had carried on within the spirit as well as within the letter of the law; if they had discountenanced violence and intimidation – then there was no agitation in the United Kingdom more deserving of untiring sympathy, and more entitled to complete success. But unfortunately they did not do that.' He told Gladstone in April 1882 that the Irish M.P.s were giving the Liberal government no help whatever in getting public support for a conciliatory policy: on the contrary, they had acted 'as if their object were to disgust, embitter and prejudice all English opinion against the cause to which they have pledged themselves.' In this situation, he went on, 'nothing would be easier at the present moment than to get up in every large town an anti-Irish agitation almost as formidable as the anti-Jewish agitation in Russia.'[47]

Still more damaging to the Irish cause were the intimidation, violence and murder promoted by the more extreme elements of the nationalist movement which Parnell, the leader of the Irish parliamentary party, was able to control only with great difficulty. During the 1880s the issue of Ireland could seldom be discussed on its merits because of the frequent distractions introduced by the methods the nationalists employed. Only a sheer accident saved the Irish Secretary W.E. Forster from being murdered on 22 April 1882: if he had not unexpectedly taken an earlier train to attend an important Cabinet meeting in London, he would have found assassins waiting for him to board the boat train.[48] The fragmented nature of the nationalist movement was not then fully appreciated: when so little was known about the dissidents, it was easy to suppose them all to be closely in league. On 6 May 1882, Lord Frederick Cavendish, Forster's successor as Irish Secretary, and Thomas Burke his Under-Secretary were stabbed to death with long surgical knives in Dublin's Phoenix Park by a band of assassins called 'the Invincibles'. According to Gladstone's private secretary, when Gladstone and his wife first heard the news

of their nephew's fate they 'threw themselves on their knees in the inner hall, and as soon as they had partially recovered themselves, they at once set out for poor Lady Frederick's.'[49] Two days later the Queen told Gladstone that the details of the event were 'all calculated to make one's blood run cold and to produce an indescribable thrill of horror.' 'London is literally aghast,' wrote Lady Knightley in her diary. Even Parnell was alarmed. On the day after the murders he called on Chamberlain 'white as a sheet, agitated and apparently altogether demoralized', afraid that he would himself be the next victim of the Irish secret societies; he began carrying a revolver in his overcoat when at Westminster.[50]

Britain in the 1880s was in some ways a more violent society than our own, but it was less tolerant of the lawless attempt at the political short cut, if only because imperial responsibilities immediately lent overseas significance to domestic unrest. Sir Alfred Lyall, the imperial administrator, wrote from India to John Morley after the murders to the effect that Britain was 'being disgraced in the eyes of the civilized world,' and asked 'what sort of a lesson are you teaching to the dangerous classes in this country, when you show that men can terrorise by assassination within a few miles of England?' But there was a further reason for the shocked contemporary response, as Violet Markham makes clear in memoirs published more than seventy years later: 'I can see as plainly as though it were yesterday my Mother's face of horror as she hurried up the garden path that Sunday afternoon to break the fatal news to my Father who was sitting in the greenhouse. The moral sense of the times had not been blunted by the large-scale cruelties and horrors of two world wars.' Ample liberal and humanitarian reasons could henceforth be found for opposing anything the Irish wanted, and Queen Victoria immediately drew out the implications for Gladstone's conciliatory strategy in her journal. In the following months, Irish secret societies lend a zest to her correspondence which is rivalled only by the exploits of Jack the Ripper later in the decade. 'Lord Spencer writes this morning with truth,' she told the Home Secretary W.V. Harcourt in February 1883, 'that we are engaged in a mortal struggle with an army of assassins.'[51]

Irish nationalist violence also involved the planting of bombs. In January 1881 one person was killed and three injured in an incident at Salford barracks; in March an unexploded bomb was found at the Mansion House shortly before the Lord Mayor's banquet was due to be held, and in May 1882 another at the same place failed to go off. By this time the Queen was thoroughly alarmed, frequently telegraphing the Home Office about the situation, urging that English detectives be sent to Dublin, and insisting that the railway lines between Osborne and Balmoral should be specially patrolled before her journey to Scotland. In January 1883 a bomb blew up a gasometer in Glasgow, and in March another at the premises of *The Times* was abortive; but a third at government offices in Whitehall achieved its objective, and in October there were two explosions on the London Underground, one of them causing seventy-two casualties. In February 1884 bombs were found at four London main-line stations, of which one went off without loss of life, and in May there were three detonations in London's West End, including one at Scotland Yard. Three conspirators were blown up by their own device at London Bridge in December 1884; several travellers on the London underground were hurt on 2 January 1885, and on 24 January there were simultaneous explosions at the Tower of London, Westminster Hall and the House of Commons, injuring several people. These events amply prepared public opinion for an increase in police resources and security precautions, thus distancing the governors still further from the governed.[52]

Harcourt told the Director of the Criminal Investigation Division (C.I.D.), Howard Vincent, in January 1881 that he was 'much disturbed at the absolute want of information in which we seem to be with regard to Fenian organization in London. All other objects should be postponed in our efforts to get some light into these dark places.'[53] The temporary secret service operation set up in response to Fenian activity in 1867 did not outlast that year, but the Phoenix Park murders of 1882 forced the government to establish another one for Ireland, and the London police had a considerable success in May when a Clerkenwell stable yielded up bayonets, 70–80,000 rounds, 400 rifles and 60 revolvers.[54] The special Irish branch established by the C.I.D. after bomb incidents in 1883 was run down with the decline in violence by the end of 1885, but not abolished, as in 1867.[55] By June 1882 Gladstone was reported as complaining that 'he never walked out to get a little fresh air without finding that he was followed by a mysterious guardian in the shape of a policeman in plain clothes.' Recalling this period many years later, Lady St Helier remembered him boasting at one of her dinners that he had for once eluded his bodyguards, yet two of the waiters behind his chair at that moment were detectives from Scotland Yard.[56] By June 1885 the House of Commons police had compiled an album containing photographs of nearly every M.P., in the hope of recognizing unauthorized persons.[57]

Despite all these obstacles to conciliation, many of them created by the nationalists themselves, Gladstone was not deterred from trying to satisfy Irish demands, and after 1886 even mounted a popular crusade to back up his policy; how was this possible for the leader of a major political party seeking an electoral majority? Gladstone's policy could be sold to his party partly because of the liberal traditions of British government, which had been learned over a long period through tackling domestic unrest with a view to forestalling an English 1789, and through handling colonial discontent in such a way as to prevent another war of independence. A Liberal government, largely officered by Whig aristocrats well versed in the arts of conciliation, had little difficulty in responding to nonconformist, libertarian and humanitarian pressures. Liberals disliked the use of force and welcomed alternative ways of dealing with the Irish problem. The Liberal Party was also relatively cosmopolitan in outlook, and Gladstone knew how Britain's overseas reputation suffered as a result of her Irish difficulties; he told the Queen in May 1885 that Dublin Castle 'continually maintains and presents in Ireland the idea of Government as a thing "foreign" and not indigenous.' Gladstone was ready to introduce temporary and exceptional curbs on liberty so as to maintain public order, but he explained in his Home Rule speech of 1886 that such curbs were becoming habitual, and some other way must be found.[58]

The apparent callousness of absentee landlords like the Marquess of Clanricarde made it somewhat easier for Gladstone to win support for conciliatory policies towards Ireland; it even induced Liberals to support schemes for land reform which repudiated economic orthodoxy on freedom of contract. By September 1889 they were using photographs of Irish eviction scenes as weapons in the by-election at Sleaford.[59] Furthermore there existed in the Liberal armoury a well tried alternative to authoritarian rule: local self-government, an expedient which enjoyed Gladstone's general sympathy. In January 1879 he told Granville that it 'opened a road for giving a considerable amount of satisfaction to persons in any way amenable to reason,' and by September 1881 he was telling Granville privately that he was 'rather advanced' on questions of Irish self-government, so long as the supremacy of the Westminster Parliament was upheld; he was even prepared to extend to Scotland any concessions made to Ireland.[60] At that stage he was not envisaging anything as radical as the nationalists' Home Rule schemes, but by May 1885 he was outlining to the Queen plans for Irish local government reform which he saw as 'in the highest sense Conservative'; their aim was 'widely, yet safely, to familiarize the people, through local matters, with the acts and responsibilities of governing, and to teach them by daily experience that governing is a business in which they have an interest and a share, not one managed by an agency which they feel to lie outside of them.'[61] From here to Home Rule there was but a short distance to travel.

Gladstone's approach towards Ireland was the more acceptable to his party because it could be presented as but the latest in a long tradition of conciliatory dealings with the leaders of dissident movements in the country at large. Gladstone grasped Parnell's situation early on in his government of 1880, and in setting out to do business with him he followed precedents shrewdly established by several of his Whig-Liberal predecessors when faced by troublesome reforming movements. As early as January 1879 he had urged Granville to cultivate good relations with 'the better Irish' through trying to meet their claims.[62] He told the Queen in February 1882 that his aim was to prevent any demand for Home Rule from being made by the Irish M.P.s in combination; there had been some danger of this in 1880 when sixty or seventy Home Rulers had been returned at the election, but 'this majority Your Majesty's Government have done their best to break up; and they have succeeded'. When, on 15 April 1882, Captain O'Shea privately urged the gains to be made from conciliating the more moderate of his fellow Irish M.P.s, Gladstone (despite nationalist behaviour – perhaps partly because of it) felt inclined to respond.[63] There followed the secret Kilmainham 'Treaty', whereby Parnell was released from gaol, to which he had been condemned for incitement in October 1881, and the possibility was opened up of closer co-operation in the future between the Liberal government and the Irish M.P.s.

Gladstone was in no position to confess his motives publicly and fully; politicians seldom are. Nor was the shrewdness of his strategy readily appreciated by the politically unsophisticated. He told the Queen in May 1882 that a Liberal government which wanted Parnell to discipline his Irish followers must refrain from attacking him 'for fear of hindering a work sacred in their eyes, by whomsoever it is done'; they must 'bear in silence reproaches which may be fatal to them ... if they have misjudged the interests of the country at so grave a crisis.'[64] It was not a line of conduct which the Queen fully grasped, and here again she was at one with many of her subjects. Nonetheless Gladstone persisted with his overall policy, despite the great setback

it received from the Phoenix Park massacres on 6 May 1882, which at once made it impossible for him to carry the Cabinet with him in meeting the reasonable claims of the Irish M.P.s; but in January 1883 he still felt able to tell Granville that his conciliatory line had 'broken down to 35 or 40 what would have been a party, in this parliament, of 65 home rulers.' This averted the danger of a Home Rule demand coming from a large majority of the Irish M.P.s: 'I can ill convey to you how clear are my thoughts,' he added, 'or how earnest my convictions, on this important subject.' In the following month he rebuked Hartington for endangering his strategy by publicly declaring against Irish local self-government.[65]

In intention, therefore, Gladstone's policy was highly conservative – and, indeed, unionist. He and many Liberals hoped to hold Ireland through affection rather than through coercion, an objective still uppermost in his mind in December 1885 when he told Hartington that the Irish question now resolved itself into a decision on whether Parnell's grouping or 'a separation or civil war party' should have the upper hand.[66] It is well known that while drafting his first Home Rule Bill of 1886 he was reading and enjoying the writings of that philosopher of conservatism Edmund Burke. Gladstone's refusal to be deflected by bombs, assassination, obstruction and intimidation does credit to his courage and consistency, yet for Conservatives and even for some members of his own party, Irish violence made his concessions look more like weakness than conciliation; fathers of families, employers of staff, people at every level with some authority to lose, found his policy more than they could stomach, and began to yearn for the firm stamp of resolute government.

In 1885 two new developments drew Gladstone in still more daring directions. The first was the outcome of the 1885 general election. Although Ireland's proportion of the United Kingdom's population had long been declining, the tighter discipline of her M.P.s in the 1880s lent them increased influence. Nor did the redistribution of parliamentary seats under the 1884 Reform Act take account of Ireland's reduced population; if seats had been allocated strictly on a population basis, her total representation in 1885 would have dropped from 103 to 92. At the 1885 election the sixty Irish nationalist M.P.s of 1880 grew to eighty-five, just enough to hold the balance between the other two parties. And whereas 101,284 Irish votes had been cast in 1880, in 1885 the total was 439,270, two-thirds of them nationalist.[67] A second influence on Gladstone at this point was the conduct of the Conservative government which succeeded his own – holding office from June 1885 to February 1886 – in breaking the long-standing two-party alignment on Ireland by abandoning the coercive policies that the Liberals had felt obliged to impose. Given the Conservatives' refusal to introduce Home Rule, Parnell's powerful position after the 1885 general election, and his willingness to play off one party against the other, Gladstone's next move seems entirely predictable to anyone with access to his private views since 1879; yet his declaration for Home Rule astonished his contemporaries, and at this point his personality and reputation injected bitterness into the whole question.

When Gladstone introduced his Irish land legislation in 1881 and his first proposal for Irish Home Rule in 1886, British aristocrats, property-owners, intellectuals, and even working men were alarmed; the resultant divisions within families and in the Liberal Party took decades to heal, and Florence Nightingale remembered nothing so disruptive of social relations since the reform crisis of 1832.[68] Gladstone's long history of making an apparent response to radical pressures on the left of his own party caused many to suspect that he would give extremists anything compatible with securing power for himself. Some Conservatives even accused the Liberal leaders of preferring policies that were popular to those that they knew were right. So when Gladstone's long sequence of equivocal and convoluted statements was followed by a commitment to Home Rule, and by consequent Irish nationalist backing for a Liberal government, many accused him of opportunism, of seeking to hold power on any terms. Political positions were then taken up largely in reference to Gladstone personally: his followers were loyal, his opponents were traitors, or *vice versa*.

However much Gladstone's eye during this crisis was cocked towards party advantage and towards his own position within his party (and these motives could hardly have been absent, though they were probably subordinate), we now know that in the long term Home Rule was the only way of dealing with nationalism compatibly with democratic values; most would now also share the Liberal conviction that even if Conservative predictions came true (as, in the event, they did after 1922), and Home Rule was progressively widened so as to become independence, a union with Catholic Ireland which could be maintained only by force was not worth preserving. Gladstone deserves the more credit when one recalls that at the same time Bismarck was expelling 37,000 Poles from East Prussia on the ground that the Prussians were being outnumbered there. *The Times* saw Bismarck's policy as springing from the practical man's recognition of antipathies

as 'ultimate facts',[69] but to these Gladstone will always be thought by some to have shown on occasion a praiseworthy indifference. He viewed the Home Rule question from the widest European perspective, and was aware of successful precedents for devolution in Norway, Finland and Austria, not to mention Canada.

Furthermore, if Gladstone's personality was in some quarters a liability, elsewhere (especially within his own party and in the country at large) it was a major asset. In 1877, when in temporary retirement, he complained to Granville of the Liberal leaders' caution: 'my opinion is and has long been that the vital principle of the Liberal party, like that of Greek art, is *action*, and that nothing but action will ever make it worthy of the name of a party.' No leading statesman was then capable of campaigning with such vigour or of evoking such idealism with his public oratory; nor have many close colleagues in British politics observed a party leader responding to a crisis with such verve and intrepidity, for at this juncture Gladstone – like Peel, his master – showed himself 'a daring pilot in extremity'. 'I have no choice,' he had told a doubting Forster in 1882 when opting for the strategy lying behind the Kilmainham Treaty: 'followed or not followed, I must go on.'[70] In 1885–6 he was again prepared if necessary to go it alone. He was well aware of his party's schismatic tendency, and knew that the radicals regarded their Whig colleagues as little better than Conservatives; but if the Liberal Party were to split, he told Hartington in November 1885, 'let it split decently, honourably, and for cause.' He knew that this was what he was risking by embracing Home Rule; he might have guessed, being in his mid seventies, that he would be branded as 'an old man in a hurry'. Yet when a colleague pointed out the political difficulties, he later recalled his reply: 'I believe it was in my mind to say, if I did not actually say it, that I was prepared to go forward without any body. That is to say without any known and positive assurance of support. This was one of the great Imperial occasions which call for such resolutions.'[71]

Unfortunately for Gladstone's strategy in 1886, he did not fully reckon with one further inflammatory factor: the growth of political self-consciousness in Ulster. He knew little of the province, and failed to include in his 1886 Cabinet James Bryce, the man who knew more. For Ulstermen, 'Rome Rule' from Dublin threatened the Anglo-Irish trade on which Belfast shipyards depended; it also seemed to affront their Protestant traditions and their ideal of a sober and rational respectability. In 1885–6, Ulster Conservatism rapidly acquired the popular party structure which

Conservatives elsewhere had created rather earlier. The influential Irish Loyal and Patriotic Union formed in southern Ireland in 1885 collaborated with Ulster's Loyalist Anti-Repeal Union, founded in January 1886 as the central core of the Conservative Party organization there. Popular Orangeism now won a new respect from the middle class and gentry who made up the local Conservative leaders. Ulster Conservative M.P.s led by E.J. Saunderson began exerting pressure on the Conservative leaders at Westminster in January 1886; during the spring, Ulster Liberals and Conservatives began moving cautiously into alliance. Preparing to resist rule from Dublin by force if necessary, they began to drill on a small scale and sought quotations for the purchase of arms. Such Protestant vigour inevitably commanded respect, even from Gladstone's followers; Liberals resisting Ireland's coercion by London could hardly oppose Ulstermen who were resisting coercion by Dublin.

The Conservatives had everything to gain from Ulster's stand, as Lord Randolph Churchill quickly appreciated: 'I decided some time ago', he wrote on 16 February 1886, 'that if the G[rand] O[ld] M[an] went for Home Rule, the Orange card would be the one to play. Please God it may turn out the ace of trumps and not the two.' In the same month he crossed to northern Ireland and promised, amid enthusiasm, that English Conservatives would rally to the Ulstermen in their time of danger; and, in a public letter, he coined the useful slogan 'Ulster will fight, Ulster will be right.' It was Churchill too who recognized the need for a broader party label which would rally the champions of 'union' against Home Rule. On 14 April 1886 anti-Gladstonian Liberals and Conservatives joined together in a big meeting at the Haymarket in London, and Lord Rowton heard 'great cheering for Union and *God Save the Queen*' coming from within: Unionism was born.[72]

At this point we reach one of the greatest dramas of modern British history, whose detailed sequence and overall significance deserve a little more discussion. The excitement which had built up by 8 April 1886, when Gladstone introduced his first Home Rule Bill into the House of Commons, shines out from many of the private letters written at the time. Diplomats crowded into the galleries, and offers of £1,000 for a seat were made in vain. Gladstone needed police help to get him to Parliament through the crowds in Downing Street and Palace Yard. Conservative hostility to the Bill was not in doubt: the question was how many Liberals could be induced to oppose it as well.

Hartington was by now a key figure among the Liberal unionists, and his restiveness at Gladstone's strategy had been obvious for some time. The murder of Lord Frederick Cavendish in Phoenix Park in 1882 had deprived him of a much-loved brother and counsellor, and had also removed a link between himself and Gladstone, who was Lord Frederick's uncle by marriage. The two men drifted ever more widely apart; by October 1882 Hartington wanted to end Gladstone's communications with Parnell via O'Shea, and by December 1883 Mrs Gladstone was convinced that the assassination had 'insensibly coloured his estimate of Irish affairs.'[73] During the Home Rule crisis of 1885–6, Hartington – whose character and judgement were widely respected outside his own party – wielded immense influence in rallying the Liberal unionists, and his speech in Parliament on 9 April 1886 recommended firm government for Ireland through collaboration between both political parties. The recollection of Lord Frederick's assassination in 1882 was not confined to Hartington. When a Gladstonian Liberal candidate was bold enough to ask, at an election meeting in Bakewell later in 1886, since when had the colours of Cavendish changed from yellow to blue, a voice from the back of the hall called out 'since they were dyed in the blood of Lord Frederick Cavendish'; whereupon the audience became so excited that the candidate was thrown into the river.[74]

Rather less predictable was Joseph Chamberlain's standpoint. British radicals tended to see Irish grievances in terms of aristocratic exploitation, but this was superficial; 'no man has the right to fix the boundary of the march of a nation,' Parnell had declared at Cork in January 1885: 'no man has a right to say, "thus far shalt thou go and no further".' British radicals were excited by nationalist movements overseas but not always enthusiastic for those nearer home. Irish nationalism in the 1880s had little to do with language – in 1881 only 1.2 per cent could speak nothing but Irish, and only 17.1 per cent were bilingual[75] – but much to do with Roman Catholicism, which to British Protestants and radicals seemed superstitious and backward-looking. An English radical like Joseph Chamberlain, strongly influenced by the French left and keen to secularize education, was particularly wary of Catholic political influence in Britain; and, as has already been seen, Chamberlain disliked the tactics the nationalists had adopted. He also felt betrayed when their political opportunism caused his strenuous efforts for Irish local government reform to fail, and considered himself bound to respond to the strongly unionist feelings he could detect among his Birmingham constituents. When the moment of decision arrived, honour demanded that he sacrifice his glowing prospects of power as a leading Liberal by ensuring that enough radical votes were cast against Gladstone's Bill to ensure its defeat.

At the end of the second-reading debate on the night of 7 June, Unionist M.P.s crowded round the door of the division lobby, eagerly counting the M.P.s as they voted. When the 336th man was notched up, and it was clear that Gladstone's Bill was dead, there was a shout of triumph: the measure was thrown out by 341 votes to 311. The Cecils sat up late at Hatfield that night to await news of the division; Lord Salisbury emerged from his room with the Persian cat Bulbul on his shoulders as they gathered at the north door to hear Lord Hugh Cecil's whoops of joy when he ran up from the post office with the telegram. The result was confirmed in the ensuing general election: 317 Conservative and 77 Liberal Unionists were returned with 51 per cent of the votes cast, as against 191 Liberals and 85 Irish Nationalists with 49 per cent. If more Gladstonian candidates had stood, the Home Rule vote would have been greater; 118 Unionists were unopposed, but only 40 Liberals. Disillusion with the Unionist government soon set in, and in the late 1880s it seemed likely that the Gladstonian Liberals, improved in energy and discipline, would regain power by a large majority; but for Parnell's divorce in 1890 and the subsequent disputes among his followers, Gladstone believed that they would have done so. Nor did even this hindrance prevent the Liberals from winning the 1892 general election with 356 M.P.s and 53 per cent of the votes cast, as against 314 Unionist M.P.s with only 47 per cent.

Irish affairs retained their drama even after 1886. The next year, when Arthur Balfour went over for the first time as Secretary for Ireland, he left a pouch with his sister-in-law which presumably contained his last wishes. The Irish Secretaryship offered few attractions in the 1880s. Forster said that he would never have taken it on if he had known what it would involve; Cavendish his successor was murdered, Sir George Trevelyan's nerve was broken by it, and even Balfour felt the need for a medical examination before undertaking the job. For some years after his appointment, Balfour was followed everywhere by two detectives, and when at the family home was required to carry a revolver; he tended to forget about it, and his niece in 1939 recalled being impressed as a child with its frequent thump on the table as Balfour flung off his overcoat.[76] Balfour's resolutely Unionist policy made police precautions seem eminently necessary, and the organized withholding of rents which the 'Plan of Campaign' entailed produced considerable excitement in

Ireland. There were also memorable scenes in Parliament after 1886, when Liberals vented their indignation at the Unionist government's renewal of coercion, and expressed their delight at the vindication of Parnell against the forged allegations about his revolutionary connections published in *The Times*; Parnell's divorce provided further occasion for drama when the Irish M.P.s split on the issue.

Parliamentary 'scenes' should not, however, be seen as necessarily divisive in their overall effect. In reality, the long-term impact of the Home Rule crisis was unifying and integrating for British society at several levels. One function of the parliamentary 'scene' is to ensure that national disagreement is focused there rather than on more violent conflicts elsewhere. The adoption of Home Rule as the policy of a major British political party helped to restrain the actions not only of Parnell but also of his more enthusiastic followers, who feared discrediting by their actions an Irish parliamentary leadership which at last seemed within sight of success. The dynamiting campaign came to an end partly because Gladstone had in effect restored the two-party system,[77] in eclipse since the mid 1870s when the Irish M.P.s drifted away from their Whig-Liberal alliance. By splitting the Liberals, the Home Rule crisis at first seemed to fragment the parties still further; yet in the outcome the fierce fight over self-government tied the Irish nationalist M.P.s once more to the Liberal Party, and so disciplined them in a manner which could hardly have been anticipated a few years before.

The need to defend the Union soon caused the gulf between Liberal Unionists and Conservatives to lose significance in the light of the need to present a united governmental front nationally and a coherent electoral front locally. Besides, for many Liberal Unionists, Home Rule was a mere excuse for effecting a change of party loyalties which they had long desired for other reasons. This applies to several of the prominent intellectuals – Huxley, Tyndall, Browning, Tennyson, Lecky, Seeley, Froude, Goldwin Smith, Martineau, Jowett and Herbert Spencer – who deserted Gladstone in 1886. Experts of all kinds, and especially scientists, had for some time been growing impatient with Liberal politicians' deference to what seemed an ignorant public – for example over legislation on vivisection, vaccination and venereal disease. In his vigorous critique of democracy published in 1886, Sir Henry Maine spoke of the 'marked antagonism between democratic opinion and scientific truth as applied to human societies'.[78] Likewise Whig aristocrats had been leaving Gladstone at least since the early 1880s for reasons only partially connected with his Irish policy. In 1880

Gladstone's Irish land measures led Lord Lansdowne to resign his post in the government, and by July 1887 the Plan of Campaign had reduced the rental of his Queen's County estate from £6,000 a year to nothing.[79] In April 1881 the Duke of Argyll resigned from the Cabinet, and the Duke of Bedford ceased supporting the government in the House of Lords.

All these new recruits brought the Conservative Party an infusion of moderate conservatism which made it easier for the leadership to resist pressures from its right; at the same time, Gladstone's Home Rule alliance made it possible for him and Parnell to restrain extremism among the Irish nationalists. Lord Salisbury might see the country in 1889 as 'in a state of bloodless civil war', with 'no common principles, no respect for common institutions or traditions' to bring together the competing groups of politicians,[80] but societies can occasionally be united by their internal conflicts, and fierce parliamentary battles can sometimes prevent even fiercer ones elsewhere. Henceforward a Prime Minister could no longer hope to reconcile his roles as party leader and head of the executive by appealing for Opposition help against his own rebels; party discipline tightened, and backbenchers lost influence and independence. Even in 1882 Private Willis in *Iolanthe* had sung of M.P.s being obliged to abandon intelligence in the division lobby 'and vote just as their leaders tell 'em to'; the Home Rule crisis carried this tendency much further.

The crisis exerted an integrating influence at another level, too, by ensuring that henceforward the Liberal Party would be better suited in the long term for meeting the demands of organized labour, and would thus encourage the socialists to follow the Irish nationalists in taking a parliamentary rather than a revolutionary direction. This change was effected in two ways: through the departure of the Whigs, and through the removal of religion as a major divisive issue between the political parties. 'As a general rule,' Gladstone announced in June 1886, 'it cannot be pretended that we are supported by the dukes, or by the

squires, or by the established clergy, or by the officers of the Army, or by any other body of very respectable persons.' Henry Broadhurst, a keen Home Ruler, recalled seeing the great London mansions 'continuously ablaze with brilliant entertainments designed to attract the rank and file of the party' to the other side.[81] At the same time as the Liberal Party lost so many of its Whigs, Home Rule caused Spurgeon, Dale, Bright, Chamberlain and Allon – all prominent Nonconformists – also to desert. Henry Broadhurst could hardly believe his eyes during the 1886 general election when he saw public-house windows decorated with Unionist appeals from Bright and Spurgeon: 'the world seemed to have turned upside down.'[82] From now on, imperialism and social reform would become the major issues between the parties; individual Nonconformists and Anglicans would enjoy greater freedom to choose whichever party they preferred.

The working classes were not of course unanimous for Gladstone in 1886. Anti-Irish and Birmingham working men, for example, huddled under Chamberlain's Radical Unionist umbrella alongside old Chartists like G.J. Harney and Thomas Cooper, and socialists regarded the Liberals' preoccupation with Irish nationalism as a diversion from the major issue. But the Home Rule crisis made it easier for the Liberals to take on a radical flavour. The aristocracy was no longer in a position to dominate every government whichever party was in power, and middle and working classes could collaborate within the Liberal Party to assault them. Gladstone needed working men as allies in his Home Rule crusade, and was beginning to lose his faith in the political instincts and popular sympathies of the British upper class. He did not welcome the aristocratic secession from his Party, but notes written the year before he died indicate that he had no serious regrets about 1886; in the light of subsequent developments neither, perhaps, have we. 'I am much more disposed to be thankful', he wrote, 'for what we then and afterwards accomplished than to murmur or to wonder at what we did not.'[83]

8.2. *The telephone ceases to be merely a novelty: the first multiple telephone switchboard at Glasgow Central Old Exchange. Undated*

8.3.4. *Post Office experiment and innovation. Horse-drawn parcel post van and twin-cycle-driven parcel post carrier* (ABOVE). *1887. The centre cycle* (BELOW) *was familiarly known as the 'hen and chickens'. Two here have front and rear panniers for parcels. 1882*

8.5 (ABOVE). *The railway age. The new Tunbridge Wells Central Station (South Eastern Railway). 1880*

8.6 (BELOW). *City streets were congested, noisy, smelly and dangerous. Oxford Circus, Ernest Milton (published by Frith & Co.), 1888*

8.7–9. Limitations on the free movement of traffic were being lifted. The East Ferry Road, North Woolwich (ABOVE LEFT), was freed from tolls as London's first municipal free ferry came into service, W. Bartier, 1889. The last Putney Bridge toll was collected in 1888 (BELOW LEFT). Horse-drawn trams penetrated the centre of cities which had successfully resisted the railways. High Street, Oxford (BELOW), Henry Taunt, undated

8.10–13. *The ever-spreading railways. Making a cutting on the Whitby-Scarborough line (North Eastern Railway) (*ABOVE*), Frank Meadow Sutcliffe, 1885. Parsons Green Station (District Railway) (*LEFT*). Beyond the bridge, the Stukeley Park Estate offers houses to let at £35–70 per annum. 1890. Chesham Station (Metropolitan Railway) (*ABOVE RIGHT*) in the year the line reached it from Rickmansworth. 1889. About to board the 12.55 workmen's train from Liverpool Street to Enfield Town (Great Eastern Railway) (*BELOW RIGHT*). 1884*

8.14.   From his election train (here halted at Warrington, Lancashire), Mr Gladstone looked out on a land of great contrasts, J. Birtles, 1885

8.15. *For northern industrial townships, civic pride required ambitious and lofty municipal buildings. Bradford Town Hall. 1891*

8.16. *The Fermanagh smithy of Robert O'Donnell, one of thousands of Irishmen forcibly evicted from their homes, Robert Banks, 1889*

Chapter 9 *Social Tensions*

Regional and national, or 'vertical', antagonisms were accompanied in the 1880s by 'horizontal' antagonisms of class. The industrialization process was itself revolutionary enough, with its constant supersession of skills and attitudes. The compilers of the 1881 census had to revise the old list of occupations completely: 'a great many terms that occurred in it', they wrote, 'had ceased any longer to be used, and, what was of more importance, several thousands that are now used had no place in it at all.' Population growth was also revolutionary in its impact, not least on education; in the United Kingdom it went up by 10.8 per cent between 1871 and 1881, and by 8.2 per cent between 1881 and 1891.[1] But it was the revolutionary ideas of individuals which impressed people in the 1880s.

Assassination as a political strategy seemed to be spreading, among the Irish at home and among anarchists abroad; William Morris was furious at the Liberal government's prosecution in summer 1881 of Johann Most, the German anarchist editor of the London paper *Freiheit*, for publishing an article in praise of the assassins of Tsar Alexander II. By 1883 the Home Secretary Sir William Harcourt was preoccupied with his police responsibilities almost to the exclusion of everything else. Most alarming of all were the economic and class questions raised by the labour move-

ment. It was not at all clear that these would eventually cut across and neutralize the contemporary battles between Christians and secularists, Nonconformists and Anglicans, English and non-English: on the contrary, subversion seemed everywhere in league. Would trade union respectability persist into an age of mass recruitment? Would this new class movement continue to work through Parliament? And through a classless Liberal Party?

For some time about 48 per cent of the national revenue had been assigned to wages and salaries, 14 per cent to rents, and the rest to profits, interest and mixed incomes; though this proportion remained stable until the First World War, it was being challenged from the 1880s. The spread of the limited liability company and (in Ireland) of absentee landlordism undermined the direct relationship between property-owner and employee or tenant at the same time as trading conditions forced the employer to reduce costs. Employers began organizing themselves, most noisily perhaps in the Liberty and Property Defence League, founded in 1882; it had 37 federated trade groups in that year, 214 in 1900. The affinity that emerged in the late 1880s between Tory gold and the distaste of some working men for the new unionism resulted in the formation of strike-breaking organizations, and culminated in the launching of the National Free Labour Association in 1893; between 1889 and 1893, 15 per cent of industrial disputes were settled by importing blackleg labour.[2]

9.1. The carnival atmosphere of many of the demonstrations and parades in the National Dock Strike was encouraged by the fine sunny weather of 1889

The employees too began organizing themselves in sheer self-defence, urged onwards by the increased integration of the economy. During the 1870s nine-year fluctuations in the trade cycle were becoming dominant, producing at the downswing an increase in what we now call 'unemployment'. The first use of 'unemployed' as a noun occurred in 1882, and Marshall introduced the term 'unemployment' into the study of economics in 1888. Neither government nor voters yet thought it feasible to manage the economy so as to flatten out the trade cycle; public order was the main preoccupation. Riots in Trafalgar Square and the West End early in 1886 and on 13 November 1887 alarmed the authorities. 'After such a breakdown of police administration,' wrote Octavia Hill in January 1886, 'one feels as if one *might* meet violence *any* where.' The Queen's correspondence in February 1886 positively bristles with '*indignation* at the monstrous riot' which Gladstone thought had 'stained the reputation of this country in the eyes of the civilised world'. When inquiry was made of 29,451 London working men on 19 March 1887, 27 per cent claimed to be unemployed on that day, and 30 per cent to have been out of work for more than twelve weeks out of the previous twenty.[3] Fortunately for the authorities, seasonal and cyclical unemployment seldom coincided, nor were the Irish and British economies pulsating in unison, so that unrest did not simultaneously present itself on both fronts.

Central in promoting the Trafalgar Square meetings was the Social Democratic Federation (S.D.F.), a pioneer socialist organization deeply influenced by Marx. Its founder H.M. Hyndman used Marxian concepts (without acknowledgement) in his *England for All* (1881), and extracts from *Capital* were translated in several socialist periodicals after 1883. Volume One of Marx's famous work first became available in English in 1887, and the first authorized English edition of *The Communist Manifesto* in 1888, but many of the key writings of Marx and Engels were not available till the 1890s or later. The S.D.F. is important for pioneering ideas which later resurfaced in organizations whose aims were quite different, and for influencing members who later moved on elsewhere, including three of the four founders of the Independent Labour Party (ancestor of the modern Labour Party) in 1893. Moreover the middle-class promoters of socialist gradualism in the Fabian Society sharpened their teeth on many S.D.F. attitudes. When William Morris left the Federation and formed the Socialist League in 1884, he did not abandon the pursuit of revolution: his aim was simply to prepare the masses the more effectively for it when it

9.12

came. The S.D.F. brought together European refugee socialists and English working men, and encouraged radicals to reject Whig-Liberalism as a satisfactory philosophy for the British left. And whereas in periods of unemployment the trade unions lost adherents, the S.D.F. (whose strategy was at this time purely political) gained them. From the mid 1880s the Federation's membership was rising; in 1889 it reached 1,926, its highest in the decade.[4]

What drove well educated and relatively wealthy men such as Morris on to socialist platforms at that period? What led Morris to read Marx's *Capital* twice, in 1883 and 1887, and to make careful notes upon it? His own explanation underlines the British labour movement's strongly ethical and aesthetic appeal at this time. 'With all the aids to a pleasant life around me which mere chance as it seems has given me,' he wrote, he nonetheless heard 'brutal and drunken voices, murdering with obscene language and coarse tones the pleasure of the fair spring Sunday.' Happy in his work as artist, writer and designer, Morris felt ashamed at his privilege. Furthermore he had been active since 1876 in resisting the current widespread and drastic 'restoration' of medieval buildings; experience in his 'anti-scrape' society nourished his increasing recognition of the philistinism of commerce and its lack of any public conscience. It was futile, wrote Bernard Shaw in *Fabian Essays*, for the well-to-do to think that they could escape to pleasant middle-class suburbs from the unsightly sources of their wealth. 'Your slaves ... breed like rabbits; and their poverty breeds filth, ugliness, dishonesty, disease, obscenity, drunkenness, and murder. In the midst of the riches which their labor piles up for you, their misery rises up too and stifles you. You withdraw in disgust to the other end of the town from them ... and yet they swarm about you still.'[5]

The doctor's loathing of disease, the temperance reformer's hatred of drunkenness, the desire of the public official and the scientist for an orderly and less wasteful society, the Christian's anguish at the loss of faith, the yearning of the middle-class eccentric and deviant for friendship with members of another class all ensured widespread middle-class sympathy for labour's aspirations. While socialist historians revealed the sufferings of working people in the past, socialist propagandists enlarged upon the future potential of industry. 'Machinery has before it possibilities almost undreamed of now' wrote Mrs Besant, the secularist, Fabian, feminist and future theosophist, in *Fabian Essays*. Like Morris, she believed that in the socialist society unpleasant inessential work would cease, while disagreeable essential work would be done by machinery: inventions would supersede the miner just as they had earlier superseded the climbing boy. Such pious hopes were reinforced by religious techniques of propaganda; for although many pioneer socialists had abandoned any formal Christian commitment, they retained its rhetoric, its appeal to the individual conscience and its readiness for self-dedication, self-sacrifice and even martyrdom. They look far from 9.12 revolutionary in photographs; in an earlier age they might have been evangelical missionaries, slum parsons or crusaders against the slave trade.

Only because the time was ripe did they gain their place in history. Their demand for increased state intervention was credible because factory inspectors had already demonstrated that it could enforce humane standards at the work-place. *Fabian Essays* argued that socialism was arriving unconsciously, almost unintentionally, and unannounced by the politician. Day-to-day administrative and legislative decisions – in Irish land laws, employers' liability and public health, for example – unobtrusively advanced the role of the state whichever party was in power. State management of industry seemed feasible now that Victorians far from socialist had eliminated corruption and created an efficient government machine, and now that limited liability was placing the manager at the centre of the stage, under supervision from a collectivity of shareholders. Bernard Shaw raised a laugh at the Industrial Remuneration Conference of 1885 when he likened the capitalist and landlord to the burglar;[6] all three, he said, ate up the profits of industry but did no work. Yet in the earlier stages of industrialism, when the capitalist was his own entrepreneur, Shaw's remark would have seemed merely absurd.

Economic orthodoxies were threatened. They had never been accepted by mid-Victorian trade unions, many of whose members from 1867 had the vote; as Bertrand Russell later wrote, 'every extension of the franchise has been followed (at a respectful distance) by a modification of the orthodox economics.' Economists dissatisfied with merely justifying the status quo were encouraged in the 1880s by many writers and intellectuals. A.R. Wallace, Herbert Spencer, Charles Darwin, John Morley, Arnold Toynbee and Joseph Chamberlain were among the distinguished men who read or recommended Henry George's *Progress and Poverty*; by 1885 it had sold over 60,000 copies in England, and its author made successful lecture-tours of Britain in 1881, 1884 and 1889.[7] His preoccupation with the land question immediately attracted British radicals because his notion of the 'unearned increment' reinforced their critique of the prevailing distribution of wealth. British socialism could also profit from Darwin's ideas on 'the survival of the fittest'; they could of course be pressed into service to support unrestricted industrial competition, but Fabians and others could also use them to justify a state intervention designed to promote the health and resources of populations locked in international rivalry.

Socialism's indirect influence was considerable. By January 1883 the radical Joseph Chamberlain, always alert to new intellectual trends, was asserting that 'the politics of the future are social politics'; a month later he told John Morley that he wanted for the nation social reforms like those he had won for Birmingham as mayor.[8] His ideas were marshalled in his so-called 'unauthorized programme' of 1885, whose introduction predicted increased state intervention 'on behalf of the weak against the strong, in the interests of labour against capital, of want and suffering against luxury and ease.' Shivers went down aristocratic spines at his rhetorical question in a speech at Birmingham in January of that year: 'I ask what ransom will property pay for the security which it enjoys?' Property had its obligations, he insisted, as well as its rights. His words carried the more weight because of the rising influence among Conservatives of the young Lord Randolph Churchill, who told a Birmingham supporter in 1884 that 'the good of the State ... stands far above freedom of contract'; his social policy consisted largely in stealing radical clothes, and his Toryism did not prevent him from maintaining close relations with leading radicals for most of the decade.[9]

The camera was hardly in a position to illuminate the steady advance of the state, but it could document the growth of trade unionism. The 672 women matchworkers of Messrs Bryant and May struck successfully 9.2 in 1888, with the backing of intellectuals and socialists; they were organized by Annie Besant, who edited the weekly socialist paper *The Link* jointly with Herbert Burrows. It was Burrows whose lecture in 1889 inspired *The Red Flag*: 'he spoke ... as if he wished to convey that Socialism was his religion,' wrote its author Jim Connell; 'this inspired me to write something in the train.' Middle-class socialist leadership was invaluable to working people in the 1880s, but the role was sometimes embarrassing; William Morris, for instance, worried about the 'great drawback that I can't talk to them roughly and unaffectedly.'[10]

Between 1888 and 1892 trade union membership rose from less than a tenth to about a fifth of the adult male working class.[11] In 1889 the gasworkers, organized by the half-literate Will Thorne from East Ham, with help from Marx's daughter Eleanor, recruited

20,000 members in four months and struck successfully for reduced working hours. A little later came the
most dramatic event of the year: the dock strike, whose
9.1 carnival atmosphere was encouraged by the fine
summer weather. With the aid of £30,000 sent by
Australian trade unionists, the dockers were out for a
month. Effectively distributing strike pay, they gained
their demand for 6d. an hour through the mediation of
Sydney Buxton and Cardinal Manning. It was a landmark for integrating Roman Catholics into English
public life and a notable triumph for the widening
recruitment of the trade unions. These events were of
course variously interpreted at the time; in the long
term they mark an important stage in the political
incorporation of the labourer, but Engels differed in his
perspective. His enthusiasm was stirred by May Day in
the following year: 'on May 4th, 1890, the *English
proletariat*, newly awakened from its forty years' winter
sleep, *again entered the movement of its class ...*' he
wrote: 'the grandchildren of the old Chartists are entering the line of battle.'[12]

These events profoundly influenced the socialists.
Trade unions had hitherto seemed so irredeemably respectable and Liberal that English Marxists diverged
from their master in pursuing a purely political and
somewhat sectarian strategy. An early English
introduction to socialist theory, J.L. Joynes's *Socialist
Catechism* (1885), does not even mention trade unions,
and in later life Fabians were surprised to discover their
neglect of them in *Fabian Essays* published four years
later. Because by European standards trade unionism
arrived so early in Britain and Marxism so late, only in
the late 1880s did an alliance between intellectuals
and trade unionists reveal itself as a viable route to the
socialist society.

In the trade union movement, the T.U.C. secretary
and Liberal M.P. Henry Broadhurst was coming under
attack; as his autobiography recalls, 'my simplest
words and actions were misconstrued and placed in a
false light.'[13] Keir Hardie's assault at the 1889 Dundee
congress was the final straw; Broadhurst triumphed on
that occasion, but retired in the following year. The
strikes of the late 1880s impressed the 25,000 members of London's two hundred radical working men's
clubs; controlling at least a fifth of the Liberal votes in
London, they offered fertile ground for socialist
propaganda.[14] Many felt that political structures were
not adapting fast enough to major economic and
intellectual changes. Property was still heavily over-
represented; although the number of electors per parliamentary seat nearly doubled between 1880 and
1892 (from 4,617 to 9,185), only two adult males in

three immediately after 1884 could vote in England
and Wales, three out of five in Scotland, and fewer still
in Ireland.[15] Rich property-owners often qualified for
votes in more than one constituency, while the vote
was denied altogether to recipients of poor relief, to
people who frequently moved house (as many working
people then did), and to most lodgers and domestic
servants living with their employers. 'Even now the
citizen is tricked out of his vote by every possible legal
and administrative technicality,' wrote Sidney Webb,
'so that more than one-third of our adult men are
unenfranchised.'[16]

The religious, diplomatic and constitutional issues
that dominated politics were of diminishing interest to
working people, who had difficulty in entering Parliament in the years before M.P.s were paid. A regular
salary was first given to an M.P. only in 1886, so the
whole political system could be represented as rigged
against the people. Socialists could also have noted that
whereas 41 per cent of Conservatives elected in 1885
were landholders, so were 28 per cent of Liberals: that
while 37 per cent of Conservative M.P.s had financial
interests, 32 per cent of Liberals had them too: and that
whereas 16 per cent of Conservative M.P.s were
lawyers, so also were 17 per cent of the Liberals.[17] At
least three prominent politicians of the period – Harcourt, Campbell-Bannerman and Edward Stanhope –
had brothers on the opposite side of the House. The
early socialists made some impact with their claim that,
for working people, there was little to choose between
the parties.

It would be wrong to regard the pioneer socialists of
the 1880s simply as ancestors of the modern Labour
Party in their ideas, for they were very varied in their
views of the world, and had not as yet been much
influenced in their political outlook by the need to win
an electoral majority, and still less by the need to
operate as an elected government. Their courage, good
intentions, imaginativeness, humane objectives, and at
times their sheer commonsense are not now in doubt;
but these qualities were overshadowed in the eyes of
many contemporaries by ideas and connections that
would seem revolutionary and eccentric in the Labour
Party today. This can perhaps best be appreciated by
glancing at the programme of the Social Democratic
Federation when it broke with the radical movement at
its annual conference in 1884.

The S.D.F.'s commitment to universal suffrage now
seems obvious for a democratic grouping, but it no
doubt appeared revolutionary at a time when women
were completely excluded from the national franchise,
and when even the feminists were advocating women's

suffrage only on a restricted property basis; nor has the S.D.F.'s aim of social and economic equality between the sexes been realized even yet. As for the idea of 'direct legislation by the people' and of giving the people the right to decide on peace or war – such notions cried out for more detail about institutional structures and for a clearer definition of terms. The very language of the Federation's commitment to 'the Socialization of the Means of Production, Distribution and Exchange to be controlled by a Democratic State in the interests of the entire community' must at the time have seemed obscure and unfamiliar.[18]

9.12   The S.D.F.'s offshoot, the Socialist League, no doubt appeared at least as subversive when it issued its manifesto in 1885, for it repudiated the commitment to the nation-state which was taken for granted at the time, declaring that 'for us there are no nations, but only varied masses of workers and friends, whose mutual sympathies are checked or perverted by groups of masters and fleecers.' The manifesto ventured on to still more dangerous territory when it mounted a full-scale attack on the family; in the socialist society, 'our modern bourgeois property-marriage', with its inevitable accompaniment of prostitution, would 'give place to kindly and human relations between the sexes.' This looks harmless enough by the standards of the day until it is made clear in a note that this means making the marriage-tie voluntary, so that women will 'share in the certainty of livelihood which would be the lot of all.'[19]

Outsiders' attitudes in the 1880s therefore owed much to the fact that the socialists of the day included relatively vociferous critics of family and religion, relatively prominent enthusiasts for class conflict, and relatively numerous sympathizers with anarchism, pacifism, feminism and vegetarianism. Dr Barnardo in his fund-raising appeals of the time spoke ominously of the need to counter 'the rapid spread of principles that would subvert orderly Government and banish the Bible from the world.' Only later was socialism securely annexed to the austere constitutionalism and Christian high-mindedness of Clement Attlee's Labour Party. Nor was socialism then necessarily seen as entrusting increased power to a bureaucratic state. Its pioneers included many who aimed at simplifying life and at applying their beliefs in their day-to-day conduct; they wanted to form small communes which would enable the state to wither away. William Morris, for example, thought it 'the business of Socialism to destroy the State and put Free Society in its place.'[20] Its early adherents therefore found themselves a persecuted and isolated group; they had to band together to uphold the right of public meeting and to protect their members from family ostracism, physical violence and even the sack. In these circumstances, socialism often of necessity became a way of life, an allegiance which profoundly affected personal relationships, daily conduct, and the routines of community life. But to outsiders it seemed a very dangerous thing.

There is always a danger when writing about a society that the stridency of discontent and rebellion will assign them a more prominent role than their contemporary importance warrants. To counteract this danger, the discussion will now turn to the stabilizing factors in the Britain of the 1880s. Numerous, and operating at several levels, they include Britain's overall geographical situation, which reduced the involvement of foreign powers in her domestic disputes; her rate of economic growth in the 1880s, which (as has already been shown) allowed substantial increases in the real income of the workforce; and her colonial connections (to be discussed later), which provided a salutary outlet for the dissident, the deprived, the ambitious and the adventurous. But it is more helpful at this stage to focus on four factors whose promotion of social and political stability was more overt and direct. The rest of this chapter and the next three will therefore concentrate on the existence in Britain of well-developed non-violent reformist traditions and structures; the influence wielded by an experienced, shrewd and popular aristocracy; the resources at the disposal of government if it needed to get its way by force; and its ceremonial and other trappings, which either concealed those resources or made it rarely necessary to use them. It will then be possible to conclude with the final themes of illness, old age and death.

If the fragmenting forces involving region and social class were important in the 1880s, as events turned out, national unity, social stability and institutional continuity were nonetheless upheld – largely, of course, because the fragmenting influences to some extent cut across one another. But the focus will now be directed elsewhere, on the opportunity extended by the political system in the 1880s to those who desired reform. There are three themes. The first is the existence at every social level in Britain of well-developed reformist traditions; this is reinforced by two structural factors – the pluralism of a decentralized government and the broad participation which stemmed from a system of competing political parties.

The more closely British society in the nineteenth century is studied, the more important in moulding its conscious and instinctive responses to the threat of social and political disruption is its experience of revolution two centuries before – an experience reinforced by observation of France between 1789 and 1792, and the dramatic sequence of events in Britain during the reform crisis of 1831–2 and the Corn Law crisis of 1845–6. Indeed, the seventeenth century has an intimate bearing on all three of the themes mentioned above.

Let us take the British reformist tradition. It was to the seventeenth century that the British Whig aristocracy looked back for its ancestry; it was from nonconformity that the British middle class derived so much of its pragmatic outlook, its social conscience, and its sense of stewardship for wealth; and it was to puritanism that the nineteenth-century leaders of the organized British working class owed so much of their influence and stature. The importance of the Whig aristocratic tradition within the party has already emerged from analysing the Liberals' handling of the Irish issue between 1880 and 1886, though attention will again turn to the political skills of the British aristocracy in the next chapter. For the present it is worth dwelling further on reformist traditions within the middle and working classes, if only because it was from these groupings that the British socialists had their best hope of recruits.

Nonconformity helped to stabilize British society in the 1880s at a number of levels. It enabled those denied full social recognition to acquire status through becoming active in the business and religious activity associated with chapel life; many nonconformists saw the chapel's hierarchy of offices and functions as a *cursus honorum* far more significant than the array of laurels and glamorous posts which public life could offer. This political quietism differed little, in its impact on social stability, from the conservatism which by the 1880s was increasingly attracting nonconformists of the politically active type. Where the latter did not opt for conservatism, however, their distance from the political elite encouraged a radicalism which profoundly affected the mood and methods of the British left, whether Liberal or Labour. It is the nonconformist connection which largely explains the compatibility of British radicalism with religious belief, and its espousal of a peaceable and gradualist route to social reform; violent revolution was difficult to reconcile with Christian and humanitarian traditions, and the notion of irreconcilable conflict jarred awkwardly with the nonconformist belief in personal responsibility and human self-determination.

W.T. Stead's judgement of the Labour M.P.s in 1906 could be accurately applied to the labour leaders of the 1880s: 'what culture they have, they obtained from the chapel, from that popular university the public library, or still more frequently from the small collection of books found in the homes of the poor.'[21] Keir Hardie, for instance, relinquished his atheism in 1879 and joined the Evangelical Union; and at the same time the sixteen-year-old Arthur Henderson was converted by the evangelist Gipsy Smith. Futhermore nonconformity profoundly affected British trade unionism – one reason why British socialists of the 1880s at first found it such uncongenial territory.

Trade union strength in 1889 should not be exaggerated: the 235 unions submitting returns had only 679,283 members, averaging at 2,891 each. Size varied from the Amalgamated Society of Engineers (60,728), the National Amalgamated Sailors' and Firemen's Union (60,525) and the huge Miners' Associations of Durham (46,000) and West Yorkshire (35,000) to the tiny Organ Builders Amalgamated Trade Society with only nine members.[22] The trade union movement – then as now – was a ramshackle coalition, inexperienced at common action, pragmatic in its approach to industrial disputes and often internally contradictory in its politics, but it could at times seem deceptively subversive.

At the Industrial Remuneration Conference at the Prince's Hall in January 1885 the chairman more than once had to fend off confrontation between capitalist and anti-capitalist. The middle-class positivist Frederic Harrison pointed out that poverty could be cured only through bringing moral influences to bear on the employers: 'as well try to moralize the lion, the boa constrictor . . .' retorted John Burns the docker.[23] Yet the mere fact that the conference could be conceived in that form and successfully held was significant, as was its impact on the chairman, Sir Charles Dilke. He had been giving an annual lunch to the parliamentary committee of the T.U.C. at the opening of Parliament since 1880, and acted as their diligent spokesman in the House for many years afterwards. This did not prevent him from encouraging the direct representation of working men in Parliament and (by offering administrative posts to trade union leaders) in government too.

The close liaison between trade unionists and M.P.s of both political parties encouraged a style of labour leadership praised by the Royal Commission on the Depression of Trade and Industry in 1886 as 'conducted with constantly increasing judgement and moderation'.[24] The Commissioners dismissed any notion that Britain's industrial difficulties were caused by strikes and factory legislation. Given this background, it is hardly surprising that Marx's British reviewers after 1887 felt no need to grapple with the subtleties of his argument: it was sufficient for them merely to assert the identity of interest between capital and labour and to rule Marx, at least in the British context, completely out of court.

What of the reformism of the middle class? Here again, nonconformist traditions and seventeenth-century memories were profoundly influential; here again pragmatism and a distaste for revolutionary change moulded political conduct. In his *Communist Manifesto*, Marx predicted that as capitalism matures 'a portion of the bourgeoisie goes over to the proletariat, and in particular, a portion of the bourgeois ideologists, who have raised themselves to the level of comprehending theoretically the historical movement as a whole.' In Britain the sequence was rather different: many of those intellectuals who supported working-class movements did so only with the aim of staving off a Marxian class alignment. Britain's middle-class intellectuals were well integrated into British institutions, and strongly reformist in mood. Their evangelical outlook made them conscious of their privileges: their pragmatism directed their consciences towards social investigation. For Engels in 1892, these middle-class socialists were 'the worst enemies of the workers – wolves in sheep's clothing', but this was not how it seemed to the East End match-girls in 1888.[25]

Significant middle-class responses can best be studied through looking more closely at two middle-class individuals and a middle-class group: at Charles Booth, Beatrice Webb, and the Fabian Society. Socialism never claimed Charles Booth, and only later did it claim Beatrice Webb; yet both in the 1880s were unconsciously preparing the way for its relatively classless twentieth-century British variant. Beatrice later came to see Booth as 'within my circle of friends, perhaps the most perfect embodiment of ... the mid-Victorian time-spirit – the union of faith in the scientific method with the transference of the emotion of self-sacrificing service from God to man.'[26] His achievement rested on years of that altruistic involvement in social problems which religious anguish so often produced in his class. A ferment of religious doubt in the 1870s had launched this young Unitarian Liverpool shipowner on his career as a social investigator; by 1888 his great survey was well under way, and he had become influential in statistical and governmental circles.

For three separate periods Booth observed working people at close quarters *incognito* as a lodger, and his wife writes of his 'set of intelligent and enlightened unwashed friends who discussed positivism and social dynamics in the dining-room.'[27] Such tastes could hardly have been predicted for a man of his wealth and occupation; yet by reducing his eating and sleeping time, and by standing up at his high office desk eating a piece of fruit at lunch time, he scraped together enough time to complete his massive survey of the poor in London, published in seventeen volumes from 1889 onwards. Systematic social research at this time was hindered by a shortage of trained investigators, by ignorance of statistical technique, by widespread working-class suspicion of inquiry in any form and by governmental ignorance of even basic information about working-class life. Booth was a Conservative; he aimed to break up the unhelpful general category 'poverty' so that its particular causes could be tackled piecemeal; individualism would then be free to operate elsewhere. To some extent he achieved the reverse of his objective. He focused public attention on poverty and pioneered its precise measurement, only to find the problem larger than he had expected; and he trained up statisticians and investigators, often only to find them later participating in the extension of state welfare schemes.

Beatrice Webb's social inquiries also at first owed much to a religious and philanthropic distaste for socialism: she was brought up in the Unitarian household of the businessman Richard Potter, moved as a young woman in the world of Herbert Spencer, and learned much from the Charity Organisation Society's case-work. She closely observed cotton workers at Bacup in 1883, while staying *incognito* with relatives. But she gradually repudiated philanthropy's excessive empiricism and individualism, and began seeking structural remedies for social problems which she eventually came to understand in a more abstract way. From her complex of domestic duties, social engagements, self-doubt and self-scrutiny there gradually emerged a trained investigator with what she called 'the consciousness of a special mission to society at large, rather than to individuals.' She rejected the lavish and leisured social round for textbooks on economics and for tours of the East End assisting Booth's survey. 'I love my work,' she wrote in her diary in August 1889; 'that is my salvation; I delight in this slow stepping towards truth. Search after truth by the careful measurement of facts is the enthusiasm of my life.'[28] She was being unconsciously prepared for her first contact, in January 1890, with the Fabian Society which enabled her to achieve so much in later years.

Fabians before 1914 were never exclusively tied to trade unions and the Labour Party, but sought support for their ideas wherever it could be found. Fabianism originated in 1884 through a secession from the Fellowship of the New Life, an organization which aimed at changing society through perfecting individual character in a type of commune. The seceders wanted more social investigation and greater contact with the working class. The Trafalgar Square riots of 1886 reinforced their search for gradualist approaches to socialism through empirical research and the permeation of existing parties and institutions. Socialism would emerge, they said, not from the class struggle, but from piecemeal legislation by aristocratic and bourgeois governments. This implied little more than collectivism, or the explicit repudiation of *laissez-faire*; but Fabian aims were so timely and their methods so effective that their achievement was considerable.

Recruited primarily from the salaried grades – from clerks, writers, architects, emancipated women, teachers, artists, professional men, civil servants – they had little to lose by extended state control. Yet they fitted so awkwardly into the existing class structure that their socialism can, in a very general sense, be seen as a form of self-interest – though few enough in the 1880s were prepared to invest in social reform the energy, time, resources and devotion lavished on it by the Fabians. The abundance of domestic servants, the shortage of careers for middle-class women and the relatively unpressured life of the middle-class administrator gave the Fabians their freedom to write, lecture, and sit on committees. They did not seek a mass following; like Marx himself, they believed in '*working behind the scenes while not appearing in public*', and despised '*being self-important in public while doing nothing.*'[29] They recognized the inevitably slow impact of legislative change, and did not underestimate the patience and skill which its enactment requires, but their youthfulness, their mutual friendship, their unsectarian political methods and their ability sometimes to laugh at themselves gave them an unusual combination of reforming drive and political shrewdness.

The success of their *Fabian Essays* was remarkable. The Society at this time numbered only about 150 members and the volume was published at a private house and not advertised in the press, yet it went through its first two editions (2,000 copies in all) in a matter of months, and by autumn 1891 had sold another 25,000.[30] In several respects, *Fabian Essays* resembles a book which emerged in the same year from a very different quarter – *Lux Mundi*. Both reflected the shared outlook of a group of friends: both responded constructively to new ideas in economics, biology and social science, and sought to win recruits for them by emphasizing their harmlessness: both reflect in their outlook and influence the flexibility and reformism of British institutions. The Fabians exploited channels of influence which had been opened up earlier – the platform, the press, the pressure group – and resembled those middle-class reformers who had achieved so much in previous decades, the Utilitarians. To quote the Fabians' historian Edward Pease, 'we did what all active politicians in a democratic country must do; we decided what the people ought to want, and endeavoured to do two things, which after all are much the same thing, to make the people want it, and to make it appear that they wanted it.'[31]

By seeking recruits among the trade unions and the middle class, socialism in the 1880s was therefore opening itself up to strongly reformist influences. But reformism was also encouraged by the pluralism associated with a decentralized governmental machine, and – among the discontented – by the concessionary response which had by now become almost instinctive among most British political leaders, as well as by a structure of governmental power which had been fragmented by the defeat of Charles I and James II in the seventeenth century. A suspicion of London was nourished by the aristocrats and gentry residing on their provincial estates, while nonconformists narrowly eyed the established church, whose infringements of liberty had oppressed their ancestors. Decentralization, Protestantism and British liberties seemed to run together, and when given their opportunity after the 1830s, nonconformists were prominent in developing the machinery of municipal self-government, especially in the manufacturing towns. So effective was the structure they erected in their localities, especially when managed by the Unitarian Joseph Chamberlain at Birmingham, that the Fabians in the 1880s urged working men to exploit the numerous opportunities that local government offered them. 'The real battles of Socialism', wrote Pease later, are not won through revolutionary action and rhetoric but 'are fought in committee rooms at Westminster and in the council chambers of Town Halls.'[32] Such activities seldom lend themselves to drama, nor can the camera illustrate the moral courage, persistence and grasp of detail they require, but if the mood of Britain in the 1880s is to be recaptured, local government must receive its due.

Centralization of prisons, police and poor law was beginning to erode local discretion just as the redistribution of parliamentary seats in 1884–5 weakened the rural community from another direction by basing the allocation of seats on population, but this trend had not yet gone very far. A grumbling Tory suspicion of cosmopolitan London could still combine, in the 1880s, with a radical and nonconformist assault on a metropolitan and corrupt aristocratic and Anglican exploitation to build up pressure for the extension of self-government beyond the towns (where it had flourished at least since the 1830s) into the countryside.

A belief in the stabilizing effects of local self-government was privately expressed by a wide range of political leaders in the 1880s. It lay at the root of Gladstone's scheme for Irish Home Rule, and inspired Joseph Chamberlain's less ambitious project of 1884–5 for Irish local government reform. As Chamberlain later recalled, 'I believed then, as I do now, that the adoption of a large yet safe proposal for the extension of local government would have cut the ground from under the feet of the agitators for independence.' Cardinal Manning, Lord Salisbury and Beatrice Webb envisaged local government performing a similar role in relation to the aspirations of the British working class. Cardinal Manning in 1882 supported a local ratepayer veto on the sale of intoxicating drinks partly, he said, because it would build up a provincial self-reliance which could neutralize London's revolutionary tendencies. 'We live in an age when the world is full of wild teachers,' Salisbury declared at Edinburgh in the same year, 'and our only security that the calm common-sense view of extravagant theories shall be taken is that the people shall be practised in their daily life in the government of their fellow-men.'[33]

In a regionally variegated and still markedly agricultural society, it was often only the local authority which possessed the intimate knowledge necessary for implementing general enactments in detail, and only they who could win the co-operation of the ratepayers. The sheer vitality of community life in the 1880s needs to be stressed; between 1870 and 1914 local government revenue from rates grew faster than national government revenue from taxes, and local government was able to draw on the services of distinguished citizens.[34] Joseph Chamberlain's successes at Birmingham rested on nonconformist reforming idealism and on the incursion of big businessmen into the city council; they alone could provide the necessary entrepreneurship and skill in financial management and in negotiation with property-owners. Any approach towards public welfare at this time took place at the local level, and not through any centralized 'welfare state'.

From 1880, municipal authorities were enabled to float consolidated municipal stock. By 1884, twenty seven towns had secured such powers, and within thirty years the local government debt in the United Kingdom had risen to £600,000,000 – almost as large as the national debt. In the five years from 1885 to 1889, central government spent £444,000,000, whereas the United Kingdom local authorities spent £227,000,000, of which 15 per cent went on poor relief, 13 per cent on highways and bridges, 8 per cent on education, 7 per cent on gas and water services. A further source of income was the exchequer grant, which contributed a rising proportion of local government revenue from the 1860s (15 per cent by 1890–91).[35] In the long term, central government power gained, because the grant could be withheld if minimum standards were not locally observed, but what impressed the late Victorians was the short-term expansion in the local authorities' sphere.

Civic events gave an excuse for robes, bunting, coats of arms, special posters and processions. Far from hiding itself away, the local elite publicly reinforced itself through participating in the structures of local authority, and its activities were commemorated in statues, paintings and foundation stones. Confronted by the outsider from overseas, from Whitehall, or even from the adjacent county or the nearest town, all classes drew together to defend their community. 9.5–8

If the reformism of urban local government in the 1880s could seldom be described as radical, local government in the countryside – dominated as it was by non-elected magistrates – lay almost entirely in the hands of local elites. Gladstone in 1877 described the English nobility as 'almost kings in their minor yet far from narrow circles', secure in the popularity which stemmed from their prominence in local affairs. In the English countryside before 1888, although the middle classes were beginning to push their way into local government, real power was shared between the gentry, who dominated the county magistracy, and the nobility, who made periodic appearances when social or legislative duties did not detain them in London. The Quarter Sessions might well comprise one or two Cabinet ministers; 'probably a clear majority of those who did the real work of the meeting', said Escott, 'had seats in the House of Commons or House of Lords, and were versed in the art of political management.'[36]

The Act of 1888 transformed this situation by giving the county council all the powers of the scattered *ad hoc* authorities which had hitherto managed rural highways, sanitation, justice and local government. No wonder Anglesey County Council felt justified in posing 9.3

for the photographer during 1889; in Wales the elections of that year produced a social and political revolution which ended the landowners' control over local affairs – 395 Liberal councillors were returned and only 184 Unionists. It was a quiet revolution which gave Wales its own form of home rule. But the Act's effects were not uniformly radical. In the south and west of England, the newly elected councils were more aristocratic in flavour than those in the north and east. The political consensus which prevailed within so many rural communities even after 1888 is reflected in the fact that in the county council elections of 1889, only 54 per cent of the 3,240 electoral divisions in England and Wales were contested, and only 74 per cent of the county electors in the contested divisions actually voted – a figure which fell to 62 per cent in contested divisions during the county council elections

9.4   of 1892. Liberals had correctly predicted that the elections would lead to the return of many country gentlemen and wealthy councillors, and knew that the reform would often be more apparent than real.[37] Any extension in the responsibilities of such authorities – over technical education, for example, in 1889 – therefore strengthened the existing social hierarchy still further.

Nonetheless Bernard Shaw welcomed the new situation in *Fabian Essays*, arguing that 'without efficient local machinery the replacing of private enterprise by State enterprise is out of the question.' The structure of local government grew up haphazardly in the nineteenth century, with administrators 'throwing out their lines until they met and formed a system'; until a coherent administrative structure was created, state management could hardly extend, either at the local or central level. But after 1888 Mrs Besant thought it worth urging councils to tackle unemployment locally, and since the 1888 Act also created the London County Council, its Lib-Lab 'progressives' could begin introducing to London the reforms which go-ahead northern municipal authorities had pioneered some time before.[38] The advent of the L.C.C. immediately improved London's fire services and encouraged ambitious public housing schemes. The 1890 Housing Act extended the power of local authorities to build and own lodging houses and dwellings, and the L.C.C.'s Boundary Street improvement scheme involved redeveloping fifteen acres in all, with blocks facing on to a central garden and flanked by wide roads.

9.8.9   Local authorities promoted ambitious projects during the 1880s. Protection against fire was ceasing to be a private responsibility, and the Public Health Act of 1875 compelled urban authorities to undertake

adequate precautions. Fire services were becoming   9.10 more efficient; street alarms were introduced after 1878, and the telephone was first used by a fire brigade at Oxford in the early 1880s. Large sums were invested in equipment and uniforms; bicycles and tricycles were also used, though horses were to remain essential for some years.

In this age of uncompensated unemployment and resolute individualism, local government work was attractive because regular and secure; employees often also enjoyed all the prestige of a uniform, and sometimes handled elaborately-maintained and expensive equipment. And by the early 1890s at least one authority, the L.C.C., had adopted a deliberate policy of improving wages and working conditions. An additional attraction of the fireman's job was the fact that, like the lifeboatman, he was a popular hero   9.11 whose bravery triumphed over the wrecks and infernos which incidentally provided the urban bystander of the day with one of his major entertainments. Captain Massey Shaw, the Metropolitan Fire Brigade's energetic but controversial chief officer, insisted that his men should control the voluntary firemen when firefighting, and instituted a regular Wednesday afternoon public drill and display in London. A very popular figure, he was an associate of the Prince of Wales, who often watched fires in his company. There was much expression of public regret when he resigned from the Brigade with a K.C.B. in 1891 after thirty years' service.

The vitality of British local government in the 1880s concealed from many contemporaries the steadily advancing role of Whitehall; this rested on the mounting quantity of social information which was becoming available, and on the civil service's greater facilities for collecting it. After the census had been launched in 1801, its detail became progressively enriched with every decade. After 1833, government inspectors were frequently appointed; in several areas of policy, this produced an almost self-generating process of increased regulation, followed by further information, followed by extended regulation. Objections to interference by central government, powerful at first, were gradually invalidated by the mid-Victorian reforms in the civil service, which became more and more efficient and free of corruption. Well before the 1880s, it was therefore able to grow; the 50,500 civil servants in 1881 rose to 79,500 in 1891 and to 116,400 in 1901.[39]

Reinforcing these continuous bureaucratic reforming pressures was an impressive battery of parliamentary techniques for intermittent social investigation

– most notably the select committee and the royal commission, which produced that great series of parliamentary papers on all aspects of British society which now load the shelves of so many university libraries. Though some critics at first branded these investigations as inquisitorial, the objection soon withered and died, and a mounting number of royal commissions was appointed from decade to decade until a peak was reached in the 1850s. There was a slow decline thereafter, but as many as forty were appointed during the 1880s, ten times as many as in the 1960s. The parliamentary select committee (whether of Lords or Commons) became more widely used at about the same time as the royal commission, and by 1880–89 the average number appointed by the House of Commons alone was thirty four, with an annual average of 370 members.[40] Politicians may sometimes have used these inquiries to postpone rather than accelerate settlement of important problems, and the formal question-and-answer technique may not now be seen as the best way of conducting social research, but they nonetheless accumulated a wealth of information sufficient to attract the admiration of Karl Marx. 'The social statistics of Germany', he wrote in 1867, 'and the rest of Continental Western Europe are, in comparison with those of England, wretchedly compiled.'[41]

With the invention of the camera, social statistics were acquiring a new immediacy. As early as 1842 a stir had been created by a few engravings which the mining commissioners included in their report on children's working conditions. Dr Barnardo's propagandist use of before-and-after photographs in the 1870s has already been discussed, and in 1877 John Thomson collaborated with Adolphe Smith (a pseudonym for Adolphe Smith Headingly) in publishing the twelve-part *Street Life in London*, one of the earliest examples of true photographic documentation, from which several Woodburytype photographs are used in this book. Writing in the *Pictorial World* of 1883, G.R. Sims is reminiscent of Henry Mayhew a generation earlier in his sense of exploration when entering the London slums and speaking of the 'wild races' to be found in the 'dark continent that is within easy walking distance of the General Post Office.'[42] By the 1880s inquiries of this type were stepping up the pressure for government involvement in improving housing conditions and relieving poverty.

The 1880s witnessed an important shift in methods of inquiry which reflects the increased role of central government. The rapid early Victorian rise in the number of royal commissions had already been reversed before the 1880s, and the decay of the select committee was not far behind; after 1890, continuous decline set in.[43] Moving into prominence in their place were two new sources of inquiry which reflect the authorities' increased need for expertise, continuity and integration when collecting social information: the departmental committee, or internal civil service investigation; and the more academic types of research conducted outside the government machine but owing so much to it in finance and inspiration.

The Board of Trade after 1886 strikingly demonstrates the power engendered by the systematic collection of information. The Industrial Remuneration Conference of 1885 had advertised the serious lack of statistics on labour questions, and the Board of Trade was entrusted with putting this right. In doing so, it was eventually able to encroach on the spheres of both the Home Office and the Local Government Board. But this was not the only contribution to the late Victorian increase in the power of central government: administrative discretion was also steadily widening, and by 1893 the number of rules and orders in council had become so great that an official collection had to be published annually which turned out already to be more bulky than the volume containing the year's crop of statutes.[44]

By the 1880s, contemporaries had become aware of the overall increase in central government's role. 'We are becoming a much governed nation,' wrote the historian F.W. Maitland in 1888, 'governed by all manner of councils and boards and officers, central and local, high and low.' Gladstone told Lord Rendel in 1892 that 'for fifty years public life in England had been an almost unbroken struggle for emancipation. Every great political movement had been in the nature of opening doors and windows', but he did not think that the next political generation would achieve improvements so satisfactory and unequivocal.[45] Figures for government expenditure had been reasonably stable between the Napoleonic and Crimean wars, but had risen to a new plateau in the 1860s; they began rising once more in the mid 1870s and did not stabilize again until after the First World War. The annual average of £70 million in 1870–74 rose to £89 million by 1885–9. In his budget speech of 1887, the Chancellor of the Exchequer G.J. Goschen pointed out that the civil service estimates for 1887–8 were almost twice as high as those for 1868–9 because 'new functions are constantly being forced on the State, and . . . new services are being demanded of it'; Chancellors were beginning to look about them for fresh sources of revenue.[46]

A visible symbol of central government's new-found growth was late Victorian Whitehall, which had now acquired some of the grandeur sketched out for it by Charles I in the seventeenth century. Soane's Board of Trade building had been completed in 1827 and expanded by Barry in 1846, the street was widened, and the meaner commercial buildings gradually retreated before the steady advance of stately bureaucratic piles. The new Home Office was built between 1868 and 1873, and the Metropolitan Police were housed at New Scotland Yard in 1891, with extensions to the Admiralty and War Office following in the 1890s. The process was not yet complete, however, and like many of his contemporaries Henry Ward, writing on Whitehall in the *Cornhill Magazine* for 1882, was less interested in comparisons with Britain in the past than with other countries. He found Britain 'behind every country in Europe' in the housing of its government machine, and deplored the fact that the War Office was scattered through ten different houses in Pall Mall, not to mention its accommodation elsewhere, and that the Admiralty was dispersed through twenty-eight houses in addition to its main building.[47] The comparison with Paris was particularly galling for patriotic Londoners. Still, by the 1880s an important beginning had been made towards transforming Whitehall into a distinguished thoroughfare, worthy of a great governmental machine.

Yet the civil service remained under continuous scrutiny from Parliament, monarchy and judiciary in the 1880s, so that even at the national level British political institutions were far from monolithic. Parliament's cause, at least since the seventeenth century, had been the people's cause, and if the traveller down Whitehall from Trafalgar Square in the 1880s was impressed by what he saw on either side, he was proceeding towards Westminster, a fitting culmination to the vista – for Parliament's great complex of buildings (replacing those destroyed in the fire of 1834) advertised its dignity and long history. Prestige and symbolism, rather than administrative efficiency, were the main architectural requirements of a legislature whose debating function was central to its role. Scenically, the outcome was a complete success: with a superbly dignified and palatial façade and a distinctive skyline, the buildings fully exploited their exposed river-bank site and rapidly gained acceptance as a national monument. Parliament thereby gained a majestic assertion of its continuing vitality, and London acquired yet another architectural asset to deploy in its continuing rivalry with the great provincial cities.

Westminster's timetable dominated the timetable of Whitehall, and Parliament's power over taxation was exercised throughout the civil service by a Treasury

which seemed ponderously to delight in saying 'no'. 'Their phraseology . . . had a certain charm,' Sir Stanley Leathes recalled in 1932: ' "My Lords are not convinced . . ." "My Lords cannot entertain the proposition . . ." "My Lords are surprised . . ." "Their Lordships view with alarm . . ." "fail to understand . . ." "are unable to conceive . . ." '[48] Parliament's continuing prestige is reflected in the fact that House of Commons procedure was imitated in many a working men's debating club or 'local parliament', each with its chairman arbitrating between government and opposition benches.

Whether at the local or national level, therefore, the opportunities for ventilating criticism and participating in government were considerable in the 1880s and produced a pluralism which (by the standards of the time) made the British political system remarkably open and accessible. From the mid eighteenth century onwards, a sequence of humanitarian and radical movements exploited the opportunities thereby presented. The nonconformists, manufacturers, humanitarians, feminists, evangelicals, writers and scientists attracted by these movements cultivated those libertarian philosophies and institutions which made it possible for British socialism in the 1880s to take a parliamentary rather than a conspiratorial direction. For Marx's critics in the 1880s, the prosperity of the United Kingdom rested on individual freedom, and it was on Parliament – as embodiment of that freedom – that so many of these movements focused their efforts. Yet their representatives, once present at Westminster, were subject to considerable temptation; for Parliament (despite the apparent predominance there of the conflict between government and opposition) combined its libertarian function with an integrating, consensus-seeking role, as can be appreciated from newcomers' reactions to it.

Radical and Irish M.P.s tried to insulate themselves against Parliament's encouragement of consensus by refusing invitations to social functions which they feared might prove corrupting. They were bewildered at having to face an irreverent audience and at the need to meet their opponents' arguments in detail. William Morris in the 1880s either discouraged socialists from aiming at Parliament altogether, or urged them if they got there simply to act as 'rebels, and not as members of the governing body prepared by passing palliative measures to keep "Society" alive.'[49] But this was to protect the purity of his socialist disciples at the price of sacrificing a major opportunity for testing their ideas against criticism, for informing themselves more fully about the working of political institutions, and for winning recruits from among their opponents. Morris also unnecessarily increased the difficulties faced by socialists in so far as his attitude ran them up against an institution which at that time enjoyed great power and popularity. But Morris was entirely correct in fearing Parliament's moderating impact on the outlook of any socialists who went there.

Samuel Smith, a Liberal philanthropist prominent in the 1880s, referred to the 'change that passed over my mental constitution' on entering Parliament. 'Like most busy men I had lived and moved pretty much in one sphere of thought. When first plunged into a maelstrom of opposing opinions the effect was rather staggering. There come into the British Parliament types of almost every conceivable opinion.' Pressures towards consensus were reinforced by Parliament's strongly pragmatic mood. 'The British Parliament ... is a wonderfully educating institution,' Smith continued; 'no man can sit there for years and follow the debates without being a much wiser man ... No man can long sit there and be an extreme dogmatist, or can fail to perceive that political truth is many sided.'[50] Furthermore, whether they succumbed to Parliament's embrace or not, the Irish nationalist M.P.s were by their very presence (however disruptive) helping to rein in the extremism of their more enthusiastic followers back home.

Parliament's defence of liberty rested on the battle between government and opposition – on the existence of a two-party system which distracted attention from, and even blurred, some major polarities within the community while simultaneously providing piecemeal reformers with many openings for influencing policy and greatly extending the opportunities for political participation. In this third dimension of British reformism in the 1880s, the seventeenth-century legacy is once again substantial, for both parties could trace an ancestry of some sort back to the reign of Charles II. The threats to the two-party system during the 1880s were serious only for brief moments and on selected issues. Although Liberal relations with the Irish nationalists between 1880 and 1885 were always strained and sometimes ruptured, such internal dissension is common in British parties of the left; as for Conservatives, their relations with the Liberal Unionists after 1886 were continuously wary and sometimes cool, but never fractious, for preservation of the Union was a major priority for both. The adversary system of debate persisted throughout the decade, and the efforts of the party leaders, together with the structure and traditions of the House of Commons, worked to restore the two-party system in its completeness; for much of the time, they succeeded.

The decade saw strenuous efforts being made to reinforce the links between the politicians at Westminster and the newly enlarged electorate in the country, and in this process three astute politicians played a conspicuous part: Gladstone, Lord Randolph Churchill and Joseph Chamberlain. All three aimed at blunting the antagonism between employer and employee, and (in their different ways) at holding Ireland within the United Kingdom. Each deserves a more extended discussion. Gladstone told Rosebery in 1880 that 'what is outside Parliament seems to me to be fast mounting ... to an importance much exceeding what is inside.'[51] Few had done more than he to bring this about; by addressing outdoor meetings, promoting a nationwide agitation on the Eastern Question in 1876, and crowning his efforts with the memorable Midlothian speeches in 1879–80, he helped to create a national political community, to convert elections into clashes of political principle, and to prepare the ground for the disciplining of M.P.s in accordance with electoral pledges on policy. During the 1880s, Liberal governments were to take this transformation of electoral practice further, with legislative curbs on corruption in 1883, with franchise extension in 1884 (for which Gladstone, more than anyone else in the government, was personally responsible), and with the Home Rule crusade after 1886. Yet for all his extra-parliamentary influence, Gladstone was a strict constitutionalist, and his career had the long-term effect of focusing the attention of even wider sections of the community on events at Westminster.

The stage was thereby set for the gladiatorial display between government and opposition, Gladstone and Disraeli. The two men might have been born for conflict; as Granville told the Queen, Disraeli 'has a power of saying in two words that which drives a person of Mr Gladstone's peculiar temperament into a great state of excitement.' Not that Disraeli ever rivalled Gladstone on the public platform; his arena was the House of Commons, and at elections he was content merely to address his constituents. Disraeli's influence with the Queen, with Parliament, the aristocracy and London opinion forced Gladstone in the 1870s to push further his earlier experiments in whipping up extra-parliamentary opinion. But by 1881 Disraeli was exhausted by ill health and old age. Sir Charles Dilke met him about a fortnight before he died, lying on a couch in his back dining room, with a bronchitis kettle on the hob and breathing with difficulty: 'but he was still the old Disraeli, and, though I think that he knew that he was dying, yet his pleasant spitefulness about "Mr G" was not abated.' 'May the Almighty be near his pillow,'

8.1

wrote Gladstone in his diary the next day.[52] In his later career Gladstone never found a comparable opponent, though for a few years Lord Randolph Churchill came near to it.

Gladstone's resort to extra-parliamentary support did not stem simply from political necessity: it owed something to his intellectual isolation at Westminster. In middle age during the 1850s he had forsaken the Conservative Party for the Liberals, and was therefore never entirely trusted in either camp. As a high church-man in a largely nonconformist and rationalistic Liberal Party, he was something of an anomaly. Fur-thermore his Liberalism was peculiar because it originated not in Whig birth, radical and secular con-viction, or Liberal political theory, but in the dilemma of a devout Christian who recognizes that modern con-ditions require a separation between politics and religion, yet who also feels obliged to carry into politics all the idealism and fervour of the Christian message.

Outside Westminster his audience consisted not only of Liberal Anglicans, Nonconformists and businessmen, but of provincial and progressive-minded people in all social classes, including working men. While Gladstone was undoubtedly exhilarated by associating with the huge audiences at his political meetings, his followers were also pressing their atten-tions on him – as three incidents must suffice to show. On 4 August 1877, 1,400 excursionists from the Bol-ton Liberal Association were allowed to roam the grounds of Gladstone's estate at Hawarden. According to *The Times*'s report, he first refused their request for an address, but they were told that he would fell a tree later in the afternoon and would speak to them then. Accordingly at about four o'clock, he and his son W.H. Gladstone emerged 'clad in rough working suits, with slouch hats' and chopped at a large ash, shedding their clothes 'till they had on only check shirts and rough light pants,' the spectators picking up the chips. The choir of the Bolton Baptist chapel was in attendance and glees were then sung, including 'Men of Harlech' and 'Gently Sighs the Evening Breeze'. Later, Mr and Mrs Gladstone joined in the hymn 'The Old Hun-dredth', and Gladstone shook hands with the ladies present. He refused to talk on party political matters and ignored interjections of 'The Eastern Question' and 'Just a little bit'; instead he delivered what was for him a short speech, which took up a third of a close-printed column in *The Times*, on urban pollution. Then, after ringing cheers for Gladstone and his family, the chopping was resumed.[53]

When about seven hundred Liberals from Lincoln descended on Hawarden on 7 June 1884, Gladstone

received one or two of their representatives in his li-brary but declined to address the group: they nonethe-less enthusiastically cheered him on the way from the castle to the rectory, and he later told Granville that the visitors seemed 'full of enthusiasm'. On 15 September, when he was travelling about the country by train during the House of Lords crisis over franchise reform, he told Granville of his 'fatiguing but remarkable day, from the almost incredible enthusiasm of the people all along the line, which made silence impossible, though I pretty much confined myself to commonplaces.' During a short stop at Carlisle on 26 September, he found himself confronted by an audience of 10,000. Yet behind the scenes, despite appearances which deceived the Queen and many others, this apparently rabble-rousing crusader was doing his utmost to get the conflict settled, in the hope that this would deprive the Liberal zealots of an excuse for mounting an assault on the second chamber; himself a strong believer in aristocratic government, he aimed to protect the upper classes against unduly weakening their own order by resisting inevitable change.[54] In his belief, a non-socialist society could readily reconcile a democratic franchise with the continued political prominence of a conscientious and responsive aristocracy.

Nonetheless, Gladstone had tangible benefits to hold out to his enthusiastic supporters. His services to provincial opinion and nonconformity have already been discussed; to businessmen and working men he could offer cheap and efficient government, oppor-tunity for talent, the democratization of an aristocratic political system, free trade, and an idealistic foreign policy, together with encouragements to thrift and re-spectability. To a working-class leader such as George Howell, whose life was spent in warding off the poverty-stricken vagrancy he had experienced for a brief nightmarish episode in childhood, Gladstone gave promise of the full incorporation of working men into British politics and the firm validation of respect-able values. To the independent type of working man in rural or mining areas – Joseph Arch or Thomas Burt, for example – he held out the inducements of religious liberty, responsible landlordism, franchise extension and (again) free trade.

From the 1860s, some politicians responded to the advent of democracy by recommending proportional representation as a safeguard for the educated classes against mass opinion. Not so Gladstone. Like Chamber-lain and Churchill he pursued the more robust course of crusading for what were initially minority views among the majority. To many excluded groups in British society, he offered above all things participation:

for many working people, this took no stronger form than listening to his speeches when he did them the courtesy of visiting their institutions and communities; but to a few, the participation offered was something more extensive, and involved mutual dependence and respect. Already by March 1882 Gladstone had his eye on the T.U.C.'s general secretary Henry Broadhurst as a parliamentary speaker. He and Thomas Burt, he thought, did honour to their class; in March 1882 he told the Queen that Broadhurst had spoken in Parliament 'as he always does with the utmost modesty and propriety, which might well teach a lesson to many, and with no small ability and clearness.' By 1886, in his crucial speech on the second reading of the Home Rule Bill, Gladstone was prepared to commit himself fully to the people. 'You have power, you have wealth, you have rank, you have station, you have organization, you have the place of power,' he told his opponents in his emotional peroration: 'what have we? We think that we have the people's heart.' His opponents would regard such emotion as sentimental claptrap, yet working men in large numbers responded with admiration; as Flora Thompson wrote of the villagers in Lark Rise, 'their faith in his power was touching.'[55]

Under Gladstone's leadership, the Liberal Party in the 1880s did much to integrate working men into the political community, amply accommodating their desire for acknowledgement of their respectable status. The fact that the party was anti-socialist and distinctly hostile to working-class candidatures in some of its constituency branches did not prevent Parliament's three working-class M.P.s from describing themselves as Liberals in 1880, eleven in 1885 and sixteen in 1892; and in 1884 the Liberal government enfranchised many rural working men. As for the specific grievances of the T.U.C., both parties were quick to enact the Bills it desired: forty-five in the 1880s, nearly twice as many as in the 1870s.[56]

Gladstone was assiduous in cultivating Henry Broadhurst; he visited his South London home, gave pleasure by wearing the carnations he grew there, and overruled his diffidence about accepting office in 1886. Liberal governments had already begun appointing working men to administrative posts; W.V. Harcourt, Home Secretary in 1880, made a point of choosing them as inspectors of mines. Liberals were also responsible for the fact that Broadhurst was the first working man to become a government minister. There was no sacrifice of self-respect here, as Broadhurst's refusal to wear court dress in 1886 testifies. 'I did not put on a black coat,' Joseph Arch the Liberal agricultural trade

union leader proudly recalled of his arrival at Westminster in 1885: '– I aped nobody – I wore my rough tweed jacket and billycock hat ... As I was, so I wished to be.' When the dockers' leader John Burns attacked the veteran Liberal John Bright at a Hyde Park demonstration of radical working men in July 1884, he was hooted and howled at, and had to be saved from a ducking in the Serpentine.[57]

Much of Gladstone's extra-parliamentary influence stemmed from resourcefulness in exploiting what we would now describe as the media. He was the first major statesman to travel the country for this purpose, let alone to speak in such passionate and high-toned language. He was not above turning the novelty of telecommunication to account for the purposes of political drama. As he neared the end of his Guildhall speech in autumn 1881, a telegram handed to him by pre-arranged plan enabled him to announce the arrest of Parnell, the man 'who ... has made himself beyond all others prominent in the attempt to destroy the authority of the law.' Gladstone was quite prepared to write signed articles in the reviews, and in the late 1880s, at the request of a dinner-party, held forth into a phonograph so eloquently that nobody noticed when the cylinder was exhausted and the needle rotating in mid-air. In 1882 the *Photographic News* was impressed that Gladstone was more accessible to photographers than Disraeli. A Mr Walker of Regent Street who asked for a sitting was told that Gladstone would visit him for the purpose on a particular day for fifteen minutes; 'he was punctual to the minute, and, with his watch on the table, posed for the stipulated quarter of an hour.'[58]

Gladstone's oratory attracted audiences large enough to arouse the Queen's jealousy. By 1884 she was telling Ponsonby that she was '*utterly* disgusted with his *stump* oratory – so unworthy of his position.' In vain she tried to stem the flow, nervously warning him before a major performance to watch his words. When she rebuked him for his whistle-stop tours in 1886, he blamed the Conservative leaders who 'have established a rule of what may be called popular agitation by addressing public meetings from time to time at places with which they were not connected.' In 1887, however, Lord Salisbury told the Queen that 'this duty of making political speeches is an aggravation of the labours of your Majesty's servants which we owe entirely to Mr Gladstone'.[59]

It is easy to see why Gladstone's opponents disliked him so intensely. His convoluted statements of policy, with their excessively fine distinctions and their superabundant dependent clauses, seemed less the phrases of a scholarly Oxford-trained high churchman

8.14

than the self-interested and self-deceiving devices of an unscrupulous and hypocritical politician. 'I never can understand Mr Gladstone in conversation', the straightforward Hartington told Granville in August 1885, 'and I thought him unusually unintelligible yesterday.'[60] To his political opponents, Gladstone seemed capable of convincing himself of anything, and, still more infuriating, of providing high-toned justifications of his latest shift of position which lent it the dignity of eternal principle and righteousness.

He could also be insensitive over personal questions, failing to understand the circumstances of people differently situated from himself; during the Home Rule crisis his mishandling of Joseph Chamberlain may well have been crucial. His combination of abstracted idealism and surpassing political agility during those dramatic months made him seem merely hypocritical and crafty to his radical critics Labouchere and Chamberlain; their letters to one another during the crisis show not a trace of the enthusiasm he could evoke in mass meetings from their followers. 'Is it not terrible to have to deal with a lunatic at large,' Labouchere asked Chamberlain on 29 May 1886, 'whose intelligence seems to be now limited to a sort of low cunning, and who cannot refrain from perpetually bringing an ace down from his sleeve, even when he has only to play fair to win the trick? ... The public do not know the object of their adoration as we do. He is still their fetish, and they regard any doubt of his divine character as sacrilege.'[61] Both the hostile and the sympathetic views of Gladstone can find support in the ample evidence he left behind him, and his personality and career are substantial enough to evoke vigorous and contrasting reactions, depending on the temperament of the observer. His character and achievements therefore retain their fascination for a twentieth-century generation whose range of interests and ideals of conduct repudiate much of what he stood for.

In a speech of 1884 Lord Randolph Churchill, a second major politician important for linking Parliament with the people in the 1880s, taunted Gladstone for his self-promotion. 'Gentlemen,' he said, 'we live in an age of advertisement, the age of Holloway's pills, of Colman's mustard, and of Horniman's pure tea.' He saw Gladstone's much-publicized tree-felling on his Hawarden estate as a stratagem of 'the greatest living master of the art of personal political advertisement'.[62] Lord Randolph was not far behind Gladstone in this art, though his methods were rather less subtle and much less scrupulous.

Churchill's undoubted courage was mingled with the spoiled child's desire to shock and attract attention.

He was always brave enough to challenge the Liberals and radicals on their home ground, whether in Ireland or in large industrial constituencies; political caricaturists therefore often drew him as a pigmy, a pug, a gnat or a wasp contending against great odds. In October 1884 he carried his campaign into the heart of the enemy camp by organizing a Conservative meeting at Aston Park, Birmingham. Many Liberals freed their employees for counter-demonstrations by closing their works; rioters broke up the open-air meetings, missiles greeted Conservative M.P.s who tried to address the crowds, the platform of the great hall was stormed and Lord Randolph was driven out. But this was a small price to pay for the publicity and for the boost thereby given to Conservative morale in Chamberlain's radical stronghold.

For a brief period, Churchill succeeded in preserving politics as a mass recreation – as a contest between two teams, each making strong claims on the loyalty of its supporters. 'Give it 'em hot, Randy,' crowds would cry in the streets, and Lord Randolph gave them what they wanted: witty, irreverent, dazzling, daring, often funny and invariably interesting speeches, with none of the Liberals' Olympian and moralistic superiority to the common man. He was a brilliant phrase-maker – a sporty, human, racy young aristocrat who delighted in shocking and surprising the puritans and the plebs.[63]

Country gentlemen, once the backbone of Toryism, in the 1880s began deserting the House of Commons, and the 1880 Parliament was the last to contain a full complement. Churchill saw that if the Conservative Party was to make headway with the electorate, it must shed its predominantly landed and aristocratic image and offer more to the urban middle and working classes. His strategy fully acknowledged the changed structure of politics. As he pointed out in 1885, the foundation of the British constitution was 'totally new, purely modern, absolutely untried ... Your new foundation is a great seething and swaying mass of some five million electors ... That is, I say, a state of things unparalleled in history.'[64]

This made it important for Churchill not only to interest the new electors, but to organize them through democratizing the structure of his party, and through advertising its sympathy with social reform under the paradoxical slogan 'Tory Democracy'. Peel and Disraeli earlier in the century had demonstrated the party's responsiveness to reforming pressures, and although Churchill lacked the constructive, experienced and imaginative mind to do more than appropriate Liberal reforming policies, he enlivened the National Union (the structure of local Conservative associations which

Disraeli had helped create in 1867) as a political machine, and he was the main architect of the Primrose League. Launched in 1883, the League mobilized snobbery, patriotism, the thirst for ceremonial and titles, and the yearning for rural garden-parties at the Great House, for the purpose of drumming up voluntary helpers and voters during election campaigns. At the general election of 1885, Primrose 'dames' led by his wife and mother helped Churchill by canvassing and addressing working men in Birmingham; at Woodstock his wife and sister-in-law toured the district in a smart tandem adorned with his racing colours of pink and brown, completely outshining two Liberal lady canvassers from Cambridge.[65] But Churchill's claim to have been the architect of his party's urban gains at the 1885 general election ignores the importance of the swing of the pendulum, the imperialist upsurge on the recent death of General Gordon (with which Churchill had little sympathy), and the segregation of urban Conservatives from urban Liberals through the creation of single-member constituencies. Churchill's major defects were less obvious to his large audiences than to those who had to work closely with him, so that it seemed possible, for that brief moment of Churchillian triumph between 1884 and 1886, that the Conservatives would rival the Liberals in reforming zeal.

In some ways, the Home Rule issue, which really launched the Primrose League, was Churchill's undoing. The League eagerly whipped up disgust at the Irish Home Rulers' violent methods, and felt no shame about the Mitchelstown meeting of 1887, where the police killed one man and wounded others; on the contrary, it took a pride in the event, and its banners displayed wild-eyed terrorists setting fire to ricks. Membership rose from 11,366 at the end of 1885 to 237,283 a year later, and from there to a million by 1891. Unhampered by the drabness of democracy or by the austerity of teetotalism, late Victorian Conservatives were usually more successful than Liberals at organizing political entertainments, and in 1889 the League innovated further by admitting child members as Primrose 'buds'. 'Vulgar?' exclaimed Lady Salisbury to objectors on one occasion: 'of course, it is vulgar! But that is why we have got on so well.'[66]

Yet the popular appeal of unionism made 'Tory Democracy' unnecessary for the Conservative Party, which was already embarrassed (as a propertied and patriotic party) by Churchill's social reform and Little Englander demands. Despite his energy and flair, Churchill had made many enemies and wounded many feelings by his ruthlessly pushing, even occasionally heartless, methods and by his aggressive manner

in Cabinet. Gladstone told Edward Hamilton in 1887 that the great danger to the country lay in 'the *men* of the future – personalities of the stamp of Randolph Churchill and Chamberlain'. It was not a criticism which came only from Gladstonians. G.J. Goschen, a prominent Liberal Unionist, regretted Churchill's promotion to leadership of the House in 1886: 'it is a premium on the arts by which he had risen into notoriety . . . as he imitated Dizzy [Disraeli] at a distance, so men of even lower *moral* may imitate Churchill.'[67] No doubt Salisbury shared this disquiet; but whatever his feeling, he and Balfour his nephew quietly prevented Churchill from recouping himself after his ill-judged resignation in December 1886.

Rather less colourful than Churchill but far more creative was his radical rival Joseph Chamberlain. His fertility in party organization and programme was remarkable. With his little political notebooks, his carefully groomed appearance, his press contacts and his secure Birmingham base, he was the first really professional politician drawn from the nonconformist world. By temperament no resigner, he was in politics to get things done. Gladstone met him in 1877 and found him 'a man worth watching and studying: of strong selfconsciousness under most pleasing manners and I should think of great tenacity of purpose: expecting to play an historical part, and probably destined to it.'[68]

Chamberlain's driving ambition was linked to a genuine distaste for aristocratic influence within his party. In 1877 he had been the leading figure in creating the National Liberal Federation, a popular constituency organization; in 1884 he was a leading campaigner for franchise extension. He told an Islington audience in 1885 that the party caucus was 'the servant of the people and not its master . . . the engine by which public opinion is concentrated,' the only weapon of the masses against 'that confederacy of class interests and selfish Conservatism which is always banded together.'[69] His campaign in that year for the 'unauthorized programme', a set of radical proposals not approved by the party leadership, was masterly, and until Gladstone out-trumped him with a Home Rule campaign which he could not conscientiously support, he seemed predestined for the Liberal leadership. As it was, he drifted after 1886, via Liberal Unionism, into a firm alliance with the Conservatives, leaving Gladstone in command of the powerful electoral machine which he, Chamberlain, had created.

Chamberlain put his faith in open government. Like Gladstone and Randolph Churchill, he was most effective on the platform. Beatrice Webb watched the audience reactions he evoked at Birmingham in 1884: 'it might have been a woman listening to the words of her lover!' she wrote: 'perfect response, and unquestioning receptivity. Who reasons with his mistress?'[70] Nor was Chamberlain popular only in Birmingham; during the campaign of 1885 his meetings were widely attended everywhere. These were the days when prominent politicians attracted huge audiences by educating the nation through oratorical sparring contests. When Churchill, at the height of his influence in October 1886, arrived at Dartford to deliver his famous social reform speech, deputations from all parts of the country presented him with nearly a hundred addresses. The town was bright with flags by day and fireworks by night, and on 2 October he addressed 12–14,000 people. Even in September 1887, after his resignation and partial eclipse, he could still attract an audience of 7,000 in the natural amphitheatre under the West Cliff on the sands at Whitby.[71]

9.13.14   The camera could scarcely capture the excitement of politics in the 1880s – so much depended on colour, sound and movement. 'Many a time at elections I fancied myself more at the Derby,' wrote the political scientist Ostrogorski; '. . . To the women and children the polling-day brings all the excitement of a fair.'[72] Not just a one-day fair, either: voting took place at different times in different constituencies. At the 1885 general election, for instance, the first contest was held on 24 November, the last not till 18 December. The introduction of the ballot in 1872 removed much of the excitement of the neck-and-neck local contest, though the completeness of its secrecy was not at first appreciated, but in the nation as a whole the results could still be totted up over a period of weeks, whereas the outcome of modern elections is clear within hours.

Legislation against electoral corruption in 1883 curbed drunkenness and extravagance, but excitement was maintained by the advent of volunteer canvassers and by the long-term increase in the number of contested elections which flowed from the redistribution of seats in 1885. Elections were still semi-recreational occasions when individuals and groups within the community squared up to one another and tested their prowess; they often gave rise to discussions on those purely local issues which at that time aroused such fervour. A high proportion of electoral expenditure was raised within the constituency. Political parties were by modern standards markedly decentralized; indeed, with the Liberals' triumph over London-based Toryism at the general election of 1880, this in a sense went one stage further. Yet within the parties, as in government, centralization was making great strides. Gladstone's Midlothian campaign advertised the party leader's mounting power, and it was noted that the Liberals gained a seat in every constituency where Gladstone stopped on his journey there on 16 March 1880. Because Gladstone so dominated the campaign for Home Rule, Lord Randolph Churchill saw the general election of 1886 as 'a pure unadulterated personal plebiscite . . . a political expedient borrowed from the last and worst days of the second Empire.'[73]

Although the country then lacked so many of the modern means of communication, the turnout secured by the politicians at the 1885 general election – 81.2 per cent in contested seats – has been exceeded in only four of the twenty-five that have taken place since: in 1906, January 1910, 1950 and 1951.[74] Parliamentary institutions in the 1880s were deeply rooted in British life, largely because they were so accessible to outside influence, so compatible with a broad political participation. But a powerful reformist tradition, a well entrenched parliamentary system and a pluralist party structure would of themselves have achieved little unless operated by a skilful, experienced and self-confident political elite whose qualities inspired widespread respect. To these aspects of Britain in the 1880s we must now turn.

*9.2. Women workers packing matches in the boxing room of
Bryant & May's old 'Centre Factory' in Bow, London. Undated*

9.3,4. New local authorities were being set up. Anglesey County Council in their Council Chamber (ABOVE), Thomas Mills, 1889. A photomontage of the members of the first Buckinghamshire County Council at County Hall, Aylesbury (BELOW), G. Jerrard, 1889–92

9.5,6. Two manifestations of burgeoning civic pride. Reading out the royal charter granted to the newly incorporated Borough of Chelmsford, Essex, 19 September 1888 (ABOVE). Birmingham's impressive new Law Courts and site for the Police Station (LEFT), J. Benjamin Stone, 1880

9.7. *Civic amenities. The opening to the public of the castle grounds, Guildford, Surrey. 1888*

9.8. Civic services. The formal start of construction at the Roall Waterworks, Pontefract, Yorkshire. 1888

9.9–11. Public services grew in scale and ambition. Lowering a 15″ water main under the bed of the River Wensum, Norwich (ABOVE), A.E. Coe, 1889. The Oxford volunteer Fire Brigade parades outside Balliol College, Broad Street, Oxford (ABOVE RIGHT), Henry Taunt, 1888. The National Lifeboat Institution's lifeboat 'The Co-operator No. 1' on its horse-drawn trolley at Cullercoats, near Newcastle (BELOW RIGHT), Walter Knott, 1884

9.12–14. The camera could capture only a shadow of the excitement of politics in the 1880s. The Hammersmith branch of the Socialist League on an outing to Epping Forest (BELOW). In the group are William and May Morris. Undated. Mr Horace Davey Q.C. and his family (ABOVE RIGHT) receive a triumphant reception at Christchurch, Hampshire, after he has been elected Liberal M.P. for the constituency, J.E. Cobb, 1880. Election transport outside Mr Wickham's Committee Room, Old Place, Tisted, Hampshire (BELOW RIGHT). c.1880

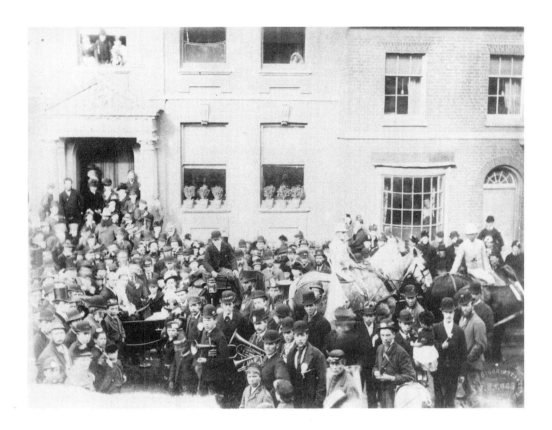

Chapter 10 *Aristocratic Magic*

The camera can record only the formal and public face of the political elite. This was important, but its essentials are difficult to recapture because so much of its significant work involved private conversations indoors and so many of its attitudes are taken for granted in the documents which survive. John Stuart Mill, whose career was largely devoted to undermining aristocratic values, pointed out that superior organization might enable the governors of a society to retain control despite inferiority to the governed in property, numbers and intelligence.[1] When to this is added self-confidence, the combination is formidable. The political staying-power of the British aristocracy, even after the introduction of a democratic franchise, was impressive.

Without ever formulating their ideas in any scientific way, the great families believed strongly in 'breeding' – which at the very least denoted the inheritance of acquired characteristics. Animal husbandry on their estates provided them with a practical and often extensive knowledge of the subject which they applied to the management of public affairs. It was a set of responses which easily degenerated into snobbery but, for Lord Lansdowne at least, it was something more than that. Throughout the 1880s he reluctantly cut himself off from the homes and relatives he loved, and took up a

10.1. The aristocracy making a spectacle of itself, supported by an army of servants below stairs. A photomontage of a fancy dress ball at Iveagh House, Dublin. 1880

series of distinguished colonial posts in the hope of restoring the failing fortunes of the family estates. 'The longer I live the more firmly do I believe in blood and breeding,' he wrote from Canada to his mother, while acting as Governor-General there in 1886. He was gloomy about the future of his order: 'many of us are poor, a good few disreputable, plenty idle and without sense of responsibility. It is not much of an army ...'[2] Nonetheless the skill of the Lansdownes, the Cecils, the Devonshires, the Derbys and a few other major aristocratic families in retaining political influence in the 1880s was considerable. Their success can perhaps best be analysed in relation to their three major spheres of operation – beginning with the largest, the international sphere, narrowing to London society and 'the season', and from there narrowing further to the social life of the country. It should then be possible to appreciate the magic of aristocracy in the 1880s, and the roots of its appeal within both middle and working classes.

A major strength of monarchy and nobility in the 1880s, even for domestic purposes, lay in their cosmopolitanism; internationally as well as nationally, they were better co-ordinated than their critics, and could achieve much through private contacts. Franchise extension encroached far less on aristocratic diplomatic preserves than Lord Salisbury (who acted as Prime Minister and Foreign Secretary for half the decade) encouraged foreigners to believe; if anything, it extended his freedom of manoeuvre by giving him excuses for avoiding binding agreements. His daughter says that 'his own conception of a perfect diplomacy was always of one whose victories come without observation.' To critics who complained after 1886 that he was too reticent on foreign affairs in his speeches, he replied that this was a subject 'about which we must all think a great deal and speak very little.' Salisbury was inexpert at the social arts then so important in diplomacy. He often had to entertain visiting foreign dignitaries at Hatfield, but his daughter says that 'the hospitalities which wealth imposed were an almost unmitigated affliction to him.' He was quite unable to identify guests at public functions and once said that he would rather compose a difficult despatch than make conversation through a long dinner-party; as for useful gossip, he displayed 'a hopeless incapacity for its accurate retention'.[3]

Peers filled the post of Foreign Secretary continuously from 1868 to 1905. The very atmosphere of the Foreign Office was aristocratic, and the reception held there on the Queen's birthday was a major event in 'the season' (the period between February and July assigned to important social functions in London). The British and overseas diplomatic elite congregated at their rendezvous, the St James's Club; with 650 members in 1898, it charged an annual subscription of eleven guineas. Until 1880 the Foreign Secretary's power of making diplomatic appointments was limited only by a 'qualifying test'. Before 1919 no candidate could sit for the entrance examination unless 'known to the Secretary of State or recommended to him by men of standing and position.' Sons of aristocrats obtained ninety-three of the 249 higher posts in the Foreign Office and diplomatic service between 1851 and 1929; they were also more likely than other recruits to get the top appointments, which were then in Europe.[4] Commercial and democratic pressures on British foreign policy were therefore filtered through a decidedly aristocratic structure; Joseph Chamberlain in Gladstone's government of 1880–85 made little headway in his efforts to convert the Board of Trade into a 'ministry of commerce' which could use Foreign Office information to foster Britain's international trade.

As for domestic affairs, aristocrats had no need of textbooks; the best of them breathed in a political sense through upbringing, schooling and social contacts. By comparison with M.P.s from other classes, they entered Parliament young, almost as a matter of course, and had plenty of leisure. The British political elite had also developed an acute sense of timing; it knew when to advance and when to retire. Its alertness to the danger of revolution, at least since 1792, and perhaps since

1642, was integral to Whig traditions, but it can also be observed in Lord Salisbury. A column of his library at Hatfield was filled with contemporary pamphlets and newspapers on the French Revolution. The knowledgeable society hostess Lady Dorothy Nevill told H.M. Hyndman that his campaign for socialism would never succeed during his lifetime: the aristocracy would stave it off by buying up the labour leaders and making judicious but modest concessions. Hyndman later recalled that this remarkably accurate prediction 'made a great impression upon me.'[5]

Political shrewdness was reinforced by a strong sense of public duty. Joseph Chamberlain's attack on Lord Salisbury in 1883 as 'the spokesman of a class ... who toil not neither do they spin' was entirely unjust in so far as the Conservative leaders were personally concerned. Salisbury saw dissipation, laziness or selfishness as the worst kind of treachery to his order, and despised clubland idleness. The pressure on ministers was mounting; bureaucratization and improved communications greatly increased the paperwork involved in traditional government activity. The Foreign Office in 1825 received only 9,059 telegrams and despatches; by 1895 the total had risen to 91,433. Lord Salisbury was forced to pore over documents late into the night; his morbid sensitivity to interruption caused him to work behind locked doors and to play hide-and-seek with his subordinates. His daughter wrote that throughout the eleven-and-a-half years when he combined the posts of Prime Minister and Foreign Secretary, he never had a day's rest except when really ill, and 'lived close to the physical breaking-point.' As for Gladstone, his rival, his appetite for work was legendary.[6]

A wider electorate and a more enterprising press rendered the politician's traditional burden still heavier because more speeches and more extra-parliamentary political activity were required. In 1885 Lord Salisbury warned Churchill against combining his departmental work at the India Office with a platform campaign. 'The strain of doing the two things together is enormous: and if you once go a step too far – if you once break the spring – you may take years to get over it.' Lord Randolph's fate in 1886 illustrates the importance the elite attached not only to hard work but to integrity, loyalty and scruple. In a two-party system, this heavy workload was not of course continuous. Nor was it as great as it is today, particularly for the ordinary M.P.; parliamentary sessions were short, ministerial posts few, and attendance was less regular. Only 30 per cent of the parliamentary divisions attracted 300 or more M.P.s in 1886; in the rather smaller Parliament in

1972–3 the figure had risen to 67 per cent.[7] In the 1880s a member was free to spend long periods at sporting functions, foreign spas or simply on his country estate. Politics was inevitably a less specialized profession when M.P.s received no salary, and when few were dependent on income from government posts.

All this reflects the interaction of political and social life, which was closer than in other European capitals. 'All the best society in London is in some degree political,' wrote Escott. 'The season' coincided with the parliamentary session, and social gatherings were essential for consolidating a political party. On the night before Parliament met, the leaders of government and opposition entertained important colleagues at a ceremonial dinner at which the Queen's speech was read out. Disraeli as Conservative leader invited the rising young men of his party to join him at breakfast, and at the gatherings held by the more sociable politicians – by W.V. Harcourt for example – disputes were quietly sorted out, enmities terminated, hostilities neutralized, and talent recruited at every level. On the other hand, embarrassment could arise, as was the case in 1886 with John Bright on receiving an invitation from Gladstone, whom he was shortly to desert on Home Rule: 'it is difficult to oppose a Minister on a critical question,' he wrote, 'and to associate with him and frequent his table.'[8]

In 1880, half the M.P.s came from families with over 2,000 acres; in 1885 a sixth (a diminishing proportion) had hereditary titles. In the Cabinets of either party, aristocrats held more than half the posts. Political honours enlarged the nobility faster than the number of great landowners. The House of Lords therefore became more representative of gradations within the landed class, and especially of its politically active elements; it contained 350 hereditary peers in 1832, over 400 by 1870 and nearly 450 by 1885.[9] It was particularly necessary for Conservative whips to enjoy close ties with the landed families. According to Escott, the party whip 'must be imperturbable in his temper, unerring in his tact'; he must 'observe everything and appear to observe nothing.' Of the party's four whips in 1887, Akers-Douglas owned 16,000 acres in four counties in 1879, Lord Arthur Hill was second son of the fourth Marquess of Downshire, Col. Walrond the son of a baronet, and the popular Hon. Sidney Herbert was the future fourteenth Earl of Pembroke; before him, as a contemporary wrote, 'the aggrieved and ill-mannered bent like willows.'[10]

The 1880s saw the culmination of the aristocracy's long-term drift towards the Conservatives. By 1885 their growing strength in the south-east and among the well-to-do gave them the edge on Liberals within London society, an asset which could be countermined only through the Liberals' increasingly popular and provincial party network. When the crucial Home Rule division was being taken on 8 June 1886, the Athenaeum emptied itself either to vote or to await the result; on Gladstone's defeat there were cries of 'bravo' and 'thank God!' from those who returned.[11] At that point, practically the whole Whig peerage – apart from Lords Spencer, Ripon, Rosebery, Kimberley and Granville – moved into alliance with the Conservatives, together with many prominent Liberal intellectuals and members of the upper class. Hence the political success of the Unionist alliance for a generation, and the defeat of Home Rule Bills in 1886 and 1893. But the long-term implications for the great British families were serious. Granville told Queen Victoria in 1880 that it was 'a great blessing to the country, and a great support to the aristocracy, that the Liberal Party had always had so large a portion of the peers and country gentlemen identified with it ... slight concessions from them to their more advanced friends do not produce the bad effect of sudden surrenders by the Conservative Party.'[12] After 1886 it would be difficult to prevent the Liberals from crusading against the House of Lords and ultimately against aristocracy itself.

The political elite was reinforced by a conspicuous display of wealth, still reflected today in the entrances to country mansions which are grandiose even in their decay. Landownership was concentrated into great estates from the late eighteenth century until 1873; only in the Edwardian period did they begin to break up. No more than 8.5 per cent of the total public revenue in 1880–89 came from death duties, and only 17.6 per cent from land, property and income tax. In 1881, excluding holdings of less than one acre, 1,200 persons owned a quarter of the land in Britain (averaging at 16,200 acres each) and 6,200 persons owned another quarter (averaging at 3,150 acres each). The largest estates were more likely to be in the north and west than in the south and east because of the great pressure on land in the London area. The 1881 census records 182,282 males between the age of twenty and sixty-five in England and Wales as being without specific occupation. Most were no more idle than the 4,458,908 females in the same age-group who were so listed. Wealth carried with it a great many unpaid and often tiresome duties; numerous claims from relatives, dependants, charities, political parties and other good causes had to be met.[13]

In the upper and even middle class, female relatives were among the dependants. Beatrice Webb later recalled that for girls whose only career was marriage, the London season was the equivalent of a university education and a professional training. Leisure was a 10.2 mark of social status, particularly among women. Gwen Raverat's Aunt Etty, who came from a decidedly middle-class family, had never done an astonishing range of things: 'ladies were ladies in those days; they did not do things themselves, they told other people what to do and how to do it.'[14] Nonetheless, women's role in the class system was crucial. An uncorrupted aristocracy can outwit its enemies, said Thomas Arnold, because 'it acts through the relations of private life, which are permanent, whereas the political excitement, which opposes it, must always be short-lived.' Through bearing numerous children, women perpetuated the family line; through conducting an elaborate correspondence and managing social occasions, they held the elite together. The radical M.P. Labouchere told Chamberlain in 1883 that the public underestimated radical strength in Parliament because radical M.P.s were divided 'and seem ashamed of their opinions. The Whigs, on the contrary, out of office act solidly together.'[15]

The London season in the 1880s was efficiently organized. Care was taken to prevent dates from clashing, and the great aristocratic mansions – Devonshire, Bridgewater, Stafford, Spencer, Apsley, Lansdowne, and many others – offered lavish entertainments over four or five months in the year. The guests usually knew one another, but, as Beatrice Webb pointed out, 'there was ... a purpose in all this apparently futile activity, the business of getting married; a business carried on by parents and other promoters, sometimes with genteel surreptitiousness, sometimes with cynical effrontery.' For her, London society radiated out from several interacting centres: the court, the leading politicians, the millionaire financiers, the racing set. There were gradations within it, and free trade in recreation did not entirely prevail; but to those who looked back from the 1920s, it all seemed well integrated and clearly defined.[16]

By modern standards, this was an age of formality and etiquette. Wives had begun to address their husbands in public by their Christian names, and many boys had ceased addressing their fathers as 'Sir', but men were not on Christian name terms unless the relationship was particularly close. Social life was riddled with unwritten rules, encrusted with elaborate symbols denoting status and connections, shot through with taboos, privacies, codes and forbidden topics. With a true Hanoverian zest for detail, the Prince of Wales presided over this world from

Marlborough House, bestowing advice, receiving confidences and interpreting the rules; he undertook virtually all the social and ceremonial functions of monarchy and operated through a circle of thirty or forty intimates. Lord Hartington was another influential social arbiter: 'I don't know why it is,' he once said, 'but whenever a man is caught cheating at cards the case is referred to me.' It was partly because of London society's tight organization of opinion, with its tribunals for settling internal disputes, that the London parks in the 1880s did not witness the duels frequently to be observed in the Bois de Boulogne.[17]

Although the British aristocracy in the 1880s presented an impressive spectacle during the London season, it was in county society that its social and political strength was most securely rooted; the capital merely linked up a series of local elites for part of the year. In her preface to Willoughby de Broke's *The Passing Years* (1924), his widow describes her husband's virtual obsession, at the end of his life, with the need to write down what he could remember of the English county society which by then was vanishing for good. Despite his enthusiasm for the task, he was unable to complete his concluding chapter on the proper relationship between the landowner and his dependants; during his first week of pain and fever, she writes, 'this idea was ever uppermost in his mind and he talked of it almost incessantly.'[18]

If given the choice, he would have been born not in 1869 but in 1810, as his grandfather was; then, as a landowner, he would have witnessed county society at its prime, reaching the age of seventy before the twin threats of agricultural depression and a democratic franchise hit the English countryside. By the 1920s Willoughby de Broke felt the need to explain to his readers what county society meant. 'One hardly ever hears "The County" being talked of at this time of day in the same tone of calm and reverent assurance that we heard when we were young,' he wrote. He goes on to explain that in social terms, 'the county' meant a hierarchy which embraced (in descending order of precedence) lord lieutenant, master of the foxhounds, agricultural landlord, bishop, chairman of quarter sessions, colonel of the yeomanry, M.P., dean, archdeacon, justice of the peace, lesser clergy and larger farmers.[19]

Gladstone moved easily within this world, and believed that 'the natural condition of a healthy society is that governing functions should be discharged in the main by a leisured class.' Many country houses were centres of judicial administration, local government and political activity. 'The great landlords of England are really the rulers of principalities,' wrote Escott: 'they are at the head of not one department, but of three or four different departments of State.'[20] A single family could wield such influence that it could even carry the local electorate with it into voting for another party; Rothschilds represented the Vale of Aylesbury continuously between 1865 and 1923 despite changes of political allegiance. Linked to the great country houses were the smaller mansions of the gentry (£1,000–£10,000 a year) and squirearchy (1,000–3,000 acres) who did not necessarily have any direct connection with London society, but were highly respected in their localities. The gentry flourished particularly in eastern England, Shropshire, Herefordshire, Oxfordshire and Gloucestershire, and in England as a whole in 1873 they owned 17 per cent of the land; the squirearchy, strong in the south-east, owned an eighth.[21]

10.3–5 At the centre of county society was the ideal of country house life. An aristocrat's status was not then in any way dependent on his personal appearance: Lord Hartington, for instance, was notorious for his conservative and even shabby dress. But his homes were lavish; Chatsworth housed priceless artistic and scholarly treasures, and the marquess was generous in welcoming students to work on them. Like many aristocrats at the time, he had little personal interest in art or humanistic scholarship, but he saw himself as a trustee for ancestors more cultivated than himself. By the 1880s the Dukes of Marlborough were among those aristocratic families already finding it necessary to sell some of their treasures; the Sunderland Library fetched nearly £60,000 in 1882–3, and the Blenheim enamels more than £73,000 in 1883. But such action was taken reluctantly, and when the eighth duke proposed to sell off some of Blenheim's finest pictures, there was considerable opposition from within the family.[22]

With Curzon at Kedleston rather later, the aristocrat's attachment to his family home became legendary, but a strong sense of local patriotism was widespread among many owners of country houses in the 1880s, not least Lord Lansdowne, whose affection for his homes amounted almost to a passion. Most of his official career was aimed at rescuing them from their financial plight. Falling revenue from his Irish estates caused him to let the family's London mansion, Lansdowne House, in 1887, and he was almost driven to selling it; but in 1888 he was able to tell his mother that becoming Viceroy of India 'means saving L[ansdowne] House for the family.' Together with an inheritance and the sale of Irish land, his viceregal income enabled the family to resume occupation in the 1890s. Lans-

downe lived to make the house over to his eldest son, Lord Kerry, in 1921, and even in 1926 to rebuild his beloved Derreen in Kerry, burned down by Irish republicans in 1922.[23]

The possession of a country house could mean as much to the *arriviste* as to the aristocrat, and its impact on house design was considerable even for those who remained within the towns. The British suburban dwelling from the late Victorian period onwards – half-timbered, perhaps, and secure within its fenced, hedged or walled garden – reflects a widespread yearning for rural independence, privacy and status. The country houses built or rebuilt in the Victorian period were concentrated in the south-east of England, especially in the London area, and testified to the persistence of what Bagehot once described as that 'struggle between what we may call the Northern and business element of English society, and the Southern and aristocratic element.' The boom period for such building, the 1870s, came to an end with the agricultural depression.[24]

Country house owners were by now drawing their income increasingly from urban sources, and often used their rural retreats primarily for a conspicuous expenditure which centred on the weekend party, with wits like Bernal Osborne and *littérateurs* like W.H. Mallock in attendance. The rambling, additive ground-plans recommended by architects like George Devey and Norman Shaw in the 1880s were ideally suited to the periodic influx of guests who stayed for two or three days and then left. 'Eat and dodle [sc. dawdle]; dodle and eat' was the phrase used by Mme Ignatieff, wife of the Russian ambassador, to describe such occasions. Mallock enjoyed the opportunities provided by the country house party for combining privacy with friendship: 'country-house conversations', he wrote, 'are like novels which, if laid down at one moment, can be taken up again the next. ... The atmosphere of a country house is one of interest pervaded by repose. Each night there is a dinner party, but there is no going out to dinner, and there is no separation afterward.'[25]

Yet a purely recreational concept of the country house differed markedly from the traditional aristocratic ideal, which envisaged an income directly drawn from farming in the surrounding area, and a continuous and highly personal relationship between landlord, tenants and estate workers. Lords Althorp and Grey in the 1830s saw London as a penance to be endured for the sake of parliamentary duties, and to be fled at the earliest opportunity for rural pursuits and relationships. It was the railway, and later the motor car, which broke down this strong aristocratic sense of locality. By the early 1920s, Willoughby de Broke was complaining that country house owners, instead of centring their social life on the Hunt Ball, were flying off to Monte Carlo and Aix-les-Bains; their dinner-parties were indistinguishable, he thought, from London ones, both in personnel and in the topics discussed.[26] Without recalling the one-time vitality of a very different pattern of country house living, the strength of the aristocratic appeal within the middle and working classes in the 1880s would be difficult to comprehend. These ramifications of the nobility among the more humble orders during the decade can now be considered in detail.

Middle-class hostility was declining by the 1880s; indeed new country houses in the mansarded French *hôtel* style reflect the trend towards aping the aristocracy. Even Joseph Chamberlain discovered the attraction: 'This luxurious society', he wrote from the Rothschild mansion at Waddesdon in 1888, '... is full of a certain charm and not altogether unprofitable. Every man and woman here is in some way gifted above the average, and ... they make life for the time very ornamental and recreative.' H.H. Asquith, the future Prime Minister, walking one day in London with Haldane, pointed to John Bright as unusual in his class for being 'the only man in public life who had risen to eminence without being corrupted by London Society.'[27] It was not long before the critics were murmuring that Asquith too had succumbed.

The social acceptance of the Rothschilds indicates the aristocracy's willingness to make terms with mere wealth; a hereditary nobility perpetuates itself only through continuously recruiting talent, wealth and beauty from the classes beneath it. By extending 'courtesy titles' to the children of a peer, but to his grandchildren only via his eldest son, the British avoided the rigidities of an aristocratic caste or 'noblesse' which would endanger relations with trade and commerce. Good looks and charm were appropriated to the aristocracy through marriage with actresses and American heiresses. Primogeniture forced the younger sons into seeking their own fortunes, and hence into middle-class company; they could pursue an energetic career in politics like Churchill or Salisbury, or marry into wealth, or embark on commercial or imperial adventures, but all three options entailed social mixing.

The aristocracy did not quickly assimilate commerce. The annual average of peerages created rose from 4 in 1830–68 to 6.5 in 1868–95, but the aristocratic reproduction-rate was falling, and the titles of duke and marquess retained all their old exclusiveness; only the ranks of viscount and baron expanded at all rapidly.[28] A landed estate was usually necessary before

a commercial family could attract a titled husband. The proportion of marriages between the late Victorian nobility and members of church or landed families declined, but this did not greatly increase the proportion of business marriages; peers began to look for wives among the daughters of foreigners or servicemen. Fewer aristocrats became entrepreneurs than in earlier decades, and those marrying into the middle class preferred to look to banking and commercial rather than to manufacturing families.[29]

Nonetheless by the 1880s distaste for Irish methods, the relative decline in agriculture, the fear of an insurgent working class *à la* Paris Commune, and also the sheer charm of the aristocratic way of life were bringing aristocracy and middle class together. Several social leaders, most notably the Prince of Wales and Lady Waldegrave, set out to extend the boundaries of fashionable acceptability. The Prince kept the monarchy in contact with the sections of British society neglected by the Queen. He also made it his business to establish good relations with Gladstone, whom she greatly disliked, and so helped to uphold the relatively recent convention that monarchy should rise above political party.

Honours aroused intense interest among the upper classes, and account for almost a quarter of Gladstone's letters to the Queen.[30] She instituted or enlarged fourteen orders, including the Victoria Cross, the Distinguished Service Order and the Star of India. Beatrice Webb says that by the 1870s London Society was open to all who possessed 'some form of power over other people'. Formal recognition, in the shape of titles, soon followed. Some old-fashioned stalwarts feigned shock when Sir Blundell Maple (of Maple's Stores) was made a baronet in 1897, but the wealth of the brewers and big industrialists could hardly be resisted at a time when the political parties needed money for their growing machines; four commercial or industrial peers were created in the ten years before 1886, as many as eighteen in the ten years after.[31] Allsopp, Guinness and Bass gained peerages in the 1880s, as did arms manufacturer William Armstrong and ironmaster Ivor Guest.

The middle classes were gaining acceptance in other ways. Decidedly bourgeois statesmen like Goschen the City banker and W.H. Smith the newsagent occupied key posts on merit even in a Conservative government. In 1886 Smith declined the Queen's offer of the G.C.B. because he felt his usefulness might be diminished '*at present* if he were to seem to the outside world to be too anxious for a decoration which, until recently at all events, has only been given to men of his social standing for very distinguished services'; but his widow became Viscountess Hambleden.[32] When the G.C.B. was offered to Joseph Chamberlain in 1888, on returning from his American mission, it is hardly surprising that (as a former radical) he refused, but he too was now inclining towards the centres of aristocratic political power.

In so far as attacks on the nobility did occur in the 1880s, they in some ways helped integrate British society by obscuring the conflict of interest between employer and employee. Snobbery and exclusiveness were so patent in the Britain of the 1880s that hostile attention could easily be focused on what might now be seen as peripheral evils such as aristocratic immorality, blood sports, the shortage of smallholdings or threats to rights of way. In the earlier stages of capitalism, wrote Marx, ' the proletarians do not fight their enemies, but the enemies of their enemies, the remnants of absolute monarchy, the landowners, the non-industrial bourgeois, the petty bourgeoisie.'[33] Attacks on aristocracy, like the Fabians' attacks on pauperism at the top and bottom of society, drew radical manufacturers and working men together, and so were easily catered for by the Liberal Party.

If wealth could find a home in both parties, even after 1886, so also could working men. The working class was itself divided – not just between Catholic and Protestant, secularist and Christian, Anglican and Nonconformist, rough and respectable – but even within the respectable grouping: on the one hand there was the rationalist who repudiated mysticism and deference, and who is usually thought of as a natural Liberal; on the other, the type whose respectability actually led him to imitate the aristocracy, and whose natural home was the Conservative Party. There he would paradoxically find himself politically allied with the rougher elements of the working class who repudiated the concept of respectability altogether, but who felt a sneaking admiration for the aristocracy's more raffish members. The three-class system was never more than a very rough approximation to the Victorian social reality, and the two-class system predicted by Marx emerged only in very limited areas at limited periods.

Conservatives reinforced their popular appeal through links with the army and the publican, with protectionism and (though only at the local level) anti-alien feeling. But the party's major source of strength lay in the pride taken by many working people, especially in the countryside, in the local social hierarchy, whose wealth was seen less as the cause of poverty than as the remedy for it: as a source of charity and employment in an insecure world. Many a working man prided himself on knowing how to distinguish between a 'man' and a 'gentleman', or fancied that somewhere in the not-so-remote past his family boasted an aristocratic forbear whose will might even now bring some windfall. 'Almost every family in the hamlet,' wrote Flora Thompson of Lark Rise, 'prided itself upon some family tradition which, in its own estimation, at least, raised it above the common mass of the wholly uninteresting.'[34]

Reinforcing such attitudes was the ideal of personal service, which then deeply influenced class and politics, if only because of the large numbers involved. In 1881 no less than 2,000,000 people (15 per cent of the British labour force) were employed in domestic and personal services, not to mention retired servants.[35] So large a figure is significant not only for itself but for the number of openings it provided for servants to influence working-class attitudes in general; there must have been few working-class families in the 1880s who had no domestic servant as a relative. Without servants, country house life could not have existed, lavish fancy-dress balls could not have been staged. The 10.1 aristocracy and gentry were themselves a spectacle at this time. Therein lay much of their strength: 'to be well-dressed is not altogether foolish,' wrote Pascal, 'for it proves that a great number of people are working for us.'[36] This army of domestic servants is the other face of that leisured country house life which now seems so attractive.

A glance at the ground plan of any country house in the 1880s, or even at the inconvenient design of any middle-class suburban house, will show why so many servants were needed. 'The remembrance of a full-blown Victorian establishment in full swing is in these days a very great treasure,' wrote Willoughby de Broke. 'It is not every one who has seen it from the inside.' He goes on to describe Compton Verney in its great days before the depression – with its park, its home-brewed beer, its roast beef and its big fires, and above all with the retinue which made all this possible. The service wing of the Victorian country house was at its most elaborate in the years up to 1870, and contracted only slowly thereafter. A host of butlers, cooks and kitchenmaids laboured for hours in preparation for the descent of the house party down the main stairs; an immense amount of work went into laying banqueting 10.6 tables and cooking upper-class meals. In those days, food was usually processed at home instead of being bought ready-made: cooking equipment was primitive: and there were few of the modern aids for cleaning kitchen paraphernalia, yet considerable emphasis on the need to polish it. Hence the emergence of large, 10.7

highly differentiated communities of servants, each with their own specialist skills. As late as 1881, 107,000 householders took out an annual licence to brew their own beer, and laundering was a complex art. Country house clothing was elaborate, high standards were required and equipment was inadequate: everything had to be done by hand.[37] The servants' area was carefully segregated, and they entered the owners' quarters only when summoned or in the very early morning; in the presence of their superiors, they had to be unobtrusive, with eyes which did not see, ears which did not hear, and movements which made no noise. In some households they were even required to sacrifice the small remaining element of their individuality by assuming a name which the employer preferred to their own.

So prevalent was domestic service that it played an important role in the economy of the working-class rural family. It was an occupation open to the teenage country working girl at just the time when the lack of local employment required her to leave home, when her parents could no longer afford to feed her, when she needed training in housekeeping, and when town life offered all the excitements of the unknown. There were 218 female domestic indoor servants per 1,000 families in England and Wales in 1881; a rising proportion of the total female labour force, domestic servants increased as agricultural and country craft occupations declined.[38] Employers' preference for country girls as servants caused the sex-ratio to vary markedly between town and country, and between town and town. In 1881 the proportion of women was high in wealthy communities like London, suburbia, and upper-class resort-towns like Brighton, Bath and Cheltenham, but low in mining and manufacturing districts, where servants were scarce. In Brighton there was one servant to eleven inhabitants, in Lancashire only one to thirty.[39]

Given the tedium which household work often entailed and the wide, closely observed differentials in wealth which prevailed in the 1880s one might have expected domestic service to be a hated occupation, and the servant-keeping classes to see their employees as potential enemies in their midst, unreliable in times of political instability. There certainly was friction. The petty jealousies, dreary vendettas and contracted views which beset relations between master and servant, and even between servant and servant, can readily be imagined. Middle-class domestic life often involved a continuous battle of wills, especially over 'waste in the kitchen'. There were other drawbacks from the employers' point of view, sometimes beginning in child-

hood, which the servant could often make miserable for children who were seldom seen by their parents. Furthermore, servants deprived employers of their privacy, and it became necessary to 'keep up appearances' even within the home; for example, such subterfuges are written all over the divorce court proceedings in 1886 which involved Sir Charles Dilke. Campbell-Bannerman felt free to discuss political personalities in the servants' presence only through denoting leading politicians by their nicknames or by the titles of their family seats. It is hardly surprising that William Stubbs, when he became Bishop of Oxford in 1889, was appalled at the thought of having to live in a large country house like Cuddesdon, and pleaded with the Archbishop of Canterbury for it to be sold: 'to live a slave to gardeners and coachmen,' he wrote, 'would be death at once both to me and to my wife ... There is no question of money in this, simply of the strain of mind and responsibility.'[40]

Yet if bad feeling between the classes had been the sole outcome of domestic service, it would hardly be relevant to discuss the subject at this point. In reality, it would be quite wrong to project on to Victorian domestic servants a modern political awareness or class conciousness; they were intensely aware of class and status, but the consequences of this were conservative rather than radical. For this, purely structural reasons were partly responsible. The servants' twofold fragmentation – into small work-groups divided between households, and into hierarchies and even specialist sub-groups within households – hardly encouraged class consciousness of the radical type. And in the larger houses, where trouble might have been expected to result from the greater number of servants, the hierarchy was yet more elaborate, the servants more specialized and therefore better paid and more fragmented, with outdoor service going to the men, indoor to the women.

The structural influences making for class harmony within the household were reinforced by ideas and attitudes with a very long ancestry: pride in the job, social emulation and mutual responsibility. Far from being seen as a humiliation, domestic service – the art of laying a table, the skills required to launder a dress-shirt, the expertise involved in keeping a cellar or grooming a horse – could be a source of great personal pride. Tools were as integral to the servant's personality as to those of other working people of the day, and uniforms as important to his own status as to that of those he served. Socially and occupationally, Victorian working people could readily be 'placed' by their clothing – particularly useful to servants who wanted to avoid the embarrassing social situations which could so easily occur in a class-conscious age, for in no occupation were these more of a hazard. Domestic service often gave men a training which could later set them up on their own, and gave women preparation for what was then their best trade of all – marriage. The country girl aimed to go into such an occupation, said Escott, 'and then to find a husband in some gentleman's footman or butler, attaining finally to the dignity of landlady of some country town inn or thriving public-house.'[41]

But social mobility did not necessarily require the servant to leave his employer and set up on his own; on the contrary, it could be acquired through long service and imitation. Gross discrepancy in wealth and status can as readily inspire emulation as resentment, pride in reflected glory as often as jealousy. If the master dressed for dinner, his butler 'dressed' too; college servants at Oxford and Cambridge even saw themselves as playing an essential part in the undergraduate's education. The role of the head gamekeeper Mr Eales in Willoughby de Broke's education has already been discussed. It was not quite social mobility which he acquired through staying on with his employer, so much as entry into a social world which was paradoxically classless in an important respect: a familiar and long-trusted servant remained fully conscious of the class hierarchy, yet he joined the family circle, and was in some sense treated as an equal. Willoughby de Broke describes Mr Eales's 'natural grace' when presented to the Prince of Wales, and goes on to say that 'Mr Eales, although he never forgot his position, always emerged with honours from the test of meeting any given company with ease and respect, as an equal talking to equals.'[42]

It was a social equality which sprang from mutual responsibility across the class divide. The employer also had his obligations: he must behave as a gentleman, and treat his servant considerately. Old retainers repeatedly feature, for instance, in the Queen's journal during the 1880s, as she visits them or records their deaths: 'my poor excellent footman Lockwood' in 1886 during his illness, 'my dear faithful old Skerrett ... most devoted and attached to me and mine' at her death in 1887, and 'poor good Kanné' who died in 1888 and 'used to think of every little thing for my pleasure and comfort.'[43]

Friendship seems often to have resulted. In several Victorian novels the lady's maid becomes her mistress's best friend, and similar situations are often reflected in autobiographies and biographies. Violet Markham, for instance, looked back on Elizabeth Downs the cook as her greatest childhood friend: 'I was as much attached to the corner of Elizabeth's dresser as I was to the corner of my Father's sofa.' Later in life her housekeeper Mildred Brown became 'for forty-one years my most beloved and trusted friend'. And the role of Mrs Everest in the life of the young Winston Churchill has already been discussed: it was to her that he poured out his troubles as a young man at Sandhurst. He later described her as 'my dearest and most intimate friend during the whole of the twenty years I had lived,' and to the end of his life her photograph hung in his room.[44]

The domestic servant's social outlook – his belief in discipline and hierarchy, and his pride in his job – reappears in the many uniformed occupations which were then recruited largely from old soldiers. Railwaymen, 10.11 for instance, were expected to identify with the employer, and therefore with his equipment and his customers; many proudly donned their company's uniform, which carefully distinguished between their many ranks and gradations.[45] But here, as in several other occupations, the ideal of personal service merges as an influence on attitudes to work with the analogy of military service, which is an important theme of the next chapter.

10.2 (RIGHT). *Well-bred young ladies were expected to be accomplished embroiderers. An unusual indoor photograph by an amateur. Undated*

10.3 (BELOW). *Weekend parties at country houses were often large enough to field two cricket teams. Ladies v. Gentlemen at Ades, Sussex. 1887*

10.4 (ABOVE). *Haddo House, Aberdeenshire, Lord Aberdeen's home, during a visit by W.E. Gladstone, G.W. Wilson & Co., 1884*

10.5 (BELOW). *Tranby Croft, East Yorkshire, with the Prince of Wales and, among others, Sir William Gordon-Cumming, who was later accused of cheating at baccarat on this occasion. 1890*

10.6–8. Aristocratic life made work for butlers, cooks and
kitchenmaids. Tables at the Waterloo Hotel, Edinburgh (ABOVE), laid
for a dinner to be given in honour of Lord Hopetoun, Bedford Lemere,
1889. The kitchen at Burton House, Sussex (ABOVE RIGHT). c.1890.
The laundry at Petworth House, Sussex (BELOW RIGHT). c.1890

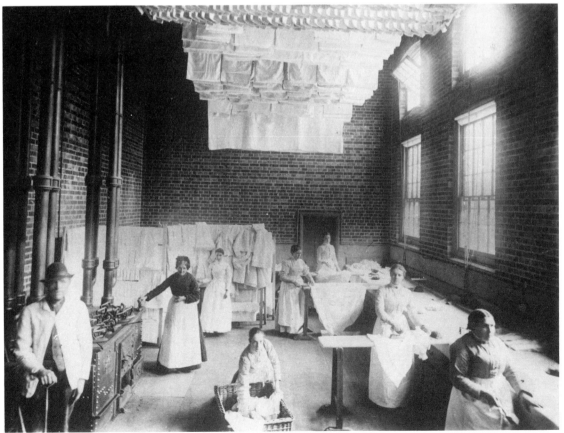

10.9. *A group of 'indoor' and 'outdoor' domestic servants with the tools of their trades. Undated*

10.10. *The ten gardeners employed by Mr T. Bass of Burton-on-Trent, Staffordshire, J. Roberts, 1880*

10.11. *Men of the North London Railway at South Acton,*
London, as proud of their uniforms as of 4–4–0 tank
locomotive No. 29. Undated

Discipline
Chapter 11 *and Authority*

In the last resort nineteenth-century government's authority could be upheld by force, and order was often maintained with vigour: against rickburners in the English countryside in the 1830s for instance, against Indian rebels in 1857, and in Ireland throughout the century. But by the standards of the time British government was slow to deploy its full strength, and gradually built up the police into an order-keeping force less provocative than the army had ever been. By the 1880s the police were more popular than they had been in the 1830s, though their intervention in the squabbles so rife in the slums was often ill-informed and clumsy. England and Wales employed 39,921 policemen in 1891; their number and density in relation to population had been rising steadily for some decades, and by 1887–8 there was one constable in 769 of the population (compare 457 in 1975).[1]

Regular employment in the 1880s was not easily had, and the forces of order could always get recruits from the numerous respectable working men of apparently sober habits and military bearing. Bernard Shaw rightly pointed out in *Fabian Essays* that, given the prevailing social structure, it would always be in the interest of some workers to repudiate socialist appeals and align themselves with their alleged oppressors. Eleanor Marx disgustedly told Liebknecht

11.1. Inside Wormwood Scrubs Prison, London. Some time before 1895

in 1881 how even Irish policemen were prepared to arrest their fellow-countrymen: outside Bow Street she had 'asked a Policeman with a very hibernian countenance if Davitt [the Irish nationalist] were still there. "No," said he "its meself put him in the van." '[2]

Police strength in relation to population differed markedly in different areas – one for 466 inhabitants in London in 1881, one for 792 in boroughs, and only one for 1,286 in the counties. It is hardly surprising that election riots proved most difficult to curb in the smaller country towns;[3] magistrates faced by the Salvation Army in such places still informally relied on the conservative mob, or 'Skeleton Army', to restrain troublesome outsiders from disturbing the peace of the community. Such expedients were unacceptable in London; but the alternative, sophistication in riot control, was not in evidence during the Trafalgar Square riots of 1886; as a result, Sir Edmund Henderson, seventeen years chief commissioner of the metropolitan police, had to resign. As a subsequent police commissioner, Sir Charles Warren, put it, in an indiscreet article published three years later, 'London was subject to a three days' reign of abject terror, pitiful and ridiculous, which only terminated because the mob was so completely astonished and taken aback at its own success, that it was not prepared to continue its depredations.' When it came to 'Bloody Sunday', however – the Trafalgar Square riots of 13 November 1887 – the police were better organized. 'I confess I was astounded at the rapidity of the thing and the ease with which military organisation got its victory,' Morris reported. 'I could see that numbers were of no avail unless led by a band of men acting in concert and each knowing his own part.'[4] But the police were not yet out of trouble: Warren was himself dismissed for undermining the Home Secretary's authority with his published statements. There was further trouble in 1890 when Warren's successor Munro supported the force's claim for higher pensions; he too lost his job, and the matter was only partially settled by the Police Act of 1890.

By comparison with some continental forces, the British police were very weak. Their decentralized structure reflected their local origins, and the plainclothes detective service was hindered by the deeply rooted English objection to government intruders and spies. Yet in one respect the weakness of the British police was their strength, as Eleanor Marx pointed out in 1874; a Prussian system for keeping order in England, she wrote, 'would do more than all the Trade Unions and Workingmen's Societies put together to bring life into the movement here.' British protest groups were less bitterly alienated from authority than elsewhere; indeed, by the 1880s the police often entrusted working-class leaders with the responsibility for maintaining order at their meetings. Not slow to employ the new methods of communication, the police already in the 1840s were making use of the railway and telegraph. Techniques of riot control steadily improved, and criminal investigation was consolidated and systematized by the Convict Supervision Office, opened in 1880 at the metropolitan police headquarters. There was close liaison with the Criminal Investigation Department (formed in 1878), whose increasing role gave it 472 officers by 1895.[5]

11.6   Photography was first applied to police purposes in 1854, when the governor of Bristol gaol began making daguerrotype pictures of his prisoners; but the rare accessible photographs of convicts reflect an impersonal, almost clinical, approach. By April 1880 the C.I.D. possessed thirty volumes, each containing five hundred portraits taken shortly before release, and classified by the type of crime committed. Offenders sentenced to penal servitude went to Pentonville for their first nine months, and all were photographed there in its special studio on the second floor. A massproduction procedure had been developed by 1881, whereby prisoners were taken in batches of six: while one sat in a high-backed chair to be photographed (with an exposure of seven seconds), another inscribed a blackboard with his number and name and held it above his head. As they sat in compulsory silence in a row on a bench in grey jackets and knickerbockers with shaven faces and cropped hair, the *Photographic News* thought they looked 'like big school boys'. By 1886 the convict officer at Scotland Yard had collected nearly 34,000 photographs dating back to 1862 in albums which each contained 6,000 portraits, together with duplicates in volumes arranged by type of crime. They were often consulted by detectives.[6]

Statistics do not necessarily reflect the incidence of crime, and in the 1880s there was little relationship between attitudes to law-breaking and the known facts about it. The traditional moralistic approach to crime was now being supplemented by two new approaches: the socialist and the urban. A straightforward socialist analysis, which argues that crime stems directly from poverty, conflicts most frontally with the evidence for this decade, in that the level of property offences in the 1880s showed some signs of being related not, as in the past, to economic depression but (in true twentieth-century style) to prosperity. In such a situation, the criminal becomes more the ally of capitalism than its victim, in that his offences reflect its competitive and accumulative values. Socialist explanations of rather a different type, however, were becoming fashionable, encouraged by a change in the nature of the prison population. They were socialist only in the weak sense that they repudiated earlier moralistic interpretations and substituted environmentalist or even psychological ones which converted the criminal into a victim of social background or parentage; in Samuel Butler's *Erewhon* (1872), for instance, it is wicked to be ill, but embezzlement is a disease.

The marked decline during the 1870s in the percentage of male and female convicts under seventeen continued more slowly during the 1880s, and for both sexes the percentage with previous gaol sentences rose markedly during the decade; prisoners were older and less literate than the population at large. This was largely because of changes in policy, which increasingly discriminated between the casual or first offender (who was given milder penalties) and the habitual offender (whose punishments were made cumulative, and whose conduct was more closely supervised when at large); the Probation of First Offenders Act in 1887 extended to adults the idea of a 'second chance' which had already been applied to children.[7] Nonetheless, it was tempting in this situation to see the criminal as a distinct 'type'; Havelock Ellis's *The Criminal* (1890), though critical of Lombroso, did much to popularize his ideas in Britain.

William Morrison offered an alternative 'urban' analysis, deducing from statistics that 'where there is most civilisation there is also most crime.' He argued that urbanization was conducive to crime in at least three ways: it increased the complexity of the law: it made conflicts more likely between individual citizens, and between them and the law: and it encouraged temptation by concentrating the ownership of property. Certainly the number of minor offences was increased by the multiplication of municipal by-laws and by legislation compelling vaccination and school attendance and protecting animals and children.[8] Yet the 'urban' theory also stumbles on the statistics. In the 1860s the level of reported crime in Lancashire, the most heavily industrialized part of the country, was twice as high as in England and Wales as a whole, yet in the 1880s crime figures there were falling faster than in the nation at large. And although Britain in the 1880s was rapidly urbanizing, the recorded rates of crime were declining markedly in relation to population, and in England and Wales the proportion of known thieves and receivers in relation to population was also declining. In 1890 there were only about 300 indictable offences known to the police in England and Wales for every 100,000 of the population, a much lower rate than prevails today.[9]

This apparent reduction in crime was accompanied by an intense interest in reading about it. The popular press had long been treating the subject sensationally, and its readership is epitomized in a respectable woman's comment to Miss Loane many years later: 'I do *enjoy* a good murder, especially when there's a long trial after.' The new penny dailies relied largely on reports of sensational law cases for 'human interest', and made leading judges and barristers into national figures. Court cases in the 1880s were often semi-recreational occasions, and when Sir Edward Clarke's speech was applauded during the Tranby Croft hearing in 1891, Lord Chief Justice Coleridge had to emphasize that the court-room was not a theatre. This was the decade when solitary strangers all over England were accused of being Jack the Ripper. The Queen was very excited: 'this new most ghastly murder shows the absolute necessity for some very decided action,' she informed Lord Salisbury in November 1888.[10] In the same year a Southsea doctor, Conan Doyle, made a major breakthrough in detective fiction with his first Sherlock Holmes story, *A Study in Scarlet*. This new genre catered more for the intellect than did the traditional approach to crime novels, and focused as much on the detective as on the criminal.

Karl Marx once emphasized the abundance of employment created by the criminal: police, the prison service, even executioners. The ranks of the lawyers

continued to swell in the 1880s despite the surprising decline in litigation when related to population. Between 1861 and 1891 the number of barristers and solicitors in England and Wales rose by 37 per cent, law clerks by 66 per cent, yet the number of writs issued fell from 3.7 per thousand of the population in 1875/8 to 2.5 per thousand in 1891/2. In absolute terms, fewer cases were begun in the superior courts in the 1890s than in the 1860s, partly reflecting a preference for the simpler procedure of the inferior (especially the county) courts, whose business increased. But, counting the cases begun at both levels together, there was still a decline when population is taken into account – from 47 per thousand of the population in 1859/62 to 41 per thousand in 1891/2. There were also not nearly so many appeals for retrial during the same period. John Macdonnell attributed the rising proportion of actions defended and coming to trial to a decline in petty litigiousness. The poorer and more backward the district, he claimed, the greater the tendency to embark on lawsuits: 'when we meet the perpetual litigant in these days he is generally found to be a half-witted dupe or a monster of egotism and vanity.' Why, then, were lawyers proliferating? Cases were no doubt becoming more complex, and contentious matters were only a small part of the attorney's business. As elsewhere among the professions, the paperwork was increasing by leaps and bounds.[11]

'The criminal produces not only crime but also the criminal law,' said Marx; 'he produces the professor who delivers lectures on this criminal law, and even the inevitable text-book in which the professor presents his lectures as a commodity for sale in the market.'[12] Great progress was made in the 1880s in getting law studied in universities. A.V. Dicey gained his chair at Oxford in 1882, Pollock followed in 1883; Maitland won his readership at Cambridge in 1884 and his chair there four years later. Dicey's *Introduction to the Study of the Law of the Constitution* duly followed in 1885 and Pollock's influential *Law of Torts* in 1887; but Maitland's lectures on the constitutional history of England, though complete by 1888, were published only posthumously in 1908. This trio helped to provide law students with their basic equipment. Pollock was chiefly responsible for founding the *Law Quarterly Review* in 1885 and continued editing it from then until 1919; Maitland founded the Selden Society in 1887 to publish documents fundamental to the history of the law, and collaborated with Pollock to produce their classic *History of English Law* in 1895.

Dicey's influence extended widely; he did not shrink from political controversy, and his *England's Case against Home Rule* (1886) was re-edited for each of the two later Home Rule Bills. Politics and the law were closely intertwined, and many distinguished lawyers sat in Parliament in the 1880s, when their colleagues contributed nearly a fifth of the M.P.s and a rising proportion of all three party groupings. Sir Henry James wielded immense influence at the highest levels, as rueful Home Rulers and woman suffragists discovered, and his young protégé H.H. Asquith jumped several rungs in the parliamentary career-ladder with his work on the Pigott forgeries case. It was a decade when the two lawsuits involving Dilke and Parnell changed the whole direction of party politics.

The 14,775 male and 2,528 female prisoners in England and Wales recorded by the 1891 census were in a sense also the products of the legal system. Despite an increase in the average length of sentence, these figures represent a 38 per cent fall since 1881. In 1881 there was one prisoner for every 931 persons, in 1891 one for 1,676. The explanation given at the time was that there were fewer criminals, and that fewer of them were being gaoled. Most were not committed for long: 72 per cent of those sentenced between 1879 and 1888 in England and Wales stayed for a month or less, 96 per cent for six months or less. Administration was centralized and standardized by the Prisons Act of 1877, and the prison force became smaller but more efficient. Small local gaols gave way to large, highly regimented institutions like Portland, visited by Sir Edward Hamilton one lunchtime in 1882. 'The order being given, each cell door was unlocked,' he wrote. 'At the word of command, "One step to the front," each man advanced and took up the plate containing his meal which had been deposited on the floor opposite his cell-door. At the further command, "One step to the rear," each convict stepped back into his cell and simultaneously closed his iron door which shuts with a spring. It was like a roar of cannon.'[13]

11.1 A combination of bluff and intimidation was inevitably used in institutions where a few officers controlled a mass of other ranks. Military formation could be obtained from quite a large body of prisoners by a small number of officers in charge. The structure of the convict service was para-military from its foundation in 11.4,6 1850; prison staff, like railway officials and policemen, adopted the soldierly bearing of an occupation regularly recruited from ex-members of the armed forces. The mystery of the law entailed secrecy: there was an annual average of thirty unobtrusive executions between 11.5 1879 and 1888 in the prisons of England and Wales. Degrading punishments like the treadmill could still be imposed at Wormwood Scrubs, and justices sentenced

3,000 people a year to be whipped between 1879 and 1888.[14] Most eloquent of all on the humiliations of life in gaol, because of its dramatic understatement, was the sight of women prisoners exercising in Wormwood 11.8 Scrubs, with regulation spacing and carrying their babies.

The insane too were regimented into large institutions, and this made it easy to collect statistics. The smaller private madhouse accounted for only half the lunatics in 1880, and by the 1890s mental asylums with as many as 2,000 beds were normal in London 11.7 and Lancashire. A similar trend was evident elsewhere, and in 1890 county borough and city asylums averaged at 802 patients. Photography had been providing physiognomic data for the study of lunacy from the 1850s, and by the 1880s portraits were often taken on entry into an asylum, usually to be pasted into casebooks, together with others taken during periods of sanity, as valuable data for the case-history. At this stage photographing the lunatic presented major difficulties. The acutely insane, wrote Dr D.G. Thomson in the *British Journal of Photography*, were 'photographically ... fiends incarnate – fractious children, express trains, sea rollers, Oxford and Cambridge boat-races, comets and other intractable subjects being as nothing to them.'[15]

The 1871 census was the first to include questions on lunacy, and in 1891 there were 97,383 insane people in England and Wales – an increase of 41 per cent on 1871, and a rising proportion of the population.[16] The reality was less alarming in so far as these figures reflect longer life, greater accuracy in statistics, and increased public provision for pauper lunatics. But they also bear witness to growing institutionalization, giving rise to a treatment which must often have been worse than the disease. Care was so poor that Mrs Fenwick excluded mental nurses from her British Nursing Association in 1895: 'everyone will agree,' she wrote, 'that no person can be considered trained who has only worked in hospitals and asylums for the insane.'[17] Not surprisingly, the major issue in mental health policy during the 1880s was the question of improper confinement: the Lunacy Laws Amendment Association capitalized on Mrs Weldon's successful suit against Dr Forbes Winslow on this score. The Lunacy Act of 1890 tightened up procedure by instituting the reception order, which involved the magistrates or courts at some stage in all cases. But for many years yet, the institutionalization of lunatics was to continue apace.

Regimentation, then, uniforms and hierarchy were far more widespread in the 1880s than now; their prevalence reflects an outlook eroded during the twentieth century by two devastating world wars. The late Victorian army and navy were far more prominent in society and politics. Repayment and servicing of the national debt, built up largely by wars in the past, was the largest single item of governmental expenditure; after 1870–74 the proportion declined, but at 29.5 per cent in the five years 1885–9 it was still substantial. Its gross total fell sharply during the 1880s, but in 1890 it still amounted to what then seemed the colossal sum of £689,000,000. Add to these figures the annual cost of the armed services (34 per cent of the total annual budget in 1885–9, only 9 per cent in 1975) and it becomes clear why politicians were so preoccupied with questions of war and peace.[18] Expenditure on modernizing the navy began rising fast after 1884; steam had superseded sail, and by 1888 the 'Admiral' class of battleship had rendered all existing vessels obsolete. Aided by the maritime scares of 1888–9 and 1893–4, the navy succeeded in overhauling its accounts and greatly increased its share of the defence budget; in 1895–6, it overtook army spending for the first time.

The number of servicemen was also impressive; a society with a much smaller population, gross national product and labour force than our own nonetheless employed an average of 269,000 people in the United Kingdom armed forces during the five-year period 1886–90 (80 per cent of the figure for 1975).[19] The close links with the aristocracy increased politicians' preoccupation with the subject, for the army was one of the few professions then open to a gentleman, and the newspapers amply reported its annual manoeuvres. A quarter of the House of Lords in 1886 were officers, and in 1877 the Queen was reluctant to make W.H. Smith, a commercial man, First Lord of the Admiralty because 'it may *not please* the Navy in which so many of *highest rank* serve, and who claim to be equal to the Army – if a man of the Middle Class is placed above them in that very high Post.'[20] The army officer belonged to a sort of club for the well-born, whose members moved freely into the upper echelons of society and married a rising proportion of the daughters of the nobility. The whole ethos of politics – with its stress on honour, chivalry, sporting prowess and male supremacy – reflected the prevailing belief in the male's predominantly military function. This was, after all, one of the reasons why aristocratic girls at the age of five between 1880 and 1949 could expect to live till 68, their brothers only till 53.[21]

In his influential *Man Versus the State* (1884) Herbert Spencer distinguished between two opposed types of social organization, the 'militant' and the 'industrial'.

As a good Liberal, he wanted to see the first of these – which rested on status rather than contractual relationships, and flourished on war rather than peace – superseded by the second. Spencer had always been an eccentric figure, and in the 1880s was rapidly becoming more so, but his classification illuminates the distaste for violence so deeply rooted in the Liberal mind; radicals associated it with aristocratic medievalism. Of the 242 M.P.s with service connections in the three parliaments of the decade, as many as 171 were Conservatives or Unionists, and this divergence between the parties widened still further in the 1890s.[22] In constituencies where military and naval connections were important – Sheffield (despite its nonconformity), Wessex and the Scottish highlands – Conservative candidates profited from the Liberals' opposition to war and empire.

The army's aristocratic links and its widening connections with the middle class encouraged public schools to cater for boys aiming at a military career. Entrance examinations were substituted for direct commissions after 1849, and in 1871 the purchase of army commissions was abolished and open competition substituted for nomination as the way into the military academies. Of the 286 entrants to Sandhurst in 1880, 15 per cent were sons of businessmen and 24 per cent sons of professional men. At Eton, Harrow and Winchester, the armed services were the most popular among the careers chosen. The major public schools contributed much of the intake to Sandhurst and Woolwich and even more of the senior army officers.[23] The prestige of the engineers and the artillery was rising, and the well-born gradually retreated into the less meritocratic havens offered by the guards regiments. Lord Wolseley in the 1880s boldly championed the cause of the more technical type of army officer and even pressed his case upon the Queen. The engineers were responsible for many major civil achievements in the nineteenth century, not least the Ordnance Survey, whose military element was in 1886 'at once the framework, the backbone, the substratum on which the stability of the whole body depends.' Middle-class progress in the profession was nonetheless slow; half the officers in the British home army in 1875 were still drawn from aristocracy and gentry.[24]

But this bourgeois advance, though limited, frustrated Richard Cobden's early Victorian hopes of an anti-militarist, anti-imperialist, anti-aristocratic middle-class culture. Here the assimilation to aristocracy occurred under decidedly aristocratic supervision. 'India and the colonies', wrote Escott, 'afford occupation for tens of thousands of young men born to decent station';

on returning home they were hardly likely to aid a Liberal Party which was lukewarm on Empire. 'The South and South-West of England is richly sprinkled with these men,' wrote J.A. Hobson, the Liberal economist, some years later: 'many of them wealthy, most of them endowed with leisure, men openly contemptuous of democracy, devoted to material luxury, social display, and the shallower arts of intellectual life.'[25]

Imperial and military considerations came to affect many political questions: feminists, for instance, encountered the physical force argument, and Home Rulers were faced by Lord Salisbury's contention in 1883 that 'the coast of Ireland, in unfriendly hands, would be something more than a pistol held to the mouths of the Clyde and the Mersey and the Severn.' Nor could the navy lightly regard the possible loss of the Belfast shipyards; Home Rule might damage an industry so heavily dependent on free trade, or even eventually remove it from British control altogether. Salisbury once said that Gladstone, in struggling for Home Rule, 'awakened the slumbering genius of Imperialism.'[26]

With nervous glances over the shoulder at industrial growth in the United States and Germany, and with the nagging worry that far-flung imperial responsibilities overstretched British military resources, politicians became increasingly absorbed in the pursuit of prestige, and continually weighed up the impact of domestic events on foreign and imperial relations. The Queen was ever preoccupied with the nation's standing abroad and, in a typically vehement letter to Gladstone on the subject in February 1884, emphasized the need to wipe out the damaging effect of British setbacks in the Sudan: 'a blow *must* be struck, or we shall *never* be able to convince the Mahomedans that they have not beaten us. – These are wild Arabs and they w[oul]d not stand ag[ain]st *regular* good Troops at all.' Lord Lansdowne, progressing through the North-West Provinces as Viceroy of India in 1889, told his mother in a letter how impressed he was at the sight of the native cavalry and infantry when they paraded beside Irish and Scottish regiments: 'when one sees these grizzled warriors, many of them 6 ft high and splendidly built, with the carriage and demeanour of a ruling race – men by the side of whom our red-coated Tommies look plebeian and insignificant – one cannot help wondering at the manner in which we have conquered and held this country.' Lord Randolph Churchill, himself just back from India, told the Primrose League in April 1885 that British rule there was 'a sheet of oil spread over the surface of, and keeping calm and quiet and unruffled by storms, an immense and profound ocean of humanity.'

Three years later he told the Czar that 250,000 people ruling a population of 250,000,000 could hardly avoid preoccupation with morale and prestige.[27]

Nervousness was increased by the weakness of the army's hold on working-class leaders. The nonconformists, who were so influential with respectable working men, had always disliked the army: of the non-commissioned officers and other ranks whose religion was recorded in the 1880s, only 4 per cent were Wesleyans, 8 per cent Presbyterians and 1 per cent Protestants of other types, whereas Anglicans accounted for 66 per cent.[28] There was little national enthusiasm for the idea of conscription. Only in 1916, in the midst of a major war, was it held to be justified; in peacetime the British armed services had to be recruited on a voluntary basis. Yet Britain's rural population, the traditional source of good personnel, was rapidly declining; and so great were the pressures for economy at the national level that really attractive wages could not be paid. A strangely ambiguous attitude towards soldiers prevailed at this time whereby they were excluded from places of public entertainment, yet praised for their courage. For the unemployed unskilled teenage boy, the army was never more than a last resort as a career. Enlistment was easiest in periods of economic depression, but fixed annual estimates prevented the recruiting sergeants from taking full advantage of this by expanding and contracting their intake in accordance with the trade cycle.

Serious disciplinary problems limited the efficiency of the soldiers secured, and the work of the recruiting sergeants, with their offers of drink and the Queen's shilling, was partly undone by desertions in the 1870s at the rate of 5,000 a year. Opposing the abolition of flogging in the armed services in 1879, Archibald Forbes argued that men of such low social grade required 'more coercive treatment than probably does the peasant of any other nationality to make him disciplined. The British soldier has always been a rough man in an enemy's territory; to blink that truth would be to ignore military history.' During the parliamentary debate on flogging in 1881, its opponents shared Forbes's view of the soldier's social status, but drew the reverse conclusion. Bradlaugh, the secularist M.P., who had once himself been in the army, said 'he had seen the lash applied – the man tied up and stripped in the sight of his comrades; he had seen the body blacken and the skin break . . .' and 'he did not know any other country in the whole world where it was a disgrace to wear the uniform of the country.' He shared the view of Osborne Morgan that a better calibre of man could be attracted 'by giving the soldier something to live for

11.9,10

and hope for, and by cultivating in his breast that sentiment of self-respect which ... was [discipline's] surest and firmest ally.' Foreign precedents and humanitarian pressure had already greatly reduced the incidence of this punishment, and later in the year it was abolished altogether in both the army and the navy.[29]

A professional army made it unnecessary to train private citizens in handling firearms, and increased the reliability of order-keeping forces during civilian unrest. Still more was this so in the Empire: beleaguered by an overwhelming majority of native peoples, thrown into close relations with their officers, the other ranks became decidedly reactionary in outlook. As George Orwell wrote many years later, 'in Burma I was constantly struck by the fact that the common soldiers were the best-hated section of the white community, and, judged simply by their behaviour, they certainly deserved to be.'[30] The respectable working man, an influence not to be ignored in British politics, joined humanitarians and moralists in deploring the degradation and immorality which this system encouraged. It made normal family life almost impossible and the resort to prostitutes almost inevitable for the serviceman. Roughly two-thirds of the mid-Victorian British army spent at least one week in hospital in any given year, and soldiers died at twice the rate of the equivalent civilian population. The Contagious Diseases Acts instituted compulsory inspection and treatment of prostitutes for venereal disease, but Josephine Butler and many of the Acts' opponents felt that the correct remedy was to abandon the whole concept of a professional army in favour of a citizen army with a healthier family life.[31]

Inadequate recruitment remained a problem throughout the 1880s. The War Office was the least prized of Cabinet posts at this time, and no Secretary of State thought out precisely what the army was for, or prevailed over the strongly entrenched traditionalists in the Horse Guards. So many soldiers were garrisoned overseas that the home reserve was undermanned for emergencies. 'We must, with our Indian Empire and large Colonies, be *prepared* for *attacks* and *wars*, *somewhere* or *other*, **continually**,' the Queen told Disraeli in 1879. 'And the *true economy* will be *to be always ready.*' Late Victorian Britain really needed (but never obtained) two armies: a long-service force staffed by conscripts or well-paid professionals; and a short-service reserve, properly trained, for emergencies. 'Our army is already so ridiculously small for all the varied duties it has to perform all over the world,' Wolseley complained to the Queen in March 1885, 'and our friendless position in Europe at this present time is so dangerous to peace, that I dread the idea of having any serious proportion of it locked up here for any length of time.'[32]

The late Victorian army upheld the reputation won for it by Wellington at Waterloo only by fighting native enemies far worse equipped than itself. Even so, the Zulus prevailed at Isandhlwana in 1879, the Afghans at Maiwand in 1880, and the Boers at Majuba Hill in 1881. The courage and resourcefulness of Sir Garnet Wolseley could not single-handed turn these defeats into victories, as he was the first to point out. Yet the decade did produce some striking military successes – Wolseley's destruction of Arabi Pasha in 1882 for example, after a completely successful night-march. More Victoria Crosses were won in the small engagements between the Crimean and Boer wars than in the Crimea itself – no less than twenty one between 1880 and 1889.[33] British society in the 1880s valued physical courage more highly than we do.

Motion and colour film could not yet alert civilians to the horrors of war, whereas journalists could emphasize all its glamour and excitement: so too could the bands and banners often seen in Victorian streets. The colour was only beginning to fade from battle: when the Queen saw the new khaki uniform in 1884 she found it 'very ugly' and wanted it used only 'for *foreign* service in *hot* climates', but the military dress of the Scottish regiments, renowned for their bravery, was still imposing. The refined distaste for violence felt by labour leaders was probably untypical of their class: the struggle for survival within the working-class community made brute force a familiar way of settling disputes. 'Nearly every family in the hamlet had its soldier son or uncle or cousin,' wrote Flora Thompson, 'and it was a common sight to see a scarlet coat going round the Rise.' Soldiering bore connotations of chivalry, courage, colour and adventure, not least in the Queen's own correspondence. She instinctively backed the man on the spot when it came to fighting abroad, and she had a romantic admiration for heroism. Much to her distress, illness prevented her in February 1885 from seeing off the Grenadier Guards who were leaving for the Sudan, but she told Ponsonby that 'her heart is with her soldiers – she *always* bid *them* farewell.'[34]

The army attracted recruits by helping to fill the recreational gap between the decline of the old rural sports and the advent of the new urban mass entertainment – through brass bands, boys' brigades, athletics, marksmanship, and even the bicycle. Watching manoeuvres and the volunteers' annual 'inspection and review' was a major pastime in itself. The volunteer movement's popularity after its launching in 1859 shows how the military spirit permeated all social levels; the rifle was the Victorians' romantic equivalent of the longbow. Recruitment was still rising in the 1880s; in 1881 there were 142,330 volunteers, 2.5 per cent of the male population aged between fifteen and forty-nine. They exploited the new recreations and enlivened local ceremonial with their processions and brass bands, thus helping to ensure that conscription never became necessary in Victorian Britain. Military values must often have been retained long after the soldier had completed his service, and greater numbers were progressively influenced by such values – not simply because of the lapse of time, but because recruits were getting younger, more working-class, and serving for shorter periods. Still, the militarism of British society in the 1880s was a frail thing by European standards: the volunteers encountered that same half-amused tolerance which later greeted the Home Guard. When a dog in Wandsworth Park was fired at by an over-enthusiastic recruit, folk memory seized on the event, and volunteers were for many years taunted in the street with the cry 'who shot the dog?'[35]

Soldiering involved long-distance travel, whose romance should not be under-estimated by an age which can get halfway across the world in a day. For officers, there was a certain exhilaration in upholding British standards in 'uncivilized' parts, assisted by an abundance of personal servants. For the other ranks, there were sport, comradeship, regimental loyalty and all the excitements of fighting itself. It was a life which accorded admirably with the masculine stereotype of the day, idealized in shelf upon shelf of schoolboy fiction and popular history, and with the half-welcomed, half-dreaded male destiny which generations of mothers, sisters and wives had been brought up to expect.

To all this there needs to be added one further attraction of soldiering overseas which has since disappeared: the seductive fascination of an empire which flourished on the missionary's dedication, the explorer's courage, the emigrant's family affection and the trader's search for markets. Late Victorian imperialism involved a half-conscious response to the need for a new religion that could replace or supplement the old one in its decline: indeed, the two were often combined in the zeal of the missionary and in the dedication of the Christian soldier.

'Descriptive geography, so far as it concerns the outlines of sea and land is now almost complete,' said *The Times* in May 1882: 'it is the physical geography of continents, their geology, biology, ethnology, and what not which now form the vastly extended field of

what is still called geographical inquiry.' A succession of British explorers into Africa's unknown interior had captured the imagination of the public, and popular fiction dwelt on the mysteries of dark continents. To the journalist, the pioneer offered excellent copy, and the *Photographic News* in 1885 even envisaged exploration becoming an exact science through copious use of the camera: 'every one, be he traveller, explorer, special correspondent, scientist, or what not, now includes a photographic apparatus amongst his *impedimenta*'.[36]

As many as 3,259,000 people, 9.3 per cent of the population of Great Britain and Ireland, emigrated between 1881 and 1890 – more than in either of the two previous decades, and a far greater proportion than in recent times (4.9 per cent of the United Kingdom population in 1966–75). It was a high gross figure by European standards, approached only by Germany, with 1,342,000; Italy, with 992,000, came a poor third. 12.4 per cent of British and Irish emigrants to non-European countries between 1881 and 1890 went to Australasia, 10.3 per cent to Canada and as many as 70 per cent to the United States. Colonial ties were reinforced by a much smaller number of immigrants to the mother country; and improved overseas communications steadily tightened the lines of contact between English-speaking peoples everywhere. During one month in 1881 no less than 3,701,100 postal items were received from Australasia (5.5 per cent of the total from overseas), followed by Canada with 4.8 per cent, India with 4.3 per cent and South Africa with 2.4 per cent – though Europe (with 54 per cent) and the United States (with 25 per cent) still dominate the field.[37] Trade reinforced the colonial connection: by the 1890s India, for example, was absorbing about a fifth of British exports and almost a fifth of Britain's entire overseas investment; it was also used as a base for extensive trading activities in Asia.

This multi-dimensional drive for expansion – religious, scientific, adventurous and entrepreneurial – was seldom wholly controlled by any one group of men; the zealous missionary and the energetic trader could hardly be restrained from crossing unpoliced frontiers. Two possibilities then opened up: that these adventurers would disrupt fragile native social structures with their beliefs or their goods – in which case the frontier would have to move forward if disorder was to be contained; or they would get into difficulties, in which case they would need to be rescued and even avenged, so as to appease an apprehensive and beleaguered local European minority obsessed by prestige. There was little opportunity for seeking advice from London until after the crucial decisions had been

11.2

11.13,14

taken. Nor were purely local considerations always uppermost on any one frontier; the British empire was composed of a series of interlocking sections, and global strategy was often involved.

The Gladstone government's difficulties with General Gordon in the Sudan in 1884–5 illustrate some of the hazards. In March 1884 Gladstone explained to the Queen 'the very imperfect knowledge with which the Government are required at the shortest notice to form conclusions in respect to a peculiar, remote, and more than half-barbarous region, with which they have but a very slight and indirect connection in the ordinary sense.'[38] The problems were compounded by Britain's simultaneous embroilment in Ireland, by the danger of war with Russia, and by deteriorating relations with Germany; even in April 1885 Lord Rosebery felt it necessary to tell Ponsonby that Britain could not possibly meet the Queen's desire to push forward in the Sudan and at the same time resist Russian ambitions in Afghanistan. Imperial lines of defence were, as usual, severely stretched. Still worse, a hero had been sent out to command the expedition who could not be relied upon to carry out his instructions.

The tragedy of Gordon's death at Khartoum on 26 January 1885 made a major national impact, but the perennial problem of the unstable frontier remained. Indeed, there was a serious danger of war with Russia in 1885 precisely because both countries were being ineluctably drawn into confrontation through failure to control their Asian borders. As Clarendon wrote in 1869, 'there was always some frontier to be improved, some broken engagement to be repaired, some faithless ally to be punished, and plausible reasons were seldom wanting for the acquisition of territory.'[39] The complexity of the factors leading to annexation can be illustrated from the justification supplied by the Earl of Derby to the Queen in 1884 for a British protectorate over part of New Guinea: 'the strong and unanimous wish of the whole Australian population; the fear entertained lest convict settlements should be formed there; the encouragement which Prince Bismarck is supposed to be giving to plans of German colonisation; and lastly the impossibility by any less stringent means of preventing disturbance and lawless acts committed on the natives by adventurers of all countries.'[40]

The whole British approach to empire was permeated by a belief in its civilizing mission. At a time when social anthropology was only beginning to comprehend the complex structures of non-European societies, and when scholars were only beginning to diffuse appreciation of the richness of Indian culture, the alternative to British order-keeping and encouragement to progress seemed often to involve anarchy, superstition, brutality and stagnation. The identification between economic growth and human advancement in such territories was hardly then questioned; still less were the values of commerce and religion thought to conflict – except with the rather peculiar trades in slaves, guns and drink. Furthermore, British parliamentary government seemed to be accompanied by such economic power and political stability as to constitute an ideal political system for English-speaking peoples and perhaps even for the world at large.

In these circumstances, the decision to withdraw from advanced imperial outposts was always painful. Lord Hartington, determined as Secretary of State for India in 1880 to relinquish the forward British position taken up in Afghanistan under the previous government, countered objections from the Viceroy with 'if there must be a period of anarchy there must.' This was not the Queen's persuasion; fearing in February 1884 that Gladstone was contemplating acquiescence in British setbacks in the Sudan, she told him that 'it w[oul]d be a disgrace to the British name' if the country's peaceful inhabitants were 'left a prey to murder and rapine and utter confusion.'[41]

In October 1882 Joseph Chamberlain complained in a Cabinet minute that discussions on the civil reorganization of Egypt since the British occupation seemed to be dominated by financial considerations, whereas in his view representative government should be extended to the area; yet he did not press the matter, and after visiting Egypt in 1890, by which time Lord Cromer's regime was well established, he wrote to say how impressed he had been with the benefits the Egyptians had gained from British rule.[42] Imperialism, a cause now espoused mainly by the extreme right, seemed in the 1880s a progressive idea which had hopes of attracting an important section of the Liberal Party in addition to the Conservatives; the death of General Gordon drew many an idealistic young politician into a Conservative and imperialist allegiance. Two important publications of the 1880s helped to strengthen this interest: J.R. Seeley's *The Expansion of England* (1883) and J.A. Froude's *Oceana* (1886). A closer look at them will perhaps help best to recapture British views of empire in the 1880s.

It was Seeley's work which caused Chamberlain to send his son Austen to Cambridge, and which was described to the Queen by her eldest daughter in 1884 as 'that *admirable* little book ... so statesmanlike, so farsighted, clear, and fair.'[43] It originated in a set of lectures delivered at Cambridge which Seeley did not at first intend to publish; but Florence Nightingale got hold of his notes and, finding them 'unspeakably important', urged him to do so, whereupon Macmillan offered to bring them out unread. Florence Nightingale was delighted with the result, and told Seeley that she studied the book daily and gave away 'many copies to deserving folk'. It sold 80,000 in the first two years, and did not go out of print till 1956.[44] History lectures do not usually hold such appeal: what qualities explain their impact here?

In the first place, their message was timely. Delivered in the year of Alexandria's bombardment, and published five months before Gordon arrived at Khartoum, their theme could hardly fail to interest. Furthermore, their uncompromising rejection of Cobdenite Liberalism caught the tide of reaction against Gladstonian attitudes on foreign policy, for by 1883 disillusionment was setting in with the Liberal government which had swept triumphantly to power in 1880. And for Seeley, the relationship between history and politics was integral. He firmly rejected that 'foppish kind of history which aims only at literary display': history for him should transcend mere recreation and fulfil a serious political function. It must also forsake mere narrative for an analytic preoccupation with problems which had implications for current policy. To these attractions he adds the *frisson* of uncompromisingly rejecting the output of his distinguished predecessors, for as a historian he spurns the trivia of social behaviour for preoccupation with the evolution and future direction of the state. History for him is exciting and relevant, and his readers can therefore luxuriate in all the enjoyment and interest it provides while at the same time feeling in tune with progressive trends and preparing themselves to understand and solve current practical problems; 'it is the welfare of your country,' Seeley tells them, 'it is your whole interest as citizens, that is in question while you study history.'[45]

Seeley feels that history should become more interesting, not less, the nearer it approaches the present. It ought not to be allowed to tail off: analysis should take up some major development which has not yet worked itself out. Despite the firm challenge it offered to Gladstonian Liberalism, *The Expansion of England* is Whig history in so far as it is oriented in a very direct way towards current affairs: the themes chosen for analysis are not those calculated to bring out the distinctiveness of bygone societies, nor were they necessarily perceived by those societies as important. Seeley is not interested in understanding the past for its own sake, nor in illuminating the present only by

contrast; for him, history's value is more immediate and direct. But he nonetheless diverges from the Whig historians in that he finds his unifying theme in the rise of empire, rather than in the rise of democracy and liberty – though he retains the Whig historian's insistence on freedom of choice at every stage in human affairs. Seeley's readers are made to feel that they are being presented with major decisions, and that the fate of their country rests on the outcome. His book ends 'with something that might be called a moral,'[46] and offers an ideal, a goal, a cause, to readers who, for whatever reason, feel increasingly adrift.

Such a history has hopes of appealing to many tastes, and as his discourse unfolds Seeley produces several more attractions. Lucid and trenchant from beginning to end, and sometimes even eloquent, his argument falls into two parts. The first combines a detailed analysis of familiar events with an integrating theory which groups them in an exciting new way. It offers a long time-span, broad vistas, bold generalizations and a new chronological framework; readers are introduced to a fascinating combination of empirical and reflective writing which imposes order on a wide scatter of events by detecting threads of causation and connection hitherto unperceived.

For Seeley, 'the great fact of modern English history' is the spread of the English-speaking peoples throughout the world,[47] and he takes as his new principle of grouping not national boundaries but Englishmen wherever in the world they settle. He takes an almost Marxian pleasure in putting his finger on the key to events undiscovered by all his predecessors, and opens up eighteenth-century history in such a way as to transcend myopic domestic rivalries at Westminster and tediously futile wars between European states; his is a saga of the dramatic and romantic contest between Britain and France for world domination, from which Britain alone among the five West European maritime empires emerges supreme. And the American revolution, far from anticipating the destiny of all the English-speaking colonies (as has hitherto been widely thought), has created a political device – federalism – which promises eventually to draw them all within a single political framework.

Seeley's second part moves away from the English colonies to India, and tells the remarkable story of how the British gained domination there as a result not of a Roman-style military conquest, but because a company of traders deployed a small British force and formed well-judged alliances with much more numerous but fragmented Indian groupings. The authoritarian mood of a conquering imperialism, which corrupted the government of Rome, had therefore never developed in India, so that liberty at home had survived intact. Nor had war and political control been incompatible with trade, as Cobden had taught his generation to expect; on the contrary, in India as elsewhere, trade followed the flag. Given expanded markets and the unprecedented improvements in communications, Seeley does not regard the secession of India from the empire as likely; the possibility therefore opens up of continuing power for a British 'world-Venice, with the sea for streets',[48] of a maritime domain straddling the oceans midway between the two great land empires of Russia and the United States. Whether this can in fact be the outcome is a matter of will. The empire acquired, in Seeley's famous phrase, 'in a fit of absence of mind' can now be rendered secure only through adopting a more positive outlook. Emigration to Britain's colonies (which incidentally helps to solve her problems of urban poverty) should be seen as a gain to the English-speaking whole, not as a loss to the British segment; the future lies with the large aggregations. The English-speaking peoples therefore have great opportunities within their grasp, but also great perils to ward off.

Froude's *Oceana* could hardly have been more different; where Seeley is taut, disciplined, compressed, analytic, Froude is discursive, descriptive, unsystematic, anecdotal, and even at times self-indulgent. A less demanding book than *The Expansion of England*, *Oceana* sold 75,000 copies in its first six months.[49] It is largely an account of Froude's journey round the world in 1884–5: by sea to South Africa, Australia, New Zealand, and California, and thence by land to New York before sailing back to Britain. While describing the scenery and the people he meets in his progress among English-speaking settlers, he pauses for the occasional interview with a colonial notability, for friendly discussions in a club, or for incidental reflections of his own. As with so many travellers, Froude's impressions were unpacked from his own baggage: he found what he was looking for, not simply in the colonies' objective situation, but in the opinions of their inhabitants. He is therefore reinforced in his scepticism about democracy, reaffirmed in his distaste for Gladstone's foreign and colonial policy, and reassured that the colonies are spontaneously moving towards closer unity with the mother country.

Froude's *Oceana* begins by mentioning the analogy drawn by Harrington between Britain and Venice, and conjures up the possibility of national greatness now that the fashion has passed for assuming that the colonies will eventually opt for secession. The whole book breathes a distaste for urban England and an exhilaration at the fact that his countrymen have successfully chosen the healthy open-air life in distant lands without losing their Englishness. Like Carlyle his master, he thinks that emigration offers the solution to problems of poverty: for him 'the life of a nation, like the life of a tree, is in its extremities.' For Froude as for Seeley, therefore, the English-speaking peoples as a whole constitute the relevant unit for analysis, the hope of continued security and influence for Britain amid the uncertainties of an increasingly threatening world. They can unite in the American manner, if only a hasty and meddling Whitehall and a waywardly inconsistent and irresolute Westminster will allow the colonies to initiate the process, and content themselves with responding to overtures when the time is ripe. Despite Froude's mellow tone, with him as with Seeley there are crucial choices to be made. The saving of England's soul is at stake: she stands at the parting of the ways. She may content herself with a mere urban and selfish accumulation of manufacturing wealth, or she can collaborate with her younger offspring to create *Oceana*, a healthier and more securely powerful trading commonwealth. The doubters receive short shrift: 'faith in a high course is the only basis of fine and noble action. "Believe and ye shall be saved", is as true in politics as in religion.'[50]

All this is a far cry from jingoism: while firmly sounding the imperial note, these two books never beat the imperialist drum. Both centre their hopes primarily on the colonies of English settlement; indeed, Froude is sympathetic to the Boers, and even less possessive than Seeley about India. Though he does not favour abandoning it, Seeley even doubts whether India really enhances British power, and dislikes the authoritarian pattern of government there. He is quite prepared to concede that there have been discreditable episodes, though he thinks these have been fewer than in the creation of some other empires. He also repudiates exaggerated and even mystical claims for the prowess of the nation's troops, especially in the growth of British India. He explicitly dissociates himself from both the 'bombastic' and the 'pessimistic' schools of empire, just as Froude continually warns British government against clumsy political initiatives, as contrasted with a cautious responsiveness, in its colonial dealings. Neither book is conscious of 'the white man's burden': neither is preoccupied with the British empire's civilizing mission to other races. Africa was not, after all, partitioned till 1890.

Given this mood, both Froude and Seeley have some hope of gaining all-party agreement to their programme, which entails repudiating Cobdenite internationalism in favour of a gradual and cautious move towards imperial federation, perhaps beginning with the co-ordination of defence. Seeley in 1883 still sees himself as resisting a Cobdenite acquiescence in an inevitable dissolution of empire as the colonies mature. He does not write as though he is playing on feelings which are already commonplace: his imperialism is missionary in tone – it seeks to change a hostile or indifferent climate, and often adopts a sermon-like mood of exhortation and admonition. For Froude in 1886, the tide has already turned; separatism is dead, and the task is now to move forward gradually towards imperial unity. For both writers, one option is firmly rejected: the authoritarian approach taken earlier by Rome and Spain, an approach which for Seeley inevitably fosters a corrupting authoritarianism at home, and which for Froude risks driving the colonies into separation. For both writers, nothing is inevitable in human history: a great future awaits the nation if she can only be made to appreciate the grandeur of the issues. Fortunately two inventions are now available which should enable Britain to strike out in unprecedented imperial directions – one technological, the other political. The first is the improvement in international communications, for, says Seeley, 'inventions have drawn the whole globe close together':[51] the second is federation, a mechanism which now makes it possible to hold together large and scattered territories.

Froude and Seeley were not of course writing in a vacuum; German and Italian unification convinced many of their generation that the future lay with larger political units. A small Colonial Defence Committee set up during the Eastern crisis of March 1878 was revived during the Anglo-Russian diplomatic crisis of 1885. When early in that year New South Wales said she was willing to finance and dispatch soldiers to Egypt, the Earl of Derby urged the Queen to send a personal acknowledgement because the offer 'deserves some special recognition.' When a similar proposal was made by South Australia, and a somewhat less generous one by Canada, Gladstone told the Queen that he would 'acknowledge these offers in terms of great warmth, and ... dwell on their historical importance.'[52]

The idea of federation was becoming fashionable not only as a means of drawing the colonies together, but even as a way of tackling the domestic overloading of the British Parliament, together with separatist dissidence within the United Kingdom. In 1882 the Canadian Parliament urged the British government to neutralize Irish disaffection and thereby boost Irish immigration to Canada by opting for a federal structure within the United Kingdom on the Canadian model which had already proved so successful. They were sent a noncommittal reply, but in 1885 federation reappears behind the scenes as an issue in British colonial affairs – this time as a remedy for problems arising from the need to co-ordinate the empire's foreign and defence policy: Sir Julius Vogel, Treasurer of New Zealand, sketches out in a memorandum his ideas for an imperial parliament which will deal with international relations, and also envisages a colonial contribution being made towards imperial defence.[53]

By mid-decade, new ideas for imperial consolidation were gaining ground at home, and though neither Seeley or Froude discusses the issue, protection was making some headway. This was partly a defensive response to the erection of tariff barriers against British goods elsewhere in the world, and to the growing industrial might of Britain's trade rivals; protection might give British manufacturers access to cheap raw-materials and assure them of outlets for their products. Preoccupation with empire was crystallized by the Imperial and Colonial Exhibition at South Kensington in 1886 and by the jubilee celebrations in the following year. The opening of the exhibition by the Queen at the Albert Hall on 4 May moved *The Times* to reflect that 'there is no political sentiment which has grown so rapidly or taken so firm a hold on the feelings and imaginations of Englishmen in all parts of the world as that of the unity of the Empire.' 'Britons hold your own' was the concluding line to each of the four verses Tennyson wrote for the occasion. There was music by Sullivan, and in her speech of acknowledgement the Queen joined in the prayer that the exhibition would draw together the trade of the empire. The ceremony concluded with a thoroughly Victorian finale: *Home Sweet Home*, *Rule Britannia* and *The Hallelujah Chorus*.

We now know that all these dreams came to nothing. The twentieth century has ample evidence that it is possible for empires to survive even into the 1980s, but not in the context of Britain's pluralistic, two-party system. It is no accident that the leading late Victorian British enthusiasts for empire often express impatience, and even disgust, at the impact of this structure on their area of concern. We have seen how in the end it ruled out the possibility of holding the line against Irish nationalist demands, and where Ireland led, other colonial peoples were to follow. Froude was no believer in democracy, and complains impatiently in *Oceana* of the fluctuations in British policy towards Ireland – of 'spasmodic violence alternating with impatient dropping of the reins; first severity and then indulgence, and then severity again.'[54]

For decades, British Liberals had included in their ranks radical champions of subordinate colonial nationalities, from Cobden to J.S. Mill to John Bright to Fawcett to W.S. Caine to Labouchere and Bradlaugh, 'the member for India', and on to the early Labour M.P.s – individuals who, in this area at least, received enthusiastic support from the Irish nationalist members. In the eyes of these radical critics of empire, Liberalism was for export as well as for home consumption. The other face of the irresolute and wavering two-party pilotage imposed on the imperial ship during the 1880s was thus self-government and the upholding of civil liberties for colonial as well as English peoples, together with the long-term protection of Britain against the arrogance and self-deception which so often accompany great political and economic power.

To the champions of imperial rule, such critics were more than mere nuisances by the 1880s: they were a real embarrassment, and in some eyes virtual traitors to their country. For Lord Salisbury, corresponding with Lansdowne in June 1890, Gladstone was numbered among them; he had 'so entirely lost all sense of responsibility, while retaining much of his old authority and all his old mastery over vague philanthropic phraseology,' that his language would inflame dangerous opinions in India. 'There is no other statesman near him or in sight,' Salisbury went on, 'who could effect a tenth part of the evil which will be caused by a few of his phrases of gorgeous reckless optimism.' The Irish Home Rule debate had always carried more than purely domestic implications. By the end of the decade the Viceroy's defenders in Parliament felt the need for fuller information about his policies in India, and for more hints about his liberal intentions there, if they were to fend off radical attack. Sir John Gorst told Lansdowne in 1888 that the Indian Congress Party had now established links with several prominent M.P.s, including Bradlaugh, and that Hyderabad might well have set a precedent for other Indian native states in keeping a permanent envoy in London for parliamentary purposes.[55]

Seeley's *Expansion of England* soon ran into opposition from the critics of empire, for the radical author John Morley reviewed the book in February 1884. He contested Seeley's view that British eighteenth-century history was often regarded as tedious, or that it was customarily interpreted from a narrowly European perspective. He also denied that the history of empire could be legitimately divorced from the history of liberty. And he dismissed Seeley's two major recommendations: emigration to English-speaking colonies and imperial federation. Governments were powerless to deflect emigrants from destinations where prosperity beckoned, that is, from the United States. Besides, what was important for Morley was not the geographical spread of a population, but the quality of its ideas and institutions.

In retrospect, Seeley's argument seems vitiated by failure to recognize the incompatibility between imperialism and the two-party system, and by its neglect of the threat to empire created by dissension between the separate nationalities which make up the United Kingdom. Morley could today have pointed out that even emigration was more damaging to empire than Seeley and Froude imagined: for if 70 per cent of British and Irish emigrants, taken together, went to the United States, the figure for the Irish alone was 80 per cent,[56] and they, on arrival, helped to generate a hatred for British imperialism which reinforced the pre-existing historical reasons for a similar attitude in the United States; during the twentieth century American power has been largely responsible for rendering Froude's 'Oceana' an insubstantial dream.

As for imperial federation, Morley rightly cites J.S. Mill on the immense difficulties which face any group of peoples striving towards such an aim, even in territories less scattered and diverse than those of the British empire; and Froude himself (let alone Seeley) rejected any more authoritarian route. It is easy now – even facile – to single out as ironic those predictions which proved wrong. Seeley, for instance, thinks that British rule in India will persist, if only because the Indians are so divided among themselves and so passive in their outlook; if the Indian population 'had a spark of that corporate life which distinguishes a nation,' he says, British rule there could not continue; 'but there is no immediate prospect of such a corporate life springing up.' Yet it was precisely during this decade that this corporate life began to manifest itself, with the enthusiastic encouragement of British radical backbenchers. Nor did Seeley envisage the possibility that European invasion of Britain might threaten control in India, for, he asks, 'what enemy could invade us but France?'[57]

Yet those who back the winning horse in history can seldom lay claim to a monopoly of the truth. Morley, for instance, greatly underestimated the strength of the imperial ties which had developed by the 1880s. He ridiculed any notion that Australia would keep her promises when committed by her representatives in an imperial parliament on the opposite side of the globe 'for a war, say, for the defence of Afghanistan against Russia, or for the defence of Belgian neutrality.'[58] In this respect, at least, Seeley was vindicated by events in

1914, because Australian support for Britain was forthcoming even without Australian representatives in an imperial parliament. And if two world wars helped to frustrate Seeley's overall programme, they frustrated Morley's optimistic Victorian Liberalism at least as completely. Besides, neither Froude nor Seeley saw imperial federation as predestined: the British peoples would in their view always remain free to turn down the option.

Finally, both Seeley and Froude were right in their major predictions: that unless British policy took an entirely new direction, the two great land-based powers, Russia and the United States, would eventually come to dominate the world: and that the British empire would then go the way of the four maritime empires which in the eighteenth century it had supplanted. If we are to understand the intellectual climate of Britain in the 1880s, we must give due attention to her involvement in a genuine and important argument about Britain's long-term international destiny: to the existence then of blueprints for her future which bear no relation at all to what has actually taken place: and even to the apparent attractiveness at that time of options which in the end were never taken.

11.2. A summer party at Murree (now Simla), Henry Hebbert, undated

11.3 (ABOVE). *A much-disliked village policeman, P.C. Rover, about to be burned in effigy at Stebbing, Essex, on Bonfire Night. 1880*

11.4 (LEFT). *A group of convicts from Portsmouth Prison, Hampshire, being marched down the road, J.H. Barber, 1883*

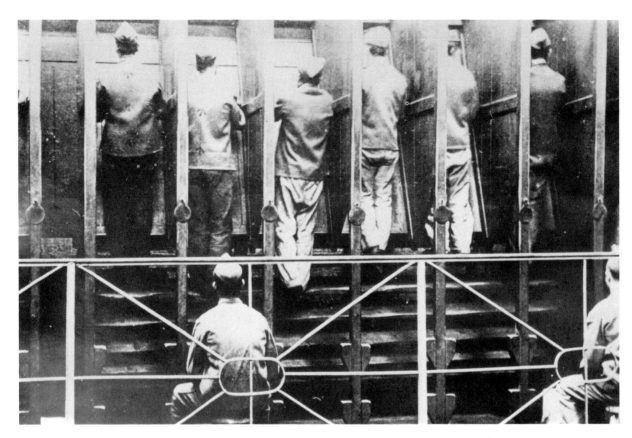

11.5,6. *Wormwood Scrubs Prison. The treadmill (ABOVE). Its speed was controlled by the prison officer turning the screw in the foreground (hence the slang term 'screw' for prison officer). The reception centre (BELOW), with a new prisoner and two prison officers. Both earlier than 1895*

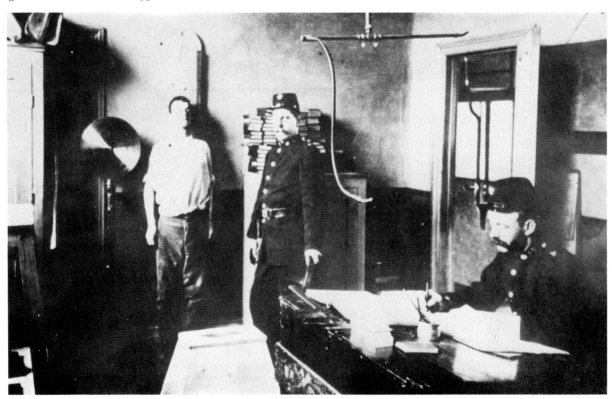

11.7 (ABOVE). *Rainhill County Lunatic Asylum, Lancashire, may have had as many as 2,000 beds, Robert Brook, 1886*

11.8 (BELOW). *Women prisoners with their babies in the exercise yard of Wormwood Scrubs Prison. Before 1895*

11.9,10. The army needed a constant supply of new soldiers to replace deserters. The Royal Field Artillery marches through Lyme Regis, Dorset (BELOW), to attract volunteers. 1888. Recruiting sergeants outside 'The Mitre and Dove', Westminster (RIGHT), ready to offer a drink and the Queen's Shilling, J. Thomson, 1877

11.11,12. *Between the Crimean and Boer Wars there were many small colonial wars against relatively ill-equipped natives. Fortified camp at Kabul (ABOVE), Second Afghan War. 1880. Mounted infantry on the banks of the Irrawaddy River (BELOW), Third Burma War. 1885*

11.13,14. Military life was losing some of its colour and glamour, and khaki was adopted for active service uniforms in 1884. But many still found the army attractive. Short haircuts for soldiers at Aldershot, Hampshire (ABOVE), Grosvenor, 1889. Off duty in camp at Aldershot (BELOW), Grosvenor, 1889

Chapter 12

Pomp and Ceremony

The photographs which survive from the 1880s exaggerate the importance of events which take place at a slow and stately pace, but they are a useful counterbalance to interpretations of the period which neglect the strong contemporary pressures for stability and continuity. Internationalism is now a sentiment so familiar that it is difficult to recapture the almost religious fervour which the nation-state in the 1880s inspired; yet the war memorials which survive in even the smallest British communities testify to its reality, right up to 1945. Government in the 1880s was therefore founded not only on reformist traditions, aristocratic competence and authoritarian structures, but on a sense of national unity which transcended yet welded together each local loyalty; and this feeling of community was frequently symbolized and consolidated in public ceremonial.

W.H. Mallock and Lord Randolph Churchill were intelligent Conservatives of the 1880s who nonetheless failed to see that it was through the magic of ceremonial, empire and tradition that their party could most effectively prevail. Mallock wanted the anti-socialist case founded on statistics, organized the Anti-Socialist Union, and took on the socialists in public debate; but he received remarkably little help from his party, and eventually gave up the struggle. Lord Randolph Churchill aimed to outmanoeuvre the radicals by stealing their clothes: to build up the popular organization and image of the Conservative Party and graft radical policies on to it. He had to fight every inch of the way, and when in December 1886 he overreached himself by resigning on impulse, Salisbury felt able to let him depart.

The strength of Conservatism in the 1880s lay rather in the continuing influence of the major institutions: of the City, the established church, the empire, the clubs, and the independent corporations throughout the country. Some years earlier, Walter Bagehot had rightly drawn attention to what he called 'the *theatrical show* of society': to the spectacle offered by the majesty of the state.[1] This was no mere touristic display: on ceremonial occasions, it could call out all the deep-seated emotions associated with family loyalty, military virtue, religious mystery, imperial grandeur and historical continuity, and epitomized a whole philosophy of government and power. Nor was it a show performed only on the London stage: it was reproduced in miniature at the periodic comings-of-age on every country estate, at the formal opening of each new town hall, and in the processions, anniversaries and festivals of friendly society, nonconformist chapel and volunteer brigade. Success against so formidable a combination would require radical leaders more persistent even than Joseph Chamberlain, and a mass following far larger than any enjoyed by the Social Democratic or even the National Liberal Federations.

12.1. *Celebrating Queen Victoria's fifty years on the throne. Decorated houses in Piccadilly, London, during Jubilee Week, W. Porter, June 1887*

The 1880s saw an unusual number of national occasions. In 1880 and 1886 the Queen opened Parliament in person. On 5 February 1880 there were two lines of spectators standing ten deep all the way from Buckingham Palace to the Horse Guards. The young Margaret Norman's everyday-book records that in 1886 'there was some fear that the Queen might be shot at by some of these beastly Irish but nothing happened.' Margaret put on two pairs of stockings and from Carlton House Gardens watched the monarch pass by in the half-melted snow. According to *The Times* 'a deafening shout of welcome' went up when she emerged from Buckingham Palace: 'this roar of acclamation was taken up along the route as the Royal carriage became visible to different masses of the spectators, the Sovereign, with her accustomed gracious courtesy, bowing right and left in acknowledgement of the welcome.'[2] When the Queen opened Epping Forest as a public park on 6 May 1882, she recorded 'nothing but loyal expressions and kind faces' in her journal. She was delighted with her visit to the international exhibition of navigation, commerce and industry at Liverpool in 1886 and got home 'quite bewildered and my head aching from the incessant perfect roar of cheering'; memories had been revived of an earlier journey there with Prince Albert in 1851.[3]

1887 saw the climax of the decade's royal ceremonial, and in its impact on the media the jubilee can perhaps be likened to the coronation of 1953. Just as the coronation marked the definitive advent of television in the 1950s, so the golden jubilee confirmed the nation's acceptance of the camera. The *British Journal of Photography* pointed out in July 1887 that 'perhaps at no previous period have so many outdoor subjects been portrayed by photography in a single week as on this occasion.' With the aid of June's good weather at the climax of the jubilee, 'cameras of all sizes and shapes, as well as every conceivable form of instantaneous shutters, were brought into requisition.' The camera did not assume its new role without difficulty: it was noted that the dust which rose from the sanded streets during the national processions produced a haze which often rendered the shots indistinct. Apart from events in the capital, the paper also recorded that 'in every provincial town, village, and hamlet there have been rejoicings, mementoes of which have been portrayed by photography.'[4]

12.2,5

Yet the camera's relationship to the jubilee has more significance than this, because it was beginning to be used in the monarchy's pursuit of favourable publicity. The Queen had long been interested in photography for domestic purposes, and in 1886 had pictures taken of her favourite dogs; the *Photographic News* claimed that she was also sufficiently aware of the need to mould her public image to stand on a concealed box, when in robes, so as to accentuate her height.[5] The Prince of Wales was an active amateur, and by 1885 he was also taking trouble to accommodate the cameraman; the *British Journal of Photography* says that on alighting from his carriage when opening a hospital at Birmingham in November he, 'with his usual good nature, uncovered his head and stood still for a few seconds while Mr Norman May, the special photographic artist of the *Pictorial World*, secured a photograph of him.' At the opening of Putney Bridge in 1886, it was noted that he and the Princess obediently submitted to the command 'now then, quite still, if you please.' In this concern for good publicity, the monarchy was not alone within the social elite: politicians, as has already been shown, were now using the photograph to get themselves known, and the high-church Bishop of Lincoln (following a precedent set by Father Mackonochie in cope and chasuble many years before) had himself taken in full canonicals; the resulting portrait was widely distributed throughout his diocese.[6]

The monarchy's concern for its image extended also to royal ceremonial occasions, though not always with enthusiasm from the monarch herself. As long as such functions had taken place exclusively before elite spectators, mistakes and mismanagement mattered little, but the gradual late Victorian selective admission of the public demanded greater professionalism. The thanksgiving service of 1872 was the first royal ceremonial occasion where the representative principle entered into the allocation of seats, a block of tickets being entrusted for distribution to nonconformist and labour leaders.[7] During the golden jubilee, journalists' needs were fully recognized: artists were allowed into the Abbey beforehand to make their sketches, and reporters received ninety good seats in the Abbey on the day.[8] To judge from complaints in the specialist magazines, photographers were less well catered for – quite apart from the dust problem, they had difficulty in getting an uninterrupted view of the complete procession. The *Photographic News* regretted 'that arrangements were not made officially, so that an adequate representation of so historical an event could have been handed down to posterity.'[9] In the case of her literary efforts, however, the Queen was prepared to go further in seeking publicity than was widely thought advisable, and even Randall Davidson's powers of discretion were taxed by the need to dissuade her from launching a third volume of the *Journal of a Life in the Highlands* on the world.[10]

Nor were the authorities slow to see the need for all the colour and glamour of honours, distinctions and medals. The Most Exalted Order of the Star of India was launched in 1861 and enlarged thereafter; in 1877 the Most Distinguished Order of St Michael and St George began to include colonial nominations, and in 1886 it took in a still broader spectrum; the Most Eminent Order of the Indian Empire followed in 1878, and the Distinguished Service Order (for military valour, and without limit of numbers) in 1886. The jubilee, together with unstable ministries in mid-decade, produced a new crop of honours; whereas only fifty-eight new peerages were created between 1870 and 1885, twenty-five were added in 1885–6 alone, and another nine in 1887. Baronetcies followed a similar course, and a special medal was struck for the jubilee – in gold for royal guests, in silver for members of the Queen's household and for officers in strategic ceremonial positions; the rest were in bronze, of which some 14,000 were distributed in all.[11] The jubilee saw the first general award of honours, and in 1888 the phrases 'new year honours' and 'birthday honours' were used for the first time: they have continued ever since.

There was little sign of enthusiasm for honours and ceremonial from some key members of the monarchy and aristocracy, though in retrospect they had much to gain from their conservative impact. Perhaps it seemed that there was a certain vulgarity in so broad a distribution – even a danger of pollution. The Queen in 1887 stubbornly opposed many of the ceremonial demands made on her, and strenuously objected to wearing elaborate clothing at her jubilee ceremonial. She offered still firmer resistance to lavish expenditure, especially where her privy purse was concerned.[12] As for Lord Salisbury, his pose in such matters was weary, even jaundiced. In 1887, when Jowett suggested an order to honour men of literature, Goschen forwarded the proposal to the Prime Minister with apologies: 'when is the "honour" correspondence to end? It is frightful ... How fearfully foolish men are about honours.'[13] Yet however reluctantly embarked upon, the whole jubilee display turned out to be a great success, and in retrospect became even a legend.

The idea of celebrating the Queen's fifty years on the throne seems to have originated with Lord Braye's rather flowery letter to *The Times* on 2 September 1885 citing the precedent set by George III in 1809. No doubt the jubilee was good for trade; commercial almanacs included coloured portraits of the Sovereign in crown and garter ribbon, which were framed and hung up in many a country cottage. The souvenir manufacturers

1.26

rapidly organized themselves; on 1 January 1887 the Queen noted in her journal that the Prince of Wales had sent her a jubilee inkstand, the first so far to have been sold: 'it is the crown, which opens, and on the inside there is a head of me. It is very pretty and useful.' Shopkeepers made much of the occasion, and *The Times* actually welcomed the lack of co-ordination in the decorations; centralized continental governments might sometimes put on a more impressive display, but 'rightly read, these very blots upon the beauty of the scene which shock the artist's eye are the signs of a goodwill which demonstrates itself freely and without prompting.'[14]

12.1

The Queen's visit to Birmingham in March for the purpose of laying the foundation-stone of the new law courts recalled her last visit in 1858; *The Times*, estimating that over half a million people watched her procession, claimed that 'at least two-thirds of this number belonged to what are probably the roughest classes of the population of England.' The Queen was surprised at the enthusiasm displayed 'in that very Radical place, amongst such a very rough population'. In some ways even more surprising was the subsequent complaint by Chamberlain at the lack of pageantry. Simplicity suits a republic, he argued, but a monarchy requires splendour. The Queen had no taste for the late Victorian pomp which so strengthened her throne, but henceforward the household cavalry accompanied her provincial processions.[15] The political purposes behind her visit to the East End on 14 May to open the People's Palace were virtually admitted by *The Times* that morning; its leader saw the venture as 'practical Socialism which works by co-operation and kindness, and not by envy and antagonism.' The climax was the service at Westminster Abbey on 21 June, and the camera was at last in a position to capture the note of eager expectation, the crowds massed on every conceivable rooftop space, the encrustation of elaborate ribbons, bunting, and ceremonial archways as the Queen drove into Pall Mall. On the following day, 30,000 children marched to Hyde Park for their own jubilee festival, and – with the Queen, Prince and Princess of Wales in attendance – were each given a meat pie, a piece of cake, an orange and a mug. Nor does this exhaust the catalogue of the decade's ceremonial: there was much festivity in July 1889 when the Shah of Persia paid a long visit, and in August there were military and naval reviews at Spithead when the German Emperor arrived with his fleet.

12.6

12.4

12.3

The jubilee ceremonial was not always taken seriously. Lady Randolph Churchill, irritated at the incessant rendering of the national anthem, announced that she had bought a special jubilee dress from Worth's which played the tune whenever she sat down; as she did so, an obliging young man, secreted beneath her couch, set off a musical box, which he stopped when she got up, to the astonishment of her friends. A more vigorous form of criticism came from William Morris, for whom the jubilee was a façade to mask the ugliness of capitalism, and his indignation swelled (as he wrote in *Commonweal*, organ of the Socialist League) 'pretty much to the bursting point' at such 'monstrous stupidity'. *Commonweal* piled up evidence of working-class hostility to the Queen – a republican resolution carried at a large open-air meeting in Bristol on jubilee day, the Queen's name hissed at a public meeting in Llanelly, and refusals to pay for sycophantic celebrations by Neath town council and Cardiff trades council.[16] The *Times* report ignored one aspect of the Queen's visit to the People's Palace: her journal notes 'the booing and hooting, of perhaps only two or three, now and again, all along the route, evidently sent there on purpose, and frequently the same people, probably Socialists and the worst Irish.' Yet the festivities in the East End were so contagious that they overcame the scepticism of the Barnetts, and even weakened their C.O.S. principles.[17]

The Irish as usual created difficulties. Eighty-four nationalist and radical M.P.s opposed assigning £17,000 for decorating the Abbey, and a five-man team of Fenians got explosives into the country to blow it up during the thanksgiving service, but the police foiled the attempt after a tip-off. The nationalist M.P.s refused to attend, arousing *The Times*'s disgust at such 'churlish conduct',[18] but any Irishman with access to the Queen's private correspondence at this time would have seen Parnell's churlishness as amply justified, for the Irish problem could hardly have been viewed with more narrowly English eyes – a royal blindness which reinforces the major indictment her reign must face.

Radical criticism of the royal finances persisted, and towards the end of the decade there were parliamentary wrangles about the civil list. *Reynolds' Newspaper*, a Sunday publication with a wide circulation, did not speak reverently of the British monarchy at this time; it vigorously condemned the Queen in 1885 for failing to come down to London or Windsor on Gladstone's resignation and refused to make allowance for the fact 'that she is dropsical, somewhat unwieldy, and unable to stand upon her legs.'[19] Nor can one assume that jubilee crowds were declaring by their presence any firmly-rooted enthusiasm for monarchy as such; many of those who moved across London from east to west to see the procession on 21 June were probably showing

no more than an entirely non-political enjoyment of a spectacle.

When reporting ceremonial functions during the 1880s the press usually expresses relief at the absence of disorder. The Trafalgar Square riots were but a recent memory, and W.H. Smith, leader of the House of Commons, told the Queen, two days after the Abbey service, that the government had been 'anxious as to the results of assembling vast crowds of people under circumstances of great excitement, but the temper and self-control of the people, and their devotion and loyalty to the Crown, augur well for the stability of the institutions of the country.'[20] In June 1887, as at a number of other key moments in modern British history – 1848, 1926, 1940 – the political elite was cheered to rediscover what it saw as the 'good sense' of the ordinary public.

Yet photographs of jubilee pageantry outside London suggest a broad-based desire to celebrate the event; all sections of the populace were brought together in ceremonial which was often most elaborate. The community sense of particular townships and the burgeoning civic consciousness of the new local authorities [12.6] came together in a massive national display of loyalty to monarchy, and the message was reinforced on the children by gifts, games, eating and drinking. Commemorative trees were gravely planted, high wires were walked, and celebratory funds were launched to finance some form of civic improvement. This is the world of 'Lord' George Sanger, the circus-proprietor, whose autobiography *Seventy Years a Showman* swells with adulation of the British monarchy. Most towns had their own thanksgiving service on the great day, with an outdoor celebration in the afternoon which mobilized the local clubs, friendly societies and volunteers; in the evening, the darkness was lit up by bonfires and blazing signal stations on the hills.[21] So the jubilee was more than a purely metropolitan and upper-class event. 'Everybody had known that the occasion of the jubilee would be remarkable,' wrote *The Times* on 22 June; 'few, perhaps, had been able to realize the fervour and the strength of the popular feeling.'

Whatever the impact of these events on the people, there can be no doubt about their impact on the Queen. Earlier in the decade, her private correspondence is still preoccupied with the death of Prince Albert. Replying to Gladstone's congratulations on the anniversary of her accession in 1881, she sees herself as wearing 'a Crown ... with many thorns'; on a similar occasion in 1884 she speaks of her widowhood as a period 'full of growing cares and unusually severe trials, bereavements and sorrows.'[22] Throughout her journal there is a tendency to select gloomy anniversaries for comment, and to mourn the passing of old friends. She makes periodic appeals to chivalrous individuals – Goschen, the Duke of Argyll, Lord Dufferin or (on church matters) the Dean of Windsor – to support her in her distress, beleaguered as she so often feels by the radicals whom Gladstone fails to restrain. She urges the young Randall Davidson's 'great charm of manner' on the Archbishop of Canterbury in 1883, when pressing him as candidate for the vacant deanery of Windsor: 'pray answer me openly,' she says, 'and think of my sadly lonely position and of the great need I have of loving and sympathetic help and of some one to lean on.'[23]

She often writes irritably to her ministers – whether Liberal or Conservative – and makes life very difficult for them with her long stays at Balmoral and Osborne. Resisting Gladstone's attempts in June 1885 to get her to come to London, she crossly brings out all her ammunition: 'the Queen is a Lady – nearer 70 than 60 – whose health and strength have been most severely taxed during the 48 years of her arduous reign and . . . she is quite unable to rush about as a younger person and a man could do.' Besides, the railway authorities need advance warning, and it is uncomfortable to be at Windsor during Ascot week.[24] Yet towards the end of the decade there is a certain lifting of the clouds which may owe something to the jubilee's demonstration of her great popularity.

Both her private correspondence and her public conduct on these ceremonial occasions indicate her pleasure. 'It was certainly a never to be forgotten reception,' she wrote after visiting Liverpool in May 1886. On the last day of 1887 she rounded off her journal with pleasant recollection: 'never, never can I forget this brilliant year, so full of the marvellous kindness, loyalty, and devotion of so many millions, which really I could hardly have expected.'[25] The newspapers noticed the pleasure she showed: at Liverpool in May 1886 she 'seemed to be much affected by the warmth of the popular manifestations,' and in her jubilee procession on 21 June she appeared 'manifestly deeply affected . . . by the unbounded enthusiasm which welcomed her throughout her progress.'[26] Whereas some of her gloom earlier in the decade probably stemmed from resentment at Gladstone's remarkable popularity, some of her zest in later years may reflect a recognition that her popularity was on a different plane from his, and not subject to the sort of eclipse which he experienced after his first Home Rule defeat in 1886. She herself did her utmost to bring about that eclipse by encouraging moderate Liberals to join the Conservatives on

1.6,7

a common Unionist platform; as early as May 1882. Gladstone had privately observed that she would 'never be happy till She has hounded me out of office.'[27]

In a decade which reinforced the monarchy's ceremonial function, its role was far more than merely symbolic. The Queen had by now accumulated a wealth of experience which she did not hesitate to use against ministers whose views she did not share. 'I remember Lord Melbourne using the same arguments many years ago,' she told Campbell-Bannerman more than fifty years later, 'but it was not true then and it is not true now.' Her relationship with Lord Rosebery, her somewhat apprehensive Foreign Secretary in 1886, was more like that of teacher to pupil: she urged him not to bring too many matters before the Cabinet 'as nothing was decided there, and it would be far better to discuss everything with me and Mr Gladstone.'[28] Here was a further basis for her power – the widening ramifications of her family connection, a source of information on foreign policy which owed nothing to her ministers.

She was not always listened to: in June 1884 she warned Gladstone against committing himself on a date for the British withdrawal from Egypt, and grumbled 'how *often and often* on many questions within the last few years have her warnings been disregarded and alas! (when too late) justified!'[29] Yet she was always formidable, even when overruled. She cultivated direct contacts with army leaders, and her zest when commenting on foreign policy, together with her impatience with unorthodox views upon it, reflect her study of the subject. Her long experience, her independent sources of information and her strong will considerably influenced appointments in Church and State. More than one 'explanation' of his former republican statements was required from Sir Charles Dilke on taking office in 1880, and the Queen's hand can be detected in Lowe's banishment to the Lords in 1880, and in Childers's failure to get the War Office and Rosebery's promotion in 1886. And if her distaste for Gladstone's methods and policies failed to deflect him, she gave him a great deal of trouble. Royal impartiality was, after all, a precarious convention only recently established.

The Prince of Wales shielded the monarchy from the taint of party bias by moving in circles neglected by his mother. He saw much of Sir Charles Dilke, for instance, in the early 1880s, and helped to overcome the Queen's objection to his entering the Cabinet in 1882. In 1886 the Prince invited the trade union leader Henry Broadhurst to Sandringham and deferred to his principled distaste for wearing a dress coat; excusing Broadhurst from formal dinner, the Prince arranged for meals to be taken to his room. The Queen was slow to admit the Prince to full knowledge of public affairs, though she told Ponsonby in 1885 that it would now be 'very judicious and desirable' to provide him with more in-'side information. But she was worried by the somewhat dubious company he kept, no doubt carrying in her mind the unpleasant memory of royal scandals during her younger days. During St Leger week in 1890 the

10.5 Prince spent three nights at Tranby Croft near Hull, home of the shipowner Arthur Wilson, where another guest, Sir William Gordon-Cumming, suspected of cheating at baccarat (which the Prince enjoyed playing wherever he went), was persuaded to sign a document agreeing 'never to play cards again as long as I live,' witnessed by the Prince in his own hand.[30] In 1891 Sir William brought an action against his accusers and the Prince was inevitably implicated, attending the court every day except the last. Some unpopularity resulted, but incidents of this type may actually have strengthened monarchy by preventing it from being too exclusively identified with 'Victorian' sections of the population.

What sort of woman emerges from the Queen's private correspondence and journal? The repeated underlinings in her letters reflect her firm opinions on many subjects – often echoed by a timid entourage – but also her increasing doubts on whether she and her country will get their way. She worries about the perpetual threats to the empire in a dangerous world; for her, national setbacks are personal humiliations. Her responsibilities weigh on her to the point of self-pity. Considering her immense experience of the British political system, she makes some remarkable misjudgements. Her belief that Parliament is gaining power at the expense of the executive, that what she describes as 'a sharp rebuke' will deter the House of Commons from inquiring into foreign policy, that Gladstone's 1880 government is dominated by the radicals, and that Gladstone is himself a radical influence in British politics – all show a surprising failure to understand the parliamentary and party system and to comprehend the pressures acting on her ministers.[31] Her views are genuinely Liberal, but while the party of the left moves on, she remains stationary.

Her reactions are often instinctively humanitarian. She is shocked by violence and cruelty wherever it occurs, but shows a certain relish in pursuing the perpetrator. Her horror at the assassinations of Czar Alexander (in 1881) and Lord Frederick Cavendish (in 1882) probably reflect her own experience of attempted assassination. In 1880 she asks Gladstone whether

'monarchical constitutional Great Britain' ought really to establish closer relations with a French republic 'which in fact approaches the Commune' and is responsible for 'frightful tyranny' in religious matters. In 1884 she telegraphs her hopes that Gladstone will not entertain Clemenceau at his home during his visit, because 'he was concerned in some most horrible acts of the Commune.' Czar Alexander's assassination leads her to hope that the police will closely watch 'the horrible foreigners we have in this Country.'[32] She had some reason for her fears. On 3 March 1882 her journal describes with remarkable coolness Maclean's attempt on her life at Windsor the previous day: 'Brown brought the revolver for me to see ... I saw the bullets ... Walked with Beatrice down to the Mausoleum, and here I knelt by my beloved one's tomb and offered up prayers of thanksgiving for my preservation to God our Heavenly Father.' She tells Gladstone in April 1883 that there should be some international agreement to deal with assassins, and welcomes legislation on explosives, 'for these Nihilists and assassins are one and the same every where and enemies to all civilisation. – *All* are threatened alike, for they care not whom they injure.'[33]

But the Queen's humanitarianism involves more than a mere concern for her own skin. Horrified that faulty machinery at Exeter has frustrated three attempts in 1885 to hang the murderer Lee, she asks the Home Secretary 'surely he cannot *now* be executed? It would be *too* cruel.' She shares her subjects' preoccupation with kindness to animals, and her detailed memorandum of August 1886 emphasizes that 'nothing brutalises human beings more than cruelty to poor dumb animals, whose plaintive looks for help ought to melt the hardest heart.' She fully shares the humanitarian justification for empire which is so widespread during the decade. In 1881, for instance, she presses on Gladstone the need to safeguard native interests in any compromise he makes with the Boers; the Transvaal had originally been annexed, she says, with their protection in mind, and they must be assured that 'we the g[rea]t supporters of *all* that helps to put down Slavery and any thing tending to crush and oppress the Natives, – we shall not abandon them to the tender mercies of a ... cruel neighbour – and in fact oppressor.'[34]

She readily enters into the sorrows of others, and sticks up for politicians who have been kind to her – Northcote, Cross, Cranbrook – when they are in difficulties. Her memory for past favours is long; she tells her eldest daughter in May 1883 how depressed she is at the death of 'my faithful, kind friend and constant companion', John Brown. Her affection for her family is revealed when – in a much-observed gesture – she kisses her numerous younger relatives after the jubilee service.[35] She loves children; in 1886 when Lord Kilmarnock apologizes because his son has written to her without his knowledge, she sends an answer to the little boy and reassures his father that she has been delighted with the letter, 'as nothing pleases her more than the artless kindness of innocent children.'[36] 'The sagacity and domestic virtue of the Sovereign' was singled out for comment by *The Times* on 19 June 1886 in its leader on the beginning of the jubilee year. A figure resembling the Queen presided over many Victorian families; the young Emmeline Pethick's 'Grandmamma Collen', for example, was Galsworthy's Aunt Ann Forsyte in real life.[37] The Queen's family role enabled many of her subjects to identify with a monarchy which might otherwise have seemed remote. Her popularity owed much to her respect for the newly developed moral values and economic might of the provincial middle class.

The Queen shares many of her subjects' interests and prejudices. She is enthralled by Stanley's African explorations, and Jack the Ripper causes her to fire off what is no doubt a redundant list of questions to her Home Secretary: have investigations been made into the number of single men occupying rooms to themselves? is there sufficient surveillance at night? have the passenger and cattle boats been examined? and so on. As for the sixty-six-year-old Baroness Burdett-Coutts's projected marriage to a twenty-nine-year-old in 1880, what does Lord Beaconsfield say to that? The Queen shares fewer of her subjects' puritan prejudices than the epithet 'Victorian' leads us to expect, but she fully enters into the late Victorian enthusiasm for empire: 'giving up what one has is always a bad thing,' she tells Lord Salisbury in 1890, squeezing herself into parting with so small a segment of it as Heligoland.[38]

Her enthusiasm for her Indian subjects leads her to suggest to the Cabinet (in vain) that she should have a bodyguard of Indian native N.C.O.s; she takes lessons in Hindustani after 1887 from the Munshi, who is brought to Balmoral as a kind of footman, but rises to higher things. After 1887 her trust in him becomes so excessive that her ministers threaten to cut her off from confidential documents. She tells the Rao of Kutch in 1887 that she greatly regrets being unable to go to India, 'but alas! at my age and dreading sea voyages as well as heat, it would be impossible.' She has no time for Russia – '*She* is our *real enemy* and *Rival*' – and detects Russian 'devilry' and 'wickedness' everywhere.[39] Her aloofness from party conflict also gives

her an impatience with partisan feeling and a contempt for politicians' apparent indecision which many of her subjects must have shared.

She has no time for extremists, either in politics or in religion, and a strong vein of common sense and fair play pervades many of her observations. Why does the Cabinet (apart from Disraeli) oppose the Sunday opening of museums, she inquires in 1879, 'for it is the only way to improve the masses and check drink.' Can't the rich be made to pay more for their wine, she asks Gladstone in June 1880: they can well afford it, whereas the poor will miss the beer they have to give up because of the new beer tax. In 1883 she wonders why the housing question does not occupy more of the government's time: the Queen 'cannot but think that there are questions of less importance than this, which are under discussion, and might wait till one involving the very existence of thousands – nay millions – had been fully considered by the Government.'[40] This sent Sir Charles Dilke on a tour of London's worst areas, and in December he pressed the local authorities to root out bad accommodation. The ultimate outcome was the royal commission on housing.

Despite Gladstone's immense popularity, events quite often justified the Queen's criticisms of his policy, and there is some reason to share Lord Salisbury's view that 'she had an extraordinary knowledge of what her people would think' – extraordinary, because she had so little daily contact with them. The phrase 'my people', which so often appeared in her public statements, reflects the sense of personal responsibility for the national welfare which, however misguided, she never ceased to feel.[41]

Her correspondence with Gladstone during the 1880s provides an opportunity for a closer character-study of these two perhaps most eminent of Victorians. It is a fascinating duet or syncopation – a contest not the less real for the fact that the objectives of the participants were invariably well-intentioned and in many ways so similar. It was tragic in its outcome because each was subject to pressure from mutually hostile groupings, both in daily life and within the family circle; each had by now adopted a set of views and responses, reinforced by formidable determination, which doomed them to mutual misunderstanding.

When Gladstone becomes Prime Minister in 1880, much to the Queen's distaste, the politenesses are fully observed. He is always dutiful, conciliatory, and perhaps excessively conscientious; he tries to please with extracts from his reading which he thinks will interest her, and in 1882 sends her a candle reflector. Despite all his other commitments, he carefully remembers birthdays and anniversaries, and offers condolences on the deaths that by this time feature so prominently in her life. The Queen responds by inquiring after his illnesses, by showing a particular affection for Mrs Gladstone, by expressing concern at his fatigue and interest in his family circumstances; in 1885 she sends him a photograph of her future son-in-law.

Yet the reality lying beneath these courtesies is an unrelenting battle between two tenacious wills. Gladstone is always respectful in tone, but he never gives way on essentials. If others in the Queen's entourage can, in their irresponsibility, evade the unpleasantness which always results from crossing her will, he cannot; he too has of course his own admiring retinue, but he is also subject to pressures from Parliament, party and public opinion which the Queen does not really attempt to comprehend. Though never didactic in manner, he nonetheless continually tries unobtrusively to educate her in the political realities. He endeavours to make her see the interrelation between political issues, to recognize the importance of timing, priorities and tact – and to understand that judicious and opportune concession may sometimes be the most effective way of weakening a dangerous enemy and strengthening a friend. Yet his efforts invariably fail. She gives way by force of necessity sometimes, but seldom from conviction, and not always with good grace; and on such occasions her capacious memory always files away facts which are readily produced in triumphant self-vindication when the moment seems ripe.

These two formidable contestants contrast notably in their devices for avoiding concession. Gladstone is prepared on occasion to postpone confrontation on lesser matters for the sake of the greater. But on issues which are important, he brings all the skills of the political controversialist and the seasoned administrator to bear. He plays the game of remorselessly citing historical precedents, for instance in relation to the appointment of Archbishop Benson at the age of fifty-three; the Queen is unseated, for her resources cannot match Gladstone's memorandum listing the ages of archbishops of Canterbury 'complete for 220 years'[42] which proves that two have been appointed at fifty, seven under sixty and none at or over seventy. Worsted in one contest by Gladstone's battery, she is sometimes obliged to retire in silent disarray; but she withdraws only to pounce unpredictably elsewhere, for her range of interests (quite apart from matters of state) is considerable, if somewhat indiscriminate – from vivisection and vaccination to mountaineering accidents and precautions against fire in London theatres.

Then there are Gladstone's long memoranda which give such pain to both parties. Their detailed reasoning and accurate, logically marshalled information often puncture the Queen's ill-considered and hasty expressions of prejudice; she is too much influenced by court gossip, private informants and Conservative newspapers which are uncritically and superficially read. Unlike the Queen, Gladstone has lived his life in a world of constant argument, and it would be surprising if she triumphed in his chosen arena. But the weapons of political controversy and administrative despatch are not necessarily appropriate, as Disraeli well knew, when seeking to convince a nineteenth-century member of the opposite sex, least of all this one. A well thought out approach is seldom hers, for she is a woman whose moderation and common sense are somewhat unexpectedly combined with strong opinions and prejudices and extreme distaste for disagreement with her views.

But the Queen too has her assets – among them an alert watchfulness for her interests, a wearing persistence that would exhaust a man of less energy and determination than Gladstone, and oft-repeated pleas relating to her age, her long experience, her womanhood, her widowhood, her loneliness, her weakness and her 'crown of thorns'. She also possesses a close understanding of sections of opinion with which Gladstone has never perhaps sufficiently reckoned. Viewpoints expressed with inferior logic are not necessarily incorrect, and even when mistaken they may nonetheless fully deserve the politician's attention. The Queen is alert to the increasing obliqueness of the Liberal Party's remedies for urban poverty in the 1880s – though she is not in a position, of course, to suggest workable remedies. In February 1886, when she asks Gladstone through Ponsonby whether public works cannot be instituted to provide labour for the unemployed, Gladstone tells her that 'to make the State minister to the poor of London at the expense of the nation would be dangerous in principle: and the machinery which puts public works in action is slow and cumbrous.'[43]

By 1882 relations were becoming seriously strained; Gladstone told Granville in December that when she was forced into admitting Lord Derby (whose recent political conduct she thoroughly disapproved) into the Liberal Cabinet, 'the lips were pinched till they were sharp as a knife's edge.' Her telegrams were strongly worded and her letters abrupt, heavily underlined and often peremptory, and at last, in September 1883, Gladstone received a communication which, he told Granville, 'has made me rather angry ... I should call the letter – for the first time – even somewhat unmannerly.' Even her motives for expressing concern over Gladstone's health become, one suspects, somewhat mixed. When sleeplessness assails him in 1883, for instance, she tells him that 'he must be *really quiet* and not occupy himself at *all* with affairs and not with *long* letters like the one he did yesterday. Perfect quiet is ordered and the prescription ought to be thoroughly obeyed and followed.' The clouds lift briefly in 1884 when the Queen successfully mediates in the dispute between Lords and Commons over franchise reform, but stormy exchanges over the 'betrayal' of General Gordon soon cause them again to descend, and Gladstone's hoarseness in 1885 is greeted with the recommendation that he should 'spare himself from speaking at public meetings for some time to come.'[44]

Thereafter the atmosphere never cleared, and it was probably only the discretion of the Queen's private secretary Sir Henry Ponsonby that made it possible for a working relationship between the two to persist – particularly in view of the Queen's preference, when faced by impasse, for operating through intermediaries. When Gladstone retired in 1894 he wrote Ponsonby a note of appreciation: 'forgive me for saying you are "to the manner born" and such a combination of tact and temper with loyalty, intelligence and truth I cannot expect to see again.' Twice soundly defeated over Home Rule, Gladstone left the Queen in full possession; yet in retrospect their long and difficult relationship seems to have ended in stalemate rather than in victory for her. Indeed, the fact that she remained on the throne at all was, in a sense, a tribute to Gladstone's success in strengthening the monarchy and to the conservative influence he exercised over its critics within his own party, for in his many battles with the Queen, Gladstone seems never even to have considered using his ultimate weapon – the threat to expose publicly the partisan nature of her conduct. His loyalty was complete, and it is therefore perhaps excusable that when he discusses his retirement in his autobiographical recollections, there is sounded a note that is rare indeed in his writings, though frequent in the Queen's – a note of self-pity. In 1894, when he at last left the arena, she failed to offer any expression of gratitude which began to measure up to his decades of service to her, nor even – as he himself said – any token adequate to the occasion: 'for I cannot reckon as anything what appeared to be a twopenny-halfpenny scrap, photographic or other, sent during the forenoon of our departure, by the hand of a footman.'[45]

12.2. Jubilee procession with 'a fine lady on a white horse', at Banbury Cross, Oxfordshire, G.A. Beales, 1887

12.3 (RIGHT). *The State Visit of the Shah of Persia: Ashridge House, Hertfordshire, with Prince Albert Victor and Lord and Lady Brownlow, W. Coles, 1889*

12.4 (BELOW). *The Queen's Jubilee Procession at Waterloo Place, London. 1887*

12.5 (LEFT). 'The British Empire', a tableau vivant *produced to mark Queen Victoria's Golden Jubilee.* 1887

12.6 (BELOW). *The elaborate Metal and Tube Trades workers' arch to welcome Queen Victoria on her visit to Birmingham in Jubilee Year.* 1887

Chapter 13 *Illness and Old Age*

Stability in a political system owes much to its institutions and to the conduct of those who operate them. But those institutions are greatly reinforced if they reflect a desire for stability which is widespread in society at large. Many factors can produce this state of affairs, and some have already received notice here; two so far omitted are illness and old age. In discussing these, we turn away from the political and social framework which has preoccupied us for the last five chapters, and revert to the individual life-cycle.

Conservatism in old age stems from at least two factors: with the passage of years, power, wealth and experience are accumulated – especially in a society which reveres the old; the Queen herself in the 1880s epitomized the increasing influence which age could bring. And for those upon whom time has not conferred such benefits, ill-health and old age often make immediate necessities so overriding that there is little energy left for wider preoccupations, and little hope of gaining by any radical change, even when it is promoted in their name. Those who have most grievance against existing social arrangements are often those least able to mount action against them.

In nineteenth-century conditions, the prevalence of illness tilts the balance of the population further towards youth, but simultaneously neutralizes any potentially radical consequences by ensuring that a higher proportion of the young and middle-aged share the disorders now associated primarily with old age. The paramount struggle for most nineteenth-century working people was not with the employer but with a measure of disease, squalor and misfortune for which he was rarely blamed. Middle-class observers often noticed that working people were seldom well; childbirth was frequent, sanitation inadequate, and in a less safety-conscious, less mechanized society, accidents were common. So was outdoor working; Joseph Arch recalled how poor food, inadequate clothing and bad weather made ill-health almost inevitable among agricultural labourers. Women were particularly vulnerable; when food was scarce, they did without, so as to ensure for the breadwinner the energy he needed. Of 12,000 Manchester men who volunteered in 1899 for service in the Boer War, 8,000 were immediately turned down; only 1,200 were accepted as fit in every respect.[1] Furthermore, the brief period of physical vitality when the younger radicals were candidates for activism coincided with relatively large family responsibilities which – in the absence of a welfare state – narrowed their preoccupations to the purely personal struggle for survival.

Urbanization in some respects made things worse. Increased road traffic enabled more and more horses to make their annual contribution of 6–7½ tons of droppings to the urban pollution problem. The annual average of dense London fogs rose from 2.4 in 1811–20 to 9.3 in 1881–90, and the number of days with

13.1. The Beaumonts enjoying a quiet old age in Kent. The country-house game of croquet appealed particularly to women and older people, William Boyer, c.1889

ordinary fog rose from 18.7 to 54.8 in the same period. The worst month in the years between 1871 and 1890 was December, followed in descending order by October, January and March. The consequences of such an escalation for bronchial diseases need only be imagined, and no doubt the situation was at least as bad in provincial manufacturing towns. Sir Douglas Strutt, in his address on 'fog and smoke' at the Museum of Hygiene in December 1887, thought that Londoners should give up burning coal in the grate and cook by gas. This is precisely what they eventually decided to do, and the number of fogs began declining in 1890, with the assistance of improved grates and stoves and, after 1899, of the Coal Smoke Abatement Society.[2]

For many who experienced the crowded living of industrial towns, adequate sanitation was either not appreciated or not feasible. Samuel Smith recalled beginning Sunday school work in Liverpool in the 1870s: 'the filth and stench of the audience were indescribable. One could hardly walk through to the platform without feeling sick. Those were the days when public baths for the poor were almost unknown, or at least unused.' Arthur Brinckman in 1885 urged ladies who reclaimed prostitutes to wear plain dresses of one colour 'so that any representatives of an unwelcome department of animal life can be readily observed. I am not going to apologize for mentioning horrors,' he went on: 'those who mean to work in this field had better be prepared for all sorts of trials that may be experienced in it.' Mrs Rackham, born in 1875, recalled a childhood in which contact with the poor on a bus or elsewhere required one's person to be searched for vermin on arriving home; she also recalled 'the awful smell which pervaded ones [sic] clothes for days' after visiting a London charitable play-centre.[3] Yet even if working people had known how to safeguard their health, they would seldom have had the resources, opportunity or time.

By the 1880s the big institutions were gradually hiding away many deformities which had hitherto been seen in public. 'Of old,' wrote 'Lord' George Sanger, the circus-proprietor, 'freaks were the mainstay of every show,' but fairs were now pursuing more humane forms of entertainment. The tragic case of 13.9 Joseph Merrick, 'The Elephant Man', vividly illustrates the cripple's gradual transition at this time from public exhibition to institutional seclusion. Suffering from a horrifying form of neurofibromatosis which is still incurable, he had been rescued in 1884 from the workhouse by the offer of Sam Torr, a Leicester music-hall proprietor, to put him on show. It was in that year that

the young surgeon Frederick Treves, who ultimately became his defender, saw 'the most disgusting specimen of humanity that I have ever seen' in a shop in the Mile End Road. By then the police were harassing the promoters of such displays, and Merrick was taken for exhibition to Europe, where he endured untold suffering before being admitted to the London Hospital in 1886. At last rescued from the prying eyes he had come to dread, Merrick nevertheless refused to condemn the showmen who had profited from his deformities: his life with them had been less of a misery than his four preceding years in Leicester workhouse, and he claimed that they had always been kind to him. Nor would the London Hospital have been an unmixed blessing but for the highly personal nature of contemporary philanthropy, which ensured that he received abundant kindnesses and visits from the benevolent which might well not be forthcoming today. As it was, an appeal for funds in *The Times* made it possible to install him in his own quarters, where he was free, among other things, to manufacture cardboard models as gifts for the many visitors he received till his death in 1890.[4]

Among the poor in the 1880s deformity was often less a source of shame than of income. Blindness, like some other misfortunes, gave one the edge over con- 13.4 temporaries in claiming the charity of the rich. The 1881 census lists 12,048 male and 10,784 female blind people in England and Wales – one for every 1,138 in the population. Of those over fifteen, only 51 per cent of the men and 19 per cent of the women were employed, whereas the equivalent figures for the rest of the population were 94 per cent and 37 per cent. The census also specifies their current or former occupations; for men, caneworking and basketmaking (772) came first, agricultural labouring (574) second, and music (496) third. Among women, the most common employments were or had been domestic service, fancy goods manufacture and laundering. As Postmaster General in 1880–84, Henry Fawcett, blinded in 1858, gave a splendid public demonstration of the limits to the crippling impact of the affliction. Inevitably he gave up some of his old sports, but he regularly attended the Oxford and Cambridge boat race till almost the end of his life, and also kept up his skating and fishing. A quick walker, 'in later years', his biographer tells us, 'he was constantly to be encountered upon the roads round Cambridge.' By the 1880s the ranks of the blind were decreasing, owing to the reduced incidence of smallpox and (according to the census) an improvement in eye medicine; but the less serious optical defects among working people remained uncorrected. A.J. Munby

made a special note in 1880 when he first noticed a
servant girl wearing spectacles.[5]

The poor often adopted a fatalistic outlook; then as
now, it was common to regard the pain as itself the
disease, and to assume that when the pain had disappeared a cure had been effected. 'It is this confusion of
ideas', wrote Miss Loane in 1909, 'which makes the
ignorant such an easy and valuable prey to the
vendors of cough mixtures, soothing syrups, and "pain
killers" of every description.' The modern ideal of
health was not universally accepted at any social level;
illness was everywhere too prevalent to be tolerable
without some degree of resignation. Nor had the old
religious notion of an association between sickness and
saintliness completely disappeared. J.R. Illingworth in
Lux Mundi tried to explain away the problem of pain by
arguing that it refines the character, and that 'martyrdom is the certain road to success in any cause.' The
vogue of genteel ill-health was still sufficiently common
among women in the early 1880s for Frances Power
Cobbe to feel that an assault on it was required, but she
was very much in tune with prevailing trends. 'The
beauty of perfect health and of high spirits', wrote
Lecky in 1896, 'has been steadily replacing, as the ideal
type, the beauty of a sickly delicacy and of weak and
tremulous nerves which in the eighteenth century was
so much admired, or at least extolled.'[6]

By the 1880s the modern cult of health was well
under way. Fitness was demanded by cycling and the
new sports, and physical education was spreading in
the schools: at first taking the form of military drill,
Prussian in origin, and as much concerned with
discipline as with health, it was taught during the
1870s by drill sergeants in the London board schools;
by 1880, 1,277 of them had it on the syllabus. With the
appointment of Miss Löfving as adviser in 1878, however, the London School Board gave a fillip to the rival
cult of Swedish gymnastics, which gained a further
boost in the 1880s from its feminist associations. It was
widely adopted in girls' secondary schools, and in 1885
the Bergman-Osterberg College was founded to train
teachers. It made a major contribution to girls' education by inventing netball and devising the gym tunic,
and in effect created a new profession for women. Sport
was simultaneously making strides in boys' public
schools. These activities flourished partly of course
because they were enjoyable: but they were also seen
at the time as a form of preventive medicine. Swedish
gymnastics originated partly as a form of health care,
and feminists embraced this new approach to exercise
in the hope of emancipation from the doctor, whose
profession they distrusted.[7]

The feminists were not alone in their suspicions.
Working people feared the medical appetite for human
material, alive or dead, for experimental purposes.
When a man named Bryan died in Spalding workhouse
infirmary in 1886, a considerable local stir was created
when it was revealed that the body had been sent to the
Cambridge School of Anatomy for dissection. As Bryan
had not been visited by relations for ten years, the
guardians felt that this was reasonable; but Bryan's
brother appeared two days later and angrily lodged a
complaint. Fortunately the body was still intact, and
was reclaimed and buried.

Self-cure had marked attractions for working people
when the sick poor were treated in the workhouse,
or in prison-like hospitals only gradually emerging
from the poor law system. An independent-minded,
intelligent and strenuously respectable working man
like the young Labour leader Keir Hardie readily embraced medical heresy; during the 1880s, before beginning his famous political career, he relieved much
suffering in his Scottish locality as an amateur
hydropathist. His enthusiasm for teetotalism, widely
shared by working people at this time, reflects the same
outlook. So does vegetarianism. 'Those who live mainly on animal food are specially liable to disease,' the
socialist prophet Edward Carpenter told the Fabians in
1888;[8] he had been experimenting with vegetarianism
since 1879. By eating and drinking correctly, and perhaps also by regularly taking Turkish baths, a man
could safeguard his own health without any of the
doctor's drugs, pills and potions, and could keep out of
the workhouse in old age into the bargain. The Victorian pursuit of thrift involved economy in more than
cash: it meant avoiding all the loss of time, energy and
security which results from bad health.

The attack on the doctors was reinforced by the
many opponents of vaccination and vivisection, who
looked on homoeopathy and other medical heresies as
potential allies. P.A. Taylor, opposing compulsory vaccination in 1883, referred in Parliament to 'the small
body of highly-paid medical gentlemen who sit behind
the throne of the President of the Local Government
Board.'[9] In the 1860s pressure from the doctors helped
to obtain the Contagious Diseases Acts, which provided
for state-regulated prostitution in garrison and seaport
towns; the incidence of venereal disease was certainly
high – it accounted for 0.500 per cent of total deaths
from natural causes in England and Wales in 1881–4,
as compared with 0.024 per cent in 1971–4 – a
contrast which is the more impressive when one recalls
the relative reticence of the time. But the success
of Josephine Butler's attack on the system shows

that many regarded such a cure as worse than the disease.[10]

Hostility to London, distaste for intellectuals and experts, enthusiasm for individual liberty, distrust of government and fear of atheism-in-science could all be worked up into a heady brew which frothed up at many a public meeting. Thomas Burt and Joseph Arch were among the many respectable working men who successfully resisted enforced vaccination. 'I had four pitched battles with the Bench at Warwick over the vaccination of my children,' Arch's autobiography proudly relates, 'and I beat them every time.' The crusade accelerated after William Tebb founded the Society for the Abolition of Compulsory Vaccination in 1880. Whereas in 1881 3.8 per cent of babies were registered as unvaccinated, by 1899 the figure was 22.7 per cent, though deaths from smallpox continued to fall.[11] Tebb secured a partially favourable report from the royal commission appointed in 1889, and complete victory in 1907.

The attack on vivisection was an allied movement, equally sceptical of recent tendencies in medical science, equally attractive to laymen at all social levels from the Queen downwards. The late Victorian growth of bacteriology and immunology greatly extended the research which depended on vivisection; by 1874, Edwin Ray Lankester was predicting a geometrically progressive increase in such experiments. In 1879, excluding simple injections performed without anaesthetic, there were 270 vivisections in Great Britain; ten years later there were 1,417. The twentieth century bore out Lankester's prediction as to the price animals would pay for medicine's transformation from art into science. 'I hope you will go on writing against this inflation of vain glory calling itself Science,' Cardinal Manning told Miss Cobbe in 1889.[12] Such sentiments were even voiced by some general practitioners, especially in the provinces. Schisms and disputes were not confined to Christians in Victorian Britain: they were rife in the church of medicine. The Victorians – in their energy, optimism and independence – tended to hold their views strongly.

Nonetheless the medical profession was steadily moving towards its present-day eminence. Its prestige was celebrated in Luke Fildes's *The Doctor*, a popular painting exhibited at the Royal Academy in 1891, showing a sick child being assiduously tended in a cottage. Major progress was being made in medical facilities, staffing and understanding. As the spread of outdoor relief gradually removed the mid-Victorian able-bodied pauper, the workhouse was free to become a hospital which could then begin to resemble the voluntary hospitals already in existence. In 1890 the state hospital still had far fewer doctors per patient than others, but the number of both public and voluntary sickbeds in England and Wales was rising fast between 1861 and 1891. The proportion of public as opposed to voluntary sickbeds actually contracted during this period (from 81 per cent of total provision to 74 per cent), but the overall number more than kept pace with population increases, and medical advances, together with changes in admissions procedure, had already launched the average length of stay on its dramatic decline. The laying of a hospital foundation stone was a major event in the life of a community, and the jubilee provided an excellent excuse for fund-raising. The Hospital for Sick Children at Great Ormond Street – one of several types of new specialist institution – seized the moment to raise the money for its new south wing, opened by the Prince and Princess of Wales in 1893. By 1879, isolation hospitals had been set up by nearly a fifth of sanitary authorities in England and Wales outside London and the seaports. There was also considerable mid-Victorian growth in out-patient departments. 13.8 If well filled, these were invaluable to any hospital anxious to build up its teaching material and its claims on financial support. But this development entailed a decline in the dispensary, an important source of nineteenth-century health care; whether supported by charity, the poor law, or patients' subscriptions, it could provide all the hospital's facilities except the sick-bed more cheaply and with less danger of infection.[13]

The proportion of doctors to population rose from one for 1,370 United Kingdom inhabitants in 1871, to one for 1,144 in 1900. Like other professions, the doctors were organizing themselves nationwide; British Medical Association membership rose from 2,000 to 18,000 between 1865 and 1900. Drs Quain, Clayton and Morell Mackenzie, together with Sir William Gull and Sir Andrew Clark, were fashionable enough to feature in Escott's *Society in London*. Escott refers to Sir Andrew's 'happy faculty of oracular utterances, the solemn aphorisms with which he clenches his counsel to his patients, the sonorous platitudes with which he emphasises the simplest of sanitary maxims.' The doctor, though not yet the psychiatrist, was replacing the clergyman as the man with the answer to every personal problem. Nonetheless, the Queen rejected Lord Salisbury's suggestion that her physician Sir William Jenner should be given a G.C.B. in 1887 – partly on personal grounds, but partly because 'no physician has ever been made a G.C.B. and the Queen owns she thinks it too much.'[14]

Under 'subordinate medical service', the 1881 census lists 35,175 women but only 1,972 men in England and Wales. The doctor was assisted by increased professionalism among these nurses, which was fostered by Florence Nightingale whom Sister Hicks saw, before leaving for the Sudan in 1885, 'propped up in bed, the pillows framing her kindly face with its lace-covered silvery hair, and twinkling eyes'; on arriving at the ship, she and her nurses found flowers waiting for them with the message 'God-speed from Florence Nightingale.'[15] Others found Miss Nightingale formidable and even ruthless as she manoeuvred unobtrusively through her agents; her great days of political manipulation were past, but her legend and her earlier work still bore rich fruit.

Hospital photographs at this time almost inevitably show everything in perfect order, but out-patient departments and dispensaries helped make socialists of many doctors. Hospital doctors giving free midwifery attendance to poor women were appalled at what they saw in working-class homes; with nothing to lose from the extension of public welfare, they had for some decades been collaborating with government in administering and extending factory legislation. Even a fashionable London practitioner like Morell Mackenzie could look on the German provisions for national insurance in 1890 as the best way of bringing order into the hospital and dispensary systems. Only twelve M.P.s in the 1885 Parliament had medical qualifications, but at the local level, where policy affected them more directly, doctors' expertise was necessary in committees concerned with public health or lunacy. The demanding nature of their occupation, however, prevented them from being very prominent in local government, and they made up only nine per cent of Wolverhampton's city councillors in 1889–90, six per cent of Birmingham's and two per cent of those in Leeds in 1882.[16]

There was also progress in medical understanding. The twin discoveries of anaesthesia and antisepsis revolutionized surgery by facilitating delicate operations and (perhaps more important) recovery from them. Medical statistics had been improving for some decades, and legislation of 1874 took this further by requiring doctors to sign certificates as to the cause of death. The slackening in the mortality rate which had begun in the 1870s continued throughout the 1880s; whereas in 1866–70 there were 23.7 male and 20.7 female deaths per thousand of each sex living in England and Wales, in 1891–5 the equivalent figures were 19.8 and 17.7. The reduced death-rate from smallpox owed much to vaccination, and there was a major late Victorian decline in the incidence of typhus, tuberculosis and scarlet fever.[17]

Yet on closer inspection there seems more to be said for the cranks, the vegetarians, the teetotalers and the medical heretics – for very little of this improvement stemmed from better medical care. Developments in surgery and even hospital treatment affected such small numbers that they could not have had any major impact on the overall death-rate. Immunization did little to ward off infectious disease until the late 1930s; sulphonamides became available only in the 1930s, and antibiotics not till after the Second World War. Medical discovery did not initiate the decline in tuberculosis, which had begun decades before the tubercle bacillus was identified in 1882. Likewise deaths from scarlet fever fell from the 1860s, yet no treatment became available till 1935. After 1870, fewer children under fifteen died from whooping cough, yet no real cure exists even today, and partially successful vaccines first appeared only in the 1950s. No impact was made on the death-rate from measles among children under fifteen until the First World War, and only recently has medical treatment become effective. Diphtheria was actually on the increase in the 1880s, largely because of improved school attendance, and the anti-toxin was not developed till 1895. Moreover, before the discovery of antisepsis in the late 1870s, hospitals – like prisons and lunatic asylums – tended actually to aggravate the evil they were designed to cure, simply because of their size. Morell Mackenzie drew the analogy with prisons in 1890, and noted that however skilful the operator, the death-rate after surgery in large hospitals was very much higher than in small.[18]

Improvements owed more to hygienic progress than to medical discovery; better sanitation helped ensure that deaths in England and Wales from typhus infection, whose source (body lice) was not pinpointed till 1909, fell from 3,297 in 1870 to 530 in 1880 to 151 in 1890. Improved hygiene also cut the death-rate from typhoid, dysentery, diarrhoea and other water-borne disease, though the rate of this decline, which had begun in the 1840s, slowed down in the 1880s.[19] The sanitarians were often severe critics of the doctor; seeing themselves merely as helping nature to do her own work, they were allied with the medical heretics. During the 1880s the great pioneer Edwin Chadwick at last received adequate acknowledgement of his immense contribution to British public health in earlier decades. In 1876 he formed the propagandist and certificating Sanitary Institute, which examined candidates in sanitary science, and in 1887 a volume of his collected works – *The Health of Nations* – was published for the first time. In 1889 he was knighted and given a public banquet. 'The greatest advance in the medical science of our generation', wrote A.J.H. Crespi in 1888, 'is the clearer and more general recognition that the power of medicine to cure disease is extremely limited.'[20]

Another non-medical influence for better health in the 1880s was improved diet. In a situation of rising real income, the proportion of the family budget spent on food was falling; so also was the intake of starchy foods (bread, cereals and potatoes) as compared with items like milk, meat and butter. The 1880s began that fall in bread consumption per head which has continued ever since. The overall change in dietary patterns emerges from comparing the figures for 1880 with those for 1962: 296 lb. potatoes were consumed per head in 1880 (214 lb. in 1962), 280 lb. wheat flour (161 lb.), 213 lb. liquid milk (325 lb.), 91 lb. meat (142 lb.), 64 lb. sugar (111 lb.), 18 lb. fish (21 lb.), 12 lb. butter (20 lb.), 11 lb. eggs (34 lb.). The average daily intake of nutrients for all classes in the late Victorian period seems to have been 2,077 kilocalories per head, whereas the equivalent figure for the 1960s was about 2,600. But averaging is very dangerous even within social classes because of the woman's tendency to give dietary priority to the man; Thomas Oliver's survey of the 1890s found women consuming only about a quarter as much calcium, a third as much fat, and half as much protein and iron as the men – with a total energy value only just over half as large.[21]

Legislation against adulteration was becoming effective, elaborated and refined by yet another new professional body; the Society of Public Analysts, founded in 1874, stimulated the growth of analytical chemistry and prescribed new criteria and tests. Through co-operation between the government and the analysts, standards improved, and during the 1880s the proportion of bread samples found to be impure fell markedly.[22] Almost simultaneously, the twentieth-century problem of preservatives and labelling made its appearance. Legislation in 1887 required margarine to be sold only under that name, and not as 'butterine'; and in the 1880s formalin was used to preserve milk, the borates and salicylates to keep cream sweet and the sulphites for meat and fruit. By the 1890s the doctors were getting alarmed at such procedures.

People do not necessarily welcome new foods, and this was certainly true of late Victorian working people. Sometimes their suspicions were justified. Changes in bread manufacture illustrate how technical innovation can actually impoverish diet. During the 1880s limited liability brought new capital and mechanized mixing equipment into baking, and the advent of roller-milling enabled the dark wheat-germ (the main source of nutrient) to be sifted off and whiter flour to be used. Only in the 1890s did the Bread Reform League make much headway in restoring the health value of bread for the minority who were aware of the problem. New foods do not necessarily improve the diet, particularly if guidance is inadequate or if nutrition as a science is insufficiently developed. Late Victorian working people relied extensively on margarine, whiter bread, commercially-produced jam, fish-and-chips and tea – not necessarily an improvement on what had gone before. The increased consumption of sugar probably damaged the nation's teeth. Toothbrushes were not at all widely used in the 1880s; in Middlesbrough in 1906 Lady Bell found that 'nearly all the women one sees have either bad teeth, or false teeth, or great gaps in their mouths.'[23] But in so far as the main dietary problem had hitherto been a simple insufficiency of food, the situation in the 1880s was improving markedly.

Medical science therefore seems to have had rather less to do with declining mortality in the 1880s than might at first sight be supposed. Changes in the pattern of disease since 1881–4 can be isolated by contrasting what were then the major killers in England and Wales with their incidence in 1971–4. No such contrast can be precise because of differing diagnoses and attributions for the cause of death; furthermore, systematic analysis would need to allow for changes in longevity, diet, stress, pollution and work-situation. Figures are even today very unreliable; still more was this the case in 1881–4, when the percentage of total deaths from natural causes in England and Wales with no specific ground assigned was as high as 24.9 (0.6 in 1971–4). Some categories of disease are now re-assigned: old age (5.380 per cent in 1881–4), convulsions (4,569 per cent), dentition (0.951 per cent) and croup (0.881 per cent). Yet these re-assignments are themselves interesting as evidence of shifts in diagnosis, and however inaccurate the statistics are as a guide to real variations in the incidence of disease, changes in the figures (for instance on cancer) profoundly affect public attitudes. The dramatic alteration in the overall picture can be gauged from the following diseases whose incidence declined markedly between the two periods: tubercular diseases 13.676 per cent of the total deaths from natural causes (0.246 per cent of the total in 1971–4), diarrhoea/dysentery 3.720 per cent (0.097 per cent), scarlet fever 2.588 per cent (0.001 per cent), whooping cough 2.413 per cent (0.002 per cent), measles 2.043 per cent (0.005 per cent), puerperal fever and diseases of childbirth 0.884 per cent (0.018 per cent), diphtheria 0.823 per cent (nil), venereal disease 0.500 per cent (0.024 per cent), erysipelas 0.455 per cent (nil), smallpox 0.382 per cent (nil), typhus 0.135 per cent (nil) and cholera 0.094 per cent (nil). The increase in the prevalence of diseases such as cancer 2.588 per cent (21.516 per cent), diabetes mellitus 0.268 per cent (0.912 per cent) and rheumatism 0.190 per cent (0.294 per cent) reflects the changing age-balance of the population.[24]

Medical progress in the 1880s had not yet moved to the point of prolonging life beyond endurance; whereas 2.4 per cent of the population in England and Wales were over eighty in 1975, only 0.5 per cent were in that age-bracket in 1881. Britain in the 1880s was composed at best of a three-generation society for most people; the proportion of the really old had not yet risen sufficiently for the present day's four-generation society to be yet in sight. The family circle and workhouse were then more often the octogenarian's destination than the hospital and the old people's home. Even where the old had lost their economic role, the strain of caring for them within the family (then so much larger) was less great than it would be now. Only 4 per cent of the male population in England and Wales were over sixty-five in 1881, 5 per cent of the female (equivalent figures for 1975, 11 per cent and 17 per cent). The old age pension and the old people's home are in a sense the natural consequences of birth control and increased longevity, in that smaller families are now less able to care for their more numerous older relations.[25]

Social stability in the 1880s stemmed partly from the immense power wielded by the old, which helped to counterbalance an age-balance which by modern standards was tipped towards youth – a fact readily brought home to anyone who saw how the younger element predominated in the nineteenth-century riot. Old people were greatly over-represented in relatively conservative areas such as the resort towns, as well as in the major centres of power – in the clubs, the Houses of Parliament, and the Cabinet. The average age of the decade's four Cabinets on taking office was, respectively, 55, 55, 56 and 56, with Prime Ministers of 70, 55, 76 and 56.[26]

Gerontocracy does not of itself bring social stability unless age is accompanied by wisdom, flexibility and experience. The British political system, in its ways of choosing leaders, was in some ways well designed to elicit these qualities. Furthermore Gladstone's example is sufficient to remind us that longevity does not necessarily go with conservative opinions. No doubt

Gladstone was in Dilke's mind when he told Chamberlain in June 1885 that 'it is in old age that power comes. An old man in English politics may exert enormous power without effort and with no drain at all upon his health and vital force. The work of thirty or forty years of political life goes in England to the building-up of political reputation and position.' At thirty five, Randall Davidson seemed to be dangerously young as candidate for the deanery of Windsor in 1883. But the Queen wryly pointed out to the Archbishop of Canterbury that youth 'is a fault which recedes quickly,' and he was appointed – though there was much critical comment among churchmen. Only aristocratic birth could normally overcome the governmental bias in favour of the old: the rich young aristocrat Lord Rosebery became Foreign Secretary at the age of thirty eight, having told Gladstone five years earlier that he did not wish 'to be buried in subordinate office till I was 60.'[27]

So highly prized was advanced age in sixteenth-century England that people tended to exaggerate their years. Even in the 1880s old people of all social classes possessed a traditional wisdom which – in a less rapidly changing society – was economically, socially and politically valued. A seasoned accumulation of knowledge and experience was then more necessary than responsiveness to new techniques and attitudes, and a great premium was placed on long service. Techniques of craftsmanship, husbandry and housekeeping, now transformed by science and technology, were then handed down from generation to generation, and the old retired from work much later in life, if at all. Hence the relative subordination of young to old, and even of the living to the dead. According to her biographer, Charlotte Yonge 'had not the slightest doubt but that the young must always and inevitably be sacrificed to the old,' and in her own life 'pushed this doctrine of filial obedience to fantastic lengths.' Numerous daughters-at-home shared her view, and even in the slums of Edwardian Salford the 'old queens', as the circle of grandmothers was called, wielded a powerfully conservative influence.[28] From the monarchy downwards, photographs reflected these attitudes: family occasions were recorded with the generations grouped hierarchically. Henry Broadhurst vividly recalled Gladstone being presented with a portrait by friends at his golden wedding in 1888. Mrs Gladstone carried a bridal bouquet and Gladstone stood beside her in semiwedding dress. Few of the forty to fifty people present could have been trusted to speak at that moment, he tells us: 'I have never witnessed a scene so rich, so full of pathos, so suggestive of the higher life.'[29]

Industrial innovation usually requires retirement from the older employee, who either moves too slowly in existing skills or cannot adapt to the new ones. Many commercial concerns therefore developed their own private pension arrangements in the late Victorian period. As for state schemes, Canon W.L. Blackley campaigned in the reviews for contributory old age pensions in the late 1870s; he was reinforced in the 1880s by German precedents, and in the 1890s by Charles Booth, who saw in the idea one way of removing large contingents of the poorest from involvement with the poor law. Joseph Chamberlain in 1891 was the first major political figure to take up the cause, though his scheme involved no more than a state payment of five per cent interest on deposits saved for old age. The movement suffered from the ignorance widespread in the area; only in 1890, for instance, was the first return of paupers by age compiled. Probably most adults at the 1891 census did not know precisely how old they were,

and as late as 1900 – after extensive sociological research and government inquiry – relevant statistics were seriously lacking.[30] Friendly societies, the major agencies outside the poor law which protected old people, understandably feared state pension schemes, nor did national policy-makers wish to discourage thrift among the poor. So even a modest state pension did not appear till 1908.

These developments had little direct bearing on the better off; old age pensions were originally introduced primarily to reduce numbers in the workhouse, where no middle-class person could reside without dramatic loss of caste. It is difficult for us now to appreciate the extent of the humiliation involved in the fact that in 1890 no less than a quarter of people over sixty-five, far more of them women than men, were receiving poor relief; within the working class, the proportion was of course still higher. There were limits, in the 1880s, to the extent of society's respect for the old.[31]

13.2. *London street vendor of medicated, peppermint-flavoured cough lozenges and 'Arabian Family Ointment', J. Thomson, 1877*

13.3. *In the 1880s, it became possible to afford spectacles even for a Barnardo's child, Roderick Johnstone(?), 1889*

13.4. *Blind people were often supported by charity. Blind man and Bible on Waterloo Bridge, Henry Rea, 1885*

13.5,6. Higher standards in surgery and medical care accompanied a greater professionalism among nurses. Florence Nightingale at Claydon House (ABOVE) with her sister Parthenope, Sir Harry and Lady Verney and a group of nurses. Undated. The dissecting room, St Thomas' Hospital, London (BELOW). 1886

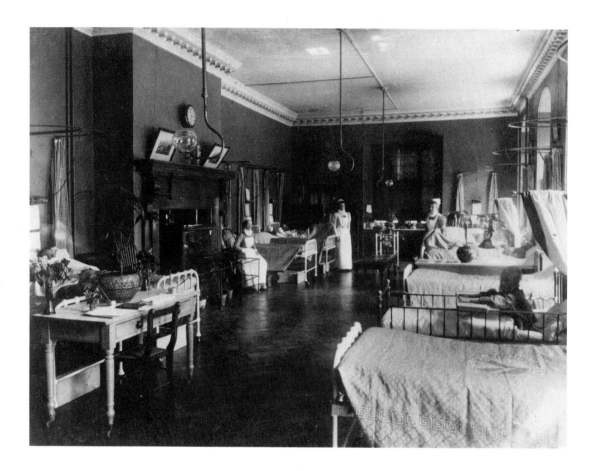

13.7 (ABOVE LEFT). *The number of sickbeds, public and voluntary, was rising fast. The Darker Ward, St Bartholomew's Hospital, London. Undated*

13.8 (BELOW LEFT). *A busy out-patients' department, such as this one at St Bartholomew's, was a valuable source of teaching material. Undated*

13.9 (RIGHT). *Joseph Merrick, the 'Elephant Man', dressed in his 'Sunday best' after being admitted to The London Hospital. 1886*

13.10 (BELOW). *The Victoria Ward, St Thomas' Hospital, with, on the left, Nurse Rutham and Nurse Helsham, and Dr W.H. Walker, Dr G. Kerr and Dr H.B. Seddon. 1887*

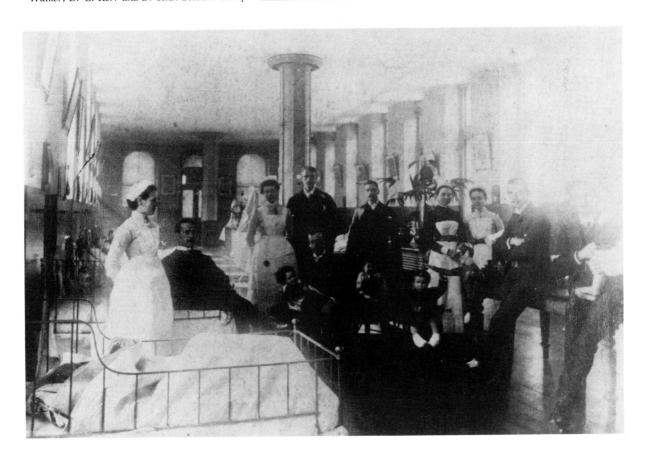

Chapter 14 *Death*

By modern standards, relatively few people had the chance to die of old age in the 1880s because disease and a violent end were relatively common earlier on in life. The proportion of the annual average contributed by deaths from violence has not altered greatly – 3.5 per cent in the four-year period 1881–4 and 3.8 per cent in 1971–4 – but there have been substantial changes within this category. In the 1880s, large families, lack of safety-consciousness, open fires in relatively combustible homes, and the tendency of mothers to entrust the younger children to the older, all greatly increased the risk of accidents in childhood. Between 1880 and 1889 in England and Wales, 654 persons per million died from violent causes, including suicide, drowning and accidents. Drowning, which accounted for 15 per cent of the total, was being tackled from several directions, especially (from 1891) by the Life Saving Society. Industrial accidents in the United Kingdom were the cause of 31,464 deaths (one third of them miners) between 1880 and 1889 – more than three times the number in Great Britain between 1965 and 1974. Mortality in railway accidents (5,212) was high, but fatal road crashes and suicide have increased since the 1880s; an annual average of 75 per million of the population living in England and Wales killed themselves between 1881 and 1884, as compared

14.1. *The Albert Memorial Chapel, Eton College, after the death of Queen Victoria's eldest grandson, Prince Albert Victor, Duke of Clarence, in 1892*

with 79 between 1971 and 1974. The individual's right to complete control over his own body was by no means conceded at this time, which may partly explain why the mean annual rate for England and Wales was so low, though the absence of so many of the modern easy routes to suicide must be relevant too.[1]

As for death from physical violence, if wars are included, twentieth-century England can show figures beyond the imaginings of the 1880s; beside these, losses in the small colonial wars of the late nineteenth century seem trivial. The number of murders in England and Wales seems to have risen somewhat: the annual average in five selected years between 1869 and 1888 was sixty-five, as compared with ninety-seven between 1971 and 1975. But in other respects, late Victorian England was a relatively violent society. The figures are unreliable, but the rate of manslaughter, assault and infanticide has probably declined markedly during the twentieth century; in the earlier period, cruel practical jokes, vendettas between and within communities and drunkenness help to explain why there were almost three times as many male as female deaths by violence.[2]

Wife-beating was widespread; when Sir Edward Clarke walked home from Parliament through the Seven Dials late at night, he often heard women crying murder and shouting for the police. Husbands were widely regarded as free to do as they liked with their own, and disgust at leniency towards wife-beaters was always a major grievance lying behind the women's suffrage movement in the 1880s. Nor were the slums free from public disputes during the day: 'verbal quarrels may fairly be accounted among the pleasures of the poor,' wrote Miss Loane in 1909. 'The retorts seem clumsy and time-worn, but they afford as exquisite a satisfaction on all sides as a large proportion of the educated derive from persiflage and repartee.'[3] Despite improved policing and higher standards of conduct, committals in England and Wales for violent offences against the person and for drunken and disorderly behaviour were falling. Imprisonment for assault from the mid 1870s shows a continuous decline when related to population, and there was a rather slower fall in committals for drunkenness. There was an obvious relationship between the two types of offence, and both were affected by fluctuations in the trade-cycle;[4] to people who could not normally count on continuous affluence, who lacked our present wealth of recreational opportunity and who had only begun to centre their ambitions on the home, it must often have seemed reasonable to live for the day and take no thought for the morrow.

So life was more precarious in the 1880s at all ages and social levels, and death was more public and more publicly discussed. For spectators, pain and death were still in a sense themselves a form of entertainment. 'One of the effects of civilization', wrote J.S. Mill, '... is, that the spectacle, and even the very idea of pain, is kept more and more out of the sight of those classes who enjoy in their fullness the benefits of civilization.' During the nineteenth century, humanitarians either legislated against ugliness or gradually segregated it into workhouses, hospitals, lunatic asylums, prisons and abattoirs; drinkers retreated behind frosted glass, public executioners behind prison walls, and deformity was no longer put on show. A similar reticence now applies to death, which in the 1880s was made the occasion for family gatherings, national ceremonial 14.2, 3 and ceaseless public debate. The dead were even photographed; in April 1888, for instance, the Empress Augusta gave Queen Victoria, then on a visit to Germany, a 'fine photograph of the late Emperor, taken after his death.' Sylvia Pankhurst says that when her brother died of diphtheria in 1888, a woman came and painted two portraits of the dead boy, but Mrs Pankhurst could not bear to look at them, and kept them in a bedroom cupboard out of sight. And when a well-known firm began selling photographs of the forger Richard Pigott taken immediately after his suicide, taboos were thought to have been breached.[5]

The poor approached the dying with reverence, so that the nurse was even discouraged from touching the patient. 'At the back of this reluctance', wrote Miss Loane in 1909, 'there seems to be some idea of impiety, a dread of appearing to take part in a struggle against inexorable fate, and also a fear of hastening the end by mistaken efforts.' In the working-class community, the drama of death was fully enacted; grandiose funerals lent a dignity to people in death who often lacked it in life, and working people could be induced to save for a 'decent burial' when they would save for nothing else. Death might even seem a consolation to those for whom life had hardly been pleasant. The 1881 census lists 1,701 male and 192 female funeral furniture makers and undertakers in England and Wales; these were the people who organized the mutes, the plumes, the crape and the elaborate expenditure on mourning clothes.[6] Such occasions introduced a moment of solemn mystery into the tedium and materialism of slum life. Blinds were drawn down, shops were closed, hats were removed as the hearse passed on its way,   14.5 prompting gestures of respect from the community. Then as now, a funeral could convey an impression of human control over unpredictable events, and endow a personal tragedy with a psychological and aesthetically satisfying neatness and harmony which in reality it often lacked.

The undertakers did not stand outside the general trend towards professionalization. The *Undertakers' and Funeral Directors' Journal*, launched in 1886, strongly favoured the idea of an Undertakers' Association, which it thought would improve knowledge and technique, promote self-respect, encourage self-defence, prevent price-cutting and improve the occupation's public image: 'the higher qualities of a man', said the paper, 'are strengthened by association with his fellows for mutual help, and by harmonious co-operation for their common welfare.' The Association was launched in Birmingham in 1888; there was a rather poor attendance, especially from London, but a good lunch was had, followed by songs and a recitation.[7]

Undertakers in the 1880s were unable to prevent the occasional disturbance at funeral services, for a whiff of hypocrisy could rouse a strong sense of popular justice. Local women were prominent in disrupting the funeral of William Bunting at Whittington Moor, near Chesterfield, in 1886: his second wife, who, it was rumoured, had refused to allow the first wife's children to see their father during his illness or after his death, was hooted on the way to the churchyard even as far as the graveside. There were cries of 'shove her in,' and police protection was needed. At Derby in June 1887, according to a press report, a crowd gathered outside the home of Mr Cupitt, whose wife had been found drowned in the Derwent a few days before, and 'hissed and hooted at him furiously' when he came out to enter the mourning coach. The police were required then and again that night, to disperse a crowd which was breaking his windows. When Thomas Oates drowned himself in Penzance harbour in 1888 after only a year of marriage, local opinion found the cause in an unhappy home with wife and mother-in-law, and two thousand people attended the funeral, laughing and talking loudly. After the clergyman had left, an attempt was made to hustle the young widow and her mother into the grave, and the widow was stripped of her wedding ring, bonnet and gloves. The police accompanied her home, 'followed by a jeering and shouting crowd, the worst offenders among whom were women.'[8]

A quite different attack was being mounted at this time by the Church of England Funeral Reform Association. It aimed to cut down expenditure: to discourage crape, scarves, feathers and velvet trappings: to reduce the provision of flowers: and to discourage excessive eating and drinking. It had both archbishops as its presidents, and patrons included almost all the bishops and many prominent laymen.[9] The Association was of course anticipating future trends; yet formal public ceremonial can be valuable in so far as it provides an opportunity for facing a painful reality without embarrassment; it also enables the community formally to demonstrate its support for the bereaved.

To judge from the private diary of the Cabinet minister Lord Carlingford, there was also a strong case for the funeral monument. Bitterly reproaching himself for failing to realize the seriousness of his wife's final illness until it was too late, he seems to have gained much consolation from frequent visits to her grave in 1885. 'I knelt before the memorial of my love', he writes on 9 January, 'and poured my heart and body out to her – and cried to her for her forgiveness, as I am always doing, for my miserable failure towards the end of our life together.' In a decade which knew nothing of the tape-recorder and the cine-film, mementos of the dead were normally less substantial than they are now – though the photograph had become available to provide some sort of consolation. In 1889 Havelock Ellis recorded in his journal that it was nearly a year since his mother had died: 'I cannot look at the curves of her cheeks in her photo', he writes, 'or think of her without tears.' The Queen, with her ample accommodation, was free to surround herself with reminders of the departed; her mother's sitting room at Frogmore was preserved as she had left it, and at Osborne the

Prince Consort's whole suite was maintained, with hot water still being brought up to his dressing room forty years after his death. The Queen used this as a sitting room and for talking to intimates, and Randall Davidson often conversed with her there with the hot water actually steaming.[10]

The accoutrements of death seemed all the more important in the case of a national figure, but here too there could be disruptions – though of a more polite nature than those at Penzance and Whittington Moor. On 9 May 1881, Gladstone made a tactful speech supporting the parliamentary motion for a monument to Disraeli in Westminster Abbey which would testify to his 'rare and splendid gifts' and 'devoted labours'. Northcote agreed, but Labouchere pleaded that such an honour should be accorded sparingly, and pointed out the inconsistency of Liberals' supporting such commemoration of a man whose dishonest policies they had repudiated at the general election they had just won. In the fourth and last speech of the debate, Arthur O'Connor reminded the House that Disraeli had never done anything for Ireland. The motion was carried by 380 votes to 54, and among the 54 were the two leading working-class M.P.s Burt and Broadhurst, two prominent radicals, Wilfrid Lawson and Jesse Collings, and several Irish M.P.s. While expressing herself '*much gratified*' by Gladstone's speech, the Queen noted that Dilke, Chamberlain and Bright – all government ministers – had not voted. Gladstone replied that Bright and Chamberlain probably felt 'too sharply committed, by declarations touching Lord Beaconsfield as contradistinguished from his policy, to make it suitable for them to vote.'[11] It was always difficult for radical backbenchers, and still more difficult for Irish M.P.s, to observe the courtesies of the two-party system in the 1880s. Nonetheless it was in those days more common for the consensus view to be lent permanence in the form of monuments, statues, vaults and mausoleums.

The intense emotion surrounding death sometimes invested funerals with political significance. *The Times* on 12 May 1882 noted that the funeral of Lord Frederick Cavendish had been 'made a public event by all who lived within reach of Chatsworth' on the previous day. A special train brought about 250 M.P.s and other official friends from London, including nearly all the members of the government; 30–40,000 were present at or near Edensor church, and there was a wreath from the Queen on the coffin. 'Nothing could be more unostentatious, and, at the same time, more imposing than the funeral procession', the paper wrote, 'as it passed very slowly between the thousands of mourners.' Somewhat incongruously, the paper also

14.1

noted that at Leicester, where his train had stopped for five minutes on the way home, Gladstone was 'the object of much popular, but not loudly-expressed interest.'[12]

The funeral and the commemoration were also occasionally used as political instruments by the critics of authority. In March 1884 on the first anniversary of Karl Marx's death William Morris, red ribbon in buttonhole, went in procession to Highgate with 1,000 others 'at the tail of various banners and a very bad band'. The police refused access to the cemetery, and it was on a piece of waste ground that the speeches had to be made and the Internationale sung. Nearly three years later, Morris participated in the public funeral of Alfred Linnell, who had been ridden down by the police after attending a meeting in Hyde Park. London socialists made considerable capital out of the funeral on 18 December 1887; their procession to Bow cemetery was led by a band playing the Dead March, and on the coffin was placed a shield inscribed 'killed in Trafalgar Square'. Morris was deeply moved, and walked quietly back with comrades in the rain; 'well, I like ceremony,' he said.[13]

These political associations of the funeral have their modern equivalents, but less familiar is the vying for status between Anglican and Nonconformist which in the 1880s so often complicated the occasion. The Nonconformist's right to burial in his parish churchyard under the ceremonial of his own denomination was hotly contested during the nineteenth century. The controversy was partly defused by the Burials Act of 1880, in which Anglicans conceded most of the Nonconformist demands. Launching the second-reading debate in the House of Lords, Bishop Wordsworth of Lincoln described the Bill as 'an Act for the burial of the Church of England herself', but the Archbishop of Canterbury thought otherwise. Disraeli broadened out the whole debate by looking forward to the day when considerations of public health would shut up all churchyards and replace them by adequate cemeteries in suitable places. He saw the Bill as 'legislation which is opposed to the circumstances in which we live,' but nonetheless supported it; triumphing by 126 votes to 101, it then went on to the House of Commons,[14] where John Bright looked forward to the closing of a subject which had exercised him, as a Quaker in politics, throughout his public life: 'it is a question on which I have spoken so often that it is not easy to say anything new or useful.' Henry Broadhurst recalled the great impact made on the House by Bright's pathos and earnestness, 'his long white locks shining in the rays of light streaming through the wes-

tern windows.' But the most interesting speech came from a Conservative, A.J. Balfour, who provoked cries of 'oh, oh!' when he said that this was just the sort of topic on which Bright could make popular but ill-reasoned speeches, embarrassing the established church (which had a good case) by forcing it to justify itself in public. The Bill was passed by 258 votes to 79.[15] In areas such as Wales, with many churchyards but few cemeteries, a grievance undoubtedly existed; and where death is involved, emotions are quickly roused. A Llanfrothen rector's refusal in 1888 to allow the burial of a Nonconformist near his daughter in the churchyard could still whip up enough emotion to launch the young Lloyd George on his famous career. But in future the debate retreated (like many other religious questions) from the forefront of politics.

There were other reasons for the prominence of death in the 1880s. It was associated with all the excitements of 'the reading of the will', all the drama of the unexpected inheritance which had fuelled the brouhaha in the 1870s about the Tichborne Claimant. In an aristocratic society, wills were key documents within the whole economic and political structure. Furthermore, at a time when aristocratic and philanthropic institutions were coming under public criticism, laws of inheritance were inevitably much discussed. And in a world of close-knit communities, low death-duties, and scrimping and saving to eke out a living, a legacy could profoundly affect personal fortunes and clarify mutual relationships in a most enthralling fashion.

Cremation was a further source of controversy – obvious as its merits now seem in an overcrowded society. The practice, which seems to have originated in Italy, was promoted amidst bitter hostility by the Cremation Society of England, founded in 1874. When Dr Price of Llantrissant tried to cremate his infant son in 1884, the police had to protect him against popular indignation; his activities on 21 March were watched by 'a vast concourse of persons ... from the hill tops around'. The undertakers were very sceptical, their newspaper describing a very gloomy visit to an ill-appointed crematorium at Woking.[16]

Yet there was a strong case for the general adoption of cremation by the 1880s. Affections might be aroused by the village churchyard, said a sympathetic *Times* leader in 1884, but they could hardly be enlisted by 'the ghastly wildernesses of stone to which our urban populations are consigned.' The parliamentary advocates of cremation in 1884, both Scottish doctors, pointed out that if all the dead were buried, 500 acres a year would be used up; they also stressed the speed,

14.4

cheapness and hygiene involved in the new practice, and Dr Farquharson demonstrated the innocuous nature of the end-product by displaying to M.P.s a small bottle containing the ashes of a cremated cow. The only serious hostile argument was that poisoners would more easily elude detection. But their confidence in popular distaste for cremation gave the advocates of burial the excuse for a rollicking, humorous debate, spiced with anti-intellectualism and replete with irrelevant classical allusions – the aristocratic Harcourt posing as the common man defending the old ways. Here again, the claims of the dead were being challenged: hygiene must prevail over sentiment and, as Labouchere put it, 'it was a question for the living, not for the dead.' It was not until 1885 that the first three cremations took place in England; by 1891 there had still been only 177 at Woking, whereas burials averaged at 550,000 a year at this time.[17]

But the major reason for the late Victorian preoccupation with death was the intense interest in the after-life, the belief that on the deathbed some indication might be given of the individual's ultimate destination. Christians and atheists alike were scrutinized in their last moments for signs of commitment or retraction. In a society where humane values had gained only a precarious acceptance, incentives to civilized conduct sometimes seemed to require reinforcement by references to the after-life that crudely anticipate the modern horror film. As the headmistress of Liverpool High School told her girls about this time, 'God would not love them and they would never go to Heaven if they did not obey the rules.' Into a painfully disordered world, heaven and hell could introduce a semblance of justice. 'The belief in a future redistribution of rewards and punishments', said *Fraser's Magazine* in 1872, 'lies at the heart of the present constitution of human society, alone explains its anomalies, and alone makes the inequalities of fortune tolerable.'[18]

Many of the intellectuals impressed by science were nonetheless concerned at two possible consequences of its impact on religion: that there would no longer be adequate sanctions for socially desirable conduct, and that the scientist would merely supplant the clergyman and create a new tyranny at least as oppressive as the old. In 1874 Henry Sidgwick, the Cambridge philosopher, joined Frederick Myers in applying the scientific method to the mystical phenomena so often ignored by scientists. In 1882 their efforts crystallized into the Society for Psychical Research, with the aim of documenting empirically the spiritual experiences which pointed to the existence of an after-life. Sidgwick made a substantial emotional investment in

this work, and underwent a serious crisis in 1887–8 when it seemed that insufficient data were emerging. Several thoughtful people in the 1880s felt that a purely secular ethic could never enforce social discipline or stave off the impending danger of amoral anarchy.[19]

For a wider audience, the same preoccupation with the supernatural and with the duality of good and evil in man created the ghost story, which reached a peak of popularity at the end of the nineteenth century. Stevenson was prompted to write *Jekyll and Hyde* (1886) partly through reading a French scientific paper on the subconscious. A similar duality (spiced with hints of evolutionary theory) pervades Oscar Wilde's *Picture of Dorian Gray* (1891) and Henry James's *Turn of the Screw* (1898); man is only precariously in control of a lower self which can take the semi-animal form of werewolf or vampire. But the ghost story had a shorter life than the detective story; by the 1930s the widespread adjustment to a relatively secularized society – perhaps supplemented by a Freudian self-consciousness about dreams and fantasies – brought the whole genre into decline.[20]

Many prominent people in the 1880s felt that the very framework of their existence depended on the reality of an after-life. The Queen was continually thinking about it, frequently brought it up in conversation, and liked it alluded to in sermons. Lady St Helier many years later recalled W.E. Forster, the prominent Liberal statesman, vigorously asserting that unless one could look beyond the grave, existence in this world would be a hideous mockery and would lack morality and standards of conduct: 'I can honestly say I have acted all through my life in the firm belief in a future state,' he said, 'and but for that belief, I should not have had the courage to face life, its difficulties and its tribulations.' Entrance to heaven was seen as conditional; 'on the track of the soul from birth to death there are two sleuth-hounds – Sin and Satan,' says the ritualist vicar of Mottringham in Mrs Humphry Ward's *Robert Elsmere*: 'Mankind for ever flies them, is for ever vanquished and devoured. I see life always as a threadlike path between abysses along which man *creeps*.'[21] Mrs Ward, whose distaste for such a view no doubt owes much to the memory of her Calvinist mother, was one of those late Victorian writers who campaigned for a more humane view of God's purposes.

The existence of hell was openly challenged from the mid nineteenth century onwards. F.W. Farrar's *Eternal Hope* (1877) created a stir by arguing that 'damnation', 'hell' and 'everlasting' should be expunged from the Bible as mistranslations. He pointed out that, except among the more sectarian and less educated religious leaders, only lip service was now paid to the old doctrines on hell, which caused anxiety to the sincere and benevolent among parishioners, not to the brutal or indifferent. Applying humane standards to Christian belief (in what earlier generations would have seen as a truly secularist fashion) he denied that physical torments would be irrevocable, eternal or widespread in the after-life. Canon Barnett was another humanizing (and, Pusey would have said, secularizing) influence in this area. He once made the mistake of inviting a hell-fire preacher to address the children in his Whitechapel parish. 'I can still see that terrible parson,' Mrs Barnett recalled many years later, 'tall, gaunt, clothed wholly in black, lifting up his arms till his gown looked like huge wings, and descending the first few steps of the lofty pulpit, saying "Down, doown, doowwnnn" as a suitable illustration of the fate of unconverted children.'[22] By the 1870s Anglo-Catholic leaders such as Pusey and Liddon, who championed the old view of eternal punishment, were very much on the defensive; with the publication of *Lux Mundi* in 1889 they were repudiated from within their own camp, and in the same year the Congregationalist leader R.W. Dale, in an important essay, noted a similar revulsion among evangelicals.[23]

The committed Christian's sigh of relief at the shedding of these old beliefs is well illustrated in the autobiography of Samuel Smith, the Liverpool philanthropist. In 1876 the Rev. E. White's *Life in Christ* showed him a way out from the traditional doctrines on eternal punishment which he had grown to detest. 'Your book came into my hands just as my mind was open to receive it,' Smith told the author; he went on to describe how the book 'has sent a thrill through my whole nature, and stirred me in a way no book has done for many years.'[24] The reasons for this shift in opinion are complex, but there can be little doubt about its impact on the rest of Christian belief. Once hell is dispensed with, divine judgement lacks meaning and sanction, and Christianity becomes a vague system of ethics hardly distinguishable from the Unitarianism which earlier Christians had condemned

as heretical. It was the judgement of posterity that now gradually became the prime concern, with the two-volume *Life and Letters* marshalling the evidence. Christianity was becoming a pleasant, sociable, compassionate faith, but lacking in precise doctrine, a positive aid to social reform in this world but decreasingly dependent on assertions about the next. By the 1880s what William James later called the religion of healthy-mindedness – the diversion of attention from disease, death and all unpleasantness – was gaining wide acceptance. Christians were becoming less and less distinct from non-religious humanitarians.[25]

The prevalence of this new outlook should not be exaggerated, because an intense conservatism surrounded the whole subject of death during the decade. The old beliefs had been cramping and even tyrannical for some, but the shift in attitudes brought loss as well as gain. For the old beliefs at their best had fostered a robust self-discipline and a contempt for the trivial and the fashionable which – together with a lifelong reflectiveness about conduct, values, and the employment of time and opportunity – cannot now be lightly set aside.

One Victorian completely out of sympathy with the new attitudes was the ageing Mr Gladstone. 'Those who deny are bold and rash against it,' he said, when discussing eternal punishment in 1896: 'those who believe hardly dare say so, and practically it is on the way to becoming obsolete.' Unlike so many of his earlier beliefs, this was one which Gladstone was not prepared to shed. In his last autobiographical note, written six months before he died, the old man described his frame of mind as he awaited the end: 'I desired to consider myself as a soldier on parade, in a line of men drawn up, ready to march, and waiting for the word of command ... without reluctance because firmly convinced that whatever He ordains for us is best for us and for all.'[26] Throughout his life Gladstone had been preparing himself for death. Such a preoccupation, unfamiliar to our more secular age, lent purpose to this best known and most controversial Englishman alive during the decade, and powerfully moulded his great career.

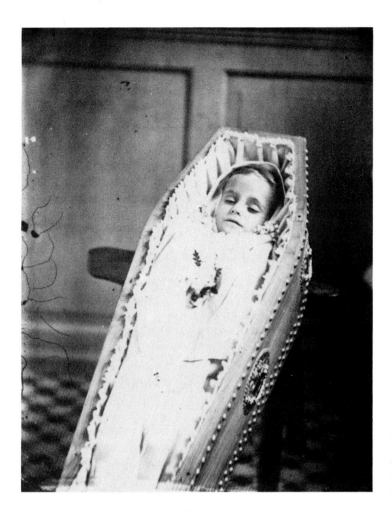

14.2,3. England in the 1880s was less reticent about the dead, whom it even photographed. Because of the high infant mortality rate, there were many portraits of dead children. Baby Hicks (LEFT). Possibly before 1880. The corpse of Lady Marling (BELOW). Robert Cox, 1885

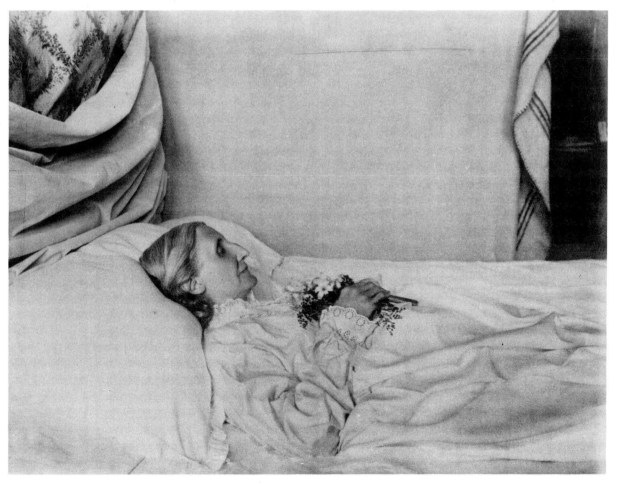

14.4. *A gravestone newly erected. William Boyer, 1882*

14.5. *A North of England funeral procession bears witness to the late Victorian love of ceremony and preoccupation with death. Undated*

Notes

Chapter 1. Introduction: Photography and Society (pp. 9–31)

1. M. Hiley, *Frank Sutcliffe* (1974), p. 58.
2. *Photographic News*, 1 Nov. 1889, p. 709.
3. *Cornhill Magazine*, May 1885, pp. 519, 528.
4. H. and A. Gernsheim, *The History of Photography* (2nd ed. 1969), p. 574; M. Hiley, *Sutcliffe*, p. 58; *Photographic News*, 6 May 1887, p. 281; G.H. Martin and D. Francis, 'The Camera's Eye', in H.J. Dyos & M. Wolff (eds.), *The Victorian City*, I (1973), p. 241.
5. Census return for Aberdeen, 1881.
6. *Photographic News*, 10 Mar. 1882, p. 115; 2 Oct. 1885, p. 636.
7. *Photographic Journal*, 23 Feb. 1883, p. 77; *List of Members, Feb. 1888* (bound in with British Library copy of the *Journal* for that year).
8. Calculated from the list of photographic societies published in H. Sturmey (ed.), *Photography Annual 1891* (1891), pp. 682 ff.
9. M. Hiley, *Sutcliffe*, p. 106.
10. *Photographic News*, 20 Feb. 1885, p. 120; *Times*, 8 Nov. 1888, p. 10.
11. H. and A. Gernsheim, *The History of Photography* (1955), p. vii (preface).
12. M. Hiley, *Sutcliffe*, p. 87.
13. P. Guedalla (ed.), *The Queen and Mr Gladstone, II (1880–1898)* (1933), p. 488.
14. W.A. Seymour (ed.), *A History of the Ordnance Survey* (Folkestone, 1980), pp. 137, 165; *Photographic News*, 2 Apr. 1880, p. 157; 6 Aug. 1881, p. 383; 3 Mar. 1882, p. 100; 23 Mar. 1888, p. 179.
15. The Society for Photographing Relics of Old London is discussed in *Photographic News*, 10 Sep. 1880, p. 433; 23 Apr. 1886, p. 265. For Barnardo, see G. Wagner, *Barnardo* (1979), pp. 44, 52, 160. For Jerome Harrison and the National Photographic Record, see Colin Ford, *Sir Benjamin Stone* (1974).
16. *Photographic News*, 28 Nov. 1884, p. 755; 3 Aug. 1888, p. 488; 1 Nov. 1889, p. 709.
17. Literally hundreds of photographers claimed to be 'Photographer to the Queen', 'Under Royal Patronage', 'Photographer Royal', 'By Special Appointment to Her Majesty', etc. For a list of the 47 who were actually given the Royal Warrant in Victoria's reign, see Colin Ford (ed.), *Happy and Glorious, 130 Years of Royal Photographers* (1977), pp. 60–61.
18. Queen Victoria, *Letters. Third Series* (ed. G.E. Buckle), I (1930), pp. 45, 62, 407.
19. Willoughby de Broke, *The Passing Years* (1924), pp. 10–11, 24; Chalon quo. in A. Scharf, *Art and Photography* (2nd ed., Pelican Books, 1974), p. 45.
20. Quotations from H. and A. Gernsheim, *The History of Photography* (2nd ed. 1969), p. 239; J.A. Froude (ed.), *Letters and Memorials of Jane Welsh Carlyle*, III (1883), pp. 15–16; *Macmillan's Magazine*, Sept. 1871, p. 382. See also M. Howell and P. Ford, *The True History of the Elephant Man* (1980), pp. 117–18, 181.
21. H. and A. Gernsheim, *The History of Photography* (2nd ed. 1969), pp. 301–2, 424; G.H. Martin and D. Francis, *op. cit.*, p. 241.
22. Quotations from *Photographic News*, 25 Mar. 1880, p. 145; 16 July 1886, p. 456; *Daily News*, 8 June 1889, p. 5. For the magic lantern, see *Photographic News*, 2 Apr. 1880, p. 157; 18 Oct. 1889, p. 680. For the mud cabin, *Photographic News*, 16 July 1886, p. 456. For Churchill, *Daily Telegraph*, 20 Oct. 1886, p. 4, cf. *Photographic News*, 22 Oct. 1886, p. 681; 10 Sept. 1886, p. 585.
23. M. Hiley, *Sutcliffe*, p. 62.
24. *ibid.*, p. 63.
25. J. Morley, *Life of William Ewart Gladstone* (2 vol. ed., 1905), II, p. 426.
26. G.H. Martin and D. Francis, *op. cit.*, p. 227.
27. Dixon in *Photographic News*, 10 Sept. 1880, p. 443. See also G. Manley, 'The Mean Temperature of Central England, 1698–1953', *Quarterly Journal of the Royal Meteorological Society* (1953), p. 261; Central Statistical Office, *Annual Abstract of Statistics 1976* (1976) (henceforth cited as *1976 Abstract*), p. 1.

Chapter 2. Childhood (pp. 33–9)

1. L.P. Hartley, *The Go-Between* (Penguin Books, 1958), p. 7.
2. B.R. Mitchell, *European Historical Statistics 1750–1970* (1975), pp. 128–9; Central Statistical Office, *1976 Abstract*, p. 48; Census returns, *Parl[iamentary] Papers* 1883 LXXX (C. 3722), p. x.
3. B.R. Mitchell and P. Deane, *Abstract of British Historical Statistics* (Cambridge, 1962) [henceforth cited as Mitchell and Deane, *Abstract*], p. 12; *1976 Abstract*, p. 15.
4. A.H. Halsey (ed.), *Trends in British Society since 1900* (1972), p. 55.
5. S. Pankhurst, *The Suffragette Movement* (1931), p. 108; L. Woolf, *Sowing. An Autobiography of the Years 1880–1904* (1960), pp. 56–7.

6. H. Mitchell, *The Hard Way Up* (ed. G. Mitchell, 1968), p. 43; cf. R. Roberts, *A Ragged Schooling* (1978 ed.), p. 108.

7. M. Greenwood, *et al.*, 'Deaths by Violence 1837–1937', *Journal of the Royal Statistical Society*, Vol. 104, 1941, p. 154.

8. Speech at Manchester, in T.E. Kebbel (ed.), *Selected Speeches of . . . the Earl of Beaconsfield* (1882), II, p. 494.

9. L. Creighton, *Life and Letters of Mandell Creighton* (1904), I, p. 258, cf. II, p. 135; K.M.E. Murray, *Caught in the Web of Words. James A.H. Murray and the 'Oxford English Dictionary'* (New Haven, 1977), p. 124.

10. In Baroness Burdett-Coutts (ed.), *Woman's Mission* (1893), pp. 66, 68.

11. *Hansard's Parliamentary Debates, Third Series*, Vol. 337 [henceforth cited as 3 Hansard 337], c. 228 (19 June 1889).

12. R. Waugh, *The Life of Benjamin Waugh* (1913), p. 284; figures from Mrs Barnardo and J. Marchant, *Memoirs of the Late Dr Barnardo* (1907), p. 384; *The First Forty Years. A Chronicle of the Church of England Waifs and Strays Society 1881–1920* (1922), p. 214. See also P. Coveney, *The Image of Childhood* (Penguin ed., 1967), pp. 29–32, 192–3, 291, 300–301.

13. A. Mason, *Association Football and British Society 1863–1915* (Hassocks, 1980), p. 82; J.O. Springhall, 'Youth and Empire: A Study of the Propagation of Imperialism' (unpublished Sussex Ph.D. thesis, 1968), p. 265.

14. W. Forrester, *Great-Grandmama's Weekly. A Celebration of the Girl's Own Paper* (Guildford, 1980), p. 145.

15. R. Churchill, *Winston S. Churchill, Vol. 1. Companion Part 1 (1874–1896)* (1967), p. 112 (letter of 29 Sept. 1885); for *Boy's Own Paper*, see H. Sturmey (ed.), *Photography Annual, 1891* (1891), p. 687.

16. R. Churchill, *Winston S. Churchill*, I (1966), pp. 49, 55; the account of Churchill which follows leans heavily on this volume, and on the associated volume of Churchill's letters, cited in note 15 above.

17. *ibid.*, p. 91.

18. S. Pankhurst, *The Suffragette Movement* (1931), p. 59; the account of Sylvia Pankhurst which follows owes much to this sensitive and informative volume, together with Sylvia's essay in M. Asquith (ed.), *Myself When Young. By Famous Women of To-Day* (1938), pp. 260ff.

19. S. Pankhurst, *Suffragette Movement*, pp. 84, 88.

20. *ibid.* p. 101.

21. J.H. Thomas, *My Story* (1937), p. 17; see also G. Blaxland, *J.H. Thomas. A Life for Unity* (1964), pp. 15–22.

Chapter 3. Education and Newspapers (pp. 47–58)

1. Census Returns, *Parl. Papers 1893–4 CVI* (C. 7222), p. 60.

2. O. Chadwick, *The Victorian Church*, II (1970), p. 257; Mitchell and Deane, *Abstract*, p. 12; R. Currie, *et al.*, *Churches and Churchgoers* (Oxford, 1977), p. 88.

3. The figure for 1882 is obtained by dividing the 3,774,000 children over 5 (there were few over 13) at inspected schools in that year by the number of children between 5 and 14 in England and Wales as a whole in 1881 (5,947,500); as most left at 13, the estimate of 63 per cent is probably below the mark. See R. Hamilton, 'Popular Education in England and Wales since 1882', *Journal of the Royal Statistical Society*, Mar. 1890, p. 89; Mitchell and Deane, *Abstract*, p. 12.

4. R. Hamilton, 'Popular Education in England and Wales before and after the Elementary Education Act of 1870', *Journal of the Royal Statistical Society*, 1883, p. 326; R. Hamilton. 'Popular Education . . . 1882', *op. cit.*, pp. 88–9.

5. R. Hamilton, 'Popular Education . . . 1870', *op. cit.*, p. 323; 'Popular Education . . . 1882', p. 95; B.R. Mitchell, *European Historical Statistics 1750–1970* (1975), pp. 753–9.

6. R. Hamilton, 'Popular Education . . . 1870', p. 323; 'Popular Education . . . 1882', pp. 94–5; *Parl. Papers 1893–4 CVI* (C. 7222), p. 39.

7. Salary figures for 1883 from T.H.S. Escott, *England: Its People, Polity, and Pursuits* (1885 ed.), p. 277; for pupil-teachers, see R. Hamilton, 'Popular Education . . . 1882', p. 95.

8. R. Hamilton, 'Popular Education . . . 1882', p. 95; *Englishwoman's Review*, 15 Apr. 1887, pp. 146ff; 15 May 1889, pp. 205ff.

9. R. Hamilton, 'Popular Education . . . 1870', p. 324; 'Popular Education . . . 1882', p. 88; D. Rubinstein, *School Attendance in London, 1870–1904: A Social History* (Hull, 1969), p. 114.

10. Quotations cited in B. Webb, *My Apprenticeship* (2nd ed., n. d.), pp. 217–18. Although Beatrice Webb remained unmarried throughout the 1880s, and was therefore known as Beatrice Potter, it seems best to use throughout the name by which she is best known.

11. R. Hamilton, 'Popular Education . . . 1870', p. 325.

12. G. Sutherland, *Policy-Making in Elementary Education 1870–1895* (1973), pp. 177, 355, 361; D. Rubinstein, *op. cit.*, pp. 84–6.

13. R. Hamilton, 'Popular Education . . . 1882', pp. 88, 95.

14. Electors in F.W.S. Craig, *British Parliamentary Election Results 1885–1918* (1974), p. 587; Irish in *Parl. Papers 1892 XC* (C. 6780), p. 3; prisoners in G. Grosvenor, 'Statistics of the Abatement in Crime in England and Wales during the Twenty Years ended 1887–88', *Journal of the Royal Statistical Society*, Sept. 1890, p. 402.

15. G. Wagner, *Barnado* (1979), p. 85; M.E. Bulkley, *The Feeding of School Children* (1914), pp. 16, 26.

16. Sheffield Central Library, *H.J. Wilson Collection*, 6009A: Joseph Edmondson to Wilson, 28 July 1877; S. Pankhurst, *The Suffragette Movement* (1931), p. 108.

17. F. Musgrove, *The Family, Education and Society* (1966), p. 22.

18. W.F. Monypenny and G.E. Buckle, *The Life of Benjamin Disraeli* (2 vol. ed., 1929), II, p. 1300; Lady G. Cecil, *Life of Robert, Marquis of Salisbury*, I (1921), p. 78.

19. G. Harries-Jenkins, *The Army in Victorian Society* (1977), pp. 139–41; T.W. Bamford, *The Rise of the Public Schools*

(1967), p. 210; *Photographic News*, 19 Feb. 1886, p. 113.

20. K. Feiling, *The Life of Neville Chamberlain* (1946), pp. 9–10.

21. *Times*, 25 Sept. 1889, p. 5; 1 Oct. 1889, p. 10.

22. F. Pethick-Lawrence, *Fate Has Been Kind* (n. d.), p. 28; T.W. Bamford, *op. cit.*, p. 210.

23. E.C. Mack, *Public Schools and British Opinion since 1860* (New York, 1941), p. 366.

24. F. Pethick-Lawrence, *op. cit.*, p. 25; G. Orwell, *Collected Essays, Journalism and Letters*, IV (Penguin ed., 1970), p. 388.

25. F. Darwin (ed.), *The Life and Letters of Charles Darwin* (1887), III, p. 177.

26. R[oyal] C[ommission] ... Depression of Trade and Industry, *Parl. Papers* 1886 XXIII (C. 4797), p. 530; T.W. Bamford, *op. cit.*, p. 210.

27. G.R. Parkin, *Edward Thring. Headmaster of Uppingham School* (1898), I, p.76.

28. 3 *Hansard* 289, c. 165 (12 June 1884). See also J. Kamm, *Indicative Past* (1971), pp. 207ff.; *Englishwoman's Year-Book*, 1890, pp. 127, 147ff.

29. B. Stephen, *Emily Davies and Girton College* (1927), p. 30.

30. B. Webb, *op. cit.*, p. 42.

31. S.M. Newton, *Health, Art and Reason* (1974), pp. 95, 107.

32. *Nineteenth Century*, June 1889, p. 782.

33. *Contemporary Review*, Dec. 1890, pp. 832, 838.

34. Census Returns, *Parl. Papers* 1883 LXXX (C. 3797), p. 30; Mitchell and Deane, *Abstract*, p. 60.

35. N.C. Soldon, *Women in British Trade Unions 1874–1976* (1978), p. 21; for the 1886 survey, see Department of Employment, *British Labour Statistics. Historical Abstract 1886–1968* (1971), p. 93; for unionization figures, see *ibid.*, p. 395; *1976 Abstract*, p. 184; B. Drake, *Women in Trade Unions* (Labour Research Dept., n. d.), appendix.

36. Memoir in A. Toynbee, *Lectures on the Industrial Revolution in England* (1884), p. xxii; see also Alice M. Gordon, 'The After-Careers of University-Educated Women', *Nineteenth Century*, XXXVII (1895). Figures for doctors from *Englishwoman's Year-Book*, 1890, pp. 202ff; *Englishwoman's Review*, 15 Feb. 1889, p. 65.

37. W.S. Churchill, *Lord Randolph Churchill* (1907 ed.), pp. 221, 266–7.

38. J. Roach, *Public Examinations in England 1850–1900* (Cambridge, 1971), pp. 129, 169; E. Welch, *The Peripatetic University* (Cambridge, 1973), p. 178.

39. Lord Ernle, 'Victorian Memoirs and Memories', *Quarterly Review*, Apr. 1923, p. 224.

40. R.M. McLeod, 'The Royal Society and the Government Grant', *Historical Journal*, 1971, p. 335.

41. K. Marx, *Capital* (tr. S. Moore and E. Aveling, New York ed., 1967), I, p. 361.

42. M. Sanderson, *The Universities and British Industry 1850–1970* (1972), pp. 136–7, 148.

43. Statistics from *Nineteenth Century*, May 1890, p. 835; *Quarterly Review*, Oct. 1880, p. 501; A.P. Wadsworth, 'Newspaper Circulations 1800–1954', *Transactions of the Manchester Statistical Society*, Session 1954–5, pp. 19–23; for newsagents, see E.A. Wrigley (ed.),

Nineteenth-Century Society (Cambridge, 1972), p. 272.

44. Arnot Reid prints an interesting content-analysis of five newspapers in the period 5–10 Apr. 1886 in *Nineteenth Century*, Sept. 1886, p. 395; journals discussed in *Quarterly Review*, Oct. 1880, pp. 523–4.

45. A. Reid, *Nineteenth Century*, Sept. 1886, p. 395.

46. For provincial papers, see *Quarterly Review*, Oct. 1880, p. 501. For London suburban papers, *ibid.*, pp. 522–3; for W.H. Smith, *ibid.*, p. 506.

47. Joseph Pennell, *Contemporary Review*, July 1890, p. 121.

48. *Nineteenth Century*, May 1890, p. 836.

49. R.R. James, *Lord Randolph Churchill* (1959), p. 296.

50. *Contemporary Review*, Nov. 1886, p. 668; *Pall Mall Gazette*, 9 July 1885, p. 2.

51. *Contemporary Review*, Nov. 1886, pp. 671–2, 675, 677–8.

52. John Bright, *Diaries* (ed. R.A.J. Walling, 1930), p. 508, entry for 26 Jan. 1884; Viscount Chilston, *W.H. Smith* (1965), p. 212; Gladstone quo. in B. Holland, *Life of Spencer Compton. Eighth Duke of Devonshire* (1911), II, pp. 99–100; see also S. Gwynn and G.M. Tuckwell, *The Life of the Rt. Hon. Sir Charles W. Dilke* (1917), II, p. 570.

53. A Reid, *Nineteenth Century*, Sept. 1886, p. 395.

54. J. Arch, *Joseph Arch. The Story of his Life* (ed. The Countess of Warwick, 3rd ed., 1898) p. 49; T.O. Lloyd, *The General Election of 1880* (1968), p. 96.

55. T.W. Reid, *Macmillan's Magazine*, May 1880, p. 25.

56. J.L. Garvin, *The Life of Joseph Chamberlain*, I (1932), p. 563; see also R. Jenkins, *Sir Charles Dilke. A Victorian Tragedy* (1958), p. 139.

57. J.S. Mill, *Representative Government* (Everyman ed., 1910), p. 195, cf. pp. 193, 288.

58. In N. St J. Stevas (ed.), *Collected Works of Walter Bagehot*, IV (1968), p. 129.

59. *Quarterly Review*, Oct. 1880, p. 536.

60. Quoted in H.M. Lynd, *England in the Eighteen-Eighties* (1945) [henceforth cited as Lynd], p. 225.

61. Hamilton Fyfe, quo. in R.C.K. Ensor, *England 1870–1914* (1936) [henceforth cited as Ensor], p. 312.

Chapter 4. Home and Family (pp. 69–76)

1. *Facts and Figures about the Church of England* (Church Information Office, 1962), p. 57.

2. E. Pethick-Lawrence, quo. in A. Rosen, *Rise Up, Women! The Militant Campaign of the Women's Social and Political Union 1903–1914* (1974), p. 61; S. Pankhurst, *The Suffragette Movement* (1931), p. 103; B. Russell, *Autobiography*, I (1967 paperback ed.), p. 40; M. Loane, *The Englishman's Castle* (1909), p. 205; R.R. James, *Lord Randolph Churchill* (1959), p. 345. For the obscene photographs, see *British Journal of Photography*, 25 Jan. 1889, p. 64.

3. H. Ellis, *Studies in the Psychology of Sex*, I (3rd ed., Philadelphia, 1910), p. xi, preface to first ed. See also Census Returns, *Parl. Papers* 1883 LXXX (C. 3722), p. 10; D. Thomas, 'The Social Origins of Marriage Partners of the British Peerage in the 18th and 19th Centuries', *Population Studies*, Mar. 1972, p. 100.

4. H. Ellis, *op. cit.*, I, p. 163. See also (for Pusey) P.T. Marsh, *The Victorian Church in Decline* (1969), p. 234; E. Lyttelton, *The Causes and Prevention of Immorality in Schools* (n. d.), p. 11.

5. For Freud and Paget, see R.P. Neuman, 'Masturbation, Madness, and the Modern Concepts of Childhood and Adolescence', *Journal of Social History*, Spring 1975, pp. 13–14; Lyttelton, *op. cit.*, pp. 22, 26. See also A.S. Dyer, *Plain Words to Young Men upon an Avoided Subject* (3rd ed., 1884), pp. 4ff.

6. Quotation from *Journal of Education*, 1 Mar. 1882, p. 85; H. Ellis, *op. cit.*, p. 250. See also H. Ellis, *ibid.*, p. 282; *Journal of Education*, 1 Nov. 1881, p. 255; 1 Dec. 1881, p. 277.

7. H. Ellis, *Sexual Inversion* (2nd ed., Philadelphia, 1908), p. 30; G. Grosvenor, 'Statistics of the Abatement in Crime in England and Wales during the Twenty Years ended 1887–88', *Journal of the Royal Statistical Society*, Sept. 1890, p. 390.

8. Quotations from Sheffield Public Library, *H.J. Wilson Collection*, 2545–15: Josephine Butler to H.J. Wilson, 10 July 1885 (copy); K. Marx, *Communist Manifesto* (ed. H. Laski, 1948), p. 142; Eleanor Marx quo. in C. Tsuzuki, *The Life of Eleanor Marx* (Oxford, 1967), p. 124; Anon, *My Secret Life* (British Library copy), VIII, p. 153.

9. P. Fitzgerald, *Music-Hall Land* (n. d.), p. 18; see also *Parl. Papers* 1889 XXV (C. 5846), pp. xli, xxxiv; *1976 Abstract*, p. 35.

10. B. Webb, *My Apprenticeship* (2nd ed., n. d.), p. 45; Countess of Warwick, *Life's Ebb and Flow* (n. d.), p. 177.

11. R.C. on Divorce, *Parl. Papers* 1912–13 XX (Cd. 6482), pp. 29, 37; G. Rowntree and N.H. Carrier, 'The Resort to Divorce in England and Wales, 1858–1957', *Population Studies*, XI (1957–8), p. 222.

12. Mitchell and Deane, *Abstract*, pp. 12, 15–16; *1976 Abstract*, p. 18.

13. Census Returns, *Parl. Papers* 1883 LXXX (C. 3797), p. 22; *Women's Suffrage Journal*, 1 Sept. 1885, pp. 150–51.

14. Mitchell and Deane, *Abstract*, pp. 29–30; for Knowlton, see J. Peel, 'The Manufacture and Retailing of Contraceptives in England', *Population Studies*, Nov. 1963, p. 115.

15. G. Grosvenor, 'Abatement in Crime', *op. cit.*, p. 390.

16. J.S. Mill, *Liberty* (Everyman ed., 1910), p. 160.

17. D.K. Sheppard, *Growth and Role of United Kingdom Financial Institutions 1880–1962* (1971), p. 150; Sir H. Bellman, *Bricks and Mortals* (n. d.), p. 221.

18. B. Webb, *op. cit.*, p. 134. See also Census Returns, *Parl. Papers* 1883 LXXIX (C. 3563), p. xix; *Parl. Papers* 1883 LXXX (C. 3797), p. 14; *Parl. Papers* 1893–4 CVI (C. 7222), p. 20; *1976 Abstract*, pp. 7, 87.

19. B. Webb, *op. cit.*, p. 237.

20. Quotation from A.S. Wohl, in S.D. Chapman (ed.), *The History of Working-Class Housing* (Newton Abbot, 1971), p. 22. See also P. Deane and W.A. Cole, *British Economic Growth 1688–1959* (2nd ed., Cambridge, 1969), p. 247.

21. Mitchell and Deane, *Abstract*, p. 239.

22. Census Returns, *Parl. Papers* 1883 LXXX (C. 3722), p. xvii.

23. Betty Balfour (ed.), *Letters of Constance Lytton* (1925), p. 130.

24. K.M.E. Murray, *Caught in the Web of Words. James A.H. Murray and the 'Oxford English Dictionary'* (New Haven, 1977), p. 125.

25. Mrs H. Ward, *Robert Elsmere* (Boston, 1911), II, pp. 124, 131, cf. pp. 137, 550, 557. See also O. Anderson's excellent 'The Incidence of Civil Marriage in Victorian England and Wales', *Past and Present*, Nov. 1975.

Chapter 5. Church and Chapel (pp. 89–97)

1. *Nonconformist and Independent*, 2 Feb. 1882, p. 106; George Eliot, *Adam Bede* (New York, 1966), p. 158.

2. O. Anderson, 'The Incidence of Civil Marriage in Victorian England and Wales', *Past and Present*, Nov. 1975, p. 62; S. Budd, 'The British Humanist Movement: 1860–1966' (unpublished Oxford D. Phil. thesis, 1968), p. 180; Census Returns, *Parl. Papers* 1893–4 CVI (C. 7222), pp. 38–9.

3. *Nonconformist and Independent*, 2 Feb. 1882, pp. 105–6; *British Weekly*, 17 Dec. 1886, p. 5. The *British Weekly's* estimate assumed that to the numbers attending the most popular service of the day should be added half those attending the other services, whereas Mann's 1851 census (more preoccupied with rural patterns of worship) added to the numbers attending the morning service half those attending the afternoon and one-third of those attending the evening services.

4. *Nonconformist and Independent*, 2 Feb. 1882, p. 107. See also O. Chadwick, *The Victorian Church*, II (1970), pp. 222, 227; R. Currie, *Methodism Divided. A Study in the Sociology of Ecumenicalism* (1968), p. 87; *Facts and Figures about the Church of England* (Church Information Office, 1962), p. 53.

5. J. Morley, *Life of William Ewart Gladstone* (2 vol. ed., 1905), II, p. 240; Mrs Ward quo. in W.S. Peterson, 'Gladstone's Review of *Robert Elsmere*: Some Unpublished Correspondence', *Review of English Studies*, 1970, p. 452. See also D. MacCarthy and A. Russell (eds.), *Lady John Russell. A Memoir* (1910), p. 264.

6. Sir E.W. Hamilton, *Diary* (ed. D.W.R. Bahlman, Oxford, 1972), II, p. 539; the estimate of atheist M.P.s is Samuel Morley's, cited in W.L. Arnstein, *The Bradlaugh Case* (1965), p. 57, cf. p. 223; on bishops, see D.H.J. Morgan, 'The Social and Educational Background of Anglican Bishops – Continuities and Changes', *British Journal of Sociology*, 1969, p. 297.

7. Ellen Wilkinson in M. Asquith (ed.), *Myself When Young* (1938), p. 401. See also H. Mitchell, *The Hard Way Up* (ed. G. Mitchell, 1968), p. 50, cf. p. 78.

8. G. Sutherland, *Policy-Making in Elementary Education 1870–1895* (1973), pp. 350, 356; R. Hamilton, 'Popular Education in England and Wales since 1882',

Journal of the Royal Statistical Society, Mar. 1890, p. 88.

9. For Eton, see E.C. Mack, *Public Schools and British Opinion since 1860* (New York, 1941), p. 366; for Rugby and Harrow, T.W. Bamford, *The Rise of the Public Schools* (1967), p. 210.

10. *Mitchell's Newspaper Press Directory*, 1880, p. iv; *Publisher's Circular*, annual summaries published in Dec. or Jan. The assertion in Ensor, p. 160, is based on too limited a selection of the statistics and antedates religious decline.

11. A. Huxley, *Beyond the Mexique Bay* (Chatto and Windus ed., 1974), p. 161. *Wiltshire and Gloucestershire Standard* 4 Oct. 1890, p. 5.

12. O. Chadwick, *The Victorian Church*, II, p. 194.

13. Mrs S.A. Barnett, *Canon Barnett. His Life, Work, and Friends* (1918) I, p. 142; for the Mothers' Union, see B. Harrison, 'For Church, Queen and Family: The Girls' Friendly Society 1874–1920', *Past and Present*, Nov. 1973, p. 109.

14. Mitchell and Deane, *Abstract*, pp. 356–7.

15. B. Webb, *My Apprenticeship* (2nd ed., n.d.), pp. 140, 147.

16. B.S. Rowntree, *Poverty. A Study of Town Life* (Nelson ed., n.d.), p. 422. For friendly society statistics, see P.H.J.H. Gosden, *Self-Help. Voluntary Associations in Nineteenth-century Britain* (1973), p. 91, cf. p. 104; for trade unions, *Parl. Papers* 1890–1 XCII (C. 6475), p. 3.

17. D.K. Sheppard, *Growth and Role of United Kingdom Financial Institutions 1880–1962* (1971), pp. 144, 146, 154; W. Ashworth, *An Economic History of England 1870–1939* (1960), p. 167.

18. Mrs S.A. Barnett, *op. cit.*, I, pp. 201–2. Statistics from Mitchell and Deane, *Abstract*, p. 416.

19. H. Spencer, *Man Versus the State* (1892 ed.), p. 363, cf. p. 358.

20. Mrs S.A. Barnett, *op. cit.*, II, p. 236; see also *ibid.*, I, pp. 84–5, 89; II, pp. 265–9.

21. British Library, *Add. MSS.* 44250 (Gladstone Papers), f. 285: Manning to Gladstone, 5 Oct. 1890.

22. R.R. James, *Rosebery* (1963), p. 209; [L.R. Phelps], *Giving, no Charity!* in Bodleian Library, Oxford, reference G.A. Oxon 4° 165.

23. R. Postgate, *The Life of George Lansbury* (1951), p. 38; see also G. Wagner, *Barnardo* (1979), p. 179.

24. L.M. Weir, *The Tragedy of Ramsay MacDonald* (1938), p. 18.

25. See the excellent article by V. Bailey, 'Salvation Army Riots, the "Skeleton Army" and Legal Authority in the Provincial Town', in A.P. Donajgrodzki (ed.), *Social Control in Nineteenth Century Britain* (1977), pp. 233–5, 241, 244–7.

26. *Nonconformist and Independent*, 2 Feb. 1882, p. 115; R. Currie *et al.*, *Churches and Churchgoers* (Oxford, 1977), pp. 208, 213.

27. Quotation from T.H.S. Escott, *England: Its People, Polity, and Pursuits* (1885 ed.), p. 9; see also L. Creighton, *Life and Letters of Mandell Creighton* (1904), II, p. 224, *Oxford English Dictionary* (1933 ed., Oxford), I, pp. xxi–xxii.

28. *Treasury* quotation cited in W.R. Lambert, 'Drink and

Sobriety in Wales, 1835–1895' (unpublished University of Wales Ph.D. thesis, 1969), p. 165; Gladstone quo. in K.O. Morgan, 'Gladstone and Wales', *Welsh History Review*, 1960, p. 70, and in J. Wilson, *CB. A Life of Sir Henry Campbell-Bannerman* (1973), p. 104.

29. *Quarterly Review*, July 1886, p. 127.

30. W.S. Churchill, *Lord Randolph Churchill* (1907 ed.), p. 204.

31. T.H.S. Escott, *England*, p. 478; J.R. Illingworth, in Charles Gore (ed.), *Lux Mundi* (7th ed., 1890), p. 181.

32. W. James, *Varieties of Religious Experience* (Fontana paperback ed., 1960), p. 345.

33. R. Currie, *Methodism Divided*, pp. 90–92; G. Sutherland, *Policy-Making*, p. 350.

34. Quotations from B. Webb, *op. cit.*, pp. 123, 154, cf. pp. 140, 155, 157.

35. *Nonconformist and Independent*, 2 Feb. 1882, p. 106. Population was 206,513, pub attendance 104,557, attendance at morning service 51,689 and at evening service 64,459. Assuming that, in towns at least, the number of attenders can be calculated from adding to the numbers attending the most popular service half the numbers attending other services, this gives a total of 83,919 attenders. See also W. Shaw, *The Three Choirs Festival* (1954), p. 54; *The Baptist*, 3 Oct. 1890, p. 195.

36. *British Weekly*, 17 Dec. 1886, p. 5; Willoughby de Broke, *The Passing Years* (1924), p. 63.

37. Mrs H. Ward, *Robert Elsmere* (Boston, 1911 ed.), II, p. 109; cf. Romanes, in O. Chadwick, *The Victorian Church*, II, p. 22.

Chapter 6. Work (pp. 111–17)

1. City of London Polytechnic, Fawcett Library Collection: *Mrs Billington-Greig MSS*, pencilled MS. in file entitled 'Childhood', in MS. box labelled 'Biographical Material (Family and Personal)'.

2. Mitchell and Deane, *Abstract*, p. 60.

3. H. Broadhurst, *The Story of his Life* (1901), p. 2.

4. Figures from Mitchell and Deane, *Abstract*, pp. 78, 80. For Denmark, see E.J. Hobsbawm, *Industry and Empire* (1968), p. 168.

5. *Quarterly Review*, Apr. 1888, p. 409; Mitchell and Deane, *Abstract*, p. 78; *Parl. Papers* 1882 LXXIV (C. 3351), p. 50.

6. C. Darwin, *On the Origin of Species* (Penguin ed., 1968), p. 90, cf. p. 99. Statistics from Census Returns, *Parl. Papers* 1883 LXXX (C. 3722), p. xii.

7. Mitchell and Deane, *Abstract*, p. 78; Charles Whitehead, in *Journal of the Royal Agricultural Society of England*, 3rd ser. I (1890), pp. 323, 336. There is an excellent discussion of migrant labour in E.J.T. Collins, 'Migrant Labour in British Agriculture in the Nineteenth Century', *Economic History Review*, Feb. 1976; see esp. pp. 41, 43, 45.

8. Wrightson, in *Journal of the Royal Agricultural Society of England*, 3rd ser., Vol. 1 (1890), p. 276; T.H.S. Escott,

England: Its People, Polity, and Pursuits (1885 ed.), p. 165, cf. p. 169.

9. David Taylor, 'The English Dairy Industry, 1860–1930', *Economic History Review*, Nov. 1976, pp. 586, 589–90; C. Booth, *Life and Labour in London* (1903 ed.), 2nd ser. III, p. 173. Milk consumption figure from T.C. Barker, *et al.*, *Our Changing Fare* (1966), p. 41.

10. Wrightson, *op. cit.*, p. 279.

11. B.R. Mitchell, *European Historical Statistics 1750–1970* (1975), p. 623; J. Rule, 'The Smacksmen of the North Sea. Labour Recruitment and Exploitation in British Deep-Sea Fishing, 1850–90', *International Review of Social History*, 1976, III, p. 390.

12. B.R. Mitchell, *op. cit.*, pp. 362–4, 393–4, 434 ff.

13. G. Stedman Jones, *Outcast London* (Oxford, 1971), p. 29.

14. Queen Victoria, *Letters, Third Series* (ed. G.E. Buckle), I (1930), p. 289.

15. Department of Employment, *British Labour Statistics. Historical Abstract 1886–1968* (1971), pp. 38, 93.

16. Sir C. Petrie, *Walter Long and his Times* (1936), p. 40; W.D. Rubinstein, 'Wealth, Elites and the Class Structure of Modern Britain', *Past and Present*, Aug. 1977, p. 102; P. Deane and W.A. Cole, *British Economic Growth 1688–1959* (2nd ed., Cambridge, 1969), p. 234; Mitchell and Deane, *Abstract*, p. 328; shipbuilding figures calculated from S. Pollard and P. Robertson, *The British Shipbuilding Industry 1870–1914* (Cambridge, Mass., 1979), pp. 250–51.

17. Mitchell and Deane, *Abstract*, pp. 366, 369; B.R. Mitchell and H.G. Jones, *Second Abstract of British Historical Statistics* (Cambridge, 1971), pp. 73–4; R.C. ... Depression of Trade and Industry, *Parl. Papers* 1886 XXIII (C. 4797), p. 522.

18. H.A. Shannon, 'The Limited Companies of 1866–1883', in E.M. Carus-Wilson (ed.), *Essays in Economic History* (1954), p. 382; Lynd, p. 43.

19. W. Ashworth, *An Economic History of England 1870–1939* (1960), p. 93; for mergers, see L. Hannah, 'Mergers in British Manufacturing Industry 1880–1918', *Oxford Economic Papers*, 1974.

20. T.H.S. Escott, *England*, p. 5; *Times*, 4 Mar. 1890, p. 10; Acworth, in *Murray's Magazine*, June 1889, p. 776; for patents, see Mitchell and Deane, *Abstract*, p. 269.

21. T.H.S. Escott, *ibid.*, p. 555. See also P. Joyce, 'The Factory Politics of Lancashire in the Later Nineteenth Century', *Historical Journal*, 1975, pp. 525–6.

22. Quo. in E.P. Thompson, *William Morris. Romantic to Revolutionary* (2nd ed., 1977), p. 734.

23. W.J. Reader, *Professional Men* (1966), p. 211.

24. W.H. Lecky, *Democracy and Liberty* (1899 ed.), II, p. 524. For clerks, see W.J. Reader, *op. cit.*, p. 211. See also E.H. Butler, *The Story of British Shorthand* (1951), pp. 138, 234 ff; E. Cohen, *The Growth of the British Civil Service 1780–1939* (1941), pp. 125, 151.

25. J.B. Jefferys, *Retail Trading in Britain 1850–1950* (Cambridge, 1954), p. 16; Census Returns, *Parl. Papers* 1893–4 CVI (C. 7222), p. 57; *Photographic News*, 6 May 1887, p. 281.

26. J.B. Jefferys, *op. cit.*, p. 182; Mitchell and Jones, *Second Abstract*, p. 63.

27. Anon., 'History of the Horse of John Rouse (Oldham) Ltd', *Fish Trades Gazette*, 18 July 1936, pp. 51 ff.

28. J.B. Jefferys, *op. cit.*, p. 22.

29. K.O. Morgan (ed.), *Lloyd George Family Letters 1885–1936* (Cardiff, 1973), p. 28; for bankruptcies, see Mitchell and Jones, *Second Abstract*, p. 208.

30. Census Returns, *Parl. Papers* 1883 LXXX (C. 3722), p. xix; 1893–4 CVI (C. 7058), pp. xviii, xix.

31. F. Harrison, *Autobiographic Memoirs* (1911), II, p. 315; A. Briggs, *Friends of the People. The Centenary History of Lewis's* (1956), pp. 85, 87.

Chapter 7. Recreation (pp. 135–47)

1. City of London Polytechnic, Fawcett Library Collection: Billington-Greig MSS., pencilled MS. in file entitled 'Childhood', in box labelled 'Biographical Material (Family and Personal)'.

2. F. Thompson, *Lark Rise to Candleford* (1948 ed.), p. 45; B. Webb, *My Apprenticeship* (2nd ed., n.d.), p. 255, cf. p. 237; L. Woolf, *Sowing. An Autobiography of the Years 1880–1904* (1960), p. 57.

3. T.H.S. Escott, *England: Its People, Polity, and Pursuits* (1885 ed.), p. 169.

4. *Parl. Papers* 1898 XXXVII (C. 8695), pp. 1 ff.

5. P. Joyce, *Work, Society and Politics. The Culture of the Factory in Later Victorian England* (Brighton, 1980), p. 269.

6. Quotation from H. Sturmey (ed.), *Photography Annual 1891* (1891), p. 691; statistics from *ibid.*, pp. 682 ff.; G.W. Simpson (ed.), *The Year-Book of Photography 1880* (1880), pp. 16 ff.; *Photographic News*, 6 Sept. 1889, p. 588.

7. There were 12,656,100 males over twenty in the United Kingdom at the 1901 census – Mitchell and Deane, *Abstract*, pp. 12–14; *Parl. Papers* 1898 XXXVII (C. 8695), p. 180 shows that there were 945,735 members in the U.K. in 1898, and specifies subscriptions and 1887 figure on pp. 1–3, 180–81. For the W.M.C.I.U., see *Parl. Papers* 1897 XXXV (C. 8523), p. 516, table VIII.

8. *Parl. Papers* 1898 XXXVII (C. 8695), pp. 181 ff.

9. For Ripon, see K. Rose, *Superior Person* (1969), p. 66; for gamekeepers, whose total number was much higher than the number who were licensed, see *Parl. Papers* 1883 LXXX (C. 3722), p. xii, where 12,633 (all male) are listed in England and Wales alone. For licences to kill game, see *Parl. Papers* 1870 XX (C. 82–I), p. 82; 1884–5 XXII (C. 4474) for p. 182 of the 28th Report of the Commissioners of Her Majesty's Inland Revenue on the Duties under their Management.

10. [T.H.S. Escott], *Society in London. By a Foreign Resident* (1885), p. 118; *Edinburgh Review*, Apr. 1880, p. 427; J. Leigh, 'What Do the Masses Read?', *Economic Review*, 15 Apr. 1904, p. 171; A. Mason, *Association Football and English Society 1863–1915* (Hassocks, 1980), pp. 187–8, 191, 193.

11. Marchioness of Londonderry, *Henry Chaplin. A Memoir* (1926), p. 225, cf. p. 247; Willoughby de Broke, *The Passing Years* (1924), pp. 49, 76.

12. See B. Harrison, 'Religion and Recreation in Nineteenth-Century England', *Past and Present*, Dec. 1967, p. 102; and *idem*, 'Animals and the State in Nineteenth-century England', *English Historical Review*, Oct. 1973, pp. 790–91. Rabies figures from *Parl. Papers* 1892 XXIV (C. 6841), p. xliv.

13. S. Alexander, *St Giles's Fair, 1830–1914* (History Workshop pamphlet No. 2, Oxford, n.d.), pp. 57, 40–41; see also pp. 44–6, 51 n.2.

14. *Contemporary Review*, 1891, p. 556.

15. S.C. Carpenter, *Winnington-Ingram* (1949), p. 35; statistics from B. Harrison, 'Religion and Recreation', *op. cit.*, p. 102.

16. Lord's Day Observance Society, *Occasional Paper*, Oct. 1886, p. 190; [T.H.S. Escott], *Society in London*, p. 162; J. Morley, *Life of William Ewart Gladstone* (2 vol. ed., 1905), II, p. 426.

17. My debt in this and the next paragraph to A. Mason, *Association Football*, is considerable; see especially pp. 16, 21, 30–31, 71, 76, 91, 93, 139, 146, 153, 158, 213, 247, 256.

18. For attendance figures, J. Walvin, *The People's Game* (1975), pp. 65, 75, and W.F. Mandle, 'Games People Played: Cricket and Football in England and Victoria in the Late Nineteenth-century', *Historical Studies, Australia and New Zealand*, Apr. 1973, p. 511.

19. Mitchell and Deane, *Abstract*, p. 417.

20. For Brabazon, see G. Stedman Jones, *Outcast London* (Oxford, 1971), p. 308, cf. p. 96 n. 93 and (for 1880 figures) *Parl. Papers* 1904 XXXII (Cd. 2175), p. 3.

21. Bury, *Nineteenth Century*, Jan. 1885, p. 96; *Times*, 31 May 1882, p. 9. See also Census Returns, *Parl. Papers* 1883 LXXX (C. 3722), p. xiii; 1893–4 CVI (C. 7058), pp. xvi, xvii.

22. *Nineteenth Century*, Jan. 1885, p. 97, cf. p. 93 (for figures). See also G. Foxall, in T. Bolas (ed.), *The Year-Book of Photography ... for 1889* (n.d.), p. 52; *Photographic News*, 12 Feb. 1886, p. 102.

23. T.H.S. Escott, *England*, p. 101; Lonsdale, *Macmillan's Magazine*, Mar. 1882, p. 394, cf. p. 398; E. Gosse, *Father and Son* (Penguin ed., 1949), p. 111; Blackpool figures from H. Cunningham, *Leisure in the Industrial Revolution c. 1780–c. 1880* (1980), p. 162.

24. T. Cooper, *The Life of Thomas Cooper* (1872 ed.), p. 394. For content-analysis, see A. Reid, *Nineteenth Century*, Sept. 1886, p. 395.

25. Quotations from *The Times*, 1 May 1882, p. 9; Lady G. Cecil, *Life of Robert, Marquis of Salisbury*, III (1931), p. 7. See also B. Kaye, *The Development of the Architectural Profession in Britain* (1960), pp. 174–5.

26. S.C. Hutchinson, *The History of the Royal Academy 1768–1968* (New York, 1968), p. 138; M.B. Huish, in *Nineteenth Century*, Jan. 1890, p. 109; Census Returns, *Parl. Papers* 1883 LXXX (C. 3722), p.x.; Queen Victoria, *Letters, Third Series* (ed. G.E. Buckle, 1930), I, pp. 260–

61. For Jowett, see J.L. Lant, *Insubstantial Pageant* (1979), pp. 189–90.

27. T.H.S. Escott, *England*, p. 334.

28. Huish, *Nineteenth Century*, Jan. 1890, pp. 102, 110 ff; Ensor, p. 135.

29. Census Returns, *Parl. Papers* 1883 LXXX (C. 3722), pp. x, xxix, xxxvii; 1893–4 CVI (C. 7058), pp. x, xi.

30. C. Ehrlich, *Social Emulation and Industrial Progress* (Inaugural Lecture, Queen's University of Belfast, 5 Feb. 1975), pp. 6, 20.

31. Queen Victoria, *Letters, Third Series*, I (*op. cit.*), p. 528.

32. J.F. Russell and J.H. Elliot, *The Brass Band Movement* (1936), pp. 102, 121, 153; *Contemporary Review*, Aug. 1887, p. 242.

33. M. Baker, *The Rise of the Victorian Actor* (1978), p. 164; G. Stedman Jones, 'Working-Class Culture and Working-Class Politics in London, 1870–1900; Notes on the Remaking of a Working Class', *Journal of Social History*, Summer 1974, p. 477.

34. [T.H.S. Escott], *Society in London*, p. 296.

35. A.G. Gardiner, *Life of Sir William Harcourt*, (1923), I, p. 608.

36. *Photographic News*, 22 May 1885, p. 328; Census Returns, *Parl. Papers* 1893–4 CVI (C. 7222), pp. x, xi.

37. *Parl. Papers* 1883 LXXX (C. 3722), p. x; 1893–4 CVI (C. 7058), pp. x, xi; information on books from *Publisher's Circular*.

38. T. Kelly, *A History of Adult Education* (Liverpool, 1962), p. 213; Mitchell and Deane, *Abstract*, p. 416; T. Kelly, *A History of Public Libraries in Great Britain, 1845–1965* (1973), p. 490, cf. pp. 32, 123.

39. *Times*, 3 Oct. 1889, p. 9.

40. *Oxford English Dictionary*, I (1933 ed.), pp. xv, xxi–xxii; K.M.E. Murray, *Caught in the Web of Words. James A.H. Murray and the 'Oxford English Dictionary'* (New Haven, 1977), p. 197.

41. Information from *Publisher's Circular*.

42. C. Darwin, *Autobiography* (ed. N. Barlow, New York ed., 1969), p. 82; L. Creighton, *Life and Letters of Mandell Creighton* (1904), I, pp. 231, 342, cf. pp. 266, 341, 344.

43. This paragraph owes much to J. Maloney, 'Marshall, Cunningham, and the Emerging Economics Profession', *Economic History Review*, Aug. 1976, pp. 441, 444, 446.

Chapter 8. Regional Loyalties (pp. 167–84)

1. Lady G. Cecil, *Life of Robert, Marquis of Salisbury*, III (1931), p. 8; Bury in *Nineteenth Century*, July 1882, p. 98. For telegrams, see B.R. Mitchell and H.G. Jones, *Second Abstract of British Historical Statistics* (Cambridge, 1971), p. 112; Birmingham, J.H. Clapham, *Free Trade and Steel 1850–1886* (Cambridge, 1932), p. 108.

2. J. Morley, *Life of William Ewart Gladstone* (2 vol. ed., 1905), I, p. 694. See also Mitchell and Jones, *Second Abstract*, pp. 109–10; Mitchell and Deane, *Abstract*, pp. 6–7.

3. P. Deane and W.A. Cole, *British Economic Growth 1688–1959* (second ed., Cambridge, 1969), p. 239.

4. For lighthouses, see *Edinburgh Review*, Jan. 1880, pp. 173, 198 ff. See also *Parl. Papers* 1888 XC (C. 5364), p. 33; O. Warner, *Life-Boat Service* (1974), pp. 57, 280 ff., 301.

5. P. Deane and W.A. Cole, *British Economic Growth*, p. 233; Mitchell and Deane, *Abstract*, p. 226; R.J. Irving, 'The Profitability and Performance of British Railways, 1870–1914', *Economic History Review*, Feb. 1978, pp. 55–9.

6. See the excellent discussion in A. Everitt, 'Country Carriers in the Nineteenth Century', *Journal of Transport History*, Feb. 1976.

7. Lady G. Cecil, *Salisbury*, III, pp. 212–13. See also F.M.L. Thompson, *Victorian England: The Horse-Drawn Society. An Inaugural Lecture* (Bedford College, London University, 1970), pp. 12, 16; *1976 Abstract*, pp. 7, 266.

8. *Times*, 25 Mar. 1889, p. 10; see also D.J. Olsen, *Town Planning in London* (New Haven, 1964), p. 145.

9. J.H. Clapham, *op. cit.*, p. 204.

10. London School of Economics, *Charles Booth Collection*, B. 297, f. 217.

11. T.H.S. Escott, *England: Its People, Polity, and Pursuits* (1885 ed.), p. 258; H.J. Dyos, 'Workmen's Fares in South London, 1860–1914', *Journal of Transport History*, May 1953, p. 8.

12. A. Palmer, *Movable Feasts* (1952), pp. 8, 16, 54, 63–4, 71–6, 97, 132, 141; J. Burnett, *Plenty and Want* (1966), pp. 54–5.

13. White in *Blackwood's Magazine*, Sept. 1886, p. 323, cf. p. 337 and *Quarterly Review*, Jan. 1895, p. 40; Sir J.S. Flett, *The First Hundred Years of the Geological Survey of Great Britain* (1937), pp. 84, 91, 95, 102, 106–7, 139.

14. D.E. Allen, *The Naturalist in Britain. A Social History* (Penguin ed., 1978), pp. 206, 212–13, 219–23.

15. H.D. Thoreau, *Walden* (1906 ed.), p. 111, cf. p. 113; Matthew Arnold, *A Southern Night*; T.H.S. Escott, *England*, p. 305; Ramsay MacDonald quo. in S. Winsten (ed.), *Salt and his Circle* (1951), p. 171. Statistics from P.E.H. Hair, 'Deaths from Violence in Britain: a Tentative Secular Survey', *Population Studies*, 1971, p. 9.

16. *Parl. Papers* 1893–4 CVI (C. 7222), pp. 7, 12–13, for counties and towns. For London, see *Parl. Papers* 1883 LXXX (C. 3797), p. 12. For Lancashire and Yorkshire see Mitchell and Deane, *Abstract*, pp. 20 ff. and (for Manchester and Birmingham) pp. 20, 22, 24–5.

17. J.S. Mill, *Liberty* (Everyman ed., 1910), p. 130.

18. Mrs H. Ward, *A Writer's Recollections* (1918), p. 286. See also L. Stephen, *Life of Henry Fawcett* (3rd ed. 1886), p. 37; C.R.L.F., *Mr Gladstone at Oxford. 1890*(1908). pp. 39, 61. Also S. Gwynn and G.M. Tuckwell, *The Life of the Rt Hon. Sir Charles W. Dilke* (1917), I, p. 196 (for Cowen) and L. Creighton, *Life and Letters of Mandell Creighton* (1904), I, pp. 158, 239.

19. E.H. Hunt, *Regional Wage Variations in Britain 1850–1914* (Oxford, 1973), pp. 70, 72, 356 (for wages); pp. 218, 239, 285 (for differentials); p. 355 (for trade union density), cf. p. 330.

20. Sir C. Petrie, *Walter Long and his Times* (1936), pp. 48–9. For uncontested seats see W.O. Aydelotte, *Quantification in History* (Reading, Mass, 1971), p. 108. See also F.D. How, *Archbishop Maclagan* (1911), p. 296; F.D. How, *Bishop Walsham How. A Memoir* (1899 ed.), pp. 253–4.

21. B. Webb, *My Apprenticeship* (2nd ed., n.d.), p. 110.

22. K. Marx, *Pre-Capitalist Economic Formations* (ed. E.J. Hobsbawm, New York, 1965), p. 127; E.R. Jones, *The Life and Speeches of Joseph Cowen, M.P.* (n.d.), p. 430.

23. T.H.S. Escott, *England*, pp. 311–12.

24. Census Returns, *Parl. Papers* 1893–4 CVI (C. 7222), p. 8; P. Deane and W.A. Cole, *op. cit.*, p. 298.

25. Quoted in P. Thompson, *The Work of William Morris* (1967), p. 253.

26. Barnes in *Photographic News*, 26 Oct. 1888, p. 675. See also W.D. Rubinstein, 'Wealth, Elites and the Class Structure of Modern Britain', *Past and Present*, Aug. 1977, pp. 105, 110. Photographic shops are listed in H. Sturmey (ed.), *Photography Annual 1891* (1891), pp. 766 ff.

27. *Pall Mall Gazette*, 24 Aug. 1885, p. 10.

28. Census Returns, *Parl. Papers* 1883 LXXX (C. 3797), p. 56; C. Bolt, *Victorian Attitudes to Race* (1971), p. 5.

29. V.D. Lipman, *Social History of the Jews in England 1850–1950* (1954), p. 94.

30. Bernard Shaw *et al.*, *Fabian Essays* (1948 ed.), p. 129.

31. G. Stedman Jones, *Outcast London* (Oxford, 1971), p. 147; Census Returns, *Parl. Papers* 1883 LXXX (C. 3797), p. 52; J.G. Kellas, *Modern Scotland* (1968), p. 238.

32. K. Marx, *Capital* (New York ed., 1967) I, p. 663; A. Thorold, *Labouchere* (1913), p. 278, cf. p. 250.

33. Sir R. Coupland, *Welsh and Scottish Nationalism* (1954), pp. 197–200.

34. *Parl. Papers* 1893–4 CVI (C. 7222), pp. 82–3.

35. Queen Victoria, *Letters, Third Series* (ed. G.E. Buckle, 1930), I, p. 528.

36. J.G. Kellas, *op. cit.*, p. 239.

37. H.J. Hanham, 'Religion and Nationality in the Mid-Victorian Army', in M.R.D. Foot (ed.), *War and Society* (1973), pp. 176–7. See also Sir R. Coupland, *op. cit.*, p. 251; R. Pares, 'A Quarter of a Millennium of Anglo-Scottish Union', *History*, Oct. 1954, p. 247; H.J. Hanham, *Scottish Nationalism* (1969), p. 105.

38. J.G. Kellas, *op. cit.*, p. 241.

39. Sir R. Coupland, *op. cit.*, p. 273.

40. Henderson quo. in D.C. Savage, 'The Origins of the Ulster Unionist Party, 1885–6', *Irish Historical Studies*, Mar. 1961, p. 196; statistics from J.G. Kellas, *op. cit.*, p. 240; D.W. Urwin, 'The Development of the Conservative Party Organisation in Scotland until 1912', *Scottish Historical Review*, Oct. 1965, p. 94.

41. Mitchell and Deane, *Abstract*, pp. 6–7.

42. Gwynn and Tuckwell, *Dilke*, II, p. 139; *Times*, 18 June 1885, p. 7.

43. H.J. Hanham, 'Religion and Nationality', *loc. cit.*; H. Cunningham, *The Volunteer Force. A Social & Political History 1859–1908* (1975), p. 156.

44. Queen Victoria, *Letters, Second Series* (ed. G.E. Buckle, 1928), III, p. 162.

45. P. Guedalla (ed.), *The Queen and Mr Gladstone, II (1880–1898)* (1933), pp. 138, 166.

46. Lord E. Fitzmaurice, *The Life of Granville George Leveson Gower, Second Earl Granville, K.G. 1815–1891* (2nd ed., 1905), II, p. 468, cf. pp. 469, 473–4; H.A.L. Fisher, *James Bryce* (1927), I, p. 206.

47. J.L. Garvin, *The Life of Joseph Chamberlain*, I (1932), p. 344; J. Chamberlain, *A Political Memoir 1880–1892* (ed. C.H.D. Howard, 1953), p. 35.

48. F.S.L. Lyons, *Charles Stewart Parnell* (1977), p. 194.

49. E.W. Hamilton, *Diary* (ed. D.W.R. Bahlman, Oxford, 1972), I, p. 265.

50. P. Guedalla (ed.), *op. cit.*, p. 191; *The Journals of Lady Knightley of Fawsley* (ed. J. Cartwright, 1915), p. 352; J. Chamberlain, *op. cit.*, p. 62.

51. Sir M. Durand, *Life of the Rt Hon. Sir Alfred Comyn Lyall* (1913), p. 258; V. Markham, *Return Passage* (1953), p. 16; Queen Victoria, *Letters, Second Series*, III, p. 410, cf. pp. 283, 285, 298.

52. This paragraph is based on K.R.M. Short, *The Dynamite War. Irish-American Bombers in Victorian Britain* (Dublin, 1979), esp. pp. 50, 55, 91–2, 104–5, 160, 162, 176, 184, 200, 205, 207–8, 229, 259.

53. *ibid.*, p. 51.

54. *ibid.*, p. 93.

55. *ibid.*, pp. 4–5, 16.

56. Queen Victoria, *Letters, Second Series*, III, p. 302; Lady St Helier, *Memories of Fifty Years* (1909), p. 219.

57. *Photographic News*, 12 June 1885, p. 376.

58. Queen Victoria, *Letters, Second Series*, III, p. 653; see also W.C. Costin and J.S. Watson (eds.), *The Law and Working of the Constitution* (2nd ed., 1964), II, p. 198.

59. *Photographic News*, 27 Sept. 1889, p. 632.

60. A. Ramm (ed.), *The Political Correspondence of Mr Gladstone and Lord Granville. 1876–1886* (Oxford, 1962), I, pp. 92, 291, cf. p. 293.

61. Queen Victoria, *Letters, Second Series*, III, p. 655.

62. A. Ramm (ed.), *op. cit.*, I, p. 92.

63. P. Guedalla (ed.), *op. cit.*, p. 177; J. Chamberlain, *op. cit.*, pp. 29–32.

64. Queen Victoria, *Letters, Second Series*, III, p. 294.

65. Quotations from A. Ramm (ed.), *op. cit.*, II, p. 11; B. Holland, *Life of Spencer Compton. Eighth Duke of Devonshire* (1911), I, p. 392; see also J. Chamberlain, *op. cit.*, pp. 62, 64.

66. B. Holland, *op. cit.*, II, p. 100.

67. N. Blewett, *The Peers, The Parties and the People. The General Elections of 1910* (1972), pp. 364–5; election statistics from C. Cook and B. Keith, *British Historical Facts 1830–1900* (1975), p. 144.

68. Sir E. Cook, *The Life of Florence Nightingale* (1914), II, p. 357.

69. Quoted in J.L. Hammond, *Gladstone and the Irish Nation* (1938), pp. 466–7.

70. A. Ramm (ed.), *op. cit.*, I, p. 40; Sir R. Peel, *Memoirs*, I (1856), p. 366; B. Holland, *op. cit.*, I, p. 349.

71. J. Morley, *Life of Gladstone*, II, p. 481, cf. p. 411; W.E.

Gladstone, *Autobiographica* (ed. J. Brooke and M. Sorensen, 1971), pp. 110–11.

72. W.S. Churchill, *Lord Randolph Churchill* (1907 ed.), p. 474; Rowton quo. in Queen Victoria, *Letters, Third Series*, I, p. 105.

73. A. Ramm (ed.), *op. cit.*, II, p. 119; see also B. Holland, *op. cit.*, I, pp. 355–6, 358–9.

74. H. Macmillan, *The Past Masters. Politics and Politicians 1906–1939* (1975), p. 190.

75. Parnell quo. in J.L. Garvin, *Chamberlain*, I (1932), p. 590; see also *Parl. Papers* 1882 LXXVI (C. 3365), p. 73; 1892 XC (C. 6780), p. 5.

76. B.E.C. Dugdale, *Arthur James Balfour* (1939), I, pp. 97–9.

77. K.R.M. Short, *op. cit.*, p. 225.

78. H.S. Maine, *Popular Government* (2nd ed., 1886), p. 37.

79. Lord Newton, *Lord Lansdowne. A Biography* (1929), p. 46, cf. p. 55.

80. Quoted in Viscount Chilston, *W.H. Smith* (1965), p. 296.

81. Gladstone quo. in H.J. Hanham (ed.), *The Nineteenth-Century Constitution 1815–1914. Documents and Commentary* (Cambridge, 1969), p. 205; H. Broadhurst, *The Story of his Life* (1901), p. 196.

82. H. Broadhurst, *op. cit.*, p. 204.

83. W.E. Gladstone, *Autobiographica*, p. 112.

Chapter 9. Social Tensions (pp. 195–212)

1. *Parl. Papers* 1883 LXXX (C. 3797), p. 26; Mitchell and Deane, *Abstract*, p. 6.

2. P. Deane and W.A. Cole, *British Economic Growth 1688–1959* (2nd ed., Cambridge, 1969), p. 247, cf. pp. 251, 255; N. Soldon, '*Laissez-Faire* as Dogma: The Liberty and Property Defence League, 1882–1914', in K.D. Brown (ed.), *Essays in Anti-Labour History. Responses to the Rise of Labour in Britain* (1974), *passim*; figures on the League from E. Bristow, 'The Liberty and Property Defence League and Individualism', *Historical Journal*, 1975, p. 767; G. Alderman, 'The National Free Labour Association', *International Review of Social History*, 1976, III, pp. 313, 327, 333.

3. C.E. Maurice (ed.), *Life of Octavia Hill as told in her Letters* (1913), p. 464; Queen Victoria, *Letters, Third Series* (ed. G.E. Buckle, 1930), I, pp. 52–3, cf. p. 58. See also M.J. Cullen, 'The 1887 Survey of the London Working Class', *International Review of Social History*, 1975, I, pp. 53, 55.

4. Membership figures in W. Kendall, *The Revolutionary Movement in Britain 1900–1921* (1969), p. 311. K. Willis, 'The Introduction and Critical Reception of Marxist Thought in Britain 1850–1900', *Historical Journal*, 1977, is valuable.

5. Morris quo. in P. Thompson, *The Work of William Morris* (1967), p. 40; Bernard Shaw *et al.*, *Fabian Essays* (1948 ed.), p. 20. See also E.P. Thompson, *William Morris. Romantic to Revolutionary* (rev. ed., 1977), pp. 227–9, 231–2, 238.

6. *Times*, 31 Jan. 1885, p. 7.

7. B. Russell, *Anti-Suffragist Anxieties* (People's Suffrage Federation, n.d.), p. 11. For George, see Lynd, pp. 142–3.

8. J.L. Garvin, *The Life of Joseph Chamberlain*, I (1932), pp. 384–5.

9. J.L. Garvin, *op. cit.*, II (1933), p. 57; I (1932), p. 549, cf. p. 551; W.S. Churchill, *Lord Randolph Churchill* (1907 ed.), p. 870.

10. Connell, quo. in D. Torr, *Tom Mann and his Times*, I (1956), p. 298; Morris quo. in P. Thompson, *op. cit.*, p. 216.

11. Lynd, p. 275, cf. p. 289.

12. Engels quo. in Lynd, p. 238.

13. H. Broadhurst, *The Story of his Life* (1901), p. 218.

14. Lynd, p. 283.

15. W.O. Aydelotte, *Quantification in History* (Reading, Mass., 1971), p. 111; H.J. Hanham, *The Reformed Electoral System in Great Britain 1832–1914* (Historical Association General Series Pamphlet, No. 69, 1968), p. 35.

16. *Fabian Essays*, p. 37.

17. J.A. Thomas, *The House of Commons 1832–1901. A Study of its Economic and Functional Character* (Cardiff, 1939), pp. 14–15.

18. E.P. Thompson, *op. cit.*, pp. 344–5.

19. *ibid.*, pp. 736, 735, 740, cf. pp. 705–6.

20. G. Wagner, *Barnardo* (1979), p. 179; P. Thompson, *op. cit.*, p. 242.

21. *Review of Reviews*, June 1906, p. 568.

22. *Parl. Papers* 1890–1 XCII (C. 6475), pp. 3, 27 ff.

23. *Times*, 31 Jan. 1885, p. 7.

24. *Parl. Papers* 1886 XXIII (C. 4797), p. 566.

25. K. Marx, *The Communist Manifesto* (ed. H.J. Laski, 1948), p. 132; F. Engels, *op. cit.*, p. 364.

26. B. Webb, *My Apprenticeship* (2nd ed., n.d.), p. 190.

27. Quoted in T.S. and M.B. Simey, *Charles Booth. Social Scientist* (1960), p. 63.

28. B. Webb, *op. cit.*, pp. 243, 338.

29. Marx quo. in Y. Kapp, *Eleanor Marx*, I (1972), p. 72. This paragraph owes much to E.J. Hobsbawm, 'The Fabians Reconsidered' in his *Labouring Men* (1964).

30. E.R. Pease, *The History of the Fabian Society* (2nd ed., 1925), p. 88.

31. *ibid.*, p. 111.

32. *ibid.*, p. 237.

33. J. Chamberlain, *A Political Memoir 1880–1892* (ed. C.H.D. Howard, 1953), p. 139, cf. pp. 137, 141; Lady G. Cecil, *Life of Robert, Marquis of Salisbury*, III (1931), p. 67, cf. B. Webb, *op. cit.*, pp. 139, 144; H.E. Manning, *The Temperance Reformation* (1882), pp. 19–20; A. Ramm (ed.), *The Political Correspondence of Mr Gladstone and Lord Granville. 1876–1886* (Oxford, 1962), II, p. 403.

34. W. Ashworth, *An Economic History of England 1870–1939* (1960), p. 233.

35. Ensor, p. 129; Lynd, p. 168; Mitchell and Deane, *Abstract*, pp. 398, 403, 416; E.P. Hennock, 'Finance and Politics in Urban Local Government in England 1835–1900', *Historical Journal*, 1963, pp. 224–5.

36. Gladstone in *Nineteenth Century*, Nov. 1877, p. 548; T.H.S. Escott, *England: Its People, Polity, and Pursuits* (1885 ed.), p. 50.

37. Figures from K.O. Morgan, *Wales in British Politics 1868–1922* (Cardiff, 1963), p. 107; J.P.D. Dunbabin, 'Expectations of the new County Councils, and their Realisation', *Historical Journal*, 1965, p. 369; see also pp. 361, 370, 378–9; G.D. Phillips, *The Diehards. Aristocratic Society and Politics in Edwardian England* (Cambridge, Mass., 1979), p. 68.

38. Shaw in B. Shaw *et al.*, *Fabian Essays* (1948 ed.), p. 174; for administrators, see G.M. Young, *Victorian England. Portrait of an Age* (2nd ed., 1953), p. 39, cf. p. 60. For Besant, see *Fabian Essays*, pp. 142–4.

39. Census figures, *Parl. Papers* 1913 LXXVIII (Cd. 7018), p. xiv; the figures exclude Post Office telegraphists and telephone operators.

40. J. Redlich, *The Procedure of the House of Commons. A Study of its History and Present Form* (tr. A.E. Steinthal, 1908), II, p. 189; T.J. Cartwright, *Royal Commissions and Departmental Committees in Britain* (1975), pp. 236, 238. See also H.McD. Clokie and J.W. Robinson, *Royal Commissions of Inquiry. The Significance of Investigations in British Politics* (Stanford, 1937), pp. 72–9.

41. K. Marx, *Capital*, I (New York ed., 1967), p. 9; cf. F. Engels, *The Condition of the Working Class in England* (tr. and ed. W.O. Henderson and W.H. Chaloner, Oxford, 1958), p. 3.

42. G.R. Sims, *How the Poor Live* (1883), p. 5.

43. H.McD. Clokie and J.W. Robinson, *op.cit.*, p. 72.

44. See R. Davidson's excellent 'Llewellyn Smith, the Labour Department and Government Growth 1886–1909' in G. Sutherland (ed.), *Studies in the Growth of Nineteenth-Century Government* (1972), pp. 227 ff. For administrative discretion, see E. Halévy, *The Rule of Democracy 1905–1914* (tr. E.I. Watkin, paperback ed., 1961), p. 263.

45. F.W. Maitland, *The Constitutional History of England* (Cambridge, 1926 ed.), p. 501; F.E. Hamer (ed.), *The Personal Papers of Lord Rendel* (1931), p. 95.

46. Goschen, 3 *Hansard* 313, c. 1427 (21 Apr. 1887), cf. Hon. A.D. Elliot, *The Life of George Joachim Goschen. First Viscount Goschen 1831–1907* (1911), II, pp. 143–4, 158–9. Figures from Mitchell and Deane, *Abstract*, pp. 397–8.

47. H.E. Ward, 'Whitehall. Past and Future', *Cornhill Magazine*, July 1882, p. 93; see also G.S. Dugdale, *Whitehall through the Centuries* (1950), p. 175.

48. In *Fifty Years. Memories and Contrasts. A Composite Picture of the Period 1882–1932* (1932), p. 157.

49. E.P. Thompson, *William Morris. Romantic to Revolutionary* (rev. ed. 1977), p. 450, cf. pp. 455–6.

50. S. Smith, *My Life-Work* (1903 ed.), pp. 145–6.

51. Quoted in B. Webb, *op. cit.*, p. 152.

52. Granville, in Queen Victoria, *Letters, Second Series* (ed. G.E. Buckle, 1928), III, p. 86; S. Gwynn and G.M. Tuckwell, *The Life of the Rt Hon. Sir Charles W. Dilke* (1917), I, p. 411; Gladstone quo. in R. Blake, *Disraeli* (1966), p. 748.

53. *Times*, 6 Aug. 1877, p. 8.

54. *Times*, 9 June 1884, p. 13; cf. A. Ramm (ed.), *op. cit.*, II, pp. 203, 257, 269; see also pp. 240, 243, 246, 268.

55. P. Guedalla (ed.), *The Queen and Mr Gladstone. II (1880–*

1898) (1933), p. 181; W.S. Churchill, *Lord Randolph Churchill* (1907 ed.), pp. 515–16; F. Thompson, *Lark Rise to Candleford. A Trilogy* (1948 ed.), p. 61.

56. Lynd, p. 156.

57. J. Arch, *Joseph Arch. The Story of his Life* (ed. Countess of Warwick, 3rd ed., 1898), p. 358. See also T. Burt, *Autobiography* (1924), p. 260; E.P. Thompson, *op. cit.*, pp. 329–30.

58. Gladstone quo. in F.S.L. Lyons, *Charles Stewart Parnell* (1977), p. 170; *Photographic News*, 3 Mar. 1882, p. 102; for the phonograph, see Lord Ernle, 'Victorian Memoirs and Memories', *Quarterly Review*, Apr. 1923, p. 227.

59. Queen Victoria, *Letters, Second Series*, III, p. 539; *Letters, Third Series* (ed. G.E. Buckle, 1930), I, pp. 150, 365, cf. p. 454.

60. B. Holland, *Life of Spencer Compton. Eighth Duke of Devonshire* (1911), II, p. 77, cf. p. 86.

61. J. Chamberlain, *Political Memoir*, p. 223.

62. W.S. Churchill, *op. cit.*, pp. 228–9.

63. *ibid.*, p. 223, cf. Lord Rosebery, *Lord Randolph Churchill* (1906), p. 168.

64. W.S. Churchill, *op. cit.*, p. 238.

65. *ibid.*, pp. 348–9; R.R. James, *Lord Randolph Churchill* (1959), pp. 193–4; this discussion also owes much to J.H. Robb, *The Primrose League 1883–1906* (New York, 1942).

66. Lady Salisbury quo. in J.H. Robb, *op. cit.*, p. 87; membership figures in W.S. Churchill, *op. cit.*, p. 209.

67. R.R. James, *op. cit.*, pp. 257, 250.

68. A. Ramm (ed.), *op. cit.*, I, p. 43.

69. *Times*, 18 June 1885, p. 7.

70. B. Webb, *op. cit.*, p. 109.

71. W.S. Churchill, *op. cit.*, pp. 558, 690.

72. M. Ostrogorski, *Democracy and the Organisation of Political Parties* (tr. F. Clarke, 1902), I, p. 466.

73. Quoted in C.S. Emden, *The People and the Constitution* (2nd ed., 1956), p. 242.

74. F.W.S. Craig, *British Parliamentary Election Results 1885–1918* (1974), p. 582, cf. D.E. Butler and A. Sloman, *British Political Facts* (4th ed., 1975), pp. 182–6.

Chapter 10. Aristocratic Magic (pp. 223–31)

1. J.S. Mill, *Representative Government* (Everyman ed., 1910), p. 183.

2. Lord Newton, *Lord Lansdowne. A Biography* (1929), p. 40.

3. Lady G. Cecil, *Life of Robert, Marquis of Salisbury*, II (1921), p. 232; IV (1932), p. 162; II, p. 6, cf. II, pp. 273, 275; III (1931), p. 25.

4. For the St James's Club, see [T.H.S. Escott], *Society in London. By a Foreign Resident* (1885), p. 63; *Parl. Papers* 1898 XXXVII (C. 8695), appendix, p. 3. Quotation and statistics from R.T. Nightingale, 'The Personnel of the British Foreign Office and Diplomatic Service, 1851–1929', *The Realist*, Dec. 1929, p. 331, 333.

5. H.M. Hyndman, *The Record of an Adventurous Life* (1911), pp. 385–6.

6. J.L. Garvin, *The Life of Joseph Chamberlain*, I (1932), p. 392; Lady G. Cecil, *op. cit.*, III, p. 202. Statistics from K. Rose, *Superior Person* (1969), p. 297.

7. W.S. Churchill, *Lord Randolph Churchill* (1907 ed.), p. 371; 1886 figures from W.O. Aydelotte, *Quantification in History* (Reading, Mass., 1971), p. 117; 1972–3 figures calculated from Hansard's *Parliamentary Debates*.

8. *Society in London*, pp. 179–81; G.M. Trevelyan, *The Life of John Bright* (1925 ed.), p. 449.

9. Figures from H.J. Hanham, *Elections and Party Management. Politics in the Time of Disraeli and Gladstone* (1959), p. xv; G.D.H. Cole, *Studies in Class Structure* (1961 ed.), p. 134; Cabinet figures from W.L. Guttsman, *The British Political Elite* (1968), p. 78; House of Lords figures from F.M.L. Thompson, *English Landed Society in the Nineteenth Century* (1963), pp. 44, 49.

10. T.H.S. Escott, *England: Its People, Polity, and Pursuits* (1885 ed.), p. 390; for Herbert, see Viscount Chilston, *Chief Whip* (1961), p. 122. See also J. Bateman, *The Great Landowners of Great Britain and Ireland* (1879 ed.), p. 131.

11. J.C. MacDonnell, *The Life and Correspondence of William Connor Magee, Archbishop of York* (1896), II, pp. 230–31.

12. Queen Victoria, *Letters, Second Series* (ed. G.E. Buckle, 1928), III, p. 132.

13. Tax figures from Mitchell and Deane, *Abstract*, p. 394; landownership figures from Lynd, p. 25; see also Census Returns, *Parl. Papers* 1883 LXXX (C. 3797), pp. 49–50.

14. G. Raverat, *Period Piece. A Cambridge Childhood* (1960 ed.), pp. 75, 119; see also B. Webb, *My Apprenticeship* (2nd ed., n.d.), p. 39, cf. p. 41.

15. A.P. Stanley, *Life and Correspondence of Thomas Arnold, D.D.* (8th ed., 1858), II, p. 87; A. Thorold, *The Life of Henry Labouchere* (1913), p. 206.

16. B. Webb, *op. cit.*, p. 42, cf. p. 40.

17. B. Holland, *Life of Spencer Compton. Eighth Duke of Devonshire* (1911), II, p. 211, n.1; see also *Society in London*, pp. 29, 320.

18. Willoughby de Broke, *The Passing Years* (1924), pp. xiv–xv.

19. *ibid.*, pp. 56–7; see also pp. 1–2, 60.

20. Gladstone quo. in G.M. Young, *Victorian Essays* (ed. W.D. Handcock, 1962), p. 106; T.H.S. Escott, *England*, p. 26.

21. F.M.L. Thompson, *op. cit.*, pp. 111–15.

22. B. Holland, *op. cit.*, pp. 228, 234, cf. Willoughby de Broke, *op. cit.*, p. 127. See also Randolph Churchill, *Winston S. Churchill*, I (1966), p. 96.

23. Lord Newton, *op. cit.*, pp. 24–5, 46, 51, 55, 129.

24. W. Bagehot, *Collected Works*, III (1968), p. 281.

25. Ignatieff quo. in Viscount Cecil of Chelwood, *All the Way* (1949), p. 20; W.H. Mallock, *Memoirs of Life and Literature* (New York ed., 1920), p. 145.

26. Willoughby de Broke, *op. cit.*, pp. 56–7.

27. J.L. Garvin, *Chamberlain*, II (1933), p. 364; for Bright see J.A. Spender and C. Asquith, *Life of Herbert Henry Asquith* (1932), I, p. 72.

28. Figures from W.L. Guttsman, *op. cit.*, p. 115; T.H. Hollingsworth, 'A Demographic Study of the British Ducal Families', in D.V. Glass and D.E.C. Eversley (eds.),

Population in History. Essays in Historical Demography (1965), pp. 367–8.

29. D. Thomas, 'The Social Origins of Marriage Partners of the British Peerage in the 18th and 19th Centuries', *Population Studies*, Mar. 1972, pp. 105–7; J.T. Ward and R.G. Wilson (eds.), *Land and Industry. The Landed Estate and the Industrial Revolution* (Newton Abbot, 1971), pp. 50–51.

30. H.J. Hanham, 'The Sale of Honours in Late Victorian England', *Victorian Studies*, III (1959–60), p. 280.

31. B. Webb, *op. cit.*, pp. 43–4; H.J. Hanham, *op. cit.*, p. 278.

32. As reported by Lord Salisbury, in Queen Victoria, *Letters, Second Series*, III, p. 17.

33. K. Marx, *The Communist Manifesto* (ed. H.J. Laski, 1948), p. 130, cf. D.A. Hamer, *Liberal Politics in the Age of Gladstone and Rosebery* (Oxford, 1972), p. 14.

34. F. Thompson, *Lark Rise to Candleford* (1948 ed.), pp. 260–61, cf. pp. 274–5.

35. P. Deane and W.A. Cole, *British Economic Growth 1688–1959* (2nd ed., Cambridge, 1969), pp. 142–3.

36. B. Pascal, *The Pensées* (Penguin ed., 1961), p. 107.

37. Willoughby de Broke, *op. cit.*, p. 3; see also J. Franklin, 'Troops of Servants: Labour and Planning in the Country House 1840–1914', *Victorian Studies*, Dec. 1975, p. 226.

38. C.V. Butler, *Domestic Service: An Enquiry by the Women's Industrial Council* (1916), p. 130; E. Richards, 'Women in the British Economy since about 1700. An Interpretation', *History*, Oct. 1974, pp. 348–9.

39. Census Returns, *Parl. Papers* 1883 LXXX (C. 3797), pp. 16, 33; P. Horn, *The Rise and Fall of the Victorian Servant* (Dublin, 1975), p. 27.

40. W.H. Hutton (ed.), *Letters of William Stubbs. Bishop of Oxford 1825–1901* (1904), p. 292.

41. T.H.S. Escott, *England*, p. 165.

42. Willoughby de Broke, *op. cit.*, p. 53.

43. Queen Victoria, *Letters, Third Series* (ed. G.E. Buckle, 1930), I, pp. 161, 344, 402–3, cf. p. 442.

44. V. Markham, *Return Passage* (1953), pp. 35–6; Lady V. Bonham-Carter, *Winston Churchill as I Knew Him* (1967 paperback ed.), pp. 26–7.

45. F. McKenna, 'Victorian Railway Workers', *History Workshop*, Spring 1976, is valuable.

Chapter 11. Discipline and Authority (pp. 239–52)

1. *Parl. Papers* 1893–4 CVI (C. 7222), p. 38; *1976 Abstract*, pp. 7, 92. See also G. Grosvenor, 'Statistics of the Abatement in Crime in England and Wales during the Twenty Years ended 1887–88', *Journal of the Royal Statistical Society*, Sept. 1890, p. 380.

2. C. Tsuzuki, *The Life of Eleanor Marx* (Oxford, 1967), p. 51. See also A.M. McBriar, *Fabian Socialism and English Politics 1884–1918* (Cambridge, 1962), pp. 19, 67.

3. V.A.C. Gatrell and T.B. Hadden, 'Criminal Statistics and their Interpretation', in E.A. Wrigley (ed.), *Nineteenth-century Society* (Cambridge, 1972), p. 359.

4. *Murray's Magazine*, Nov. 1888, p. 578; E.P. Thompson,

William Morris. Romantic to Revolutionary (rev. ed., 1977), p. 490, cf. p. 498.

5. Y. Kapp, *Eleanor Marx*, I (1972), p. 168; for the C.I.D. see W.L.M. Lee, *A History of the Police in England* (1901), pp. 359–60, 370.

6. *Photographic News*, 2 Apr. 1880, p. 158; 21 Jan. 1881, p. 27; 13 Aug. 1886, p. 520.

7. Gatrell and Hadden, *op. cit.*, pp. 378–9, 382–3, 385; W.L.M. Lee, *op. cit.*, p. 355.

8. Morrison, *Nineteenth Century*, June 1892, pp. 955–7; G. Grosvenor, *op. cit.*, p. 386.

9. Gatrell and Hadden, *op. cit.*, pp. 374, 377; G. Grosvenor, *op. cit.*, p. 382.

10. M. Loane, *An Englishman's Castle* (1909), p. 33; Queen Victoria, *Letters, Third Series*, (ed. G.E. Buckle, 1930), I, p. 447. See also D. Walker-Smith and E. Clarke, *The Life of Sir Edward Clarke* (1939), p. 217.

11. Quotation from J. Macdonnell, 'Statistics of Litigation in England and Wales since 1859', *Journal of the Royal Statistical Society*, Sept. 1894, p. 509; this valuable article also supplies all the statistics in this paragraph. See also T.B. Bottomore and M. Rubel, *Karl Marx. Selected Writings in Sociology and Social Philosophy* (1961 ed.), p. 159.

12. Bottomore and Rubel, *op. cit.*, p. 158.

13. Sir E.W. Hamilton, *Diary* (ed. D.W.R. Bahlman, Oxford, 1972), I, p. 318; figures from *Parl. Papers* 1893–4 CVI (C. 7222), pp. 79–80; G. Grosvenor, *op. cit.*, pp. 406–7, 412–13.

14. G. Grosvenor, *op. cit.*, pp. 406–7, 412–13.

15. Thomson in *British Journal of Photography*, 16 Dec. 1881, p. 649, cf. *Photographic News*, 23 Mar. 1888, p. 179; see also W.Ll. Parry-Jones, *The Trade in Lunacy* (1972), p. 56; F.N.L. Poynter (ed.), *The Evolution of Hospitals in Britain* (1964), pp. 136–7; K. Jones, *Mental Health and Social Policy 1845–1959* (1960), p. 210.

16. *Parl. Papers* 1893–4 CVI (C. 7222), p. 75, cf. K. Jones, *op. cit.*, p. 207.

17. *Nursing Record*, 1896, quo. in F.R. Adams, 'From Association to Union: Professional Organisation of Asylum Attendants, 1869–1919', *British Journal of Sociology*, 1969, pp. 12 ff.

18. Mitchell and Deane, *Abstract*, pp. 397–8, 403; *1976 Abstract*, p. 349.

19. Department of Employment, *British Labour Statistics. Historical Abstract 1886–1968* (1971), p. 300; *1976 Abstract*, p. 149.

20. K. Rose, *Superior Person* (1969), p. 133; statistic from G. Harries-Jenkins, *The Army in Victorian Society* (1977), p. 218.

21. T.H. Hollingsworth, 'A Demographic Study of the British Ducal Families', in D.V. Glass and D.E.C. Eversley (eds.), *Population in History. Essays in Historical Demography* (1965), p. 360.

22. J.A. Thomas, *The House of Commons 1832–1901* (Cardiff, 1939), pp. 14–17; it is connections which are being counted here, not individuals.

23. C.B. Otley, 'The Social Origins of British Army Officers', *Sociological Review*, 1970, pp. 224 ff; 'Public School and

Army', *New Society*, 17 Nov. 1966, pp. 754–6; T.W. Bamford, *The Rise of the Public Schools* (1967), pp. 210–12.

24. *Blackwood's Edinburgh Magazine*, Sept. 1886, p. 335, cf. p. 324. Statistic from P.E. Razzell, 'Social Origins of Officers in the Indian and British Home Army, 1758–1962', *British Journal of Sociology*, 1963, p. 253.

25. T.H.S. Escott, *England: Its People, Polity, and Pursuits* (1885 ed.), p. 5; J.A. Hobson, *Imperialism. A Study* (paperback ed., Ann Arbor, 1967), p. 151.

26. Lady G. Cecil, *Life of Robert, Marquis of Salisbury*, III (1931), p. 76; W.S. Churchill, *Lord Randolph Churchill* (1907 ed.), p. 520.

27. P. Guedalla (ed.), *The Queen and Mr Gladstone, II (1880–1898)* (1933), p. 259; Lord Newton, *Lord Lansdowne. A Biography* (1929), p. 72; R.R. James, *Lord Randolph Churchill* (1959), p. 162; cf. W.S. Churchill, *op. cit.*, p. 720.

28. H.J. Hanham, 'Religion and Nationality in the Mid-Victorian Army', in M.R.D. Foot (ed.), *War and Society* (1973), p. 180.

29. Forbes, *Nineteenth Century*, Oct. 1879, p. 606; Bradlaugh in *3 Hansard 260*, c. 35 (28 Mar. 1881); Morgan, *ibid.*, cc. 20 ff.; for desertions, see B. Bond, 'Recruiting the Victorian Army 1870–92', *Victorian Studies*, June 1962, p. 334.

30. G. Orwell, *Collected Essays, Journalism and Letters*, I (Penguin ed., 1970), p. 443.

31. F.B. Smith, 'Ethics and Disease in the Later Nineteenth Century: The Contagious Diseases Acts', *Historical Studies, Australia and New Zealand*, Oct. 1971, p. 122.

32. Queen Victoria, *Letters, Second Series* (ed. G. E. Buckle, 1928), III, pp. 38, 632.

33. Sir J. Smyth, *The Story of the Victoria Cross 1856–1963* (1963), pp. 91, 123–9.

34. Queen Victoria, *Letters, Second Series*, III, p. 472; F. Thompson, *Lark Rise to Candleford* (1948 ed.), p. 182; Queen Victoria, *Letters, Second Series*, III, p. 608.

35. H. Cunningham, *The Volunteer Force. A Social and Political History 1859–1908* (1975), p. 49 (for statistics); see also pp. 33–4, 42–5, 49, 69, 71, 78–9, 104–5, 112–13, 119, 129–31.

36. *Times*, 24 May 1882, p. 10; *Photographic News*, 5 June 1885, p. 360.

37. B.R. Mitchell, *European Historical Statistics 1750–1970* (1975), p. 135; Mitchell and Deane, *Abstract*, p. 50; *1976 Abstract*, pp. 7, 26–7; 28th Report of the Post Master General, in *Parl. Papers*, 1882 XXI (C. 3324), pp. 50 ff.

38. P. Guedalla (ed.), *op. cit.*, II, p. 265, cf. p. 52, and Lord E. Fitzmaurice, *The Life of Granville George Leveson Gower. Second Earl Granville, K.G. 1815–1891* (2nd ed., 1905) II, p. 399.

39. Lord E. Fitzmaurice, *op. cit.*, pp. 407–8.

40. Queen Victoria, *Letters, Second Series*, III, p. 525; see also R. Robinson and J. Gallagher, *Africa and the Victorians* (1967 ed.), p. 11.

41. B. Holland, *Life of Spencer Compton. Eighth Duke of Devonshire* (1911), I, p. 311; P. Guedalla (ed.), *op. cit.*, II,

p. 259, cf. pp. 342, 346, and B. Holland, *op. cit.*, II, pp. 44–5.

42. J. Chamberlain, *A Political Memoir 1880–1892* (ed. C.H.D. Howard, 1953), pp. 75–6, 314.

43. Queen Victoria, *Letters, Second Series*, III, p. 506.

44. D. Wormell, *Sir John Seeley and the Uses of History* (Cambridge, 1980), pp. 94, 199; statistics from p. 154.

45. J.R. Seeley, *The Expansion of England. Two Courses of Lectures* (2nd ed., 1895), pp. 193, 201.

46. *ibid.*, p. 1.

47. *ibid.*, p. 15.

48. *ibid.*, p. 334.

49. D. Wormell, *op. cit.*, p. 154.

50. J.A. Froude, *Oceana, Or England and her Colonies* (1886), pp. 387, 356.

51. J.R. Seeley, *op. cit.*, p. 297.

52. Queen Victoria, *Letters, Second Series*, III, pp. 607, 611.

53. A.B. Keith (ed.), *Selected Speeches and Documents on British Colonial Policy 1763–1917* (1933 ed.), II, pp. 193–5, 199, 201.

54. J.A. Froude, *op. cit.*, p. 67, cf. p. 395.

55. Lord Newton, *op. cit.*, pp. 74, 60–61, cf. p. 110.

56. Mitchell and Deane, *Abstract*, pp. 50, 52.

57. J.R. Seeley, *op. cit.*, pp. 321, 339.

58. J. Morley, 'The Expansion of England', *Macmillan's Magazine*, Feb. 1884, p. 250.

Chapter 12. Pomp and Ceremony (pp. 261–9)

1. W. Bagehot, *The English Constitution* (Fontana ed., 1963), p. 248.

2. Quotations from Margaret Norman's *Every-Day Book*, 21 Jan. 1886 (in the possession of Mrs Decima Curtis); *Times*, 22 Jan. 1886, p. 6. See also *Times*, 6 Feb. 1880, p. 6.

3. Queen Victoria, *Letters, Second Series* (ed. G.E. Buckle, 1928), III, p. 282; *Letters, Third Series* (ed. G.E. Buckle, 1930), I, pp. 125–7.

4. *British Journal of Photography*, 1 July 1887, p. 402.

5. *Photographic News*, 8 Oct. 1886, p. 648; 6 Aug. 1886, p. 504.

6. *British Journal of Photography*, 4 Dec. 1885, p. 784; *Photographic News*, 4 June 1886, p. 360. See also *ibid.*, 5 Apr. 1889, p. 216.

7. J.L. Lant, *Insubstantial Pageant. Ceremony and Confusion at Queen Victoria's Court* (1979), pp. 24, 77–83.

8. *ibid.*, p. 85.

9. *Photographic News*, 22 July 1887, p. 456, cf. *British Journal of Photography*, 1 July 1887, p. 402.

10. G.K.A. Bell, *Randall Davidson. Archbishop of Canterbury* (1935), I, pp. 92, 95.

11. J.L. Lant, *op. cit.*, pp. 185–9, 199.

12. *ibid.*, pp. 155–6, 166, 174, 216, 218.

13. *ibid.*, pp. 189–90.

14. Queen Victoria, *Letters, Third Series*, I, p. 245; *Times*, 20 June 1887, p. 6; see also F. Thompson, *Lark Rise to Candleford* (1948 ed.), p. 226.

15. *Times*, 24 Mar. 1887, p. 6; Queen Victoria, *Letters, Third Series*, I, p. 289, cf. p. 293.

16. *Commonweal*, 25 June 1887, p. 204; see also E.P. Thompson, *William Morris. Romantic to Revolutionary* (rev. ed., 1977), p. 480; R.R. James, *Lord Randolph Churchill* (1959), p. 324.

17. Queen Victoria, *Letters, Third Series*, I, p. 308, cf. p. 310; see also Mrs S.A. Barnett, *Canon Barnett. His Life, Work, and Friends* (1918), II, pp. 74–6.

18. *Times*, 23 June 1887, p. 9; see also K.R.M. Short, *The Dynamite War. Irish-American Bombers in Victorian Britain* (Dublin, 1979), pp. 232–3.

19. Quoted in Lynd, p. 195.

20. Queen Victoria, *Letters, Third Series*, I, p. 331.

21. J.L. Lant, *op. cit.*, p. 174.

22. Sir E.W. Hamilton, *Diary* (ed. D.W.R. Bahlman, Oxford, 1972), I, p. 148; P. Guedalla (ed.), *The Queen and Mr Gladstone, II (1880–1898)* (1933), p. 277.

23. G.K.A. Bell, *op. cit.*, p. 64.

24. P. Guedalla (ed.), *op. cit.*, II, p. 364.

25. Queen Victoria, *Letters, Third Series*, I, pp. 127, 369, cf. pp. 338, 341.

26. *Times*, 12 May 1886, p. 9; 22 June 1887, p. 9, cf. the curious incident at Hyde Park Corner in L. Housman, *The Unexpected Years* (1937), p. 220.

27. Sir E.W. Hamilton, *op. cit.*, p. 269.

28. J. Wilson, *CB. A Life of Sir Henry Campbell-Bannerman* (1973), p. 165; Queen Victoria, *Letters, Third Series*, I, p. 48.

29. P. Guedalla (ed.), *op. cit.*, p. 274.

30. *ibid.*, p. 359; P. Magnus, *King Edward the Seventh* (Penguin ed., 1967), pp. 279 ff.

31. Quotation from Queen Victoria, *Letters, Second Series*, III, p. 114; for other misjudgements, see *ibid.*, pp. 108–9, and F. Hardie, *The Political Influence of Queen Victoria, 1861–1901* (2nd ed., 1938), p. 79. For Gladstone see H.J. Hanham, *The Nineteenth-Century Constitution 1815–1914. Documents and Commentary* (Cambridge, 1969), p. 50.

32. P. Guedalla (ed.), *op. cit.*, pp. 120, 261, 147.

33. Queen Victoria, *Letters, Second Series*, III, p. 267; P. Guedalla (ed.), *op. cit.*, p. 233.

34. Queen Victoria, *Letters, Second Series*, III, p. 612, see also pp. 254, 266; *Letters, Third Series*, I, pp. 176–7; P. Guedalla (ed.), *op. cit.*, p. 167.

35. Queen Victoria, *Further Letters* (ed. H. Bolitho, 1938), p. 251; for the service, see *Letters, Third Series*, I. p. 324.

36. Queen Victoria, *Letters, Third Series*, I. p. 228.

37. E. Pethick-Lawrence, *My Part in a Changing World* (1938), p. 21.

38. Quotation from *Letters, Third Series*, I, p. 615; see also pp. 447, 449, and *Letters, Second Series*, III, pp. 134, 144.

39. Queen Victoria, *Letters, Third Series*, I, p. 354; P. Guedalla (ed.), *op. cit.*, p. 105. For the bodyguard, see S. Gwynn and G.M. Tuckwell, *The Life of the Rt Hon. Sir Charles W. Dilke* (1917), I, p. 522; for the Munshi, see V. Mallet (ed.), *Life with Queen Victoria* (1968), p. xxii.

40. Queen Victoria, *Letters, Second Series*, III, pp. 16, 452; see also P. Guedalla (ed.), *op. cit.*, p. 103, cf. p. 30.

41. Lady G. Cecil, *Life of Robert, Marquis of Salisbury*, III (1931), p. 186, cf. p. 187.

42. G.K.A. Bell, *op. cit.*, p. 60.

43. P. Guedalla (ed.), *op. cit.*, p. 392.

44. A. Ramm (ed.), *The Political Correspondence of Mr Gladstone and Lord Granville. 1876–1886* (Oxford, 1962), I, p. 470; II, p. 90; P. Guedalla (ed.), *op. cit.*, pp. 229, 380.

45. Quotations from P. Guedalla (ed.), *op. cit.*, p. 495; W.E. Gladstone, *Autobiographica* (ed. J. Brooke and M. Sorensen, 1971), p. 169.

Chapter 13. Illness and Old Age (pp. 273–80)

1. For volunteers, see Ensor, p. 513; see also J. Arch, *The Story of his Life* (ed. Countess of Warwick, 3rd ed., n. d.), p. 29.

2. F.M.L. Thompson, *Victorian England: The Horse-Drawn Society. An Inaugural Lecture* (Bedford College, London University, 1970), p. 10; H.T. Bernstein, 'The Mysterious Disappearance of Edwardian London Fog', *London Journal*, Vol. 1, No. 2 (Nov. 1975), pp. 192–3, 205.

3. S. Smith, *My Life-Work* (1903 ed.), p. 107; A. Brinckman, *Notes on Rescue Work* (1885), p. 87, cf. p. 64; Mrs Clara Rackham, 'Recollections of Childhood 1875–1891', MS. in the care of Miss Mary Tabor of Stevenage.

4. Quotation from 'Lord' George Sanger, *Seventy Years a Showman* (1927 ed.), p. 16; see also M. Howell and P. Ford, *The True History of the Elephant Man* (1980).

5. L. Stephen, *Life of Henry Fawcett* (3rd ed., 1886), pp. 56–8, 60, 63; Census Returns, *Parl. Papers* 1883 LXXX (C. 3722), pp. xlvii, xlviii; 1883 LXXX (C. 3797), pp. 60, 62; D. Hudson, *Munby. Man of Two Worlds* (Boston, 1972), p. 401.

6. M. Loane, *An Englishman's Castle* (1909), p. 249, cf. R. Roberts, *The Classic Slum* (Pelican ed., 1973), pp. 125ff.; J.R. Illingworth, 'The Problem of Pain', in C. Gore (ed.), *Lux Mundi* (7th ed., 1890), pp. 117–18; W.E.H. Lecky, *Democracy and Liberty* (1899 ed.), II, p. 531. See also F.P. Cobbe, *The Life of Frances Power Cobbe* (2nd ed., 1894), II, pp. 226–7.

7. This paragraph relies heavily on P.C. McIntosh, *Physical Education in England since 1800* (1968 ed.), esp. pp. 108–13, 115, 136–7, 140–41.

8. E. Carpenter, *Civilisation: Its Cause and Cure and Other Essays* (1921 ed.), p. 61. See also *Undertakers' and Funeral Directors' Journal*, 22 Sept. 1886, p. 175.

9. 3 *Hansard* 280, c. 994 (19 June 1883).

10. *Parl. Papers* 1892 XXIV (C. 6841), p. xliv; *1976 Abstract*, p. 45.

11. J. Arch, *Joseph Arch. The Story of his Life* (ed. Countess of Warwick, 3rd ed., 1898), p. 54; J.L. Brand, *Doctors and the State* (Baltimore, 1965), pp. 48–51.

12. F.P. Cobbe, *op. cit.*, II, p. 170; *Parl. Papers* 1880 LVI (125), p. 3; 1890 LVIII (150), p. 5.

13. For doctors per patient, see M. Mackenzie, *Contemporary*

Review, Oct. 1890, p. 503; other figures in R. Pinker, *English Hospital Statistics 1861–1938* (1966), pp. 49–50, 52, 111. See also I.S.L. Londun, 'Historical Importance of Outpatients', *British Medical Journal*, 1978, I, pp. 974–7.

14. [T.H.S. Escott], *Society in London. By a Foreign Resident* (1885), pp. 169–71; J.L. Lant, *Insubstantial Pageant, Ceremony and Confusion at Queen Victoria's Court* (1979), p. 198: figures from J.L. Brand, *op. cit.*, pp. 148, 158.

15. Sir E. Cook, *Life of Florence Nightingale* (1914) II, p. 349; *Parl. Papers* 1883 LXXX (C. 3722), p. x.

16. Mackenzie, *Contemporary Review*, Oct. 1890, p. 513; G.D.H. Cole, *Studies in Class Structure* (1961 ed.), p. 135; E.P. Hennock, *Fit and Proper Persons* (1973), pp. 34, 37, 207.

17. Figures from W.J. Martin, 'A Comparison of the Trends of Male and Female Mortality', *Journal of the Royal Statistical Society*, Vol. 114, Series A (1951), p. 296. See also T. McKeown, *The Modern Rise of Population* (1976), pp. 99, 101; T. McKeown, *Medicine in Modern Society* (1965), p. 43.

18. Mackenzie, *Contemporary Review*, Oct. 1890, p. 503. For diphtheria, see J.L. Brand, *op. cit.*, p. 56; other statistics from T. McKeown, *op. cit.*, (1976), pp. 92–7, 109.

19. J.L. Brand, *op. cit.*, pp. 53–5; T. McKeown, *op. cit.* (1976), pp. 120–21.

20. Crespi, *Edinburgh Review*, Oct. 1888, p. 495, cf. Mann, in *Edinburgh Review*, Apr. 1883, p. 483. See also S.E. Finer, *The Life and Times of Sir Edwin Chadwick* (1952), pp. 510–12.

21. J.P. Greaves and D.F. Hollingsworth, 'Trends in Food Consumption in the United Kingdom', in G.H. Bourne (ed.), *World Review of Nutrition and Dietetics*, VI (1966), pp. 38–9; D.J. Oddy, 'Working-Class Diets in Late Nineteenth-Century Britain', *Economic History Review*, Aug. 1970, pp. 319–21.

22. J. Burnett, *Plenty and Want* (1966), p. 210.

23. Lady Bell, *At the Works. A Study of a Manufacturing Town* (Nelson ed., 1911), pp. 303, 315; F. Thompson, *Lark Rise to Candleford* (1948 ed.), p. 127.

24. *Parl. Papers* 1892 XXIV (C. 6481), pp. xliv–xlv; *1976 Abstract*, p. 45; Office of Population Censuses and Surveys, *Trends in Mortality 1951–1975* (1978), pp. 10 ff.

25. Mitchell and Deane, *Abstract*, p. 12; *1976 Abstract*, p. 15.

26. Calculation based on information in C. Cook and B. Keith, *British Historical Facts 1830–1900* (1975), p. 15.

27. J.L. Garvin, *Life of Joseph Chamberlain*, II (1933), p. 40, cf. S. Gwynn and G.M. Tuckwell, *The Life of the Rt Hon. Sir Charles W. Dilke* (1917), II, p. 153; G.K.A. Bell, *Randall Davidson. Archbishop of Canterbury* (1935), I, p. 64, cf. p. 67; R.R. James, *Rosebery* (1963), p. 121.

28. G. Battiscombe, *Charlotte Mary Yonge* (1943), p. 75. See also P. Laslett, *The World We Have Lost* (1965), p. 99; R. Roberts, *The Classic Slum*, p. 43.

29. H. Broadhurst, *The Story of his Life* (1901), pp. 301–11.

30. E.A. Wrigley (ed.), *Nineteenth-Century Society* (Cambridge, 1972), p. 21; cf. p. 75; D. Collins, 'The Introduction of Old Age Pensions in Great Britain', *Historical Journal*, 1965, p. 246.

31. D. Collins, *op. cit.*, pp. 247–8.

Chapter 14. Death (pp. 287–92)

1. Deaths from violence, *Parl. Papers* 1892 XXIV (C. 6841), pp. xliv–xlv; *1976 Abstract*, p. 45; M. Greenwood *et al.*, 'Deaths by Violence 1837–1937', *Journal of the Royal Statistical Society*, 1941, p. 148. For industrial accidents, see Department of Employment, *British Labour Statistics. Historical Abstract 1886–1968* (1971), p. 399; *1976 Abstract*, p. 86; cf. J. Benson, 'English Coal-Miners' Trade-Union Accident Funds, 1850–1900', *Economic History Review*, Aug. 1975. For suicides, see *Parl. Papers* 1892 XXIV (C. 6841), p. xlvii; *1976 Abstract*, p. 45.

2. M. Greenwood *et al.*, *op. cit.*, pp. 151, 162; *1976 Abstract*, p. 95; G. Grosvenor, 'Statistics of the Abatement in Crime in England and Wales during the Twenty Years ended 1887–8', *Journal of the Royal Statistical Society*, Sept. 1890, p. 390.

3. M. Loane, *An Englishman's Castle* (1909), p. 79; see also Sir E. Clarke, *The Story of My Life* (1923 ed.), p. 198.

4. E.A. Wrigley (ed.), *Nineteenth-Century Society* (Cambridge, 1972), pp. 365, 371, 391.

5. J.S. Mill, *Essays on Politics and Culture* (ed. G. Himmelfarb, Anchor Books, 1963), p. 57; Queen Victoria, *Letters, Third Series*, I (1930), p. 405; see also S. Pankhurst, *The Suffragette Movement* (1931), p. 88; *The Globe*, 5 Apr. 1889, p. 2.

6. M. Loane, *op. cit.*, p. 137; *Parl. Papers* 1883 LXXX (C. 3722), p. xiii.

7. *Undertakers' and Funeral Directors' Journal*, 22 Sept. 1886, p. 171; see also *ibid.*, 22 July 1888, p. 83.

8. *ibid.*, 22 July 1886, p. 120; 22 July 1887, p. 85; 23 July 1888, p. 87.

9. *ibid.*, 22 Oct. 1886, p. 192.

10. Quoted in A.B. Cooke and J. Vincent (eds.), *Lord Carlingford's Journal. Reflections of a Cabinet Minister. 1885* (Oxford, 1971), p. 50; P. Grosskurth, *Havelock Ellis. A Biography* (1980), p. 6; G.K.A. Bell, *Randall Davidson, Archbishop of Canterbury* (1935), I, pp. 84–5.

11. P. Guedalla (ed.), *The Queen and Mr Gladstone*, II *(1880–1898)* (1933), pp. 155–6.

12. *Times*, 12 May 1885, p. 5.

13. E.P. Thompson, *William Morris. Romantic to Revolutionary* (rev. ed., 1977), pp. 314, 495.

14. *3 Hansard* 252, c. 1018 (3 June 1880); *3 Hansard* 253, c. 695 (24 June 1880).

15. Bright, *3 Hansard* 255, c. 1059 (12 Aug. 1880); H. Broadhurst, *The Story of his Life* (1901), p. 296; Balfour, *3 Hansard* 255, c. 1044 (12 Aug. 1880).

16. Price, in *Times*, 24 Mar. 1884, p. 6; 1 May 1884, p. 9; *Undertakers' and Funeral Directors' Journal*, 22 June 1888, pp. 63–4.

17. Labouchere, *3 Hansard* 287, c. 993 (30 Apr. 1884); Sir A. Wilson and H. Levy, *Burial Reform and Funeral Costs* (1938), p. 51.

18. Headmistress quo. in J. Kamm, *Indicative Past* (1971), p. 73; *Fraser's Magazine*, Jan. 1872, p. 6.

19. This paragraph owes a great deal to F.M. Turner's excellent *Between Science and Religion. The Reaction to Scientific Naturalism in Late Victorian England* (New Haven, 1974), esp. pp. 2, 6–7, 51–9, 118, 177, 250–51.

20. This discussion is much indebted to J. Briggs, *Night Visitors. The Rise and Fall of the English Ghost Story* (1977), esp. pp. 14–24, 52, 65–9.

21. Forster, quo. in Lady St Helier, *Memories of Fifty Years* (1909), p. 176; Mrs H. Ward, *Robert Elsmere* (Boston, 1911 ed.), I, p. 300. See also G.K.A. Bell, *op. cit.*, I, p. 82.

22. Mrs S.A. Barnett, *Canon Barnett. His Life, Work, and Friends* (1918), I, p. 198.

23. R.W. Dale, *The Old Evangelicalism and the New* (1889), pp. 39–41.

24. S. Smith, *My Life-Work* (1903 ed.), pp. 97–8.

25. W. James, *The Varieties of Religious Experience* (Fontana paperback ed., 1960), pp. 101, 103; cf. R. Currie, *Methodism Divided* (1968), pp. 124–5.

26. D.C. Lathbury (ed.), *Correspondence on Church and Religion of William Ewart Gladstone* (1910), II, p. 124; W.E. Gladstone, *Autobiographica* (ed. J. Brooke and M. Sorensen, 1971), p. 175 (Nov. 1897).

Further Reading

This guide to further reading follows the arrangement of the chapters in the book. In a text which surveys so many subjects so briefly, many readers will want further information on particular topics, and the intention here is simultaneously to guide them on their way and to fill out footnotes which have been confined to identifying quotations and statistics. This is not a complete bibliography: the literature on any one decade in modern Britain is too huge for that. It does not even include all the items cited in the footnotes, though it does include some items not cited there. All items are published in London unless otherwise stated.

For a superbly comprehensive coverage, see H.J. Hanham's *Bibliography of British History 1851–1914* (Oxford, 1976); the annotated bibliography in R.C.K. Ensor's *England 1870–1914* (1936), is also useful, but needs supplementing with more recent research. Conveniently concise is J.L. Altholz, *Victorian England 1837–1901* (Conference on British Studies Bibliographical Handbook, Cambridge, 1970), but D. Nicholls' *Nineteenth-Century Britain 1815–1914* (Folkestone, 1978) is annotated and more up-to-date. Continuous updating is provided by the annual bibliography attached to *Victorian Studies*; the *Annual Bibliography of British and Irish History* (ed. G. Elton) published from 1975 by the Royal Historical Society; and the summaries in *Historical Abstracts* (published by ABC-Clio, Inc.).

S.P. Bell's *Dissertations on British History, 1815–1914. An Index to British and American Theses* (Metuchen, New Jersey, 1974) provides guidance to the wealth of unpublished secondary research on the period, and can be kept up to date with the twin guides published by London University's Institute of Historical Research – *Theses in Progress* and *Theses Completed*. The Association of Special Libraries and Information Bureaux [A.S.L.I.B.] publishes an annual *Index to Theses Accepted for Higher Degrees in the Universities of Great Britain and Ireland*; American theses are summarized in *Dissertation Abstracts*, and research in labour history is periodically listed in *The Bulletin of the Society for the Study of Labour History*.

Several sources have been drawn upon for more than one chapter in this book. *The Times* is the more valuable because of its detailed index. Hansard's *Parliamentary Debates* are less well indexed, but contain a wealth of contemporary views. The climate of educated opinion is best assessed in the fortnightly, monthly and quarterly reviews; these are being superbly indexed in W.E. Houghton (ed.), *The Wellesley Index to Victorian Periodicals*, I (1966) and II (1972), which has identified many of the anonymous articles used in this book. There is a useful subject-index of this material in W.F. Poole and W.I. Fletcher (eds.), *Poole's Index to Periodical Literature* (6 vols., Boston, 1882–1908). T.H.S. Escott's *England: Its People, Polity, and Pursuits* (1885 ed.), shrewd and wide-ranging, does for the 1880s what Anthony Sampson did for a later age. Beatrice Webb's sensitive and penetrating *My Apprenticeship* (1926) is a major source throughout.

As for secondary sources on the 1880s, H.M. Lynd's *England in the Eighteen-Eighties* (Frank Cass reprint, 1968) is a fine predecessor, though its aims differ somewhat from those of this book. It is obvious that investigation of any one decade must draw on sources covering a much wider time-span. Two general surveys which include the 1880s, though published in the 1930s, have not been surpassed: they are G.M. Young, *Victorian England. Portrait of an Age* (annotated ed. by G. Kitson Clark, Cambridge, 1977) and R.C.K. Ensor, *England 1870–1914* (1936). Young's is a brilliant short evocation of the Victorian period, and Ensor is comprehensive and judicious. A more up-to-date introduction is R.T. Shannon, *The Crisis of Imperialism. 1865–1915* (1974). For economic aspects, see W. Ashworth, *An Economic History of England 1870–1939* (1960) and E.J. Hobsbawm, *Industry and*

Empire. An Economic History of Britain since 1750 (1968).

There is a wealth of material in the census volumes *Parl. Papers* 1883 LXXX (C. 3722), LXXX (C. 3797); 1893–4 CVI (C. 7222), but a broader statistical sequence needs to be drawn upon, and fortunately this is now available through several valuable and recently-compiled collections, most notably P. Deane and W.A. Cole, *British Economic Growth 1688–1959* (2nd ed., Cambridge, 1969); C. Cook and B. Keith, *British Historical Facts 1830–1900* (1975); B.R. Mitchell and P. Deane, *Abstract of British Historical Statistics* (Cambridge, 1962); B.R. Mitchell and H.G. Jones, *Second Abstract of British Historical Statistics* (Cambridge, 1971); the Department of Employment's *British Labour Statistics. Historical Abstract 1886–1968* (1971); and F.W.S. Craig's two volumes, *British Parliamentary Election Results 1832–1885* (1977) and *British Parliamentary Election Results 1885–1918* (1974). B.R. Mitchell's *European Historical Statistics 1750–1970* (1975) provides a comparative perspective, and the Central Statistical Office's *Annual Abstract of Statistics* sets nineteenth-century figures into a present-day British context; the volume for 1976 has been used in this book. Individual bibliographies now follow under the book's chapter-headings.

Chapter 1. Introduction: Photography and Society

Photographs can be located through John Wall, *Directory of British Photographic Collections* (1977) and G.W.A. Nunn (ed.), *British Sources of Photographs and Pictures* (1952). Context and problems of method are raised in H. and A. Gernsheim, *The History of Photography* (2nd ed., 1969); G.H. Martin and D. Francis, 'The Camera's Eye', in H.J. Dyos and M. Wolff (eds.), *The Victorian City*, I (1973); and in A. Scharf, *Art and Photography* (Pelican ed., 1974).

Valuable studies of individual photographers active in the 1880s include P. Turner and R. Wood, *P.H. Emerson, Photographer of Norfolk* (1974); B. Jay, *Victorian Cameraman* (Newton Abbot, 1973) about Francis Frith; R. Flukinger, L. Schaaf and S. Meacham, *Paul Martin, Victorian Photographer* (Austin, Texas, 1977) and B. Jay, *Victorian Candid Camera* (Newton Abbot, 1973) about Paul Martin; M. Moss, S. Elson and J. Hume, *A Plumber's Pastime* (Burnley, 1975?), about Matthew Morrison; C. Ford, *Sir Benjamin Stone* (1974) and B. Jay, *Customs and Faces* (Newton Abbot, 1972) about Benjamin Stone; M. Hiley, *Frank Sutcliffe* (1974) and B.E. Shaw, *Frank Meadow Sutcliffe, Photographer* (Whitby, 1974); B. Brown (ed.), *The England of Henry Taunt* (1973) and M. Graham, *Henry Taunt of Oxford* (Oxford, 1973); R. Taylor, *George Washington Wilson* (Aberdeen, 1981). Useful information on cameras and techniques used in the 1880s can be found in E.S. Lothrop Jr, *A Century of Cameras* (Dobbs Ferry, New York, 1973), B. Coe, *George Eastman and the Early Photographers* (1973), B. Coe and P. Gates, *The Snapshot Photograph* (1977), O. Mathews, *The Album* (1974) and D.B. Thomas, *From Today Painting is Dead* (1972). Painters of the period are discussed by J. Maas, *Victorian Painters* (2nd ed, 1978).

The series on 'Victorian and Edwardian Britain from Old

Photographs' is a particularly useful guide to sources of contemporary photographs. The volumes on cities and counties are: D. McCulla, *Birmingham* (1973), J. Betjeman and J.S. Gray, *Brighton* (1972), M. Lawson and I.S. Parkes, *Buckinghamshire* (1976), F.A. Reeve, *Cambridge* (1971), F.A. Reeve, *Cambridgeshire* (1976), J. Betjeman and A.L. Rowse, *Cornwall* (1974), B. Chugg, *Devon* (1975), M. Gorham, *Dublin* (1972), C.S. Minto, *Edinburgh* (1973), S. Jarvis, *Essex* (1973), J. Norwood, *Hampshire and the Isle of Wight* (1973), R. Whitmore, *Hertfordshire* (1976), M. Crouch and W. Bergess, *Kent* (1974), J. Marshall and M. Davies, *Lake District* (1976), I. Cruickshank and A. Chinnery, *Leicestershire* (1977), G. Chandler, *Liverpool and the Northwest* (1972), J. Betjeman, *London* (1969), G. Chandler, *Manchester and East Lancashire* (1974), I. Murray, *Middlesex* (1977), P. Hepworth, *Norfolk* (1972), J.W. Thompson and D. Bond, *Northumbria* (1976), S. Cooke, *Nottinghamshire* (1976), C.S. Minto, *Scotland* (1970), D. Bromwich and R. Dunning, *Somerset* (1977), C. Harrison, *Suffolk* (1973), M. Goff, *Surrey* (1972), J.S. Gray, *Sussex* (1973), E.D. Jones, *Wales* (1972), D. McCulla and M. Hampson, *Warwickshire* (1976) and A.B. Craven, *Yorkshire* (1971).

Collections have also appeared on particular aspects of social life. On monarchy there are C. Ford (ed.), *Happy and Glorious. 130 Years of Royal Photographs* (1977) and H. and A. Gernsheim, *Queen Victoria: A Biography in Word and Picture* (1959). For the army see Carman and J. Fabb, *The Victorian and Edwardian Army from Old Photographs* (1975); B. Mollo, *The British Army from Old Photographs* (1975); D. Clammer, *The Victorian Army in Photographs* (Newton Abbot, 1975). On empire see A.T. Embree, *The Last Empire. Photography in British India 1855–1911* (1977) and the National Army Museum's *The Army in India 1850–1914: A Photographic Record* (1968). For nautical aspects see W.P. Trotter, *The Royal Navy in Old Photographs* (1975); B. Greenhill and A. Giffard's *Victorian and Edwardian Ships and Harbours from Old Photographs* (1978) and *Victorian and Edwardian Sailing Ships from Old Photographs* (1976); B. Greenhill, *A Quayside Camera, 1845–1917* (Newton Abbot, 1975); R. Simper, *Victorian and Edwardian Yachting from Old Photographs* (1978); D.D.F. Gladwin, *Victorian and Edwardian Canals from Old Photographs* (1976) and W. Ware, *A Canalside Camera. The Heyday of the Canal System Studied* (Newton Abbot, 1976).

On entertainment see R. Mander and J. Mitchenson, *Victorian and Edwardian Entertainment from Old Photographs* (1978); V. Glasstone, *Victorian and Edwardian Theatres* (1975); R. Southern, *The Victorian Theatre: A Pictorial Survey* (Newton Abbot, 1970); J.N.P. Watson, *Victorian and Edwardian Field Sports from Old Photographs* (1978); A.B. de Maus, *Victorian and Edwardian Cycling and Motoring from Old Photographs* (1977). See also J. Spence, *Victorian and Edwardian Railways from Old Photographs* (1975); P.S.H. Lawrence, *An Eton Camera 1850–1919* (1980); J.K. Major and M. Watts, *Victorian and Edwardian Windmills and Watermills from Old Photographs* (1977); J.S. Creasey, *Victorian and Edwardian Country Life from Old Photographs* (1977); R. Whitmore, *Victorian and Edwardian Crime and Punishment from Old Photographs* (1978); J. Calder, *The Victorian and Edwardian Home from Old Photographs* (1979). The following collections have also been consulted: *Victorian Life in Photographs* (introduction by W. Sansom, 1974), Paul Martin, *Victorian Snapshots* (1939), R. Whitmore, ... *Of Uncommon Interest* (Bourne End, 1975) and G. Winter, *A Country Camera, 1844–1914.*

Chapter 2. Childhood

J. Springhall pioneered the history of youth organizations with his *Youth, Empire and Society. British Youth Movements 1883–1940* (1977), but there is remarkably little scholarly literature on the history of childbirth, child-rearing, children's books, dress and toys, child labour, children's games, and servants, or even on child cruelty. W. Forrester, *Great-Grandmama's Weekly. A Celebration of the Girls' Own Paper* (Guildford, 1980) gives the flavour of this important periodical, but there is need for a serious study both of this and of *Boys' Own Paper*. There is no scholarly history of the N.S.P.C.C. or of the ragged schools, though R. Waugh, *The Life of Benjamin Waugh* (1913) and Mrs Barnardo and J. Marchant, *Memoirs of the Late Dr Barnardo* (1907) are useful. P. Coveney's *The Image of Childhood* (Penguin ed., 1967) is stimulating but (as the author himself confesses) covers only a small area of the relevant territory.

Chapter 3. Education and Newspapers

There is little on education within the family, but F. Musgrove, 'The Decline of the Educative Family', *Universities Quarterly*, XIV (1959–60), may be consulted. On the statistics of elementary education, the two articles by R. Hamilton are invaluable: 'Popular Education in England and Wales before and after the Elementary Education Act of 1870', *J[ournal] of the R[oyal] S[tatistical] S[ociety]*, 1883; and 'Popular Education in England and Wales since 1882', *J.R.S.S.*, Mar. 1890. There is all too little on what was actually taught within the schools and how, but D. Rubinstein's *School Attendance in London, 1870–1904: A Social History* (Hull University Occasional Papers in Economic and Social History, No. 1, 1969) makes an important contribution; see also B. Simon's *Education and the Labour Movement 1870–1920* (1965), F.M. Turner's *The Greek Heritage in Victorian Britain* (New Haven, 1981), and R. Jenkyns' *The Victorians and Ancient Greece* (Oxford, 1980). A. Digby and P. Searby (eds.), *Children, School and Society in Nineteenth-Century England* (1981) print documents which succeed in illuminating what went on in the classroom. On administrative aspects, see G. Sutherland, *Policy-making in Elementary Education, 1870–1895* (1973). On school buildings, see M. Seaborne and R. Lowe, *The English School. Its Architecture and Organisation. II. 1870–1970* (1977).

There are numerous histories of individual public schools, but little that is analytic or comparative apart from T.W. Bamford's useful *The Rise of the Public Schools* (1967), D. Newsome's *Godliness and Good Learning. Four Studies on a Victorian Ideal* (1961), and E.C. Mack's *Public Schools and British Opinion since 1860* (New York, 1941). G.R. Parkin's *Edward Thring. Headmaster of Uppingham School* (2 vols., 1898) does justice to an important and creative figure. For

women's education, see S. Fletcher, *Feminists and Bureaucrats. A Study in the Development of Girls' Education in the Nineteenth Century* (Cambridge, 1980) and J.N. Burstyn, *Victorian Education and the Ideal of Womanhood* (1980). On girls' secondary schools see J. Kamm, *Indicative Past. A Hundred Years of the Girls' Public Day School Trust* (1971) and E. Raikes, *Dorothea Beale of Cheltenham* (1908). On women's university education see B. Stephen's *Emily Davies and Girton College* (1927), G. Battiscombe's *Reluctant Pioneer. A Life of Elizabeth Wordsworth* (1978) and R. McWilliams-Tullberg's *Women at Cambridge* (1975).

On university education M. Sanderson's *The Universities and British Industry 1850–1970* (1972) is indispensable for its linking of universities with wider currents. S. Rothblatt's *The Revolution of the Dons. Cambridge and Society in Victorian England* (1968) is one of the few books to relate the history of Oxford and Cambridge to wider social themes. For a major Oxford personality, see G. Faber, *Jowett. A Portrait with Background* (1957), and for university extension, E. Welch, *The Peripatetic University* (Cambridge, 1973) in conjunction with T. Kelly, *A History of Adult Education* (Liverpool, 1962). J. Roach tackles an important subject in his *Public Examinations in England 1850–1900* (Cambridge, 1971); see also Auberon Herbert (ed.), *The Sacrifice of Education to Examination. Letters from all Sorts and Conditions of Men* (1889).

On the press, A.P. Wadsworth, 'Newspaper Circulations 1800–1954', *Transactions of the Manchester Statistical Society*, Session 1954–5 is excellent. See also A.J. Lee, *The Origins of the Popular Press in England, 1855–1914* (1977). Arnot Reid, 'How a Provincial Paper is Managed', *Nineteenth Century*, Sept. 1886 conducts a most useful content-analysis. See also T.W. Reid, 'Our London Correspondent', *Macmillan's Magazine*, May 1880; F. Hitchman, 'The Newspaper Press', *Quarterly Review*, Oct. 1880; and F. Greenwood's two articles, 'The Newspaper Press', *Nineteenth Century*, May 1890 and 'The Press and Government', *Nineteenth Century*, July 1890. R.L. Shults, *Crusader in Babylon. W.T. Stead and the Pall Mall Gazette* (Lincoln, Nebraska, 1972) is good, and should be read in conjunction with Stead's remarkable 'The Future of Journalism', *Contemporary Review*, Nov. 1886. See also S. Koss, *The Rise and Fall of the Political Press in Britain. I. The Nineteenth Century* (1981).

Chapter 4. Home and Family

No aspect of Victorian sexuality is studied as capably as birth control in A. McLaren's *Birth Control in Nineteenth-Century England* (1978); but see J. Weeks, *Sex, Politics and Society. The Regulation of Sexuality since 1800* (1981). For prostitution, see F. Finnegan, *Poverty and Prostitution. A Study of Victorian Prostitutes in York* (Cambridge, 1979) and J.R. Walkowitz, *Prostitution and Victorian Society. Women, Class and the State* (Cambridge, 1980). Diet is another aspect of family life which has been treated only patchily. J.P. Greaves and D.F. Hollingsworth, 'Trends in Food Consumption in the United Kingdom', in G.H. Bourne (ed.), *World Review of Nutrition and Dietetics*, VI (1966) is an excellent short introduction to the subject; fuller studies are J. Burnett, *Plenty and Want* (1966) and J.C.

Drummond and A. Wilbraham, *The Englishman's Food. A History of Five Centuries of English Diet* (rev. ed. 1957). See also T.C. Barker *et al.*, *Our Changing Fare. Two Hundred Years of British Food Habits* (1966) and D.J. Oddy, 'Working Class Diets in Late Nineteenth-Century Britain', *Economic History Review*, Aug. 1970. It would be helpful to have more studies of individual foods as able as V. Cheke's *The Story of Cheese-Making in Britain* (1959) and J.H. van Stuyvenberg (ed.), *Margarine, An Economic, Social and Scientific History 1869–1969* (Liverpool, 1969).

A. Palmer's charming *Movable Feasts* (1952) plots the history of mealtimes, though primarily from middle-class and literary sources. A good introduction to the subject of drinking is J.A. Spring and D.H. Buss, 'Three Centuries of Alcohol in the British Diet', *Nature*, 15 Dec. 1977. The statistics are in G.B. Wilson, *Alcohol and the Nation (A Contribution to the Study of the Liquor Problem in the United Kingdom from 1800 to 1935)* (1940). See also A.E. Dingle, 'Drink and Working-Class Living Standards in Britain, 1870 –1914', *Economic History Review*, Nov. 1972.

For life in the slums, there are several perceptive studies by middle-class observers writing rather later than the 1880s – notably Lady F.E.E. Bell's *At the Works. A Study of a Manufacturing Town* (1907), Robert Roberts's *The Classic Slum* (Pelican ed., 1973), and the various works of Miss M.E. Loane – *The Queen's Poor* (1905), *The Next Street But One* (1907), *From Their Point of View* (1908), *An Englishman's Castle* (1909) and *Neighbours and Friends* (1910). On working-class housing see J.N. Tarn, *Five Per Cent Philanthropy. An Account of Housing in Urban Areas between 1840 and 1914* (Cambridge, 1973) and E. Gauldie, *Cruel Habitations. A History of Working-Class Housing 1780–1918* (1974). For middle-class housing see M. Girouard's excellent *Sweetness and Light. The 'Queen Anne' Movement 1860–1900* (Oxford, 1977), but there is no comprehensive study of the building society movement, and architectural historians tell us more about exteriors than about what went on inside the home.

P. Branca, *Silent Sisterhood. Middle Class Women in the Victorian Home* (1975) rightly embraces more than the history of feminists. For divorce, see G. Rowntree and N.H. Carrier, 'The Resort to Divorce in England and Wales, 1858 –1957', *Population Studies*, XI (1957–8) and O.R. McGregor, *Divorce in England* (1957). Women's education led many in feminist directions; see A.M. Gordon's interesting 'The After-Careers of University-Educated Women', *Nineteenth Century*, June 1895. There is valuable statistical and other information on women's organizations in the various editions of the *Englishwoman's Year-Book*. Little of value has been written on the history of clothing, but see S.M. Newton, *Health, Art and Reason. Dress Reformers of the 19th Century* (1974). See also Brian Harrison's 'Women's Health and the Women's Movement in Britain: 1840–1940', in C. Webster (ed.), *Biology, Medicine and Society 1840–1940* (Cambridge, 1981).

For suffragism, Ray Strachey's *'The Cause'. A Short History of the Women's Movement in Great Britain* (1928) is still a good guide, supplemented by her *Millicent Garrett Fawcett* (1931) and C. Rover's *Women's Suffrage and Party Politics in Britain 1866–1914* (1967). But these were minority causes; most women probably shared the outlook of 'An Appeal against Female Suffrage', in *Nineteenth Century*, June 1889; the anti-

suffragists are discussed in Brian Harrison's *Separate Spheres. The Opposition to Women's Suffrage in Britain* (1978). Prominent anti-feminist women are portrayed in G. Battiscombe, *Charlotte Mary Yonge* (1943) and J.P. Trevelyan, *The Life of Mrs Humphry Ward* (1923). Anti-suffragism encouraged rather than prevented such women from being active in religious work; for this see Brian Harrison's 'For Church, Queen and Family: The Girls' Friendly Society 1874–1920', *Past and Present*, Nov. 1973.

Chapter 5. Church and Chapel

The best short introduction is A.D. Gilbert's excellent *Religion and Society in Industrial England. Church, Chapel and Social Change 1740–1914* (1976), and religious statistics are most conveniently collected in R. Currie *et al.*, *Churches and Churchgoers* (Oxford, 1977). See also *Facts and Figures about the Church of England* (Church Information Office, several eds.). O. Chadwick, *The Victorian Church*, I (1966) and II (1970) is best on the established church. R. Currie's *Methodism Divided. A Study in the Sociology of Ecumenicalism* (1968) achieves the double feat of conducting an important theoretical argument and writing the best denominational history for the period that we possess. Also good is E. Isichei's *Victorian Quakers* (1970), but there are no comparable histories for other religious groups. We even lack a scholarly modern biography of that major Baptist leader, C. H. Spurgeon. A.W.W. Dale's *Life of R.W. Dale of Birmingham* (2nd ed., 1899) chronicles the diverse activities of an influential provincial Congregationalist. There is no good history of the Salvation Army, but an excellent study of its opponents is V. Bailey's 'Salvation Army Riots, the "Skeleton Army" and Legal Authority in the Provincial Town', in A.P. Donajgrodzki (ed.), *Social Control in Nineteenth Century Britain* (1977). For Catholics, see G.A. Beck (ed.), *The English Catholics. 1850–1950* (1950) and E.S. Purcell's valuable *Life of Cardinal Manning* (2 vols., 1895).

The relationship between religion and social reform in the 1880s is best approached through M. Richter's *The Politics of Conscience. T.H. Green and His Age* (1964) and Mrs Humphry Ward's novel, *Robert Elsmere* (1888), which is analysed in W.S. Peterson's *Victorian Heretic. Mrs Humphry Ward's 'Robert Elsmere'* (Leicester, 1976). For the moralistic background to late Victorian charity see Brian Harrison's 'State Intervention and Moral Reform', in P. Hollis (ed.), *Pressure from Without in Early Victorian England* (1974). The poor law system is best introduced in M.E. Rose, *The Relief of Poverty 1834–1914* (Economic History Society booklet, 1972). Supplementing the poor law system were a host of philanthropists, of whom the most famous is enshrined in E. Hodder's *Life and Work of the Seventh Earl of Shaftesbury K.G.* (3 vols., 1886); there is also much of interest in G. Wagner, *Barnardo* (1979). For two nonconformist philanthropists, see E. Hodder, *Life of Samuel Morley* (2nd ed., 1887) and S. Smith, *My Life-Work* (1902). For a clergyman involved in philanthropy in all its dimensions, see Mrs S.A. Barnett's comprehensive and refreshingly analytic *Canon Barnett. His Life, Work, and Friends* (2 vols., 1918). Aggressive in defence of philanthropy as a social panacea were Octavia Hill – best studied through C.E. Maurice (ed.), *Life of Octavia Hill as Told in Her Letters* (1913) and E.M. Bell, *Octavia Hill. A Biography* (1942) – and the Charity Organisation Society, on which see M. Rooff, *A Hundred Years of Family Welfare* (1972) and C.L. Mowat, *The Charity Organisation Society 1869–1913* (1961).

The negative aspects of religion's relationship with recreation are studied in Brian Harrison's 'Religion and Recreation in Nineteenth-Century England', *Past and Present*, Dec. 1967; the positive aspects shine out from the weakness of Victorian irreligion. Austin Harrison's *Frederic Harrison. Thoughts and Memories* (1926) is a sensitive portrait of a positivist leader who tried to create a secular religion. The political aspects of secularism are covered in W.L. Arnstein, *The Bradlaugh Case* (1965), but its social dimension needs filling out with F.B. Smith, 'The Atheist Mission', in R. Robson (ed.), *Ideas and Institutions of Victorian Britain* (1967), and S. Budd, *Varieties of Unbelief. Atheists and Agnostics in English Society 1850–1960* (1977). Secularization, as distinct from secularism, awaits its historian, but relevant to that story is O. Anderson's valuable article on 'The Incidence of Civil Marriage in Victorian England and Wales', *Past and Present*, Nov. 1975.

Chapter 6. Work

Lord Ernle's *English Farming Past and Present* (6th ed., 1961) is the classic starting-point, supplemented for the 1880s by T.W. Fletcher, 'The Great Depression of English Agriculture 1873–96', *Economic History Review*, XIII (1960–61) and J. Wrightson's 'The Agricultural Lessons of the Eighties', *Journal of the Royal Agricultural Society of England*, 3rd ser., I (1890). David Taylor's 'The English Dairy Industry 1860–1930', *Economic History Review*, Nov. 1976 and E.H. Whetham's 'The London Milk Trade 1860–1900', *Economic History Review*, Dec. 1964 chronicle one of agriculture's several growth-areas in the 1880s. E.J.T. Collins, 'Migrant Labour in British Agriculture in the Nineteenth Century', *Economic History Review*, Feb. 1976 is valuable, and the essence of rural life is brilliantly re-created in Flora Thompson's *Lark Rise to Candleford. A Trilogy* (1945); almost as evocative is M.K. Ashby, *Joseph Ashby of Tysoe. 1859–1919. A Study of Village Life* (Cambridge, 1961). Though crucial to agricultural life, the weather is often neglected by historians; see G. Manley, 'The Mean Temperature of Central England, 1698–1953', *Quarterly Journal of the Royal Meteorological Society*, 1953. It is also crucial to an industry whose neglected history J. Rule pioneers in 'The Smacksmen of the North Sea. Labour Recruitment and Exploitation in British Deep-Sea Fishing 1850–90', I[nternational] R[eview] of S[ocial] H[istory], 1976.

Vols. 2 and 3 of J.H. Clapham's massive *Economic History of Modern Britain – Free Trade and Steel 1850–1886* (Cambridge, 1932) and *Machines and National Rivalries 1887 –1914. With an Epilogue (1914–1929)* (Cambridge, 1938) – are still essential, supplemented by D.H. Aldcroft (ed.), *The Development of British Industry and Foreign Competition 1875 –1914* (1968). The final report of the Royal Commission on the Depression of Trade and Industry, *Parl. Papers* 1886 XXIII (C. 4797), shows that the phrase 'great depression' was

controversial at the time as well as later. See A.E. Musson, 'The Great Depression in Britain 1873–1896: a Reappraisal', *Journal of Economic History*, 1959; D.J. Coppock, 'The Causes of the Great Depression', *Manchester School*, Sept. 1961; C. Wilson, 'Economy and Society in Late Victorian Britain', *Economic History Review*, Aug. 1965; S.B. Saul, *The Myth of the Great Depression, 1873–1896* (Economic History Society booklet, 1969). L. Hannah, 'Mergers in British Manufacturing Industry 1880–1918', *Oxford Economic Papers*, 1974 is important, and W.J. Reader, *Imperial Chemical Industries. A History, Vol. 1: The Forerunners 1870–1926* (1970) analyses one of several industrial growth-areas in the period. W.M. Acworth, 'The Manchester Ship Canal', *Murray's Magazine*, June 1889 chronicles one of those major engineering achievements of the period which deserve more attention from the historian.

It is surprising how little secondary literature there is on the routines of management and the work-process – as opposed to industrial relations and economic history of the more impersonal type, as Raphael Samuel points out in his remarkable article, 'The Workshop of the World: Steam Power and Hand Technology in mid-Victorian Britain', *History Workshop Journal*, No. 3 (Spring 1977). Air pollution, the daily realities of life in the factory and workshop, apprenticeship, industrial welfare, model estates and many kindred subjects await their historian. M.A. Bienefeld, *Working Hours in British Industry. An Economic History* (1972) ably covers important ground; Patrick Joyce, *Work, Society and Politics. The Culture of the Factory in Later Victorian England* (Brighton, 1980) is the first to draw out sensitively and comprehensively the social and political implications of the work experience. Office management and the bureaucratization of industry are another neglected field. E.M. Carus-Wilson (ed.), *Essays in Economic History* (1954) contains two important essays relevant here – H.A. Shannon's 'The Limited Companies of 1866–1883', and J.B. Jefferys' 'The Denomination and Character of Shares, 1855–1885'. W.D. Rubinstein analyses millionaires interestingly in 'Wealth, Elites and the Class Structure of Modern Britain', *Past and Present*, Aug. 1977, but there is no good history of the department store which made so many fortunes. J.B. Jefferys, *Retail Trading in Britain 1850–1950* (Cambridge, 1954) is good, but much more needs to be done on shops and on the tertiary sector generally.

D.K. Sheppard, *The Growth and Role of United Kingdom Financial Institutions 1880–1962* (1971) charts one area where professional people abounded, and W.J. Reader's *Professional Men* (1966) was a pioneering attempt to describe the process. N. Stacey's *English Accountancy. A Study in Social and Economic History 1800–1954* (1954) would be worth following up in more detail, and B. Kaye's *The Development of the Architectural Profession in Britain* (1960) is a good case-study of an individual profession. Professionalism in science is viewed as making menacing strides in D.E. Allen's excellent and well-written *The Naturalist in Britain. A Social History* (Penguin ed., 1978) but is sympathetically recorded in F. Darwin (ed.), *Life and Letters of Charles Darwin* (3 vols., 1887). The enemies of the new scientist can be found in R.D. French, *Antivivisection and Medical Science in Victorian Society* (Princeton, 1975) and R.M. Macleod, 'Law, Medicine and

Public Opinion: The Resistance to Compulsory Health Legislation 1870–1907', *Public Law*, 1967, as well as in E.M. Bell's *Josephine Butler. Flame of Fire* (1962). Her assault on the Contagious Diseases Acts has been skilfully analysed by P. McHugh in his *Prostitution and Victorian Social Reform* (1980), and see F.B. Smith, 'Ethics and Disease in the Later Nineteenth Century: The Contagious Diseases Acts', *Historical Studies, Australia and New Zealand*, Oct. 1971.

For professionalism elsewhere in academic life, see (for example) J. Maloney, 'Marshall, Cunningham, and the Emerging Economics Profession', *Economic History Review*, Aug. 1976. J.F. Unstead, 'H.J. Mackinder and the New Geography', *Geographical Journal*, 1949, and E.W. Gilbert, 'The Rt Hon. Sir Halford J. Mackinder, P.C. 1861–1947', *Geographical Journal*, 1948 illustrate the need for a really good intellectual portrait of this influential figure. Boris Ford (ed.), *The Pelican Guide to English Literature. VI: From Dickens to Hardy* (Penguin, 1969) is a good entrée to literature in the 1880s, supplemented by J. Gross, *The Rise and Fall of the Man of Letters* (1969), but the period cries out for a literary historian of Kathleen Tillotson's calibre. Noel Annan's brilliant *Leslie Stephen* (1951) and 'The Intellectual Aristocracy' in J.H. Plumb (ed.), *Studies in Social History* (1955) illuminate many aspects of the period. K.M.E. Murray's *Caught in a Web of Words. James A.H. Murray and the 'Oxford English Dictionary'* (New Haven, 1977) does far more than illuminate how a major intellectual enterprise came to fruition: in fascinating detail, it goes to the heart of intellectual activity, with all its excitement and drudgery, jealous vanity and selfless dedication.

Chapter 7. Recreation

Sociable activity in the 1880s was more likely to take place in clubs and pubs than in the home. There is useful statistical information on clubs in *Parl. Papers* 1898 XXXVII (C. 8695) and interesting comment in S. Shipley, *Club Life and Socialism in Mid-Victorian London* (History Workshop pamphlet no. 5, Oxford, n. d.), but Pall Mall's important role deserves more than the antiquarian interest it has so far received. For pubs see M. Girouard, *Victorian Pubs* (1975) for buildings and furniture, and Brian Harrison's 'Pubs' in H.J. Dyos and M. Wolff (eds.), *The Victorian City*, I (1973) for social function. The enemies of the pub can be found in A.E. Dingle, *The Campaign for Prohibition in Victorian England. The United Kingdom Alliance 1872–1895* (1980).

Animals were central to Victorian leisure, as W. Vamplew's *The Turf. A Social and Economic History of Horse Racing* (1976) makes clear; see also J.G. Bertram's helpful 'Modern Horse-racing', *Edinburgh Review*, Apr. 1880, 'Lord' George Sanger's *Seventy Years a Showman* (1910) and Brian Harrison's 'Animals and the State in Nineteenth-Century England', *English Historical Review*, Oct. 1973. S. Alexander pioneered a neglected subject with her *St Giles's Fair. 1830–1914* (History Workshop pamphlet No. 2, Oxford, n. d.) but has had no successors. See also D. Braithwaite, *Fairground Architecture* (Cambridge, 1968).

For football, see A. Mason, *Association Football and English Society 1863–1915* (Hassocks, 1980), and W.F. Mandle,

'Games People Played: Cricket and Football in England and Victoria in the Late Nineteenth-Century', *Historical Studies, Australia and New Zealand*, Apr. 1973. There are no good historical studies of cricket, tennis, boxing, golf, fishing, swimming and many other sports. Viscount Bury is useful on 'Cycling and Cyclists', in *Nineteenth Century*, Jan. 1885, and E.W. Gilbert is illuminating as usual in 'The Growth of Inland and Seaside Resorts in England', *Scottish Geographical Magazine*, 1939. A history of British freemasonry is much needed.

In *The Rise of the Victorian Actor* (1978) Michael Baker rescues an important subject from antiquarianism, and G. Stedman Jones, 'Working-Class Culture and Working-Class Politics in London, 1870–1900. Notes on the Remaking of a Working Class', *Journal of Social History*, Summer 1974, leads into the neglected subject of the music-hall. The history of music is an almost untilled field, but see J.S. Curwen, 'The Progress of Popular Music', *Contemporary Review*, Aug. 1887 and J.F. Russell and J.H. Elliot, *The Brass Band Movement* (1936). C. Ehrlich, *Social Emulation and Industrial Progress* (Inaugural Lecture, Queen's University of Belfast, 5 Feb. 1975) rather unexpectedly turns out to be a valuable piece of piano history. M.B. Huish is good on 'Ten Years of British Art', in *Nineteenth Century*, Jan. 1890, but the history of British art has not so far benefited from an expert as historically aware as Mark Girouard on architecture. T. Kelly's *A History of Public Libraries in Great Britain 1845–1965* (1973) is useful, but there is no really good general study of where the books came from – that is, of Victorian publishing.

Chapter 8. Regional Loyalties

Transport is best approached through H.J. Dyos and D.H. Aldcroft, *British Transport. An Economic Survey from the Seventeenth Century to the Twentieth* (Leicester, 1969). There is surprisingly little secondary literature on the history of sea transport, especially on coastal routes, but there are good statistics on wrecks in *Parl. Papers* 1888 XC (C. 5364), and F.F. Conder's 'British Lighthouses', *Edinburgh Review*, Jan. 1880 is useful. A. Everitt's 'Country Carriers in the Nineteenth Century', *Journal of Transport History*, Feb. 1976 is a model article, and F.M.L. Thompson opens up an important subject in his *Victorian England: The Horse-Drawn Society. An Inaugural Lecture* (Bedford College, London University, 1970). The history of engineering, surveying and geological exploration needs a historian, though T.P. White's 'The National [Ordnance] Survey', *Blackwood's Magazine*, Sept. 1886 is helpful, and W.A. Seymour (ed.), *A History of the Ordnance Survey* (Folkestone, 1980) is splendidly comprehensive. A thorough study of the Victorian explorer – whether at home or overseas – would be well worth while.

For railways see R.J. Irving, 'The Profitability and Performance of British Railways, 1870–1914', *Economic History Review*, Feb. 1978. J.R. Kellett, *The Impact of Railways on Victorian Cities* (1969) and H.J. Dyos, 'Workmen's Fares in South London, 1860–1914', *Journal of Transport History*, May 1953 skilfully link transport developments to the important theme of suburbanization. J.P. McKay's *Tramways and Trolleys. The Rise of Urban Mass Transport in Europe* (Princeton, 1976) does the same for road transport, and S.J. Low in 'The Rise of the Suburbs. A Lesson of the Census', *Contemporary Review*, Oct. 1891 was alert to the trend at the time. Two studies of individual suburbs are H.J. Dyos, *Victorian Suburb. A Study of the Growth of Camberwell* (Leicester, 1966) and F.M.L. Thompson, *Hampstead. Building a Borough, 1650–1964* (1974). There is all too little historical literature on attitudes to time, but Derek Howse's *Greenwich Time and the Discovery of the Longitude* (Oxford, 1980) is helpful. As for immigrants, there is no good book on Irish immigration, but Jews are well covered in L. Gartner, *The Jewish Immigrant in England 1870–1914* (1960) and in V.D. Lipman, *The Social History of the Jews in England 1850–1950* (1954).

There is no historical study of London in the 1880s, despite its political prominence, but Birmingham is done justice in A. Briggs, *History of Birmingham, II: Borough and City 1865–1938* (1952), and H. Pelling's *Social Geography of British Elections 1885–1910* (1967) most valuably documents the regional diversity of British politics. E.H. Hunt's penetrating *Regional Wage Variations in Britain 1850–1914* (Oxford, 1973) does rather the same for economic life.

K.O. Morgan is the best guide for Welsh history – most notably in his *Wales in British Politics 1868–1922* (Cardiff, 1963) and 'Gladstone and Wales', *Welsh History Review*, 1960. Sir R. Coupland is stimulating on *Welsh and Scottish Nationalism* (1954) and J.G. Kellas's *Modern Scotland* (1968) is a good introduction. See also D.W. Crowley, 'The Crofters' Party, 1885–1892', *Scottish Historical Review*, 1956, and D.W. Urwin, 'The Development of the Conservative Party Organisation in Scotland until 1912', *Scottish Historical Review*, Oct. 1965.

F.S.L. Lyons's *Ireland since the Famine* (1971) is the best general introduction, but E. Strauss, *Irish Nationalism and British Democracy* (1951) is stimulating. On the political aspects, J.L. Hammond, *Gladstone and the Irish Nation* (1938) is a classic, ably complemented by C.C. O'Brien, *Parnell and His Party 1880–90* (Oxford, 1957). For detailed discussion of the political sequence, see F.S.L. Lyons's *Charles Stewart Parnell* (1977) and A.B. Cooke and J.R. Vincent's often dazzling *The Governing Passion. Cabinet Government and Party Politics in Britain 1885–1886* (Brighton, 1974). Three articles document interesting by-products of the Home Rule crisis: H. Berrington's insufficiently-known 'Partisanship and Dissidence in the Nineteenth-Century House of Commons', *Parliamentary Affairs*, XXI (1967–8); J. Roach's 'Liberalism and the Victorian Intelligentsia', *Cambridge Historical Journal*, 1957; and J.M. Lee, 'Parliament and the Appointment of Magistrates. The Origin of Advisory Committees', *Parliamentary Affairs*, XIII (1959–60). There is fascinating material in K.R.M. Short's rather unintegrated *The Dynamite War. Irish-American Bombers in Victorian Britain* (Dublin, 1979).

Chapter 9. Social Tensions

The best introduction to the rise of the Labour Party is H. Pelling's pioneer work, *The Origins of the Labour Party 1880–1900* (1954). Overseas influences on British labour are documented in E.P. Lawrence, *Henry George in the British Isles* (East Lansing, Mich., 1957) and in K. Willis's valuable 'The Introduction and Critical Reception of Marxist Thought in Britain, 1850–1900', *Historical Journal*, 1977. For the revolutionary left, see H. Collins's 'The Marxism of the Social Democratic Federation', in A. Briggs and J. Saville (eds.), *Essays in Labour History 1886–1923* (1971) and Paul Thompson's *Socialists, Liberals and Labour. The Struggle for London 1885–1914* (1967). Of more than merely political relevance is G. Stedman Jones's important *Outcast London* (Oxford, 1971). Important biographies of personalities active on the left are C. Tsuzuki, *Life of Eleanor Marx* (Oxford, 1967); Y. Kapp, *Eleanor Marx*, I (1972), II (1977); E.P. Thompson, *William Morris. Romantic to Revolutionary* (rev. ed., 1977); and Paul Thompson, *The Work of William Morris* (1967). Socialists with intriguing side-interests feature in A.H. Nethercot, *The First Five Lives of Annie Besant* (1960) and Edward Carpenter, *My Days and Dreams* (1916).

Much less has been written on the ideas and institutions combated by the socialists. 'Business history' is less active and enterprising than 'labour history', and K.D. Brown (ed.), *Essays in Anti-Labour History. Responses to the Rise of Labour in Britain* (1974), by concentrating on formal anti-socialist activity, risks focusing only on the peripheral. See also G. Alderman, 'The National Free Labour Association', *I.R.S.H.*, 1976. There is an abundant literature on the influences producing social cohesion. The Liberal Party's vitality as channel for reforming aspirations in the 1880s is best appreciated through D.A. Hamer's perceptive *Liberal Politics in the Age of Gladstone and Rosebery* (Oxford, 1972). For the pressure groups to which Liberals responded, see his *The Politics of Electoral Pressure. A Study in the History of Victorian Reform Organisations* (Hassocks, 1977), especially for prohibitionist and liberationist pressure. They contributed, by attraction and repulsion, to the growth of mass parties – a process analysed in H.J. Hanham's important *Elections and Party Management. Politics in the Time of Disraeli and Gladstone* (1959). On the interaction between pressure-groups and politicians, see Brian Harrison's 'A Genealogy of Reform in Modern Britain', in C. Bolt and S. Drescher (eds.), *Anti-Slavery, Religion, and Reform* (Folkestone, 1980).

The parties are seen in action in the sole election study to be published for the decade – T.O. Lloyd's *General Election of 1880* (1968); studies of the 1885 and 1886 general elections would be equally interesting. M. Ostrogorski, *Democracy and the Organisation of Political Parties*, I (tr. F. Clarke, 1902) still has much of value, and N. Blewett's 'The Franchise in the United Kingdom 1885–1918', *Past and Present*, Dec. 1965 illuminates the working of the reformed electoral system.

Gladstone did more than anyone else simultaneously to channel anti-system feelings towards Westminster and to moderate them. Andrew Jones tells the inside story of Gladstone's major role in broadening out the electorate in his *The Politics of Reform. 1884* (Cambridge, 1972). The classic biography is J. Morley's *Life of William Ewart Gladstone* (3 vols., 1903); see also Gladstone's *Speeches* (ed. A. Tilney Bassett, 1916). One can get closer to the man through his *Autobiographica* (ed. J. Brooke and M. Sorensen, 1971) and C.R.L.F.'s *Mr Gladstone at Oxford. 1890* (1908), an intriguing account of his table-talk on a visit to All Souls. For his secretary's admiration, and much else on the 1880s besides, see Sir E.W. Hamilton's *Diary* (ed. D.W.R. Bahlman, 2 vols., Oxford, 1972).

Useful biographies of Liberal firebrands are J.L. Garvin's excellent *Life of Joseph Chamberlain*, I (1932) and II (1933), supplemented by the illuminating correspondence in A. Thorold, *Labouchere* (1913) and Chamberlain's *A Political Memoir 1880–1892* (ed. C.H.D. Howard, 1953). Briefer and more recent studies are D. Judd's *Radical Joe* (1977) and R. Jay, *Joseph Chamberlain. A Political Study* (Oxford, 1981). S. Gwynn and G.M. Tuckwell, *The Life of the Rt Hon. Sir Charles W. Dilke* (2 vols., 1917), ample on what it chooses to reveal, should be supplemented by R. Jenkins, *Sir Charles Dilke. A Victorian Tragedy* (1958). See also G.M. Trevelyan's *The Life of John Bright* (1913), a politician somewhat less than radical by the 1880s, and G.W.E. Russell, *Sir Wilfrid Lawson. A Memoir* (1909).

Essential to Liberal vitality was a group of passionately Liberal labour leaders, of whom the following have biographies: H. Broadhurst, *The Story of his Life* (1901); T. Burt, *Autobiography* (1924); J. Arch, *Joseph Arch, The Story of his Life* (ed. Countess of Warwick, 1898); and F.M. Leventhal, *Respectable Radical. George Howell and Victorian Working Class Politics* (1971) – the only modern biography of this type of labour leader. Aspects of their outlook are captured in P.H.J.H. Gosden, *Self-Help. Voluntary Associations in Nineteenth-century Britain* (1973) and in H. Pelling, 'The Working Class and the Origins of the Welfare State', in his provocative *Popular Politics and Society in Late Victorian Britain* (1968).

Conservatives, too, were strengthening the links between Parliament and the people, as two important articles by J.P. Cornford reveal – 'The Transformation of Conservatism in the late Nineteenth Century', *Victorian Studies*, Sept. 1963 and 'The Adoption of Mass Organisation by the British Conservative Party', *Transactions of the Westermarck Society*, X (1964). See also J.H. Robb, *The Primrose League 1883–1906* (New York, 1942); B.H. Brown, *The Tariff Reform Movement in Great Britain 1881–1895* (New York, 1943); and R. McKenzie and A. Silver, *Angels in Marble. Working Class Conservatives in Urban England* (1968). Solid legislative achievement for social reform lay behind 'Tory Democracy', as the career of Lord Shaftesbury shows. See G.B.A.M. Finlayson, *The Seventh Earl of Shaftesbury 1801–1885* (1981). But the key figure in popularizing Conservatism was Lord Randolph Churchill; the biography by his son (2 vols., 1906) is good, but Lord Rosebery's *Lord Randolph Churchill* (1906) is a brilliant personal portrait, and R.F. Foster, *Lord Randolph Churchill. A Political Life* (1981) is more up-to-date.

Basic membership figures for trade unions – major reformist institutions of the period – are in *Parl. Papers 1890–91* XCII (C. 6475). H. Pelling's *History of British Trade Unionism* (3rd ed., 1977) is a good introduction. For fuller treatment, see S. and B. Webb's classic *History of Trade Unionism* (rev. ed. 1920) and H.A. Clegg *et al.*, *A History of British Trade Unions since 1889: I: 1889–1910* (Oxford, 1964). No study of women's trade unionism does justice to the subject, but see N.C. Soldon, *Women in British Trade Unions. 1870–1914* (1978). See also J. Lovell, *Stevedores and Dockers.*

A Study of Trade Unionism in the Port of London, 1870–1914 (1969) and B. Potter [later Webb], *The Co-operative Movement in Great Britain* (1891). Systematic social investigation in the 1880s grows largely out of the world of philanthropy; see especially T.S. and M.B. Simey, *Charles Booth. Social Scientist* (1960).

K.B. Smellie provides a good brief introduction to local government in his *A History of Local Government* (1946); fuller is J. Redlich, *Local Government in England* (ed. F.W. Hirst, 2 vols., 1903). For rural local government, see C.H.E. Zangerl, 'The Social Composition of the County Magistracy in England and Wales, 1831–1887', *Journal of British Studies*, Nov. 1971; J.P.D. Dunbabin's two articles, 'The Politics of the Establishment of County Councils', *Historical Journal*, 1963, and 'Expectations of the new County Councils, and their Realisation', *Historical Journal*, 1965; and J.M. Lee, *Social Leaders and Public Persons. A Study of County Government in Cheshire since 1888* (Oxford, 1963).

For urban local government, E.P. Hennock's *Fit and Proper Persons. Ideal and Reality in Nineteenth-Century Urban Government* (1973) provides the best introduction, supplemented by his two articles, 'Finance and Politics in Urban Local Government in England 1835–1900', *Historical Journal*, 1963 and 'The Social Composition of Borough Councils in Two Large Cities, 1835–1914', in H.J. Dyos (ed.), *The Study of Urban History* (1968). A. Redford and I.S. Russell, *The History of Local Government in Manchester* (III, 1940) is a substantial local study. See also G.V. Blackstone, *A History of the British Fire Service* (1957) and C. Cunningham, *Victorian and Edwardian Town Halls* (1981).

For the Fabians, the 1948 ed. of Bernard Shaw *et al.*, *Fabian Essays* is the best introduction. The best study is A.M. McBriar, *Fabian Socialism and English Politics 1884–1918* (Cambridge, 1962) but see also E.J. Hobsbawm, 'The Fabians Reconsidered', in his *Labouring Men* (1964), a volume which also contains valuable essays on 'The Tramping Artisan', the labour aristocracy, and various aspects of late Victorian trade union history. For a more biographical approach, see N. and J. MacKenzie, *The First Fabians* (1977); M. Cole (ed.), *The Webbs and their Work* (1949) contains some useful analytical essays.

Chapter 10. Aristocratic Magic

Historians have not so far concerned themselves much with the social history of the Victorian aristocracy, though its architecture is splendidly portrayed in Mark Girouard's *The Victorian Country House* (Yale ed., revised and enlarged, 1979); see also J. Franklin, *The Gentleman's Country House and its Plan 1835–1914* (1981). Willoughby de Broke's *The Passing Years* (1924) is a gem, and there is valuable material in T.H.S. Escott's anonymous *Society in London. By a Foreign Resident* (1885) – but there is no good history of domestic service in the period, though C.V. Butler's *Domestic Service. An Enquiry by the Women's Industrial Council* (1916) is useful. The literature on 'deference' has become quite extensive, and is touched upon below; but F. McKenna's 'Victorian Railway Workers', *History Workshop*. Spring 1976 breaks out of the narrowly political framework usually dominant here.

The economic and political history of the late Victorian aristocracy has been excellently handled in F.M.L. Thompson's *English Landed Society in the Nineteenth Century* (1963). For statistical information, see W.L. Guttman, *The British Political Elite* (1968) and the several editions of J. Bateman's *The Great Landowners of Great Britain and Ireland*. James Cornford has provided a penetrating introduction to the aristocracy's political role with his 'The Parliamentary Foundations of the Hotel Cecil', in R. Robson (ed.), *Ideas and Institutions of Victorian Britain* (1967).

For the weighting of the political system in favour of wealth, see H.J. Hanham, 'The Sale of Honours in Late Victorian England', *Victorian Studies*, III (1959–60); N. Blewett, 'The Franchise in the United Kingdom 1885–1918', *Past and Present*, Dec. 1965; and C.C. O'Leary, *The Elimination of Corrupt Practices in British Elections 1868–1911* (Oxford, 1962). J.A. Thomas's *The House of Commons. 1832–1901. A Study of its Economic and Functional Character* (Cardiff, 1939) is valuable on functional representation in the House of Commons, but there is no analytic and descriptive account of Parliament as an institution in the 1880s, and no thorough study of the House of Lords in the period. For the workings of the constitution, there is no rival to Walter Bagehot's *The English Constitution* (Fontana ed., 1963), which can be supplemented by H.J. Hanham's valuable collection of documents in his *The Nineteenth-Century Constitution 1815–1914* (Cambridge, 1969) and J.P. Mackintosh's *The British Cabinet* (3rd ed., 1977).

There are many biographies of the politicians prominent in the 1880s. Of major importance is Lady G. Cecil's brilliant life of her father, *The Life of Robert, Marquis of Salisbury*, I (1921), II (1921); vol. III (1931) covers the period 1880–86 and vol. IV (1932) the years from 1886 to 1892. Paul Smith's introduction to *Lord Salisbury on Politics. A Selection from his Articles in the Quarterly Review, 1860–1883* (Cambridge, 1972) is valuable; see also L. Penson's *Foreign Affairs under the Third Marquis of Salisbury* (Creighton Lecture, 1960), published in 1962. Other notable biographies are A.G. Gardiner, *Life of Sir William Harcourt* (2 vols., 1923); D.A. Hamer, *John Morley. Liberal Intellectual in Politics* (Oxford, 1968); R.R. James, *Rosebery* (1963); and Viscount Chilston, *W.H. Smith* (1965).

Late Victorian Whitehall has been almost as neglected by historians as late Victorian Pall Mall, though there are some valuable essays on the Colonial Office, Foreign Office and Labour Department in G. Sutherland (ed.), *Studies in the Growth of Nineteenth-Century Government* (1972). Particularly good on the Foreign Office are R.T. Nightingale, 'The Personnel of the British Foreign Office and Diplomatic Service, 1851–1929', *The Realist*, Dec. 1929, and D.C.M. Platt, *Finance, Trade, and Politics in British Foreign Policy 1815–1914* (Oxford, 1968). The growth of late Victorian bureaucracy was recorded memorably and with suspicion from a theoretical perspective in A.V. Dicey's *Lectures on the Relation between Law and Public Opinion in England during the Nineteenth Century* (1905), and with downright hostility in Herbert Spencer's *Man Versus the State* (1884).

Chapter 11. Discipline and Authority

Little enough is known even about modern patterns of crime, which are very imperfectly recorded in the statistics: still less was known in the 1880s. V.A.C. Gatrell and T.B. Hadden's 'Criminal Statistics and their Interpretation' is the only systematic attempt to detect patterns in the wealth of late Victorian crime statistics – in E.A. Wrigley (ed.), *Nineteenth-Century Society* (Cambridge, 1972). G. Grosvenor's 'Statistics of the Abatement in Crime in England and Wales during the Twenty Years ended 1887–88', *J.R.S.S.*, Sept. 1890 is admirable. W.D. Morrison's 'The Increase of Crime', *Nineteenth Century*, June 1892, is stimulating, but much remains to be discovered in this area, and a good account of detective fiction is much needed.

The lack of a satisfactory history of the police is one of the major hindrances to a proper understanding of late Victorian Britain; W.L.M. Lee's *History of the Police in England* (1901) is entirely inadequate, but see Sir Charles Warren's interesting 'The Police of the Metropolis', *Murray's Magazine*, Nov. 1888. There is little on prisons, though J.E. Thomas's *The English Prison Officer since 1850. A Study in Conflict* (1972) is useful. We are equally ignorant about asylums, though K. Jones, *Mental Health and Social Policy 1845–1959* (1960) covers some of the ground.

For lack of contemporary work on late Victorian legal history the general historian is forced back on J. Macdonnell's excellent 'Statistics of Litigation in England and Wales since 1859', *J.R.S.S.*, Sept. 1894. Three useful biographies are G. Feaver's *From Status to Contract. A Biography of Sir Henry Maine 1822–1888* (1969); Leslie Stephen's *Life of Sir James Fitzjames Stephen* (1895); and R.S. Rait (ed.), *Memorials of Albert Venn Dicey* (1925), which if studied in conjunction with H.S. Maine's *Popular Government* (1885) illustrate the Conservative directions some influential lawyers were taking in the 1880s.

With the history of the late Victorian army, as with the history of schools, we know more about administrative aspects than about what the institution felt like to those who experienced it; see, for example, B. Bond's *The Victorian Army and the Staff College 1854–1914* (1972); W.S. Hamer's *The British Army. Civil-Military Relations 1885–1905* (Oxford, 1970); B. Bond's 'The Effect of the Cardwell Reforms in Army Organisation 1874–1904', *Journal of the Royal United Services Institution*, CV (1960); and A. Forbes, 'Flogging in the Army', *Nineteenth Century*, Oct. 1879. Some useful work has been done on the status of officers – see P.E. Razzell, 'Social Origins of Officers in the Indian and British Home Army 1758–1962', *British Journal of Sociology*, 1963 and C.B. Otley, 'The Social Origins of British Army Officers', *Sociological Review*, 1970. H.J. Hanham's 'Religion and Nationality in the Mid-Victorian Army', in M.R.D. Foot (ed.), *War and Society* (1973), discusses an important aspect, but no study extends to the army that preoccupation with the other ranks and with wider social functions which lends distinction to H. Cunningham's *The Volunteer Force. A Social and Political History 1859–1908* (1975).

Useful introductions to imperialism can be found in R. Hyam, *Britain's Imperial Century 1815–1914. A Study of Empire and Expansion* (1976) and D.K. Fieldhouse, *Economics and Empire. 1830–1914* (1973). R. Robinson and J. Gallagher, *Africa and the Victorians* (1961) is a brilliant monograph. Well worth detailed study is the Earl of Cromer's *Modern Egypt* (2 vols., 1908) as a record of achievement which greatly impressed observers in the 1880s. See also the Marquess of Zetland's *Lord Cromer* (1932) and John Marlowe's *Cromer in Egypt* (1970). Another influential imperialist is captured well in D. Wormell, *Sir John Seeley and the Uses of History* (Cambridge, 1980). For Liberal reactions to Empire, see D. Schreuder's *Gladstone and Kruger: Liberal Government and Colonial 'Home Rule', 1880–85* (1969), which displays a splendid perception of how things happen in politics. There is a helpful discussion of missionary organizations in *Quarterly Review*, July 1886, but the great influence of the missionary ideal on Victorian life has yet to find its historian. So also have the imperial contacts and connections of the British churches, and the important subject of improvements in internal communication within the empire.

Chapter 12. Pomp and Ceremony

Surprisingly little has been written even on the constitutional aspects of late Victorian monarchy, let alone on its important and growing ceremonial role. F. Hardie's *The Political Influence of Queen Victoria 1861–1901* (2nd ed., 1938) is still almost alone in the field, though see also D.W.R. Bahlman, 'The Queen, Mr Gladstone, and Church Patronage', *Victorian Studies*, June 1960, and P. Magnus, *King Edward the Seventh* (Penguin ed., 1967). Philip Guedalla's *The Queen and Mr Gladstone Vol. 2 (1880–1898)* (1933) contains a wealth of splendid material on a historic relationship. Queen Victoria's *Letters, Second Series*, III (ed. G.E. Buckle, 1928) and *Letters, Third Series*, I (ed. G.E. Buckle, 1930) give a glimpse of the wealth of material in the royal archives which could give a more rounded picture of monarchy's late Victorian role. J.L. Lant, *Insubstantial Pageant. Ceremony and Confusion at Queen Victoria's Court* (1979) does not exploit its important subject to the full.

Chapter 13. Illness and Old Age

Mortality trends are comprehensively analysed for 1867–91 in *Parl. Papers* 1892 XXIV (C. 6481). Particularly valuable are two articles, W.J. Martin's 'A Comparison of the Trends of Male and Female Mortality', *J.R.S.S.*, CXIV Series A (1951), and M. Greenwood *et al.*, 'Deaths by Violence 1837–1937', *J.R.S.S.*, CIV (1941). Three valuable books on the neglected area of medical history for the period are J.L. Brand, *Doctors and the State* (Baltimore, 1965); R. Pinker, *English Hospital Statistics. 1861–1938* (1966); and F.B. Smith, *The People's Health 1830–1910* (1979). B. Abel-Smith's *History of the Nursing Profession* (1960) is disappointingly institutional in approach; a social history of nursing is much needed. See also M. MacKenzie's 'The Use and Abuse of Hospitals', *Contemporary Review*, Oct. 1890, and B. Abel-Smith's *The Hospitals 1800–1948. A Study in Social Administration in England and Wales* (1964). There is no good historical study of dentistry.

For the exhibition of freaks, see Michael Howell and Peter Ford's extraordinary *The True History of the Elephant Man* (1980).

T. McKeown's work is of major importance for getting the activities of doctors and hospitals into perspective: see his *Medicine in Modern Society* (1965) and *The Modern Rise of Population* (1976). He emphasizes the achievement of late Victorian public health reformers, who have received less attention than their early Victorian predecessors, though see C.F. Brockington, *A Short History of Public Health* (1966). It also plays up the importance of environmental factors on health, and retrospectively lends some credit to the advocates of medical self-help. For one such group, see P.C. McIntosh's useful *Physical Education in England since 1800* (2nd ed., 1968).

No comprehensive study so far exists of old age in the Victorian period; significantly, the only relevant article is on its implications for government policy – D. Collins's 'The Introduction of Old Age Pensions in Great Britain', *Historical Journal*, 1965. On the occupational, family, political and social role of old people – or even on the relationship between the generations – nothing has been written.

Chapter 14. Death

Here too is an important but neglected subject. There is no scholarly history of Victorian funeral customs or attitudes to death, though fruitful lines of investigation are suggested in F.M. Turner's excellent *Between Science and Religion. The Reaction to Scientific Naturalism in Late Victorian England* (New Haven, 1974) and J. Briggs, *Night Visitors. The Rise and Fall of the English Ghost Story* (1977).

Conclusion

The above discussion shows how precariously the 'general' historian of Britain in the 1880s skates over large patches of ignorance. With more research on the history of law, sport, music, science, medicine, childhood, painting, sculpture, insurance, literature, geology, exploration, furniture, domestic interiors, missionary work, clothing, shopping, death, the navy, the professions, the civil service, domestic service, and crime – to take only a few instances – a much better account of England in the 1880s could be written. This discussion also throws into relief the historical importance of more general themes: the growth of suburbs and professions, secularization and institutionalization: reformism and pressures towards social integration – all of which deserve more sustained discussion. But a conclusion should more properly strike a note of appreciation than of complaint. The historian who tries to describe a whole society over a decade inevitably depends heavily on those scholarly pioneers whose thorough, well-documented and often unsung labours within their chosen area succeed in making the way plain. Our debt to them is great, and merits something more than a mere footnote reference.

YEAR	POLITICAL (major events in capitals)	LEGISLATIVE	OVERSEAS
1880	Dilke begins his lunches for T.U.C parliamentary committee 5 Feb: Queen opens Parliament in state 8 Mar: dissolution of Parliament announced 31 Mar: first day of polling in general election 18 Apr: DISRAELI RESIGNS AFTER ELECTION DEFEAT (354 LIBERALS, 238 CONSERVATIVES, 60 HOME RULE) 23 Apr: GLADSTONE PRIME MINISTER 3 May: Bradlaugh tries to affirm instead of taking the oath 17 May: Parnell elected chairman of Home Rule M.P.s 22 June: Bradlaugh arrested on failing to withdraw from House of Commons 2 July: Bradlaugh takes seat, legality contested, and he is unseated 3 Aug: House of Lords rejects Compensation for Disturbance Bill 22 Sept: boycotting begins in Ireland	Ground Game Act Liberals allow Irish Coercion to lapse Burials Act relieves Nonconformist grievances Statutes (Definition of Time) Bill makes Greenwich time legal time	27 July: Afghan victory at Maiwand Sept: Afghan war ends 13 Oct: Transvaal declares independence 16 Oct: War in Transvaal starts
1881	14 Jan: Fenian bomb injures three at Salford 31 Jan – 2 Feb: forty-one hours continuous session till Speaker ends obstruction by taking vote 16 Mar: unexploded bomb at Mansion House 7 Apr: Gladstone brings in Irish Land Bill Apr: Duke of Argyll resigns in consequence 9 Apr: Bradlaugh re-elected at Northampton 19 Apr: DISRAELI DIES 5 May: Tory peers choose Salisbury as their leader 3 Aug: Bradlaugh tries to enter House of Commons, but is ejected 13 Oct: PARNELL ARRESTED AND IMPRISONED AT KILMAINHAM for inciting the Irish to intimidate tenants taking advantage of the Land Act 18 Oct: government declares Irish Land League illegal	Welsh Sunday Closing Act Irish Land Act gives fair rents Coercion Act for Ireland	26 Feb: Boer victory at Majuba Hill 6 Mar: armistice with Boers 13 Mar: Czar Alexander II of Russia assassinated 8 Aug: Pretoria Convention with the Boers Dec: Canadian Pacific Railway founded
1882	21 Feb: Bradlaugh tries to take oath on his own Bible, but is expelled 2 Mar: Bradlaugh re-elected at Northampton 2 Mar: Maclean fires at the Queen at Windsor May: W.E. Forster resigns when 'Kilmainham Treaty' produces Liberal conciliation of Parnell 6 May: PHOENIX PARK MURDERS OF CAVENDISH AND BURKE 11 May: Harcourt introduces Prevention of Crimes Bill increasing police powers in Ireland for three years 12 May: unexploded Fenian bomb at Mansion House 17 June: large seizure of Fenian arms in London 17 July: Bright resigns from Cabinet over Egyptian invasion 17 Aug: Maamstrasna murders in Ireland	Settled Land Act eases land transfers Married Women's Property Act Municipal Corporations Act removes property qualification for borough councillors July: Prevention of Crimes Bill for Ireland suspends trial by jury and extends police powers	Triple Alliance (Austria, Germany, Italy) 11 July: Alexandria bombarded 13 Sept: British victory at Tel-el-Kebir followed by occupation of Egypt and Sudan
1883	Bomb incidents cause C.I.D. to establish special Irish branch 20 Jan: Fenian bomb blows up Glasgow gasometer 15 Mar: Fenian bomb explodes in Whitehall 19 Mar: Churchill and Wolff conceive idea of Primrose League 30 Mar: Chamberlain's attack on Salisbury at Birmingham as belonging to a class 'who toil not, neither do they spin' 3 May: Affirmation Bill rejected by three votes 9 May: Bradlaugh excluded from House of Commons by resolution 30 Oct: two Fenian explosions, one injuring seventy-two	Explosives Act increases penalties for implication Corrupt and Illegal Practices Act reduces electoral corruption Contagious Diseases Acts suspended Arrears Act	16 Apr: Kruger President South African Republic 11 Sept: Sir Evelyn Baring (later Lord Cromer) arrives in Egypt as British agent and consul-general to establish civil administration
1884	11 Feb: Bradlaugh again excluded from House of Commons 19 Feb: Bradlaugh re-elected for Northampton for third time 26 Feb: bombs at four London mainline stations, one explodes 28 Feb: Gladstone introduces his franchise Bill 7 Apr: Liberal majority of 130 on second reading of franchise Bill 30 May: three Fenian explosions in London's West End Autumn: W.T. Stead's articles on 'The Truth about the Navy', in *Pall Mall Gazette* 13 Oct: franchise reform riots disrupt Conservative meeting at Birmingham's Aston Park 26 Oct: over 80,000 protest in Hyde Park at House of Lords resistance to franchise reform 13 Dec: three Irish conspirators blown up by their own bomb at London Bridge	Representation of the People Act	18 Jan: Gordon sent to Sudan 30 Aug: Wolseley leaves for Cairo 13 Oct: the Mahdi takes Omdurman 18 Nov: first meeting of Imperial Federation League 6 Dec: Froude leaves for world tour
1885	Unionists in southern Ireland form Irish Loyal and Patriotic Union 2 Jan: Fenian bomb on London underground injures several 5 Jan: Chamberlain's 'ransom' speech at Birmingham 24 Jan: Fenian bombs at Tower and Westminster injure several 7 Apr: Prince and Princess of Wales official visit to Ireland 15 May: Gladstone announces renewal of Prevention of Crimes Bill 9 June: GLADSTONE GOVERNMENT RESIGNS	Ashbourne's Land Purchase Act (helps Irish tenants buy out landlords) Redistribution Act (establishes modern pattern of parliamentary constituencies)	26 Jan: death of Gordon 28 Jan: Wolseley reaches Khartoum 12 Feb: New South Wales offers troops for Sudan 26 Feb: Leopold II of Belgium establishes Congo State

SOCIAL/ECONOMIC	CULTURAL	YEAR

Tebb's London Society for the Abolition of Compulsory Vaccination founded
Elementary education made compulsory
Institute of Chartered Accountants formed
Albert Dock opens in London
Parcel post introduced in England
  2 Feb: Australian meat arrives in London in good condition
    on S.S. *Strathleven*
	Newnes's *Tit-Bits* launched
	Henry George's *Progress and Poverty*
	Mason College, Birmingham, opens
	Guildhall School of Music founded
	Alfred Waterhouse's Natural History Museum completed
	Owen's College becomes Manchester University
	Gilbert and Sullivan, *Pirates of Penzance*
	May: John Morley editor of *Pall Mall Gazette*
	22 Dec: 'George Eliot' dies
		1880

Henry George's first British lecture tour
A.R. Wallace founds Land Nationalization Society
Surveyors chartered
24 Feb: Cambridge admits women to honours examinations
19 Mar: Rev. S. Green, ritualist, imprisoned at Lancaster
  3 Apr: census day
  8 June: Democratic Federation inaugural conference
	Gilbert and Sullivan, *Patience*
	Morris opens weaving works at Merton Abbey
	Ibsen's *Ghosts*
	Morley's *Cobden*
	Poems by Oscar Wilde
	T.H. Green's *Liberal Legislation and Freedom of Contract*
	Natural History Museum opened at Kensington
	  5 Feb: death of Carlyle
	17 May: revised version of New Testament published
		1881

Beatty v. Gillbanks upholds right of public meeting
Highland Land Law Reform Association (from 1887, Highland Land
  League) formed
Forth Bridge begun
S.S. *Dunedin* brings first imported frozen New Zealand meat
16 Sept: Pusey, Oxford high church leader and professor of Hebrew, dies
  3 Dec: Tait, Archbishop of Canterbury, dies: his successor E.W. Benson
    enthroned 29 Apr. 1883
	Law chair for A.V. Dicey at Oxford
	University College Liverpool founded
	Dictionary of National Biography begins
	Creighton's *History of the Papacy* begins
	Jackson's Examination Schools in Oxford
	Society for Psychical Research founded
	Wilson Carlile founds Church Army
	Gilbert and Sullivan, *Iolanthe*
	26 Mar: T.H. Green dies
	19 Apr: Charles Darwin dies
	  6 Dec: Trollope dies
		1882

28 Sept: electric tramway opened at Portrush
  4 Oct: Boys' Brigade launched
24 Oct: Fellowship of the New Life launched
	R.L. Stevenson's *Treasure Island*
	T.H. Green's *Prolegomena to Ethics*
	J.A. Symonds's *A Problem in Greek Ethics* (homosexuality)
	Mearns's *Bitter Cry of Outcast London*
	Pollock professor of jurisprudence, Oxford
	University College Cardiff founded
	Sullivan knighted
	Seeley's *Expansion of England*
	Stead edits *Pall Mall Gazette*
	14 Mar: death of Karl Marx
	  7 May: Royal College of Music formally opened
	30 Nov: peerage for Tennyson
		1883

First Anglo-Australian test match
Gaelic Athletic Association founded
Institute of Chemistry chartered
Henry George's second British lecture-tour
  4 Jan: Fabian Society emerges from split in Fellowship of the New Life
13 Jan: Dr Price tries to cremate his dead child
  4 Mar: royal commission on housing of working classes appointed
Apr: first Fabian Tract published (on *Why are the Many Poor?*)
30 Apr: Cameron's Bill to legalize cremation defeated by 147 to 79 votes
Aug: Democratic Federation becomes Social Democratic Federation
27 Dec: Socialist League splits from S.D.F.
	Toynbee's *Industrial Revolution*
	Spencer's *Man Versus the State*
	Burne-Jones's *King Cophetua and the Beggar Maid*
	Marshall professor of economics at Cambridge
	Manchester, Leeds and Liverpool universities combine
	  into the Victoria University
	University College Bangor founded
	Gilbert and Sullivan, *Mikado*
	  1 Feb: *Oxford English Dictionary* begins publication
		1884

Industrial Remuneration Conference
Safety bicycle first built at Coventry
10 Jan: Toynbee Hall opens
28 Jan: Bishop Temple moves to see of London
31 Jan: Dr King Bishop of Lincoln
24 Mar: first cremation at Woking
22 Aug: mass Hyde Park meeting against
  vice in London
  1 Oct: death of Lord Shaftesbury
10 Nov: Stead imprisoned
	Society for Utilisation of the Welsh Language in Education formed
	Oxford University Dramatic Society formed
	Law Quarterly Review starts
	Maine's *Popular Government*
	Dicey's *Introduction to the Law of the Constitution*
	Rider Haggard's *King Solomon's Mines*
	Dictionary of National Biography begins publication
		1885

POLITICAL	LEGISLATIVE

1885 13 June: LORD SALISBURY AGREES TO FORM A CONSERVATIVE GOVERNMENT
    6 July: Bradlaugh again excluded from House of Commons
   13 July: Speaker refuses to allow any objections to Bradlaugh's taking the oath
   17 Aug: Duke of Richmond first Secretary of State for Scotland
   Sept: Joseph Chamberlain campaigns for 'unauthorized programme'
   21 Nov: Parnell's manifesto urges Irish nationalists in Britain to vote Conservative
   24 Nov: general election begins
   17 Dec: Hawarden 'Kite' publicizes Gladstone's ideas on Home Rule
   18 Dec: GENERAL ELECTION ENDS (334 LIBERALS, 250 CONSERVATIVES,
      86 IRISH NATIONALISTS)

Legislative: Criminal Law Amendment Act raises age of consent for women from 13 to 16, and bans homosexuality
14 Aug: Conservatives allow Prevention of Crimes Bill to lapse

1886 Scottish Home Rule Association launched
Ulster Loyalist Anti-Repeal Union formed
   12 Jan: Caernarvon's resignation indicates Tory hardline policy on Ireland henceforward
   21 Jan: Queen opens Parliament in state
   26 Jan: Conservative government announces it will resume coercion in Ireland
   27 Jan: CONSERVATIVE GOVERNMENT DEFEATED IN HOUSE OF COMMONS BY 329 VOTES TO 250
   29 Jan: GLADSTONE PRIME MINISTER
   12 Feb: Dilke cited as co-respondent in divorce case
   22 Feb: Churchill addresses enthusiastic public meeting in Belfast
   27 Mar: Chamberlain and G.O. Trevelyan resign from Cabinet over Gladstone's Home Rule Scheme
    5 Apr: death of W.E. Forster
    8 Apr: Gladstone introduces Home Rule Bill in House of Commons
   14 Apr: Unionists gain boost from important Haymarket meeting chaired by Earl Cowper
   10 May: Gladstone moves second reading of Home Rule Bill
    7 June: HOME RULE BILL DEFEATED ON SECOND READING BY 341 VOTES TO 311
   10 June: Gladstone announces dissolution
   30 June: general election campaign begins
   17 July: GENERAL ELECTION CAMPAIGN ENDS (191 LIBERALS, 317 CONSERVATIVES,
      85 IRISH NATIONALISTS, 77 LIBERAL UNIONISTS)
July – Sept: serious riots in Belfast
   20 July: GLADSTONE GOVERNMENT RESIGNS
   25 July: SALISBURY TAKES OFFICE AS PRIME MINISTER OF A CONSERVATIVE GOVERNMENT
    2 Oct: Churchill's Dartford speech announces his programme of Conservative reform
   20 Nov: O'Brien and Dillon draw up 'Plan of Campaign' to organize Irish tenants
   23 Dec: CHURCHILL RESIGNS AS CHANCELLOR OF THE EXCHEQUER, and his resignation is accepted

Legislative: C.D. Acts repealed
Crofters Act gives security of tenure and fair rents in Scotland

1887   4 Jan: Goschen becomes Chancellor of the Exchequer
   12 Jan: Stafford Northcote (Earl of Iddesleigh) dies
   13 Jan: Round Table for Liberal reunion meets
   24 Feb: jury fail to agree in Dublin trial of Plan of Campaign leaders
    5 Mar: A.J. BALFOUR BECOMES CHIEF SECRETARY FOR IRELAND
   28 Mar: Balfour introduces Crimes Bill without time limit
   11 Apr: great Hyde Park meeting to protest against Crimes Bill
   18 Apr: *Times* publishes forged documents alleging that Parnell had been implicated in the
      Phoenix Park murders
   12 May: motion to reduce Westminster Abbey jubilee expenditure defeated
   17 June: government successfully moves guillotine motion
   23 July: naval review at Spithead by the Queen
    9 Sept: POLICE FIRE ON CROWD AT MITCHELSTOWN, LEADING TO THREE DEATHS
   22 Nov: protectionist resolution overwhelmingly carried at twentieth Conservative Party conference

Legislative: Probation of First Offenders Act extends probation idea to adults
Balfour's Crimes Act

1888 11 Aug: Parnell initiates action against *Times* claiming £100,000
      damages (£5,000 paid 3 Feb. 1890)
    4 Sep: Gladstone attends Eisteddfod at Wrexham
   17 Sep: royal commission on *Times* articles attacking Parnell first meets

Legislative: Bradlaugh's Oaths Act enables affirmation to replace oath
Local Government Act establishes county councils

1889 Jan: Lloyd George chosen Liberal candidate for Caernarvon
   23 Jan: first meeting of the new county councils
    1 Mar: Richard Pigott's suicide at Madrid
   27 Mar: John Bright dies
   23 July: Board of Agriculture created
    5 Aug: Spithead Naval Review in honour of German Emperor's visit
   28 Dec: CAPTAIN O'SHEA FILES PETITION FOR DIVORCE, CITING
      PARNELL'S ADULTERY WITH HIS WIFE

Legislative: Prevention of Cruelty to Children Act
Naval Defence Act lays down eight battleships
Welsh Intermediate Education Act allows Welsh county councils to set up and support secondary schools

OVERSEAS	SOCIAL/ECONOMIC	CULTURAL	YEAR
Mar: British Protectorate of North Bechuanaland begins 3 Mar: New South Wales contingent leaves Sydney 30 Mar: Russia occupies Penjdeh 27 Apr: Vote of Credit for £11,000,000 helps deter Russia 16 May: Germany annexes northern New Guinea 13 Nov: war formally declared against King of Burma Dec: British protectorate over southern New Guinea		Meredith's *Diana of the Crossways* 24 June: baronetcy for Millais: Watts declines it	*1885*
Indian National Congress founded Transvaal gold rush 1 Jan: Upper Burma annexed 4 May: Queen opens Imperial and Colonial Exhibition in London June: Britain annexes Zululand	Royal Commission on Depression in Trade and Industry reports Tilbury docks open 20 Jan: Mersey Tunnel opens 8 Feb: Trafalgar Square riots cause extensive clubland damage 21 Feb: S.D.F. mass meeting in Hyde Park: many hurt in police charge 27 Mar: Warren replaces Henderson as Chief Commissioner of Metropolitan Police 11 May: Queen opens International Exhibition of Navigation and Commerce, Liverpool 28 June: Prince of Wales lays foundation stone of Queen's Hall in East End Sept: Fabian Society declares unequivocally for parliamentary strategy 1 Sept: Severn Tunnel open for goods traffic	New English Art Club formed Hardy's *The Mayor of Casterbridge* *Dream of John Ball* published in *Commonweal* Anson's *Law and Custom of the Constitution* Froude's *Oceana* *English Historical Review* founded Gissing's *Demos* St Hugh's College, Oxford founded 14 Apr: Social Science Association dissolves 21 June: Tower Bridge begun 30 June: Queen opens Royal Holloway College, Egham R.L. Stevenson's *Dr Jekyll and Mr Hyde*	*1886*
4 Apr: first Colonial Conference assembles 4 July: Queen lays foundation stone of Imperial Institute	First international short-hand congress, London 7 Jan: socialists seriously disrupt Brabazon's emigration meeting at Clerkenwell 26 Feb: new Charing Cross Road opened 27 Feb: socialists disrupt St Paul's service 14 May: Queen opens People's Palace 21 June: jubilee service in Westminster Abbey 24 Aug: Cardiff docks completed Sept: Keir Hardie challenges Broadhurst at Swansea T.U.C. 17 Oct: Trafalgar Square riots of unemployed 23 Oct: socialists disrupt Westminster Abbey service 11 Nov: work on Manchester Ship Canal begins 13 Nov: 'Bloody Sunday' riots in West End, John Burns arrested 17 Nov: *c.* 6,000 special constables enrolled to curb future riots 18 Dec: funeral of Alfred Linnell	J.L. Pearson's Truro Cathedral consecrated Agneta Ramsay placed above the senior classic at Cambridge Maitland founds Selden Society Important National Gallery extensions Conan Doyle's *Study in Scarlet* Stevenson's *Kidnapped* Marx's *Capital*, Vol. 1, first available in English Pollock's *Law of Torts* Gilbert and Sullivan's *Ruddigore* Hardy's *The Woodlanders* 23 Mar: Queen lays foundation stone of new Law Courts	*1887*
11 Feb: King Lobengula of Matabele accepts British protection 17 Mar: British protectorate over Sarawak 12 May: British protectorate over North Borneo and Brunei 15 June: Frederick III of Germany dies 3 Sept: British East Africa Company chartered	J.B Dunlop's pneumatic tyre patented First British nature reserve created (in Norfolk) 18 Jan: Burns and Cunninghame Graham imprisoned for inciting Trafalgar Square riot 27 Apr: Keir Hardie defeated as candidate for Mid-Lanark 5 June: Church Association decides to prosecute Bishop King of Lincoln for high church practices 5 July: Bryant & May match girls strike Aug onwards: Jack the Ripper murders in East London 25 Aug: inaugural conference of Scottish Labour Party 27 Nov: James Monro succeeds Warren as Chief Commissioner of Metropolitan Police	Wilde's *The Happy Princess and Other Tales* Mrs Ward's *Robert Elsmere* First authorized English edition of *Communist Manifesto* Bellamy's *Looking Backward* Kipling's *Plain Tales from the Hills* Newnes launches weekly *Answers to Correspondents* Maitland professor of law at Cambridge First exhibition of Arts and Crafts Guild George Eastman's Kodak box camera Mark Rutherford's *Revolution in Tanner's Lane* Lawn Tennis Association founded 15 Apr: Matthew Arnold dies 31 Oct: Vizetelly fined for publishing English translations of Zola	*1888*
Milner becomes director-general of accounts in Egypt 1 July: Shah of Persia visits Britain 15 Oct: Royal Charter for South Africa Company	Metropolitan Railway reaches Chesham Henry George's third British lecture-tour Keir Hardie attacks Broadhurst at T.U.C. Dundee congress 12 Feb: Lord Rosebery elected first chairman of the L.C.C. Mar: Will Thorne founds National Union of Gas Workers and General Labourers 23 Mar: first free ferry between Woolwich and North Woolwich opened by L.C.C. 19 Aug – 14 Sept: London dock strike	George Eastman produces a celluloid roll film Gilbert and Sullivan's *Gondoliers* Ibsen's *Doll's House* performed in London Curzon's *Russia in Central Asia* *Lux Mundi* Norman Shaw's *Scotland Yard* Dec 1889: *Fabian Essays* 2 Dec: Robert Browning dies	*1889*

Index

Where several entries appear under one heading, the most important of them feature in **bold** type. Individuals appear under the name by which they are best known (thus 'Disraeli', not 'Beaconsfield'). As in the book itself, photographs and prose are brought together, but the photographs are distinguished here by the use of *italic* type. As also in the book itself, county boundary changes since 1974 have been disregarded.